Rights, Resc
Rural Development

Community-based Natural Resource
Management in Southern Africa

EDITED BY

CHRISTO FABRICIUS AND EDDIE KOCH
WITH
HECTOR MAGOME AND STEPHEN TURNER

London • Sterling, VA

First published by Earthscan in the UK and USA in 2004

ISBN: 1-84407-009-3 paperback
       1-84407-010-7 hardback

Typesetting by MapSet Ltd, Gateshead, UK
Printed and bound in the UK by Cromwell Press Ltd
Cover design by Danny Gillespie
Cover illustrations © Richard Kilpert

For a full list of publications please contact:

Earthscan
8–12 Camden High Street
London, NW1 0JH, UK
Tel: +44 (0)20 7387 8558
Fax: +44 (0)20 7387 8998
Email: earthinfo@earthscan.co.uk
Web: **www.earthscan.co.uk**

22883 Quicksilver Drive, Sterling, VA 20166-2012, USA

Earthscan publishes in association with WWF-UK and the International Institute for
Environment and Development

A catalogue record for this book is available from the British Library

Library of Congress Cataloging-in-Publication Data

Rights, resources & rural development : community based natural resource
management in Southern Africa / edited by Christo Fabricius ... [et al.].
     p. cm.
   Includes bibliographical references and index.
   ISBN 1-84407-009-3 (pbk.) — ISBN 1-84407-010-7 (hb)
     1. Natural resources—Africa, Southern—Management. 2. Conservation of
natural resources—Economic aspects—Africa, Southern. 3. Rural development—
Environmental aspects—Africa, Southern. 4. Local government—Africa, Southern.
I. Title: Rights, resources and rural development. II. Fabricius, Christo, 1956–

HC900.Z65R54 2004
333.7'0968–dc22
                                                                      2003014962

Contents

List of figures, tables and boxes   *v*
List of contributors   *vii*
Acknowledgements   *ix*
List of acronyms and abbreviations   *x*

Introduction   xiii
Christo Fabricius and Eddie Koch

PART 1: SYNTHESIS

1   The fundamentals of community-based natural resource
     management   3
     Christo Fabricius
2   Community-based natural resource management and rural
     livelihoods   44
     Stephen Turner
3   Political economy, governance and community-based natural
     resource management   66
     Eddie Koch
4   Putting out fires: Does the 'C' in CBNRM stand for community
     or centrifuge?   78
     Eddie Koch
5   Reconciling biodiversity conservation with rural development:
     The Holy Grail of CBNRM?   93
     Hector Magome and Christo Fabricius

PART 2: CASE STUDIES

6   Community-based natural resource management, traditional
     governance and spiritual ecology in southern Africa: The case of
     chiefs, diviners and spirit mediums   115
     Penny Bernard and Sibongiseni Kumalo
7   The contribution of bees to livelihoods in southern Africa   127
     Etienne Nel and Pete Illgner

8   Everyday resources are valuable enough for community-based
    natural resource management programme support: Evidence from
    South Africa   135
    Sheona Shackleton and Charlie Shackleton

9   Community-based natural resource management in the
    Okavango Delta   147
    Lesley Boggs

10 Local ecological knowledge and the Basarwa in the
    Okavango Delta: The case of Xaxaba, Ngamiland District   160
    Masego Madzwamuse and Christo Fabricius

11 A land without fences: Range management in Lesotho   174
    Stephen Turner

12 Beach village committees as a vehicle for community participation:
    Lake Malombe/Upper Shire River Participatory Programme   182
    Mafaniso Hara

13 Key issues in Namibia's communal conservancy movement   194
    Colin Nott and Margaret Jacobsohn

14 The Torra Conservancy in Namibia   200
    Colin Nott, Anna Davis and Bernard Roman

15 The Tchumo Tchato project in Mozambique: Community-based
    natural resource management in transition   210
    Steve Johnson

16 The Richtersveld and Makuleke contractual parks in South Africa:
    Win–win for communities and conservation?   223
    Hannah Reid and Stephen Turner

17 The Luangwa Integrated Rural Development Project, Zambia   235
    Brian Child

18 Community wildlife management in Zimbabwe: The case of
    CAMPFIRE in the Zambezi Valley   248
    Backson Sibanda

19 New configurations of power around Mafungautsi State Forest
    in Zimbabwe   259
    Bevlyne Sithole

**Conclusions and recommendations: What we have learned from a
decade of experimentation**   271
*Christo Fabricius, Eddie Koch, Stephen Turner, Hector Magome
and Lawrence Sisitka*

Index   282

List of figures, tables and boxes

FIGURES

1.1	The environmental entitlements approach and its application to people–natural resource relationships	26
1.2	The participatory resource management continuum	31
8.1	Contribution of woodland products to rural livelihoods	137
10.1	The adaptive renewal cycle	161
12.1	Estimated total catch from Lake Malombe	183
12.2	Estimated catch from the Upper Shire River	184
17.1	The pre-1996 top-down structure of the community programme	242
17.2	Changes to the programme following the introduction of a policy emphasizing fiscal devolution at village level in 1996	243
17.3	Illustration of the difference between first- and second-generation CBNRM and its impacts on the public–private nature of resources and community attitudes	244
19.1	Control of key positions in different committees of the RMCs by the *kraalhead*'s family in Mrembwe village	264
19.2	Positions held by the most influential person in Mrembwe village	265
20.1	A CBNRM systems model	273

TABLES

1.1	The characteristics of case-by-case management	20
1.2	A typology of participation	29
1.3	Intangible benefits from CBNRM	34
2.1	Annual, gross direct-use values (in South African rand) per household of timber use by rural households from various sites	51
2.2	Quantum and per household direct financial benefits from CBNRM	56
5.1	Conditions for effective CBNRM	102
5.2	Five incomplete arguments in the new protectionist paradigm	104
9.1	Direct financial benefits from the joint venture to Sankuyo, 1996–2000	153
10.1	Livelihood options in Xaxaba and Khwai	169

14.1   Estimated game numbers for Kunene region and Torra
        Conservancy   202
14.2   Income and expenditure from commercial tourism and wildlife
        activities in Torra Conservancy   107
17.1   Principles embodied in LIRDP's 1996 CBNRM proposal,
        stipulating conditions for the release of wildlife funds   238
17.2   The application of the CAMPFIRE principles of CBNRM to
        the Lupande project   245

BOXES

1.1   International agreements affecting people–natural resource
        relationships in southern Africa   11
1.2   CAMPFIRE principles of CBNRM   16
1.3   Rules for lasting common property institutions   17
1.4   Principles for improving the chances of success of CBNRM
        initiatives, and criteria for evaluating them   18
8.1   The story of everyday resources in an ordinary rural life   144

List of contributors

Penny Bernard is a lecturer in the Department of Anthropology, Rhodes University, Grahamstown, South Africa.

Lesley Boggs is an independent researcher and consultant, based in Botswana and Canada.

Brian Child is coordinator of the Luangwa Integrated Rural Development Project (LIRDP) in Zambia.

Anna Davis is an independent researcher in Namibia.

Christo Fabricius is Professor of Environmental Science, Rhodes University, Grahamstown, South Africa.

Mafaniso Hara is a senior researcher in the Programme for Land and Agrarian Studies, University of the Western Cape, South Africa.

Pete Illgner is an environmental consultant with Coastal and Environmental Services in Grahamstown, South Africa.

Margaret Jacobsohn is Director of Integrated Rural Development and Nature Conservation in Namibia.

Steve Johnson is a researcher with IUCN–World Conservation Union in Botswana.

Eddie Koch is a Director of Mafisa Research and Development, South Africa.

Sibongiseni Kumalo is a post-graduate student in the Department of Anthropology, Rhodes University.

Masego Madzwamuse is country coordinator of IUCN–World Conservation Union in Botswana.

Hector Magome is Director of the Conservation Services in South African National Parks.

Etienne Nel is Head of the Department of Geography, Rhodes University, South Africa.

Colin Nott is a freelance consultant in Namibia.

Hannah Reid is a research associate with the International Institute for Environment and Development (IIED) in London.

Bernard Roman is an independent researcher in Namibia.

Charlie Shackleton is Associate Professor in the Department of Environmental Science, Rhodes University, South Africa.

Sheona Shackleton is a research associate in the Department of Environmental Science, Rhodes University, South Africa.

Backson Sibanda is Chief Evaluation Specialist with UNESCO in Paris, France.

Lawrence Sisitka is an independent environmental education and development consultant in Grahamstown, South Africa.

Bevlyne Sithole is a freelance researcher in Jakarta, Indonesia.

Stephen Turner is a researcher in the Resource Development Unit, Centre for Development Cooperation Services, Vrije Universiteit, Amsterdam.

Acknowledgements

The editors wish to thank the Ford Foundation and the Deutsche Gesellschaft für Technische Zusammenarbeit (GTZ) Transform project for the generous financial support that made this book possible. Thanks are due, in particular, to James Murombedzi (formerly of the Ford Foundation) and Johannes Baumgart (Transform) for their patience, and to Sue Southwood, Andrew Ainslie and Samantha Browne for their good proof-reading. We are indebted to the many government officials, facilitators and rural people throughout southern Africa who helped us to learn about natural resource management. Christo Fabricius wishes to thank his colleagues and students, past and present, for their support and stimulation, and Rhodes University for the time and freedom to edit this book.

List of acronyms and abbreviations

ADC   area development committee
ADMADE   Administrative Management Design for Game Management Areas (Zambia)
BVC   beach village committee
CAMPFIRE   Communal Areas Management Programme for Indigenous Resources (Zimbabwe)
CASS   Centre for Applied Social Studies (University of Zimbabwe)
CBD   Convention on Biological Diversity
CBNRM   community-based natural resource management
CBO   community-based organization
CCD   Convention to Combat Desertification
CDO   community development organization
CHA   controlled hunting area
CITES   Convention on International Trade in Endangered Species of Wild Fauna and Flora
CMA   community management area
CPA   Communal Property Association
CPPPs   community private–public partnerships
CPR   common pool resource
CPT   common property theory
DFID   Department for International Development (UK)
DNPWLM   Department of National Parks and Wildlife Management (Zimbabwe)
DWNP   Department of Wildlife and National Parks (Botswana)
EEC   European Economic Community
FAO   Food and Agriculture Organization of the United Nations
FD   Fisheries Department (Malawi)
GA   grazing association
GDP   gross domestic product
GEF   Global Environment Facility
GMA   game management area
GRZ   Government of the Republic of Zambia
GTZ   Deutsche Gesellschaft für Technische Zusammenarbeit (German government agency for international cooperation)
ICDP   Integrated Conservation Development Project
IDP   Integrated Development Plan
IIED   International Institute for Environment and Development

ILO	International Labour Organization
IRDNC	Integrated Rural Development and Nature Conservation Project (Namibia)
IUCN	World Conservation Union
JMB	joint management board
JVA	joint venture agreement
JVP	joint venture partner
KNP	Kruger National Park
KZN	KwaZulu-Natal
LHWP	Lesotho Highlands Water Project
LIFE	Living in a Finite Environment (Namibia)
LIRDP	Luangwa Integrated Rural Development Project
MAB	Man and the Biosphere Programme (UNESCO)
MET	Ministry of Environment and Tourism (Namibia)
NACOBTA	Namibian Community-Based Tourism Association
NACSO	Namibian Association of CBNRM Support Organizations
NG18	Ngamiland Area 18 (Botswana)
NG32	Ngamiland Area 32 (Botswana)
NG34	Ngamiland Area 34 (Botswana)
NGO	non-governmental organization
NORAD	Norwegian Agency for International Development
NRM	natural resource management
NRMP	Natural Resources Management Project (Botswana)
NTFP	non-timber forest product
ODA	Overseas Development Administration
OKMCT	Okavango Kopano Mokoro Trust (CBO)
PACT	Partnership Agencies Collaborating Together
PFM	participatory forest management
PFMP	Lake Malombe/Upper Shire River Participatory Fisheries Management Programme
PRA	participatory rural appraisal
RALE	representative and accountable legal entity
RDC	rural district council
RMA	range management area
RMC	resource management committee
RNP	Richtersveld National Park
SADC	Southern African Development Community
SANP	*see* SANParks
SANParks	South African National Parks (*formerly* SANP)
SDI	Spatial Development Initiative
SL	sustainable livelihoods
SLAMU	South Luangwa Area Management Unit
SLNP	South Luangwa National Park
TGLP	Tribal Grazing Land Policy (Botswana)
UK	United Kingdom
UNDP	United Nations Development Programme

UNESCO	United Nations Educational, Scientific and Cultural Organization
US	United States
USAID	United States Agency for International Development
VAG	village action group
VDC	village development council
VTC	village trust committee
WINDFALL	Wildlife Industries New Development For All (Zimbabwe)
WMA	wildlife management area
WSN	Wilderness Safaris Namibia
WTO	World Trade Organization
WWF	World Wide Fund For Nature
ZAWA	Zambia Wildlife Authority

Introduction

CHRISTO FABRICIUS AND EDDIE KOCH

Throughout southern Africa, ordinary men and women are managing and using natural resources (for example, plants, animals, forests, wildlife and crops) in ways that enhance their lives. They get their food, fuel, building materials and spiritual nourishment from natural resources and, either consciously or unconsciously, manage these resources through the local rules, taboos and belief systems that they have developed in particular contexts. Although natural resources have long been an integral part of rural southern African livelihoods, it is only in recent decades that outsiders have sought to promote natural resource management as a rural development strategy – which is partly why this book is being written. The concern of governments and donor agencies with community-based natural resource management (CBNRM) arose mainly from a widespread assumption that the rural poor are exerting unsustainable pressure on their natural environment. Better use practices, policies and management systems, it was argued, could halt this environmental degradation. This led to the formulation and implementation of 'formal' CBNRM programmes in many countries of the subcontinent, most of which were driven, and often even initiated, by a combination of government, non-governmental organizations (NGOs), community-based organizations (CBOs) and, sometimes, the private sector.

In this book, we examine the relationship between people and natural resources from a CBNRM perspective. We take a utilitarian view of the role of ecosystems in people's lives, considering the wild resources that millions of people live with to be a crucial component of their livelihood strategies. Our definition of natural resources is broad, covering agriculture, forestry, conservation, tourism, fisheries and 'everyday' resources such as bees, brush, water and fuelwood. We draw on case study material from almost every country in the subregion, supplemented by the literature.

Part 1 synthesizes existing information and provides a 'state of the art' summary of a debate that surrounds CBNRM as a strategy for promoting both conservation and local economic development. Christo Fabricius (Chapter 1) provides a summary of the concepts and issues in the relationship between people and natural resources. He charts the evolution of CBNRM, explains key definitions and concepts relevant to CBNRM and maps the structure of the book. He also explains why CBNRM has become important in the subregion and globally, against the backdrop of ecological degradation, poverty, political neglect, decreasing government budgets, changing notions of the development process, urban–rural interactions and political change. He concludes by outlining new problems and challenges, as well as opportunities and possibilities.

Stephen Turner (Chapter 2) describes and assesses the revenues and other livelihood benefits generated by CBNRM. While a number of attempts to 'squeeze' tangible benefits from meagre resources for large numbers of people have often only raised and then frustrated local expectations, some initiatives have been able to deliver tangible benefits that are significant enough to improve the livelihoods of local people. Turner explores the importance of intangible benefits that can be generated by these projects, such as the diversification of subsistence options and opportunities for local people, risk reduction, group cohesion and identity, increased management capacity, pride and self-confidence. He also looks at factors that impede or enhance the ability of CBNRM to improve the quality of life of the rural poor, in both tangible and intangible ways. The chapter further highlights a number of seemingly incongruous phenomena, such as the apparent reluctance of some communities to spend the revenue that they have earned from CBNRM projects, even though they appear to be living in abject poverty.

Eddie Koch (Chapter 3) deals with the role of local groups in natural resource management. Local people and organizations are unpredictable and often appear unstable, with 'communities' constantly defining and redefining themselves. One of the reasons is internal conflict over access to revenues and benefits. Another is the different way in which local people and outside 'experts' view their relations to the natural world. These issues often frustrate project managers and officials, while local role players seem more willing to accept these vagaries as a fact of life. Koch provides insights into how to plan for and deal with conflict, and how to make peace with the many paradoxes and quirks thrown up by these interactions.

In Chapter 4 Koch discusses the way in which national and global politics influence resource management. All over southern Africa, community-based initiatives are being affected by a range of national political forces. The crisis around land reform in Zimbabwe is a graphic example of how power and the state can affect the performance of local development projects. In Namibia, for example, the innovative conservancy movement is, in some cases, opposed by national politicians and their business allies, an alliance whose interests are not always served by official policy that promotes CBNRM programmes that give substantial rights to the rural poor. In the Okavango Delta of Botswana, the ruling elite is challenging pro-poor tourism programmes that allow local residents to receive most of the rents from lucrative wildlife tourism and trophy hunting projects. In many countries, including South Africa, some factions of the state are supportive of CBNRM, while others are indifferent or hostile. This chapter explores the problems that arise from the wider political forces and draws important lessons from the ways in which various projects have tried to cope with them.

Hector Magome and Christo Fabricius (Chapter 5) address the dual objectives of CBNRM: the desire to conserve natural resources while, at the same time, reducing poverty. The question is whether conservation objectives are met through CBNRM and how these resources can be conserved while simultaneously being used. Magome and Fabricius address the tension between conservation and development, and provide new insights into how these seemingly conflicting goals might be reconciled. How is the conservation fraternity responding to the delegation of authority to local communities? And how much are local people really investing in conservation? This chapter critically assesses one of the central tenets of CBNRM – namely, that decentralization leads to greater custodianship by local people.

Part 2 consists of 14 case studies that each deal with the relationship between people and natural resources. These case studies cover many of the variants in people–natural resource relationships in settings where people use and manage wildlife, forestry, fisheries, tourism and agricultural resources. Some of the case studies also deal with 'everyday' resources such as fuelwood, honey and landscapes that have special spiritual significance.

The book concludes with a set of management recommendations and offers a conceptual model for understanding the relationship between people and natural resources. This final chapter summarizes the key management and policy lessons highlighted in Parts 1 and 2. It also revisits the fundamental issues and controversies raised in Chapter 1.

Part 1

Synthesis

Chapter 1

The fundamentals of community-based natural resource management

CHRISTO FABRICIUS

HISTORICAL BACKGROUND TO COMMUNITY-BASED NATURAL RESOURCE MANAGEMENT

Although not well documented, there is some evidence that elaborate resource management systems prevailed among indigenous African people before the arrival of European colonists. Traditional institutions such as kings, chiefs, headmen and healers played an important role in regulating and monitoring resource use. Examples include the royal hunting preserves of the amaZulu and amaSwati people, and the *kgotla* system of land management practised by the Batswana people.

> *It is too often assumed that the traditional systems were characterized by a free-for-all anarchic exploitation of resources. While it is possible that in some exceptionally richly endowed regions with very sparse populations the regulatory may have been minimal or even non-existent, most communities had evolved systems which in varying degrees conserved resources and ensured their equitable distribution among households* (Ghai, 1992).

Traditionally, people relied heavily on the abundant wild natural resources that surrounded them. As a result, people in Africa generally appreciated the value of nature, and incorporated nature into their worldviews, metaphors, folklore and belief systems (see Chapter 6). Many of their systems of governance included rules and procedures designed to regulate the use and management of natural resources. Practices that were geared towards enhancing ecosystem services and maintaining their resilience were developed through adaptive management or 'trial and error'. These practices have been carried over from generation to generation through oral testimony and are now recognized as customary (Folke et al, 1998).

The range of people's resilience-enhancing practices included customs that created small-scale disturbances – for example, 'pulse' hunting, where animals were heavily hunted during certain months and then left alone for the rest of the year (see Chapter 18) and patch burning to enrich grazing for wildlife (Feely, 1986; Kepe and Scoones, 1999) – and customs to nurture biodiversity stocks to assist renewal after resource depletion – for example, taboos where certain resources were prohibited from being used at certain times of the month or year, or where certain plants and animals are out of bounds for certain families or clans. Food taboos were broken in times of extreme scarcity, suggesting that their function was partly to nurture resources upon which to fall back during crises (see Chapter 10). Animals such as the python and lion were believed to be the custodians of important landscapes and resources, often through human spirit mediums that represented these animals. Sacred forests are scattered all over the southern African landscape (Barrow, 1996); these forests, together with abandoned fields and settlements, result in a rich mosaic of habitat patches that are strongly influenced by human impacts. In Botswana, hunter-gatherer Basarwa were able to move around in response to ecosystem change and wildlife dynamics, burn vegetation selectively, and choose a livelihood strategy from a range of possibilities that would best suit their particular circumstances. Although many of these practices still exist, they were much more prevalent and effective in the past than now because of low human population densities, people's minimal impact on the land and their lifestyles, which were often nomadic.

Local institutions such as chiefs and headmen also played an important ecological role, setting boundaries that restricted natural resource use and enforcing them. In the Eastern Cape Province, South Africa, research conducted among local communities showed a clear decline in the condition of indigenous forests after the headman (*Ibhodi*) system collapsed (primarily due to the corrupting influences of apartheid-era social engineering) (Rhodes University et al, 2001). In Lesotho's communal rangelands, chiefs and headmen controlled the use of grazing and managed a system of controlled grazing areas (*maboella*), often with the assistance of the people themselves. These comprised grazing land set aside to recover; scarce resource areas; fields that were periodically opened to everyone – for example, for the grazing of crop residues; and special grazing reserves in the lowlands (see Chapter 11). These traditional leaders often got their legitimacy from the spirit mediums mentioned above. The link between leadership, land and life was undisputed, implicit and strong.

The arrival of colonial powers in southern Africa

The colonists arrived in the Cape during the mid 17th century and steadily worked their way northwards. Soon after their arrival, the Portuguese, British and particularly the Dutch colonists started hunting large quantities of game, especially elephant. They would disappear into the interior for months and return with wagonloads of ivory (Mostert, 1992). Products of the hunt, especially ivory, were also traded throughout the subcontinent, and local chiefs and their followers in some regions began to intensify their hunting efforts in order to be part of the growing trade in ivory and other animal products during this period. British administrators and the wealthier settler farmers engaged in hunting for recreation and sport. The combined impact of these intensified hunting activities caused a severe drop in animal numbers throughout southern Africa. Some writers speak of a 'killing spree' by African and settler hunting parties (Carruthers, 1989). Constant hunting resulted in piles of skulls of plains animals such as black wildebeest and springbok being visible across the veld, in what Mostert (1992) describes as scenes of 'perpetual havoc'.

In 1775, a Swedish botanist at the Cape named A Sparmann pointed out that the Dutch farmers, who were producing meat and milk for the market, could have damaged the land much more than the nomadic *Khoikhoi*, who constantly moved their livestock before grazing could have a lasting impact on the land (Wilson, 1970). Economic pressure on the land during the late 18th and early 19th centuries induced a change in traditional practices. While the Africans used hoes to till the soil, the Europeans brought ploughs that were unsuitable to the African climate (Maquet, 1972), accelerating soil erosion and disturbing natural soil profiles and processes. This played an important role in the development of the environmental degradation experienced today. Many invasive alien plant species and animals were brought by the colonial military. Invasive alien species such as *Opuntia monacantha*, deliberately introduced by the French to southern Africa, caused tremendous damage as these plants were able to outcompete indigenous vegetation (McNeely, 2002).

The tribal population increased rapidly as a result of the cattle revolution; however, simultaneously, the land to the south was gradually taken over by Europeans (Kuper, 1963; Yudelman, 1964). Conflicts over land and resources escalated. The Kruger National Park, for example, has been characterized by conflicts of interest since its inception:

> *White farmers wanted game reserves to be opened for grazing, the Department of Mines raised the question of valuable minerals in the reserves, land owners wanted to control hunting in their private farms, the Department of Lands wanted the reserve for white settlement, while the Department of Native Affairs wanted land for the relocation of Africans* (Carruthers, 1993).

Perceptions of scarcity: The emergence of top-down preservation

By the early 1920s, law-makers started realizing that natural resources would not last for ever, and that something needed to be done to conserve the dwindling wildlife and forests, and to combat land degradation (Schroeder, 1999). The first signs of preservationist sentiment emerged from the ranks of colonial administrators on the Indian Ocean islands off the east coast of the subcontinent. Because these islands, which were used by ships plying the Cape trading route from Europe to the Middle East, were small, it was possible to detect land degradation and deforestation much earlier than on mainland Africa. The proportional impact was also much higher. Because of this, early conservation legislation was developed on these islands and then exported to the Cape Colony (Beinart, 1990; Carruthers, 1989).

Conservation ideologies in southern Africa were heavily influenced by political and economic events on other continents. Impressionist paintings of Edenic landscapes, devoid of labour and portraying peace and tranquility, reflected a popular consciousness that underlay the British colonial drive for 'wild' protected areas, without people, where animals could be observed in 'pristine' environments (Neuman, 1998). Colonial administrators, alarmed by the American dust bowl of the depression during the 1930s, made soil conservation compulsory for peasant farmers (Schroeder, 1999). Management ideologies such as the concept of 'climax' vegetation – that is, pristine vegetation at the pinnacle of its development, with no or minimal disturbance (Schroeder, 1999) – Hardin's (1968) 'Tragedy of the commons' essay and beliefs in Malthusian economics, which postulated that resources eventually have to run out if human populations keep growing, further fuelled the move towards conserving landscapes devoid of people and towards returning disturbed landscapes to their 'original' undisturbed form.

In 1900, foreign ministers representing the African colonial powers – Britain, France, Belgium, Italy, Portugal and Spain – gathered in London to sign the world's first international conservation treaty: the Convention for the Preservation of Animals. In its report on the conference, the *Times of London* described the situation in southern Africa:

> *It is necessary to go far into the interior to find the nobler forms of antelope, and still further if the hunter wants to pursue the elephant, the rhinoceros or the giraffe. It is perfectly clear that very soon those animals, unless something is done to prevent their extermination, will be stamped out as completely as the dodo. To some extent this process is inevitable. The advance of civilization, with its noise and agitation, is fatally disturbing the primitive forms of animal life. Commerce, moreover, discovers continually some new demand for trophies of the chase. The horns, the skins and the plumage of beasts and birds have an increasing market value. It is not surprising, therefore, that men of science have become alarmed at the prospect of the extinction of many of the most interesting and characteristic types of zoological development* (Bonner, 1993).

In the early part of the century, an influential lobby of landowners, mining magnates and colonial administrators in the colonies secured tighter legislation for the preservation of game reserves, largely to protect wildlife (Beinart, 1990). But many people were excluded in the process:

> *Africans and poorer whites – those for whom hunting was still of some importance in subsistence and survival – were finally to be excluded from hunting on private lands and in the new game reserves. Hunting for subsistence or trade goods – 'biltong hunting' – was conceived as laziness, a term increasingly identified with the capacity to avoid wage labour. Trespass onto private land to hunt animals, which still in law belonged to no one, became poaching* (Beinart, 1990).

Beinart argues that because whites had disproportionate political power in South Africa, game reserves were usually located in the segregated ethnic 'homelands' or on lands made marginal by low rainfall, poor soils, malaria and tsetse fly. People in these areas were poor and lacked political representation, and were less able to resist land alienation than people in the commercial agricultural regions. Conservation thus became highly politicized and was intricately bound up with the political imperatives of segregation, (Koch et al, 1990).

The colony of Rhodesia, later to become the independent states of Zimbabwe and Zambia, was colonized during the late 19th century by British settlers. The preservationist laws that had been developed in the Cape Colony were thus extended north into the British colonies across the Limpopo River. In Rhodesia, tribal areas became buffer zones where subsistence and commercial hunting was allowed around most protected areas.

In the Portuguese colonies of Mozambique (Portuguese East Africa) and Angola, legislation to create formally protected wildlife areas was only passed during the 1960s and 1970s. In Mozambique, the Banine, Zinave and Maputa elephant reserves were promulgated as late as 1969 (Meneses, 1994). In Angola, proposals were made during the same period to create a network of new protected areas that would set aside 6 per cent of the land and protect up to 90 per cent of the country's biological richness. War in the post-colonial period ensured that these plans were stillborn (Huntley and Matos, 1992).

In the then Basutoland, the colonial administration became very concerned about land and soil degradation during the 1930s. During the 1970s, a number of donor-funded land reclamation initiatives were launched in independent Lesotho. Researchers made wild claims that the rangeland was 200 to 300 per cent overstocked, not taking into account local coping strategies, such as the use of crop residues to supplement grazing (see Chapter 11). More recent estimates are that Lesotho's rangelands are only around 20 per cent overstocked.

Natural resource legislation has generally failed to take into account the intricate relationships between people and nature that were typical of the culture of most African societies. Traditional African institutions that prevented the overuse of natural resources were replaced by Western institutions and practices, such as courts of law, fines and fences. The development of agriculture and pastoralism by local peoples was seen as unnatural and ecologically unsound. The cause of rural degradation was seen as unsustainable land-use methods, accentuated by high population densities in African settlements (Bell, 1987). The main emphasis became how to restrict the use of wildlife resources, rather than the development of strategies to ensure their long-term utilization and ecosystem renewal. In terms of the colonial paradigm of conservation, subsistence hunters became defined as poachers by the same settler population who had once relied on this form of economic activity for its survival (Crush, 1980). Paramilitary conservation authorities, tasked with policing the protected areas under their control, were a logical product of this preservationist outlook. Enforcement strategies ignored local sentiments and did not understand that poaching was often a rational response to the fencing-off of parks that made them inaccessible, while there were food shortages in the surrounding villages (Crush, 1980). In many southern African states, armed confrontations between 'poachers' and rangers become commonplace by the middle of the 20th century (Bell, 1987).

By this time in southern Africa, the state controlled most natural resources and it became impossible for anyone wishing to make a living from natural ecosystem products to do so without breaking one law or another. In the conservation sector, the sentiment that only Europeans knew how to conserve nature prevailed. Protected areas were proclaimed one by one, people were forcibly removed from them and anti-hunting laws were rigidly enforced. In the forestry and fisheries sectors, legislation was less rigid and people were allowed limited consumptive use (see Chapter 12). Permits to harvest indigenous trees could be obtained from local headmen or government officials, which, to this day, remains unthinkable for wildlife harvesting. In agriculture, land degradation became synonymous with communal and subsistence agriculture (De Bruyn and Scogings, 1998).

The era of conflict

Because of this inappropriate and foreign approach to conservation, biodiversity protection in southern Africa became charged with political conflict. As Abel and Blaikie (1986) point out, resource conservation in the region became part of an ideological and political struggle:

> *Government policy has created areas called national parks that are officially designated for a particular and exclusive use. However, competing groups such as local hunter-cultivators or commercial poachers also have claims upon these natural resources and manage sometimes to press them successfully... Viewed in this way, a particular national park at any moment is like the resultant in a parallelogram of forces in an analogy with elementary physics. The forces are contradictory and unequal, the strongest having the greatest influence upon the way resources of a national park are used. Each is used by different groups in a different direction* (Abel and Blaikie, 1986, p736).

The top-down approaches of governments and the efforts of private landowners did, indeed, save several species from the brink of extinction. Formally protected areas made an important contribution to the survival of white rhinoceros, black wildebeest, roan antelope, oribi, tsessebe, bontebok and sable antelope in the subregion. Carnivores such as lion, leopard, cheetah and many large birds of prey rely on wildlife reserves for their core home ranges, and it would have been inappropriate for people and these species to continue to coexist. In Namibia, South Africa and Zimbabwe, commercial game ranchers spearheaded the conservation, through sustainable use, of wildlife outside protected areas (SASUSG, 1997). The concept of conservancies – where groups of private landowners formed institutions to collectively manage their land – become popular during the 1980s and set the scene for communal conservancies in Namibia (Jones, 1999; Jones and Murphree 2001).

More recently, racist policies resulted in the forced removal of people from land earmarked for conservation, forestry and agricultural development. In South Africa alone, some 3.5 million people were forcibly removed in an attempt by the government of the day to divide the country geographically along racial and ethnic lines (Surplus People Project, 1985). As part of this ideology of centralized control, people were also removed from land containing rich biodiversity resources in order to incorporate such land into protected areas. The Makuleke (see Chapter 16; Reid, 2001) and Dwesa-Cwebe cases (Timmermans, 1999) are among the best known in South Africa. Fabricius and de Wet (2002) discuss eight South African cases of forced removal and conservation. In Botswana during the period of 1910 to 1968, the San bushmen of the Kalahari and Okavango Delta were severely restricted in their hunting and movement patterns (see Chapter 10). Displaced people were worse off than before in every way imaginable (Fabricius and de Wet, 2002).

Forcibly removed people shared a similar plight in that they were inadequately compensated. They were further impoverished because of their loss of access to natural resources and their social situation became more fragmented than before. Resettled people were centrally and politically controlled and their traditional institutions eroded as the government tightened its control over rural politics. Settlement areas were generally more densely populated, less productive and poorer in biodiversity than the land from which people were removed. But, contrary to expectations, resettlement was also bad for resource conservation: there was more pressure on natural resources than before and the traditional local institutions that governed natural resource use were undermined. At the same time, local people became hostile to conservation and conservationists, and 'poaching' increased (Fabricius and de Wet, 2002).

It is now widely accepted that the particular style of official natural resource management that emerged in southern Africa during the colonial and apartheid periods generated a range of social conflicts that now endanger the future of natural resources. An awareness of the damaging effects of colonial approaches to resource management is a major reason for the recent popularity of the new people-centred approach to natural resource management.

The era of democratization

During the mid 1980s, and even earlier in some cases, natural resource management agencies in southern Africa began to realize that they lacked the financial and human resources to effectively prevent resource degradation. At roughly the same time, democracy found its way to the subregion. Natural resource management agencies experienced pressure from newly elected governments to consider the demands and pleas of local communities for greater recognition and improved access to ecosystem services.

New and innovative programmes, aimed at removing or reducing the conflict between protected areas and people, signalled a shift in international thinking on conservation issues. The World Bank's 1986 policy on wildlands recognized that the protection of natural areas needed to be integrated within regional economic planning. In 1985, the World Wildlife Fund launched its Wildlife and Human Needs Programme, which consists of some 20 projects in developing countries that attempted to combine conservation and development:

> These [Integrated Conservation and Development] projects attempt to ensure the conservation of biological diversity by reconciling the management of protected areas with the social and economic needs of local people. The smaller Integrated Conservation Development Projects (ICDPs) include biosphere reserves, multiple-use areas, and a variety of initiatives on the boundaries of protected areas, including buffer zones. Larger projects include the implementation of land-use plans with protected area components, as well as large-scale development projects with links to nearby protected areas (Wells and Brandon, 1992).

Another important milestone was the Rio Declaration in 1992, out of which flowed the Convention on Biological Diversity (CBD). This was one of the first international conservation policies that demonstrated the move towards people-centred conservation. Significantly, two out of three of its principles (the fair and equitable sharing of benefits and sustainable use) imply that people are an integral part of conservation. Other international agreements that facilitate CBNRM are summarized in Box 1.1.

Inspired by a number of innovative projects in which rural groups were able to improve their livelihoods through the use of wildlife – most notably, the Communal Areas Management Programme for Indigenous Resources (CAMPFIRE) in Zimbabwe – government officials and non-governmental organizations (NGOs) around southern Africa began realizing that biodiversity resources could play an important role in the lives of impoverished rural people, and that the productive use of plant and animal resources could play a role in rural development (Matzke and Nabane, 1996). Throughout southern Africa and the rest of the world, authorities began experimenting with new approaches to the management of natural resources. During the mid 1980s,

Box 1.1 International agreements affecting people–natural resource relationships in southern Africa

Southern African Development Community (SADC) protocol on tourism, wildlife conservation and law enforcement

Objective: each state party shall ensure the conservation and sustainable use of wildlife resources under its jurisdiction. Parties shall take measures facilitating community-based natural resource management (CBNRM) practices in wildlife management and wildlife law enforcement. The protocol also calls for economic and social incentives for the conservation and sustainable use of wildlife.

SADC protocol on shared watercourses

Objective: to foster closer cooperation for judicious, sustainable and coordinated management, protection and utilization of shared watercourses and regional integration and poverty alleviation. State parties undertake to respect the existing rules of customary or general international law relating to the utilization and management of the resources of shared watercourses.

Convention concerning the protection of the world cultural and natural heritage (World Heritage Convention)

Objective: to promote cooperation among nations to protect natural and cultural heritage of outstanding universal value, of concern to all people. It promotes multi-sectoral initiatives and integrates cultural and biological conservation.

Convention on Biological Diversity (CBD)

Objective: to effect international cooperation in the conservation of biological diversity, and to promote the sustainable use of living natural resources worldwide, as well as the sharing of the benefits arising from the use of biological resources. Article 8j relates to safeguarding intellectual property rights and benefit-sharing. Signatories are obliged to develop their capacity to pursue the convention's objectives.

Convention to Combat Desertification (CCD)

This convention applies to those countries experiencing serious drought and/or desertification, particularly in Africa. The CCD encourages integrated development to prevent or reduce land degradation, and to rehabilitate and reclaim land. Its core principles are the participation of local communities, partnerships and cooperation at all levels and consideration of the needs of developing countries.

Convention on International Trade in Endangered Species of Wild Fauna and Flora (CITES)

Objective: the control and monitoring of illegal international trade in endangered species and their products by means of a system of import/export permits.

Convention on Wetlands of International Importance especially as Waterfowl Habitat (Ramsar Convention)

Objective: advocates the conservation, management and wise use of wetlands. The contracting parties note their conviction that wetlands constitute a resource of great economic, cultural, scientific and recreational value, the loss of which would be irreparable.

International Covenant on Civil and Political Rights

According to Human Rights Committee, General Comment 23, Article 27 (1994):

> ...the Committee observes that culture manifests itself in many forms, including a particular way of life associated with the use of land resources, especially in the case of indigenous peoples. That right may include such traditional activities as fishing or hunting and the right to live in reserves protected by law.

The covenant stresses the rights of all people to land and equal participation in decision-making.

International Labour Organization (ILO) Convention

The ILO Convention specifies that rights to land of indigenous people should be recognized (Article 11). 'Aboriginal title' is embedded in memory and does not necessarily depend upon any act of the state.

Dana Declaration on Mobile People and Conservation

This declaration, signed by a group of concerned individuals in April 2002, recognizes the contribution that 'mobile people' (a subset of indigenous people whose livelihoods depend upon the use of mobility as a management strategy) could make to conservation. It calls for mutually beneficial partnerships between mobile peoples and those involved in conservation.

IUCN–World Conservation Union principles and guidelines on indigenous and traditional peoples and protected areas (IUCN Resolution 1.53 of 1996, amended in 1998)

These principles call for the development of policies for protected areas that safeguard the interests of indigenous people, taking into account customary resource practices and traditional land tenure systems. It promotes the recognition of indigenous people's rights, agreements between them and conservation agencies, decentralization and transparency, and benefit-sharing arrangements.

United Nations Educational, Scientific and Cultural Organization (UNESCO) Man and the Biosphere (MAB) Programme guidelines

Man and the Biosphere (MAB) is an approach to conservation that allows conservation agencies to register a system of core conservation areas surrounded by buffer zones. It enables the linking of communal lands to core conservation areas.

examples of good private-sector wildlife management and forestry practices outside of protected areas were noticed and documented. Governments and parastatals across East Africa, Zimbabwe, Zambia, Botswana, Namibia, South Africa and Mozambique switched to new approaches (SASUSG, 1997).

Factors catalysing the shift towards a more people-centred approach

The pressure to promote natural resource-related development in rural areas, and the need to diversify the economy to include tourism and the commercial use of biodiversity, gave further impetus to this shift in approach. In Botswana, there was a realization that government-promoted livestock development programmes were undermining traditional resource use by remote rural communities (Boggs, 2000), and that they were prone to international trends such as consumer aversion, especially because of disease scares. More recently in South Africa, the government has launched a number of Spatial Development Initiatives (SDIs) to diversify the rural economy, notably the Wild Coast SDI (Timmermans, 1999; Kepe et al, 2000), the Maputo Corridor and the Lubombo SDI – all of which are aimed at stimulating nature tourism industries based on the landscape, wildlife and other natural assets in these regions. All of these programmes stress the need for rural residents, previously excluded from the mainstream of the rural economy by discriminatory practices, to participate as entrepreneurs and beneficiaries in the new resource-based industries that are being stimulated.

Another catalyst for the change in emphasis was the lack of resources for law enforcement, and the view that devolution of authority to communities would reduce the transaction costs of managing natural resources (see Chapter 12). Rural groups started using subversion as a tactic to coerce authorities into providing better access to land and natural resources.

During the early and mid 1990s, a number of communities began organizing to claim back title to land in protected areas from which they were removed during colonial and apartheid times. NGOs began to play an important support role in this regard (SASUSG, 1997). The Luangwa Integrated Rural Development Project (LIRDP) in Zambia was initiated as a tactic to reduce poaching (see Chapter 17), as was the Integrated Rural Development and Nature Conservation (IRDNC) programme in Namibia (see Chapter 13). Community forestry in Zimbabwe gained popularity because the government did not have the personnel and other resources to conserve forests, leading to the subsequent co-opting of local forest committees as agents of government (see Chapter 19).

This same pressure from local people was spectacularly evident in the Eastern Cape region of South Africa when, as a symbolic act of defiance staged during 1995, residents of settlements around the Dwesa, Cwebe and Mkambati reserves staged headline-grabbing invasions of the reserves. Once there, they began plundering shellfish in the marine reserves and decimating indigenous inland forests (Timmermans, 1999). The South African government, in this case, quickly started feeling the pressure to deal with their grievances that included the expediting of land claims. In most countries in the subregion, then, the change towards a more community-centred approach was thus strongly motivated by a desire to change communities' attitudes to wildlife and conservation (see Chapter 9), with the expectation that the status of natural resources would improve.

Political expediency and a recognition by governments that rural voters are important also played a role in fostering the new people-centred approach. In Zimbabwe, the government started claiming responsibility for the successes of CAMPFIRE, while simultaneously giving its district councils an increasingly controlling role in the programme (Hasler, 1999). In Zambia, the LIRDP gained the acceptance of President Kenneth Kaunda partially on the basis of its political benefits (Barry Dalal-Clayton, pers comm; Richard Bell, pers comm). In Namibia, communal conservancies arose, in part, because of an attempt by the post-apartheid Namibian government to redress the imbalances of the past (see Chapter 13). In Malawi, the government adopted a policy of decentralization to appease local government and rural voters (see Chapter 12).

For their part, conservation organizations saw community-based natural resource management (CBNRM) as an opportunity to expand southern Africa's conservation estate, as well as an opportunity to conserve natural resources outside existing protected areas. In some cases, conservation agencies were able to expand the size of the protected wildlife estate by entering into negotiations with local residents and negotiating for 'contract parks' in which communal land was incorporated within game reserves so that it could be used for conservation and development purposes. In South Africa, the Richtersveld and the West Coast National Parks, along with the more recent agreement with the Makuleke people around the northern parts of the Kruger National Park, are examples (SANParks, 2000). Land restitution in South Africa has generally had positive spin-offs for conservation: in most instances, land was gained for conservation and local people become more supportive of resource conservation (Fabricius and de Wet, 2002). One of the claims of the success of the CAMPFIRE programme is its contribution to the conservation estate in Zimbabwe (Hasler, 1999).

The advent of common property theory

Also in the early 1980s, social scientists began having an impact on the natural resource management debate and catalysed a more people-centred approach. Their key contribution was to alert ecologists and range scientists to common property theory and its value in CBNRM. Zimbabwe's CAMPFIRE programme set the scene, with social scientists from the University of Zimbabwe's Centre for Applied Social Studies (CASS), and economists of the World Wide Fund For Nature (WWF) in Zimbabwe playing a pivotal role (Murphree, 1997). The myth that common property management always led to an abuse of natural resources was consistently questioned. The new challenge, however, was how to manage common pool resources, such as ecosystems, sustainably and, in particular, how to set up lasting institutions for their management. According to Lesley Boggs:

Centralized and privatized control of resources has been the predominating management strategy since the early 20th century. This already established strategy was strengthened by Garrett Hardin's widely acclaimed 1968 theory described as 'The Tragedy of the Commons' (Hardin, 1968). Hardin argued that common ownership of a resource cannot succeed, as the innate human desire to maximize individual benefits will inevitably cause overuse of a common resource leading to ultimate resource degradation. Partly because of frequent and chronic declines in state managed resources and in direct challenge to Hardin's theory, in the last decade there has been a growing body of theory and discussion in the social sciences dedicated to the study of local management and decentralization. Central to this shift is a body of theory collectively known as common property theory (CPT), which argues for the potential success of commonly managed resources and identifies several broad but crucial criteria for success in commonly managed natural resources (Boggs, 2000).

Common property theory (CPT) has now become one of the foundations of CBNRM (Campbell et al, 2001). The 'CAMPFIRE principles', pioneered by Marshall Murphree of CASS (Murphree, 1997) and the more recently adapted and refined 'principles of second generation CBNRM' (see Chapter 17) reflect the influence of CPT (see Box 1.2).

Ostrӧm (1990) documented eight widely accepted principles for lasting common property institutions (see Box 1.3). These rules are valuable and have been used to initiate conservancies on communal land in Namibia (Jones, 1999), and have formed the basis for CBNRM principles developed by Shackleton (2000) (Box 1.4).

We are, however, discovering that a more rigorous and nuanced social analysis of the processes of political and economic change at the country level, and the specific social, political and biological conditions at the local level, is required, rather than adopting sets of rules in a blueprint way. Murphree, for example, has made the critical point that the CAMPFIRE approach is based on the specific demographic conditions that apply in parts of Zimbabwe:

Small institutions increase the efficiency and willingness to take responsibility and decrease the likelihood for corruption. They enhance a sense of 'collective identity' and make it more practicable to enforce rules. From a social dynamics perspective, scale is an important consideration: large-scale structures tend to be ineffective, increasing the potential for inefficiency, corruption and the evasion of responsibility. Conversely, a communal resource management regime is enhanced if it is small enough (in membership size) for all members to be in occasional face-to-face contact, enforce conformity to rules through peer pressure and has a long-standing collectively identity... CAMPFIRE has been

---

Box 1.2 CAMPFIRE principles of CBNRM

1 The unit of production should be the unit of management and benefit.
2 Producer communities should be small enough that all households can participate face to face.
3 Community corporate bodies should be accountable to their constituency.
4 Functions should be conducted at the lowest appropriate level.
5 The link between production and benefit should be transparent and immediate.
6 Communities must have full choice in the use of wildlife revenues, including household cash.
7 All marketing should be open and competitive and should be done by the wildlife producers themselves.
8 The rates of taxation of wildlife should be similar to that of other resources.
9 Activities or investment should not be undertaken unless they can be managed and sustained locally.
10 Government is the ultimate authority for wildlife.
11 Devolving authority and developing community management capacity is a process.
12 Co-management is necessary, especially in the shift from central to community management systems.

Source: Murphree (1997)

---

developed in a national context by nationals for a national objective. The intent has never been that of a package export of the programme in its specifics to other countries (Murphree, 1997).

Fortmann et al (2001) calls this 'case-by-case management' – that is, analysing each case on its own merits. They postulate that the performance record of case-by-case management will be a mix of positive and negative outcomes, varying from one case to another, which is why strategies for enhancing CBNRM are so difficult to generalize or replicate. Each case differs in terms of ecosystem properties, people's beliefs about ecosystems being managed, the types of models (decision systems) used to understand and predict ecosystem functioning, the modes of learning, and how success and failure is measured (see Table 1.1).

Most policy-makers now accept that top-down decision-making in resource management is likely to precipitate a spiral of conflict that places natural resources at risk. It is also generally accepted that the social aspects of resource management have been neglected. This over-concentration on the biological and ecological aspects of resource protection has contributed to the hazards that face natural resources in the region. Fortmann et al (2001) conclude that 'devolution now!' is the only really effective policy instrument in case-specific situations. It is clear that the new, more open, approach to

---

BOX 1.3 RULES FOR LASTING COMMON PROPERTY INSTITUTIONS

1 *Clearly defined boundaries:* Individuals or households who have rights to use resources must be clearly defined, as must the boundaries of the resource itself.

2 *Rules governing use or provision of the resource must be appropriate to local conditions:* Rules for using the resource or providing it to resource users, such as restricting time, place, technology and how much can be used, must be appropriate to the resource itself, including availability.

3 *Collective-choice arrangements:* Most individuals affected by the operational rules can participate in changing the rules.

4 *Monitoring:* Those monitoring the rules and the use of the resource are either resource users themselves or accountable to the users.

5 *Graduated sanctions:* Resource users who break the rules are likely to face various degrees of punishment, depending upon the seriousness and context of the offence. Punishments are decided by other resource users, by officials accountable to them, or by both.

6 *Conflict resolution mechanisms:* Resource users and their officials have rapid access to low-cost local mechanisms to resolve conflicts among users or between users and officials.

7 *Recognition of legitimacy:* Government supports, or at least does not challenge, the rights of resource users to devise their own institutions.

8 *Nested enterprises* (for common property resources that are part of larger systems): Resource use or provision, monitoring, enforcement, conflict resolution and governance activities are organized in multiple layers of nested institutions, where rights and responsibilities are clearly defined.

Source: Öström (1990)

---

resource management has come to stay. Dialogue and participation is the expected norm in southern Africa, and the expectations among communities and politicians are high. As Hulme and Murphree (1999) put it:

> *Of one thing there can be no doubt, however: the old orthodoxy of conservation purely as state enforced protection, that evolved in the colonial era and was continued by the elites who took control of independent Africa in the 1950s and 1960s, is no longer presented as a viable option by any serious actors.*

Certainly, these days, proponents of a revival of blanket 'fines-and-fences' approaches to natural resource management are not taken seriously by most donors, policy-makers and local communities in southern Africa. The challenge is to understand the conditions under which devolution and community-based management of resources are likely, or are less likely, to be successful. This is what this book is about.

Box 1.4 PRINCIPLES FOR IMPROVING THE CHANCES OF SUCCESS OF
CBNRM INITIATIVES, AND CRITERIA FOR EVALUATING THEM

1 A diverse and flexible range of livelihood options exist and are maintained

- A diversity of resource types is maintained.
- A diversity of economic opportunities is developed and maintained.
- The community can easily switch from one livelihood strategy and resource to another as the need arises.
- There is room for ecological and social systems to renew themselves: change and adaptive renewal in social and ecological systems are not obstructed.

2 The production potential of the resource base must be maintained or improved

- Key resources keep on producing.
- Biodiversity is maintained.
- Perennial streams continue to flow and erosion gullies do not increase.
- Soils remain fertile.
- Patches of natural habitat remain.
- People plant trees, grow crops or breed animals to compensate for scarcity of wild resources.
- Sound rules for resource management exist; rules are based on local knowledge.
- There is an environmental management plan in place and it is being implemented.
- Participatory ecological monitoring systems are in place.

3 Institutions for local governance and land and resource management must be in place, and they must be effective

- The institution for resource management operates at a local level.
- The institution and its management structure are strong.
- The institution and its management structure are legitimate.
- The institution and its management structure are adaptive, flexible and evolve.
- The institution and its management structure are efficient in their operation.
- Common property is legitimate in law (local rights recognized and enforceable; legislation exists for institutions at grassroots level).
- The community has secure access to land and resources.
- Outside institutions support the local CBNRM institution.
- Acceptable rules are in place.
- Everyone is clear about their roles.
- Grassroots institutions are not dominated by those higher up.
- There is agreement over the use and management of shared resources that span group boundaries.
- There are good social relations within the community and no unmanageable conflicts.
- Benefits are not biased or appropriated by one sector in the community only.
- The distribution of benefits is fair: those who deserve to benefit do so.

4 There must be economic and other benefits to provide an incentive for the wise use of resources

- The type of CBNRM makes economic sense; it is a viable form of land use.
- Resource degradation is not severe.
- External subsidies are limited.
- The perceived and actual benefits outweigh the costs.
- Everyone understands and sees the costs and benefits.
- Some revenue from CBNRM is held back to support local resource management functions.
- Community members have been trained in relevant skills.
- Both individual entrepreneurs and community groups take part in the initiative.
- Partnerships exist.
- There are local enterprises that add value to resources (for example, furniture making from wood and tourism accommodation).

5 There are effective policies and laws; they are implemented, and authority is handed down to the lowest level where there is capacity

- There is political stability.
- Policies that promote devolution are in place.
- The state is committed to local control over resources.
- Outsiders' access can be limited.

6 There should be sensitive and responsible facilitation from outside

- There is empowerment and re-empowerment of resource users.
- The process is adaptive.

7 Local-level power relations are favourable for CBNRM, and local relationships are understood

- There is little evidence of division within the community; conflicts can be managed.
- Own agendas and vested interests do not dominate the process; the weaker role players – for example, the poor and women – can speak openly.

Source: adapted from Shackleton (2000)

New problems on the horizon

More recently, however, researchers and project managers are discovering flaws in the design of most CBNRM initiatives. Responses range from outright and hostile criticism (Spinage, 1998) to approaches that question some of the assumptions of CBNRM and suggest modifications to current methodologies (Fabricius et al, 2001; Adams and Hulme, 2001).

There is also a growing realization that the theoretical foundations of CBNRM are on shaky ground: our predictive understanding of the relationship between people and natural resources is weak, as is our understanding of the

Table 1.1 *The characteristics of case-by-case management*

Criterion	Characteristic
Ecosystem properties	'Patchy', anthropogenic landscapes with zones of conflict; natural features are overlaid and emphasized by 'human artifacts'.
Beliefs about ecosystem being managed	Each ecosystem is its own case, where managers improve ecosystem performance but with varying success.
Types and foci of models employed	A variety of formal and informal models are used and they differ in importance, depending upon the merits of each case. The focus is on increasing the ability to predict, often through using multiple decision systems.
Modes of learning	Learning takes place through real-time management and constant evaluation; each case is treated in its own right; learning is passed on from one generation to the next.
Measure of success	Success is measured against multiple criteria and is, over time, always mixed with failure.
Measure of failure	Failure is, to some degree, inevitable because of multiple criteria; success cannot be generalized beyond the case being managed.

Source: adapted from Fortmann et al (2001)

factors that shape the outcome of this relationship. But is predicting the functioning of complex systems a feasible objective, in the first place? Madzwamuse and Fabricius (Chapter 10) attempt this, adopting the model refined by Gunderson and Holling (2002).

Researchers, project managers and natural resource management professionals have come to realize that nature-based rural development is associated with many problems and flawed assumptions, notably:

- *Policies that simply do not work:* Policies that govern the participation of local people in natural resource management are often poorly coordinated, and inter-departmental cooperation is weak or non-existent. Most policies are broadly defined and lay out the basic principles of the role of natural resources in rural development and people's involvement in natural resource management. Implementation guidelines, stipulating how to put such policies into practice, are scarce (but see DEAT, 2003). Most government policies aim to devolve the *responsibility* (and often the costs) for natural resource management to local people, without giving them decision-making authority. Not surprisingly then, governments' expectations of improved custodianship and a change in attitude in communities have not been met (see Chapters 12, 15 and 18).
- *Different definitions of participation:* Although the policy trend is towards increased participation and devolution of natural resource management to communities, the interpretation of 'participation' on the ground varies

widely. The state will always have a role in natural resource management (see Chapter 17), but many natural resource professionals feel that the state should control access and decision-making over natural resources, and that communities should be passive participants (see Chapter 15).

- *Incapable professionals:* Officials remain poorly equipped to deal with a people-centred approach to natural resource management. While many officials go along with the new approach, there are signs that others would quite happily revert to orthodox, top-down approaches (Fabricius and de Wet, 2002). Donor funds are sometimes used to prop up bureaucracies that then crumble when the donors disappear (see Chapter 15). Officials do not treat rural communities with the same respect that they would extend to private landowners and apply the law differentially. The same officials often delay progress by being too thinly spread and by not being available for meetings and other activities in which they insist on participating (see Chapter 14).

- *Differences in worldviews between outsiders and local people:* Donors, project managers and officials often do not understand the belief systems of people in rural areas and erroneously assume that profits alone will lead to development and resource conservation. The importance of spirit mediums (see Chapters 6 and 15) is often overlooked; witchcraft accusations and behaviour attributed by outsiders to 'superstition' can precipitate unexpected events (see Chapter 19); democratic elections of community structures often do not meet expectations (see Chapters 12 and 17); and people's values of wildlife and their beliefs about the use of resources differ from those of project managers. Overseas hunters, for instance, are often perceived as privileged individuals who are allowed to break laws that the local people themselves are expected to uphold and abide by (see Chapter 18). This happens when decisions about resource harvesting and hunting quotas are taken elsewhere and not communicated to local people.

- *Naive assumptions about custodianship:* The assumption that local people, when given opportunities to participate and benefit from biodiversity, will automatically become custodians of the natural resource base is naive (see Chapter 9). The engagement of local people in biodiversity conservation requires a range of critical ingredients that vary from one context to another. The lack of meaningful devolution of authority and the lack of land ownership has, no doubt, contributed to apathy in many communities (see Chapter 18).

- *Intra-community conflicts:* Conflicts within communities abound, ranging from stock theft (see Chapter 11) to squabbles over leadership, land and revenue (see Chapter 9), and poaching by community members of their own wildlife (see Chapter 15). Many of these conflicts are not appropriately managed or resolved. Elites attempt to get hold of an unfair share of the benefits from rangelands, hunting and donor funds at the expense of ordinary people (especially the weakest and poorest who are in greatest need of development) (see Chapters 11, 15 and 17). Conflicts have also emerged between elected representatives and co-management organizations, and traditional leadership who often expect their share of the benefits from wildlife by virtue of only their positions (see Chapters 12 and 17). Newly formed institutions can also become co-opted by government and start acting like agents of the state rather than as elected community representatives (see Chapters 12 and 19).

- *Elusive communities:* The expectation that local people should 'speak with one voice' and have a single vision that encompasses all the aspirations of the group often does not hold. It is becoming apparent that the term 'community' is difficult to define, at least, because local groupings constantly redefine and re-align themselves and reformulate their objectives (see Chapter 15). Moreover, 'indigenous people' refuse to subscribe to the stereotype assigned to them by donors and NGOs of 'pristine hunter-gatherers'. But they also do not fit the development stereotype of 'civilized' Western citizens. The !khomani San, for example, are now split between a loin-cloth-wearing 'traditional' faction and a Westernized, Afrikaans-speaking 'hybrid' faction, after being successful in a lucrative land claim where they showed remarkable solidarity in public (Robins, 2001). Koch expands on this theme in Chapter 4.
- *Overestimated financial benefits:* The benefits from formal, project-related nature-based enterprises is generally overestimated (see Chapter 15). Most of the formal community-based tourism and wildlife management projects produce meagre dividends per household (see Chapter 18). Non-financial benefits, on the other hand, are more valued and underestimated (see Chapters 15 and 18; Ashley, 1998). Turner expands on this in Chapter 2.
- *Weak institutions:* Local institutions are often weak and unstable, or unacceptably flexible, and traditional institutions are disappearing and are being replaced by open-access systems and lawlessness (see Chapter 11). Furthermore, the amount of effort and resources required to sufficiently develop local institutions has been grossly underestimated. The extent and duration of facilitation and assistance to local communities that is required has equally been underestimated; project managers now realize that project cycles should be measured in decades rather than years (Jones, 1999).
- *Poor local administrative capacity:* Local people's ability to manage and administer revenues from natural resources is primarily weak. Because of decades of poverty and experiences of being marginalized, the temptation to be corrupt is often too great. New elites, for example, often try their utmost to gain a disproportionate share of the benefits from biodiversity projects (see Chapter 9). The much-promoted partnerships between communities and the private sector are also not the panacea they were anticipated to be: joint venture partners often approach community-based enterprises with caution because of the high risks involved, the high potential for corruption and manipulation, and uncertainties about their rights and obligations (see Chapter 9; Andrew et al, 2000).

- *Globalization:* These days local people are as keen as most other citizens to spend their money on modern conveniences such as cellular phones and vehicles, and are much more mobile than before (see Chapter 9). Many rural villages consist of school children and old people, with everyone of working age either looking for a job in the urban areas or already working there. This has profound implications for capacity development in rural communities. This aspect is dealt with in more detail by Koch in Chapters 3 and 4.

Boggs (2000) sums it up by arguing that:

> Community-based natural resource management programmes have been implemented throughout the world, including Botswana, in the past decade. Eagerly embracing the theory and principles of common property theory and decentralization, the primary goals of the Natural Resource Management Programme are:
>
> 1   to increase rural economic development; and
> 2   to improve natural resource management through improved attitudes to wildlife.
>
> However, there have been few examples of long-term success of community-based initiatives as these have a high incidence of degeneration through time. The assumptions underlying the programmes, specifically that improved incomes will improve attitudes towards wildlife, require systematic research and validation.

It is now becoming evident that success in formal CBNRM is elusive, and that, in any event, long-term success cannot be guaranteed. In many instances, CBNRM is not the answer and other development pathways or conservation strategies are required (Hulme and Murphree, 1999). Furthermore, Fortmann et al's (2001) case-by-case philosophy implies that there will almost always be a mix of losses and gains, and that all-out success or failure seldom occurs when dealing with people–natural resource relationships.

Describing people–natural resource relationships

'Everyday' resource use

'Everyday resources' include fuelwood, medicinal plants, water, bees, rivers and other water-related ecosystems, and rangelands, all contained in urban and rural landscapes (see Chapters 6, 7, 8 and 11). Everyday resource use covers the complete range of available resources in a locality at any particular time, and people incorporate a selection (or 'bundle') of resources and landscapes in their day-to-day lives.

Culture is intricately bound up with the use and management of natural resources, and conservation, consumptive use and local belief systems form part of a way of living (see Chapter 6). Local and traditional knowledge often play a signficant role in the management of everyday natural resource use. Traditional institutions have, over many generations, incorporated techniques to monitor resources, created rules to control the amount and rate of natural resource use, and developed sanctions that govern and restrain the consumption of resources (see Chapters 6 and 11). Many of these rules are tacit rather than explicit, and have become intertwined with religion, belief systems and customs. Traditional customs constantly change, however, in response to outside political and other influences, local events, changes in leadership, outside interventions and intermixing between ethnic groups and clans (see Chapter 10).

In many instances, donors have stepped in to augment the existing capacity of communities – for example, in the case of community beekeeping. They have played a role by finding markets and improving existing practices (see Chapter 7). In water resources management, facilitators are strengthening local institutions and assisting them in formalizing their management structures into water users' forums (Motteaux, 2001). In range management, donors introduced grazing schemes to reduce overstocking. But interference in informal CBNRM practices is risky. Local people, more often than not, resist changes to traditional practices. This failure by outsiders to understand local tenure and institutional arrangements often has disastrous consequences, such as the sabotaging of projects by groups who feel marginalized (see Chapter 11). Magome and Fabricius provide a more extensive discussion of biodiversity in CBNRM in Chapter 5. Turner discusses CBNRM in rural livelihoods in more detail in Chapter 2.

'Formal' community-based natural resource management projects

Local people and external role players (government and NGOs) also engage in more formalized forms of resource use and management. These initiatives are more commercially oriented, usually make explicit reference to resource conservation, and are typically framed by funded projects or other external interventions. This is where the development industry is investing most of its effort. This is the synthetic 'big' CBNRM that development and conservation agencies are constructing with rural people. Examples of this type of natural resource management initiatives are joint forest management (see Chapter 19), community conservation (see Chapters 13, 15 and 16), community fisheries (see Chapter 12), nature tourism (see Chapters 9 and 10), sustainable rural livelihood initiatives (Fabricius et al, 2002), participatory watershed management (Motteaux, 2001), biological trade agreements (Wynberg and Swiderska, 2001) and agricultural development schemes (Andrew et al, 2000). Formal CBNRM requires collaboration between donors, NGOs, government and, of course, local communities. Many of these initiatives were started because authorities and donors perceived them as a 'quick fix' to solve natural resource-related problems such as illegal use or perceived degradation (see Chapter 17), as a way of protecting threatened natural resources outside protected areas (see Chapters 13 and 18), or because governments want to diversify their economies (see Chapter 15). In other instances, governments attempt to devolve natural resource use because it is unable to afford institutional controls (see Chapter 12).

Understanding how people gain access to natural resources is important in understanding natural resource use. Leach et al (1997) developed a generalized theory of access to natural resources called 'environmental entitlements'. Local people are constantly in search of power and control (entitlements) over natural resources in order to attain other end goals. Resource management initiatives (at any point in time) can only claim to work if the main role players have acquired specific capabilities through effectively using natural resources (see Figure 1.1). A second feature of the entitlements approach is that the untapped ecosystem goods and services (populations of plants and animals, abiotic resources, habitats and ecosystems) in an area become useful through the impact of transforming structures or institutions (Leach et al, 1997). These mechanisms act like catalysts that convert ecosystem goods and services from resources with potential benefits, to resources over which local people have rights and which they can put to use (called 'endowments' by Leach et al, 1997).

These transforming structures and institutions are of particular relevance in formal CBNRM: they are the main driving forces that determine whether ecosystems can become useful to communities as commodities over which they have rights, and as sets of benefits over which they have effective command and control. At any point in time, the key criterion for success is whether local people have attained their goals and increased their capabilities. Based on the environmental entitlements framework, a number of key criteria relating to structures and institutions that affect the achievements of CBNRM initiatives have emerged (see Figure 1.1). These include:

- international, national and sub-national policies and strategies (for example, approaches to law enforcement, and policies about land and resource ownership);
- the capacity of communities to manage natural resources and, in particular, the existence and strength of traditional knowledge;
- the existence, and application, of local regulations and restrictions;
- the strength of community-based organizations;
- the mechanisms by which benefits are shared;
- the size of financial and non-financial benefits, and whether they exceed the costs to local people; and
- the balance between benefits received, and the amount of effort (or other costs) that people are required to put into management (those who put more in should get more out).

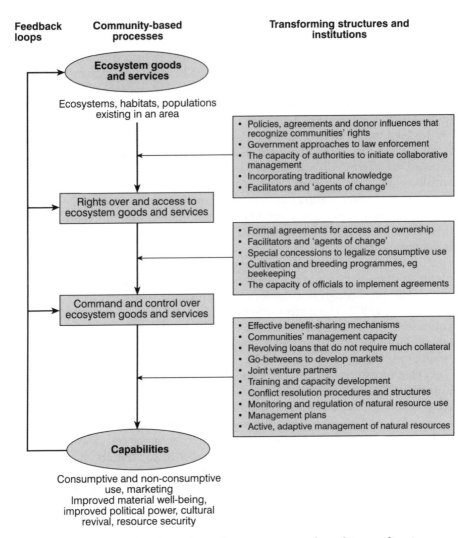

Figure 1.1 *The environmental entitlements approach and its application to people–natural resource relationships*

The problem with the environmental entitlements approach is that it portrays this succession – from untapped goods and services, to entitlements to capabilities – as a linear process. This is exactly what Murphree (1997) warns against when he states, that:

> ...*success [in CBNRM] is too often seen, often unthinkingly, as a linear progression towards a predetermined set of fixed goals. Analytically, this is convenient as it enables us to set criteria and measure progress along a spectrum of degrees of accomplishment, in governance and community capacity as well as the other*

> *themes chosen for the programme... in reality, we know that 'progress' in CBNRM projects and programmes is not linear. What, in the light of our own criteria, is judged as static or recalcitrant may shift to what we consider 'success,' while 'success cases' may seem to falter and fail. Nor is 'progress' in CBNRM predictable. Our predetermination of goals can never be more than partial and indeterminate.*

Natural and social scientists now agree that success in CBNRM is elusive and variable. But 'communities' always knew this. This explains why many local groups do not take kindly to efforts to introduce stable management systems and rigid, Western-style institutions into CBNRM.

The core elements of people–natural resource relationships in southern Africa

Flexibility through diversity: A diversity of landscapes, livelihood assets and resources allows people to be flexible, to switch from one livelihood strategy to another as the need arises, and to put their livelihood eggs in many different baskets.

Participation: Local people are involved in the planning and implementation of local initiatives.

Ownership: Ownership (or at least legally recognized and secure use rights) or tenure of land or resources lies with the group as a whole.

Motivations: Both short-term and long-term incentives exist to help promote collective action and the wise use of resources.

Benefits: Benefits accrue to those community members who make a contribution to the initiative.

Institutions: Management, regulation and decision-making occur at the local level through an acceptable local body.

Local knowledge: Management systems incorporate local traditions and institutions, including traditional knowledge systems.

State cooperation: The state respects local-level control and enables and facilitates its development.

Facilitation and conflict management: Mechanisms exist to manage conflicts, often with the assistance of external individuals or organizations.

Institutions: These are the codes of conduct, rules and norms that govern local behaviour. They can take the form of local 'dos and don'ts', constitutions, regulations, management plans, policies and laws. As will be shown later, institutional factors and criteria have an extensive influence on natural resource management.

Flexibility through diversity

Conventional definitions of CBNRM stress the participatory aspect but a recently identified key characteristic is the maintenance of a flexible range of livelihood options (Carney, 1998). One of the key differences between CBNRM and other natural resource-based enterprises is its focus on livelihoods, and the diversity of strategies, opportunities and resources that make up a livelihood. CBNRM is truly about keeping as many options as possible open for local people, maintaining flexibility and avoiding an undue emphasis on any one type of resource or livelihood strategy.

The adaptive renewal cycle (Gunderson and Holling, 2002) is a useful model to rationalize diversity and flexibility as a strategy (see Chapter 10 and Figure 10.1). Local people in southern Africa have discovered, over many generations of experimentation, that diversity means being in control, being able to cope with shocks and surprises, and slowing down the release phase of the adaptive renewal cycle. Furthermore, they have developed strategies to slow down the rate of the release phase ('putting the brakes on release', *sensu* Gunderson and Holling, 2002). These include using fire and ritual hunting to prevent build-up of biomass in ecosystems (see Chapter 10); seasonal movements of people and livestock (see Chapter 11); spiritual belief systems that allowed resources to rest by, for example, prohibiting resource use on certain days or certain periods (see Chapters 6 and 18); rules to prevent overuse (see Chapter 11); avoiding inflexible management systems, such as the use of fences in livestock grazing (see Chapter 11); and a total ban on hunting in delineated areas or of certain species (see Chapters 10 and 18).

Maintaining a diversity of opportunities, or options, in the system facilitates the movement between various semi-stable states in the social–ecological system. This increases flexibility and maintains the ability of societies or ecosystems to cope with unexpected events (shocks and surprise). Traditional communities used the strategy of investing in diversity to maintain their resilience in the face of uncertainty and unpredictability (not putting all of their livelihood eggs in one basket). Examples of unexpected or unpredictable events are droughts, floods, movements of animals or disease. Political surprises can take the form of conflicts, local and national political events, and changes in power relations (see Chapter 4). When this adaptive ability is neutralized, eg by prohibiting consumptive use and preventing mobility and burning of the veld, then communities can suffer disastrous consequences and are easily outcompeted by other groups (see Chapter 10).

Participation

Participation is generally believed to be a good thing in development theory and a key feature of CBNRM, but it comes in many different forms. There are strong reasons why CBNRM should be participatory. The user is typically part of the system and has his finger on the pulse (Walker et al, 2002); effective participation by members of the group is essential for the legitimacy of

Table 1.2 *A typology of participation*

Type of participation	Description
1 Passive participation	People being told what is going to happen or has already happened. Unilateral announcement without any listening to people's responses. The information being shared belongs only to external professionals.
2 Participation in information giving	People answering questions; questionnaire surveys or similar approaches. People do not have the opportunity to influence proceedings; findings are neither shared nor checked for accuracy.
3 Participation by consultation	People are being consulted and external agents listen to views. External agents define both problems and solutions; may modify these in the light of people's responses. Does not concede any share in decision-making; professionals are under no obligation.
4 Participation for material incentives	People provide resources – for example, labour – in return for food, cash or other material incentives. Much in-situ research and bioprospecting falls in this category.
5 Functional participation	People form groups to meet predetermined objectives; can involve the development of externally initiated committees, etc. Does not tend to be at early stages of project cycles or planning; rather, it occurs after major decisions have been made. Initially dependent upon external initiators and facilitators; may become self-dependent.
6 Interactive participation	Joint analysis, leading to action plans and the formation of new local groups or the strengthening of existing ones. Involves interdisciplinary methodologies, multiple perspectives and learning processes. Groups take control over local decisions; people have a stake in maintaining structures.
7 Self-mobilization	Initiatives taken independently of external institutions. May challenge existing inequitable distributions.

Source: Pretty et al (1994)

initiatives; and local people mistrust authorities and want to be involved and informed because of bad historical experiences. Pretty et al (1994) highlighted seven categories of participation, along a gradient of community involvement and empowerment (see Table 1.2). At the least participatory end of the spectrum, people are merely informed and do not contribute information or views. At the most participatory end, CBNRM is self-initiated; *'everyday CBNRM'* falls in this category (see Figure 1.2).

As authority gets transferred and the locus of control shifts from government to other stakeholders, expectations on all sides unavoidably increase. It is an unrealistic aim to 'never raise expectations'. One case study after another has taught us that the mere transfer of responsibility automatically results in raised expectations, irrespective of whether participants wanted this to happen or not. Project managers and officials need to be prepared for the symptoms of raised expectations in communities and to deal with these from the start.

The shift in power and delegation of responsibilities requires much more commitment, investment of resources and capacity development than before. CBNRM is not a cheap or low-key option. High-quality, light-touch facilitation is one of the key ingredients of success of CBNRM, as demonstrated in Namibia's community conservancies (see Chapter 13; Jones, 1999).

Dictatorships, though highly effective for a while, inevitably lead to unmanageable conflicts and the collapse of the system. But analysts are not unanimous in their assessment of whether top-down approaches can be sustainable. Barrow and Fabricius (2002) conclude that natural resources must contribute to people's well-being and that local people must be involved in their management:

> *The ground rules have changed: no protected area is an island, and people and conservation cannot be separated... Ultimately, conservation and protected areas in contemporary Africa must either contribute to national and local livelihoods, or fail in their biodiversity goals* (Barrow and Fabricius, 2002).

Brockington (pers comm) believes, however, that 'fortress conservation' is a reality, and that it can (albeit unjustly) be sustained under certain conditions, such as those in Nkomazi Game Reserve in Tanzania where he worked:

> *The lessons of history are that new mechanisms of natural resource use and management can be imposed by powerful groups on weaker, marginal peoples, and that this situation has continued without effective challenge for many years...we have to acknowledge the existence of the powerful forces mitigating against just solutions in order that the justices which community conservation portends might become reality* (Dan Brockington, pers comm).

Ownership and the concept of community

Much of the debate taking place in CBNRM is on the unit of ownership, and whether a natural resource management initiative has to be wholly community owned to qualify as CBNRM. The reality is that most, if not all, initiatives involve a combination of community and privately owned endeavours. CBNRM is multifaceted and involves an integration of different types of assets. In a typical village, for example, private and communal resources are managed side by side. Moreover, a particular resource (for example, a field) might be managed as a private resource during one period and communally during another, often after its abandonment.

Communities can be functionally identified in several ways through the type of organizations representing them; ethnic or clan affiliations; geography;

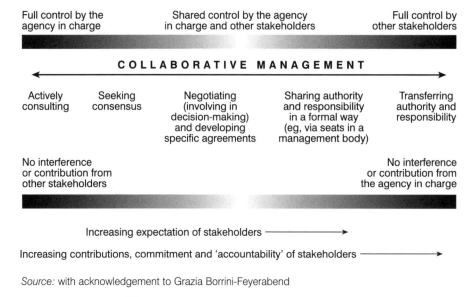

Source: with acknowledgement to Grazia Borrini-Feyerabend

Figure 1.2 *The participatory resource management continuum*

common interest; utilizing the same resource; or practising the same type of land use (Barrow and Murphree, 1998). The participatory approach advocated in most southern African CBNRM-type policies is, however, often premised on a homogeneous notion of 'community'. Working with communities requires flexible definitions and adaptability, as such entities constantly define and redefine themselves (Fabricius et al, 2001).

Donors and project managers are beginning to realize that it does not necessarily save time to group people together, and that working with fewer groups seldom fast-tracks a project. If the groupings within a community and the differences between groups are not taken into account, then conflicts emerge that are difficult to resolve. Different villages are, nevertheless, often grouped together as single entities for the sake of convenience, only for facilitators or project managers to discover that the groups vary greatly in terms of their skills, socio-economic backgrounds and attitudes. At Madikwe, for example, a single community development forum failed to address the needs of three villages that differed in their support for conservation, social dynamics and socio-economic profiles (Magome et al, 2000).

This fluidity does not apply only to geographical communities, but also to 'communities of interest'. In the Mkambati area, Kepe et al (2000) identified seven groupings who earned their livelihoods in different ways within the same village. These 'livelihood clusters' had different needs and used natural resources differently. For project managers to approach the entire community as if it is a single, like-minded entity would be a mistake.

There is also a tendency to define communities along geographic boundaries; but this could be equally misguided. In Namibia, several communities were grouped together within the same conservancy because of the legislative requirement that conservancies should have clearly defined boundaries. A geographic definition of boundaries was used that did not correspond with the local political boundaries. This roused dormant disputes over land, and the ensuing struggle over land and group membership hamstrung the development of the conservancy for a long time (Jones, 1999).

Incentives

There is often the assumption that the greater the material benefit, the wiser the natural resource base will be managed. This has, however, been refuted in some cases (see Chapters 5 and 9). Incentives motivate communities and other role players to not only participate in projects, but also to manage natural resources sustainably. Incentives also encourage local residents to engage in planning, to participate in the creation of new local institutions and rules, and, generally, to engage and sacrifice their time for many years or even decades. It is, however, comparatively easy to get people interested in a CBNRM initiative at the start – they often attend meetings and show an interest because it might be new to them, or because they are inquisitive. Residents tend initially to decide to become involved in CBNRM because of a heightened awareness that something has changed: a resource has become scarcer, funds have become available, or facilitation and capacity-building services are on hand. Ongoing interest and participation is a different matter, and therefore the incentives for initial participation differ from those for *ongoing* participation.

In most cases, local people are involved in CBNRM (and, especially, everyday resource management) because they have to be. Natural resources are their safety net to reduce risk, and natural resource management is one of the few fall-back mechanisms that will carry them through difficult economic and climatic cycles. CBNRM enables a level of flexibility and adaptability that is unparalleled in other livelihood strategies. The Basarwa in the Okavango Delta, for example, rely on natural resources to cope in an environment that is naturally dynamic, with constant changes in the availability of wildlife, plant and aquatic resources (see Chapter 10).

In addition to the material incentives to participate, there are many spiritual incentives for communities to engage in CBNRM. Spiritual incentives stem from ancestral belief systems – for example, in the water spirits that are found with remarkable consistency throughout the subregion (see Chapter 6). In participatory monitoring programmes, communities often voluntarily select water-related indicators to monitor ecosystem health (Rhodes University et al, 2001), and communities engaged in participatory catchment management processes seem to, as a rule, be highly motivated (Motteaux, 2001). In Zimbabwe, the Tonga believe that natural resources need to be used and managed in a manner that pleases the ancestors and God. They believe in preserving clan animals, and this inter-linking of worldviews, religion, customs and traditional knowledge greatly influences the way in which they regard wild animals (see Chapter 18).

Thus, people are primarily motivated by several incentives, whether a push by government and NGOs, the desire to apply their traditional knowledge, a vision of wildlife conservation (see Chapter 13), the promise of donor funding (see Chapter 15), or the hope of development which collectively motivated communities, as in Namibia, to participate in conservancies (see Chapter 13).

Benefits

The underlying assumption in CBNRM is that benefits from natural resources will result in benefits to the natural resource base and to society, and that this is a mutually reinforcing relationship (Ashley, 1998). These benefits can be tangible (measurable in monetary terms) or intangible. In reality, the distinction is less clear. But if the beneficiaries are uncertain about their future, then they tend to base their decisions on short-term gain only. Hara (Chapter 12), for example, found that crew members who did not own fishing gear tended to break the law purely to meet the targets imposed by the gear owners for whom they worked. Gear owners, who carried the legal responsibility, ignored locally made rules.

Many CBNRM projects deliver large quantum benefits to entire communities. CAMPFIRE, for example, delivered US$9.4 million over seven years (1989–1996) (Bond, 2001), while LIRDP delivered US$220,000 to 10,000 households between 1997 and 2001 (Brian Child, pers comm). The tangible benefits from wild resources used in people's everyday lives are consistently underestimated (see Chapters 2, 5 and 8).

The emphasis on tangible benefits can, however, create unexpected problems. Village Beach Committee members in Malawi, for example, refuse to serve voluntarily on committees; instead, they demand payment for this sacrifice (see Chapter 12).

Ashley (1998) documented a number of intangible benefits to communities who become involved in community wildlife management initiatives in Namibia. These benefits can broadly be grouped into four main categories (see Table 1.3).

During a 1998 project evaluation, members of the West Caprivi Conservancy Management Committee were asked: 'What is your vision of the benefits that you will receive in five years' time by forming a conservancy?' Their unanimous response was: ' To be able to control and manage our own natural resources.' This was after some US$70,000 per annum was generated from trophy hunting (Ashley, 1998).

Local knowledge

One of the hallmarks of CBNRM is its attention to the local and traditional knowledge base. This knowledge is constantly evolving and is embedded in local institutions. These are the local 'memory' for natural resource management. One important characteristic of traditional knowledge is that it is mostly tacit, whereas scientific knowledge is mostly explicit. Traditional knowledge is often transferred orally from one generation to another and has

Table 1.3 *Intangible benefits from CBNRM*

Category	Intangible dividend
Capacity-building and empowerment	Improved institutions and organizations More accountable leadership Defined membership More open processes for making decisions and sharing information Greater equality for weaker community members, especially women More cohesive social units New skills Confidence in dealing with outsiders Greater recognition Greater self-belief and an increased sense of control.
More secure livelihoods	Diversification and risk reduction More secure access to resources Ability to cope with change and surprise
Enhancement of cultural and aesthetic values	Revival of traditions and traditional knowledge Awareness by outsiders of community worldviews and belief systems
Improvements to the natural resource base	Better management when communities and the state cooperate

Source: adapted from Ashley (1998)

its roots in trial and error, and lessons learned over many centuries of successes and failures (Folke et al, 1998).

Why is local and traditional knowledge important? Although political correctness and responsiveness to donor needs is often cited as a reason for incorporating local knowledge within CBNRM, the most compelling reason is its practical value. Local knowledge is mostly undocumented and is transferred through stories and legends over countless generations. It is developed through 'learning the hard way', by trial and error and through adaptive management. The Basarwa, for example, have developed elaborate systems to cope with the harsh and unpredictable Okavango Delta environment. These systems include flexibility in their livelihood strategies. They elect different leaders for different tasks and use wildlife, plant and soil resources in a complementary manner. They know how to use fire to attract wildlife and to maintain the ecosystem in a state of constant renewal. They also believe that hunting is essential to keep animal populations healthy and at manageable levels, where they do not constantly clash with humans. It would take many years of experimentation to develop a comparable level of understanding through formal science (see Chapter 10).

The Tonga of Zimbabwe believe that an abundance of natural resources depends not only on the ecosystem, but also on the people using the resources 'in a manner that is in harmony with nature and pleases the ancestors and

God' (see Chapter 18). The Tonga believe that one should only hunt as much as one can eat, and then only after the meat from the previous hunt has been finished. Disregarding this rule would cause the lion spirit to take revenge, killing people and livestock. Certain animals – for example, eland and elephant – are sacred; accidentally killing one of them in a snare would result in a lengthy cleansing ceremony by the chief and the spirit medium.

Traditional knowledge constitutes a wealth of experience about management strategies that work, especially in unpredictable southern African environments. Local people think and act across sectoral or disciplinary divides – for example, communities do not separate their rangelands and forests from water, wildlife or fisheries. This puts local knowledge at the forefront of interdisciplinarity, something which academics are still struggling to come to terms with. Local users can detect and respond to changes in ecosystems much earlier than managers and researchers who do not live with their resources. They also know about fine-grained changes, such as early warnings of soil erosion or changes in water quality, long before these are detected at coarser levels with high-technology methods, such as satellite images or aerial photographs.

Local knowledge is a rich store of historical information about ecosystem change. This history is primarily unavailable in documented form, and will be either very expensive or impossible to obtain through conventional methods. Local knowledge is one of the few sources of information about the cultural value of natural resources: without tapping into people's local knowledge, much of the information about spiritual values (see Chapter 6), traditional adaptations (see Chapter 10) and traditional institutions (see Chapter 15) would not be available to planners and implementers of CBNRM initiatives.

One of the limitations of traditional ecological knowledge is that its reference framework is almost entirely based on local contexts and local historical events. In many instances, this local context does not take into account larger-scale contexts, such as the rarity of plant or animal species. At Dwesa, local people are unaware that the indigenous forest and intertidal ecosystems, common in their area, have special conservation significance (Palmer et al, 2002). In Botswana, the communities in the Okavango Delta are generally unaware that the wildlife that is abundant around them has all but disappeared from other parts of the country, and that the elephants causing them anguish might be going through a population crisis, if viewed at larger scales (see Chapter 9).

In southern Africa, at least, traditional knowledge is seldom linked to knowledge of political and institutional processes at the district/provincial, national and international levels. Where this hierarchical linkage does exist – for example, in the case of Dwesa Cwebe (Palmer et al, 2002) and the Namibian community conservancies (see Chapter 13) – then the effect on communities' awareness can be profound. 'Formal' CBNRM generally creates and relies on links between the holders of knowledge at the local level and those at higher levels, whereas 'everyday' resource management is generally developed locally. There is, however, an increasing number of exceptions where everyday resource management has managed to break through the scale barrier (for instance, when traditional healers travel to other countries; Penny Bernard, pers com) or where space is created around the 'policy fire' for those who have a direct stake in the natural resource base (Mayers and Fabricius, 1997).

There is, however, growing consensus that the traditional knowledge base is fast disappearing. The youth are not always interested in traditions and take issue with the discernible lack of democracy associated with traditional institutions (see Chapter 18). Many young people want to get out of rural areas and disappear as soon as they can find a job, often thanks to the training they received while participating in a CBNRM project (see Chapter 9; Boggs, 2000). Globalization and consumerism have found their way into remote rural areas, and traditional knowledge is, to a large extent, a relic of days gone by (see Chapters 12 and 18).

State cooperation

Governments have a major role to play in CBNRM, at three levels. Firstly, governments are party to *international* treaties and decide whether or not to commit to international agreements. They also decide to what extent and how they should honour these international commitments. Governments are often the main link between communities and international donors. Secondly, government is tasked with formulating policy at the *national and provincial* levels. While the pace of change at the policy level is much slower than local management processes, these processes have profound effects on the way in which CBNRM is enacted. Thirdly, government is often the main facilitator and capacity developer at the *local* level. The Namibian government, for example, played a crucial role in resolving conflicts around community conservancies in Namibia (Jones, 1999), while the Botswana government is a crucial link in the Botswana CBNRM programme (see Chapter 10).

However, many of the case studies in this volume have demonstrated the potentially obstructive role that government can play in CBNRM. Examples include:

- imposing taxes and other types of levies on CBNRM that do not apply to other natural resource enterprises (Chapter 17);
- making policies that marginalize local people and cause them to lose social capital, relinquish their access to natural resources and lose their capacity to adapt (Chapter 10);
- launching programmes that are insensitive to local belief systems (Chapter 18);
- co-opting communities and community institutions to become little more than extensions of the state machinery (Chapter 19);
- insisting on playing a role in CBNRM, but then withdrawing due to lack of capacity (Chapter 12); and
- over-regulating communities' ability to manage their own natural resources, especially where communities have been successful in claiming land inside protected areas (Chapter 16).

While legislative reforms in southern Africa have been substantial and are still evolving, there continue to be many shortcomings. In particular, the relationship between traditional authorities and formal legal systems has not been clarified and there are no policies that explicitly incorporate customary practices (see Chapter 12).

Facilitation and conflict management

Community wildlife management in southern Africa seems to be characterized by conflict (Roe et al, 2000) and it seems logical that other types of CBNRM should show the same characteristics. Conflicts in CBNRM escalated because of the typical factors that fuel conflict (Anstey, 1999). In an analysis of conflict and conservation in southern Africa, the following factors were found to exacerbate conflicts between protected area managers and communities (Fabricius et al, 2001):

- *The number of issues at stake:* Conflict managers widely accept that the level of conflict increases as the complexity of issues involved increases. In the case of CBNRM, the initial conflict precipitated by lack of access to natural resources and land in many instances became complicated by 'add-on' grievances over heavy-handed and unfair treatment of community members, violence on both sides, unilateral decisions over boundaries and quotas, nepotism in the appointment of staff, and increasingly disruptive and illegal actions by communities.
- *The level of investment by role players:* According to conflict management theory, conflict is positively correlated with how many resources the different parties have invested in obtaining their goals. Rural communities' investment in natural resources is considerable: most of southern Africa's rural people rely extensively on wild plants and animals for building materials, fuelwood, fodder and protein (see Chapter 8). Natural resource management officials, on the other hand, have made personal sacrifices, such as working exceptionally long hours, risking their lives during law enforcement operations, and personally contributing to the construction of infrastructure, such as roads and fences, in game reserves and forests. Their careers are on the line.
- *Meeting of goals:* When all of the parties are doing well, the potential for conflict is low; but conflict escalates rapidly when some role players lose, or when one or more role players harm the others. Natural resource management in the colonial era hurt rural communities through forced removals and disenfranchisement, with little gain for biodiversity conservation (Fabricius and de Wet, 2002).
- *Perceptions:* When perceptions are non-evaluative, conflicts tend to remain at manageable levels; but when the role players engage in negative stereotyping and 'enemy' perceptions, conflicts often escalate sharply. Many natural resource managers were (and still are), for example, highly sceptical about the sustainability of common property resource management, in keeping with sentiments expressed by early theorists such

as Garrett Hardin in his 'Tragedy of the commons' essay (1968). Many of them also have a weak understanding of the importance of natural resources and land in local people's lives. Communities, on the other hand, often see conservation, forestry and fisheries staff as the evil perpetrators of land evictions and heavy-handed policing.

- *Communication:* Low levels of conflict are associated with open and regular communication, while the absence of communication or the selective giving of information is associated with heightened conflict. Many of the past conflicts arose from differences in knowledge and understanding between communities and natural resource professionals.
- *Relations:* The association of state-driven natural resource management with injustice and suffering, especially because of forced relocation from traditional land, had a lasting impact on local people.
- *Types of tactics used:* Conflicts remain low when problem-solving tactics are employed; but when these are replaced by coercive behaviour, threats or violence, then conflicts tend to grow. Over the past century, strategies and actions on both sides became increasingly violent and coercive. Communities tended to respond to unjust treatment by government with the only source of power at their disposal: subversive behaviour such as land invasions, poaching and vandalism.

Institutions

Institutions are defined as 'the rules of the game' – rules and norms that govern human behaviour and provide a common understanding of what may and may not be done. Leach et al (1997) speak of institutions as 'regularized patterns of behaviour based on rules in use'. It is important to distinguish between the terms *institution* and *organization*. Organizations are groups of individuals bound together by some common purpose to achieve objectives, while institutions form the framework upon which organizations are based.

The decentralization debate has led to a greater recognition of the relevance of local knowledge and institutions. This was mainly precipitated by governments' realization of their lack of capacity (see Chapters 17 and 18), but also, in part, stemmed from a romantic belief that rural people have been able to live in harmony with their resources before colonialism took its toll (Ghai, 1992).

Stable and lasting institutions are the essential ingredient that makes the difference between communally managed and open-access systems (Ostrōm, 1990); institutions make decisions, formulate rules and enforce them. In Lesotho, traditional institutions administered by chiefs and headmen regulate all movements of livestock and have recently taken the step of proclaiming livestock-free ecological areas dedicated to tourism (see Chapter 11).

In southern Africa, many local institutions are not geared towards a 'winner takes all' democracy through simple voting. Decisions are either made through consensus or autocratically by traditional leaders. Traditional leaders, for example, regard it as their inherited right to receive benefits from natural resources, such as *mawe*, the weekly gift of fish to headmen around Lake Malawi (see Chapter 12). This important reality is often misunderstood by donors and governments when they insist on proper elections or referendum-type processes in decision-making and needs to be accepted as a given (or as part of the complicated cultural politics of rural Africa) (see Chapter 17).

CONCLUSIONS

A critical review of the historical, conceptual and global background of CBNRM, such as has been conducted in this chapter, is essential in order to improve our understanding of the relationship between people and natural resources in southern Africa. We need to recognize that this relationship is highly value laden and agenda driven. Objectivity in CBNRM is a myth – everyone has a motive and the motives do not necessarily converge. There are three distinct agendas: a conservationist and somewhat social democratic egalitarian agenda, advocated by well-meaning donors and project managers; a spiritual and traditional agenda, driven by communities who live close to natural resources and who are dependent upon them for their survival; and a materialistic, capitalist agenda, driven by the private sector and individual members of the local community, who choose to have a more selective engagement with conservation, egalitarianism or tradition and who see wild plants and animals as the road to affluence.

These agendas need to find common ground around five issues that all role players agree upon – namely:

- policies that devolve responsibility and make it easier for people to benefit materially from natural resources;
- clarity about land and resource ownership;
- the need to resolve conflicts;
- capacity development; and
- effective management systems.

If strategies can be developed around these five common strategic areas, then the three CBNRM agendas mentioned above might find common ground.

In exploring and intervening in this relationship between people and natural resources, practitioners, policy-makers, donors, communities and facilitators are, essentially, part of a movement towards a new, more just, social order. The new order sees people and natural resources as part of the same system, and links culture to nature. The end result will, hopefully, one day combine the best of private and common property regimes and lead to more efficient natural resource use and management.

REFERENCES

Abel, N and Blaikie, P (1986) 'Elephants, people, parks and development: The case of the Luangwa Valley, Zambia', *Environmental Management* 10: 735–751

Adams, W M and Hulme, D (2001) 'If community conservation is the answer, what is the question?' *Oryx* 35: 193–200

Andrew, M Fabricius, C and Timmermans, H (2000) *An Overview of Private Sector Community Partnerships in Forestry and Other Natural Resources in Eastern Cape.* Report produced for Huntings Technical Services for the Forest Enterprise Development Office, and Environmentek, Council for Scientific and Industrial Research (CSIR), Pretoria

Anstey, M (1999) *Managing Change, Negotiating Conflict.* Juta and Co, Cape Town

Ashley, C (1998) *Intangibles Matter: Non-Financial Dividends of Community-Based Natural Resource Management in Namibia.* Report for the World Wildlife Fund Living in a Finite Environment (LIFE) programme, Windhoek

Barrow, E G C (1996) *The Drylands of Africa: Local Participation in Tree Management.* Initiatives Publishers, Nairobi

Barrow, E and Fabricius, C (2002) 'Do rural people really benefit from protected areas: Rhetoric or reality?' *Parks* 12: 67–79

Barrow, E and Murphree, M W (1998) *Community Conservation from Concept to Practice: A Practical Framework.* Research Paper No 8 in the series Community Conservation Research in Africa: Principles and Comparative Practice. Institute for Development Policy and Management, University of Manchester, Manchester

Beinart, W (1990) 'Introduction: The politics of colonial conservation', *Journal of Southern African Studies* 15(2): 143–162

Bell, R H V (1987) 'Conservation with a human face: Conflict and reconciliation in African land use planning', in Anderson, D and Grove, R (eds) *Conservation in Africa: People, Policies and Practice.* Cambridge University Press, Cambridge

Boggs, L P (2000) 'Community power, participation, conflict and development choice: Community wildlife conservation in the Okavango region of Northern Botswana', *Evaluating Eden Discussion Paper* No 17. International Institute for Environment and Development, London

Bond, I (2001) 'CAMPFIRE and the incentives for institutional change', in Hulme, D and Murphree, M (eds) *African Wildlife and Livelihoods: The Promise and Performance of Community Conservation.* James Currey, Oxford, pp227–243

Bonner, R (1993) *At the Hand of Man: Perils and Hope for Africa's Wildlife.* Vintage Books, New York

Campbell, B, Mandondo, A, Sithole, B, De Jong, W, Luckert, M and Matose, F (2001) 'Challenges to the proponents of common property resource systems: Despairing voices from the social forests of Zimbabwe', *World Development* 29(4): 589–600

Carney, D (ed) (1998) *Sustainable Rural Livelihoods: What Contribution Can We Make?* Department for International Development, London

Carruthers, J (1989) 'Creating a national park, 1910 to 1926', *Journal of Southern African Studies* 15(2): 188–216

Carruthers, J (1993) '"Police Boys" and poachers: Africans, wildlife protection and national parks, the Transvaal 1902 to 1950', *Koedoe* 36(2): 11–22

Crush, J S (1980) 'National parks in Africa: A note on a problem of indigenisation', *African Studies Review* 23(3): 21–32

De Bruyn, T D and Scogings, P F (eds) (1998) 'Communal rangelands in southern Africa: A synthesis of knowledge. Proceedings of a symposium on policy making for the sustainable use of southern African communal rangelands', Department of Livestock and Pasture Science, University of Fort Hare, Alice

DEAT (2003) *Guidelines for the Implementation of Community-based Natural Resource Management (CBNRM) in South Africa*. Department of Environmental Affairs and Tourism, Pretoria

Fabricius, C and de Wet, C (2002) 'The influence of forced removals and land restitution on conservation in South Africa', in Chatty, D and Colchester, M (eds) *Conservation and Mobile Indigenous Peoples: Displacement, Forced Resettlement and Conservation*. Berghahn Books, Oxford, pp142–157

Fabricius, C, Koch, E and Magome, H (2001) 'Community wildlife management in southern Africa: challenging the assumptions of Eden', *Evaluating Eden Discussion Paper* No 6. International Institute for Environment and Development, London

Feely, J M (1986) *The Distribution of Iron Age Farming Settlements in the Transkei*. MA thesis, University of Natal, Durban

Folke, K, Berkes, F and Colding, J (1998) 'Ecological practices and social mechanisms for building resilience and sustainability', in Berkes, F and Folke, K (eds) *Linking Social and Ecological Systems*. Cambridge University Press, Cambridge, pp414–436

Fortmann, L, Roe, E and Van Eeten, M (2001) 'At the threshold between governance and management: Community-based natural resource management in southern Africa', *Public Administration and Development* 21: 171–185

Ghai, D (1992) *Conservation, Livelihood and Democracy: Social Dynamics of Environmental Changes in Africa*, Discussion Paper 33. United Nations Research Institute for Social Development, Paris

Gunderson, L H and Holling, C S (2002) *Panarchy: Understanding Transformations in Human and Natural Systems*. Island Press, Washington, DC

Hardin G (1968) 'Tragedy of the commons', *Science* 162: 1243–1248

Hasler, R (1999) 'An overview of the social, ecological and economic achievements and challenges of Zimbabwe's CAMPFIRE project', *Evaluating Eden Discussion Paper* No 3. International Institute for Environment and Development, London

Hulme, D and Murphree, M (1999) 'Communities, wildlife and the "new conservation" in Africa', *Journal for International Development* 11: 277–285

Huntley, B J and Matos, E (1992) *Biodiversity: Angolan Environmental Status Quo*. Assessment Report, IUCN/Regional Office for Southern Africa, Harare

Jones, B T B (1999) 'Rights, revenue and resources: The problems and potential of conservancies as community wildlife management institutions in Namibia', *Evaluating Eden Discussion Paper* No 2. International Institute for Environment and Development, London

Jones, B and Murphree, M W (2001) 'The evolution of policy on community conservation in Namibia and Zimbabwe', in Hulme, D and Murphree, M W (eds) *African Wildlife and Livelihoods: The Promise and Performance of Community Conservation*. James Currey, Oxford, pp38–58

Kepe, T, Cousins, B and Turner, S (2000) 'Resource tenure and power relations in community wildlife contexts: The case of the Mkambati area on the Wild Coast of South Africa', *Evaluating Eden Discussion Paper* No 16. International Institute for Environment and Development, London

Kepe, T and Scoones, I (1999) 'Creating grasslands: Social institutions and environmental change in Mkambati Area, South Africa', *Human Ecology* 27(1): 29–54

Koch, E, Cooper, D and Coetzee, H (1990) *Water, Waste and Wildlife: The Politics of Ecology in South Africa*. Penguin, Cape Town

Kuper, H (1963) *The Swazi: A South African Kingdom.* Holt, Rinehart and Winston, Austin, TX

Leach, M, Mearns, R and Scoones, I (1997) 'Challenges to community-based sustainable development: Dynamics, entitlements, institutions', *IDS Bulletin* 28(4): 4–14

Magome, H, Grossman, D, Fakir, S and Stowell, Y (2000) 'Partnerships in conservation: The state, private sector and the community at Madikwe Game Reserve', *Evaluating Eden Discussion Paper* No 7. International Institute for Environment and Development, London

Maquet, J (1972) *Civilizations of Black Africa.* Oxford University Press, New York

Matzke, G E and Nabane, N (1996) 'Outcomes of a community-controlled wildlife utilization programme in a Zambezi Valley community', *Human Ecology* 24: 65–86

Mayers, J and Fabricius, C (1997) 'Who sits by the policy fire?' Paper presented at an IUCN Global Biodiversity Forum, Harare, July

McNeely, J A (2002) *An Introduction to the Human Dimension of Invasive Alien Species*: www.iucn.org/biodiversityday/historical.html

Meneses, C (1994) *Legal and Constitutional Aspects of Land Tenure, Wildlife Utilisation and Protected Areas.* Environment Development Group, Global Environment Facility (GEF) Transfrontier Conservation Areas and Institution Strengthening Project, Draft Final Report, March

Mostert, N (1992) *Frontiers.* Pimlico, London

Motteaux, N (2001) *The Development and Co-ordination of Catchment Fora Through the Empowerment of Rural Communities.* Water Research Commission Report No 1014/1/01, Water Research Commission, Pretoria

Murphree, M W (1997) 'Articulating voices from the commons, interpretation, translation and facilitation: Roles and modes for common property scholarship', *Society and Natural Resources* 10: 415–417

Neuman, R P (1998) *Imposing Wilderness: Struggles over Livelihood and Nature Preservation in Africa.* University of California Press, Berkeley

Oström, E (1990) *Governing the Commons: The Evolution of Institutions for Collective Action.* Cambridge University Press, Cambridge

Palmer, R, Timmermans, H and Fay, D (2002) *From Conflict to Negotiation: Nature-based Development on South Africa's Wild Coast.* Human Sciences Research Council, Pretoria

Pretty, J, Guijt, I, Scoones, I, and Thompson, J (1994) 'A trainer's guide to participatory learning and interaction', *IIED Training Series* No 2. International Institute for Environment and Development, London

Reid, H (2001) 'Contractual national parks and the Makuleke community', *Human Ecology* 29: 135–155

Rhodes University, Unitra and Fort Cox (2001) *A Monitoring System for Community Forestry: Combining Scientific and Local Knowledge in the Eastern Cape.* Report to the Department of Water Affairs and Forestry, DWAF project RU1/100, Pretoria

Robins, S (2001) 'NGOs, "Bushmen" and double vision: The !khomani San land claim and the cultural politics of "community" and "development" in the Kalahari', *Journal of Southern African Studies* 27: 833–853

Roe, D, Mayers, J, Greig-Gran, M, Kothari, A, Fabricius, C and Hughes, R (2000) *Evaluating Eden: Exploring the Myths and Realities of Community-based Wildlife Management.* International Institute for Environment and Development, London

SANParks, (2000) *Visions of Change: Social Ecology and South African National Parks,* South African National Parks, Pretoria

SASUSG, (1997) *Community Wildlife Management in Southern Africa: A Regional Review*, IUCN Regional Office for Southern Africa, Sustainable Use Specialist Group, Harare

Schroeder, R A (1999) 'Geographies of environmental intervention in Africa', *Progress in Human Geography* 23: 359–378

Shackleton, S (2000) *Generic Criteria and Indicators for Assessing the Sustainability of Common Property/Community-Based Natural Resource Management Systems.* Report ENV-P-1-2000-042, CSIR, Pretoria

Spinage, C (1998) 'Social change and conservation misrepresentation in Africa', *Oryx* 32(4): 265–276

Surplus People Project (1985) *The Surplus People.* Raven Press, Johannesburg

Timmermans, H (1999) *Perceptions, Goals and Actions: Their Role in Shaping Relations of Power at Dwesa and Cwebe Wildlife and Marine Reserves.* Unpublished report, IIED *Evaluating Eden* Project, International Institute for Environment and Development, London

Walker, B, Carpenter, S, Anderies, J, Abel, N, Cumming, G, Janssen, M, Lebel, L, Norberg, G, Peterson, G and Pritchard, R (2002) 'Resilience management in social-ecological systems: A working hypothesis for a participatory approach', *Conservation Ecology* 16(1): 14, www.consecol.org/vol6/iss1/art14

Wells, M and Brandon, K (1992) *People and Parks: Linking Protected Area Management with Local Communities.* World Bank, WWF and USAID, Washington, DC

Wilson, M (1970) *The Thousand Years Before Van Riebeeck.* Witwatersrand University Press, Johannesburg

Wynberg, R and Swiderska, K (2001) *South Africa's Experience in Developing a Policy on Biodiversity and Access to Genetic Resources.* Participation in Access and Benefit-Sharing Policy Case Study No 1. International Institute for Environment and Development, London

Yudelman, M (1964) *Africans on the Land.* Harvard University Press, Massachusetts

Chapter 2

Community-based natural resource management and rural livelihoods

STEPHEN TURNER

INTRODUCTION

The concept of livelihoods is now common currency in development planning and debate. A number of livelihood models are usefully summarized by Carney et al (1999). They all agree that the livelihoods concept has social, cultural and political dimensions, as well as material ones. Beyond physical assets, nutrition, health, production, consumption and other tangible components, livelihoods comprise social networks, institutional frameworks, human rights, skills, abilities, religious values and duties – to name a few.

One of the most influential approaches to understanding livelihoods is the sustainable livelihoods (SL) framework developed by the UK Department for International Development (DFID, undated). DFID stresses that it is a framework, not a theoretical model. It is designed to allow an examination of the array of factors, forces and relationships that show how people build their lives, what their quality of life is and how that quality can be sustainably enhanced in a particular place and time.

The SL framework identifies livelihood assets in terms of five types of capital with which people are differentially endowed: human capital, social capital, physical capital, financial capital and natural capital. In community-based natural resource management (CBNRM) terms, natural resources correspond to natural capital. For these resources to be managed through community-based institutions, human and social capital must be available and appropriately deployed. The status, networks, roles and relationships that shape how people interact in their access to, use and governance of natural resources are elements of social capital. Various forms of physical capital (such as infrastructure) and financial capital are likely to be needed for CBNRM to succeed. People's ability to use these five types of capital is influenced by the vulnerability context that frames their lives – a range of shocks, stresses, trends and seasonal patterns that constrain their economic and institutional endeavours.

The SL framework shows how people pursue a range of livelihood strategies in order to achieve livelihood outcomes, both material and intangible. These outcomes can be thought of in terms of income and food security, but also in less material terms, such as well-being, social, cultural or religious status or human rights. Reduced vulnerability and enhanced environmental sustainability are other commonly desirable types of livelihood outcome. The framework also shows that a number of 'transforming structures and processes' can influence the efficacy with which local assets are used in the pursuit of livelihood strategies. In this framework, 'structures' are the organizational hardware (both public and private sector) that influences people's lives and to which people may (or may not) have access: legislatures, government departments, non-governmental organizations (NGOs), private corporations and so on. 'Processes' are the many structured and less-structured ways in which people behave towards each other – for example, policies, cultural practices, legislation, gender relations, political power structures, local institutions and market structures. These structures and processes are at the heart of our concern with CBNRM, since CBNRM is a structured way for people to interact with each other in their relations with natural resources.

A key distinction that this chapter will seek to draw out is between the tangible and intangible dimensions of livelihoods and of the livelihood benefits that CBNRM can generate. Like a number of dualities that the chapter suggests, this is an oversimplification of highly complex realities. For example, community infrastructure such as roads and schools is tangible, but offers indirect and sometimes intangible livelihood benefits, as well as material ones. The road may enable a farmer to sell more crops; the school may help households to develop their human capital and livelihood capabilities. The ownership and management of such infrastructural assets may increase communities' and individuals' political confidence, dignity and self-esteem – all of which are important elements of livelihoods.

CBNRM: THE LINKS WITH LIVELIHOODS

Rural livelihoods thus have many facets. As was shown in Chapter 1, there are many dimensions of CBNRM and many different scenarios in which CBNRM may occur in practice. Therefore, it is useful to sum up the ways in which CBNRM – and the activities for which it provides a framework – may be part of rural livelihoods.

The natural resource base that CBNRM aims to govern is one of the foundations of rural livelihoods, constituting the natural capital referred to above. It may comprise the whole landscape, as in informal and everyday CBNRM, or one or more specific natural resources through which formal CBNRM is intended to frame profitable livelihood strategies – such as the charismatic mega-fauna that are central to several of the Botswana and Namibia CBNRM initiatives discussed in this volume (see Chapters 9 and 13). Livelihood strategies that depend upon this resource base include subsistence and commercial resource harvesting (see the case studies in Chapters 8 and 14, respectively). Crop and livestock production are other key livelihood strategies that depend upon the governance of the resource base through CBNRM.

The human capital available to households and communities is of central importance to the pursuit of natural resource-based livelihood strategies and to the ways in which transforming structures and processes shape the links between those strategies, the natural resource base and other livelihood assets. In informal CBNRM programmes, the most important form of human capital is usually the technical and political experience that local leadership can deploy. In formal CBNRM initiatives, externally supported training programmes often seek to enhance human capital in fields such as wildlife conservation, tourism and business management. Donors have funded such programmes in a number of the South African, Namibian and Botswana cases described in this volume.

As a governance activity, informal and everyday CBNRM is central to the institutional and social life of rural communities in most of southern Africa. This kind of resource management takes place through the core institutions of these communities – for example, the chief and the council of elders, or the local administrative committee(s). The case study of Lesotho in Chapter 11 is an example of how much overlap there can be between general local governance and informal systems of resource management. In the sustainable livelihoods terminology outlined above, informal systems of resource management are intertwined with the local structures and processes that influence how local livelihood strategies can make use of livelihood assets. 'Local' is stressed twice here because 'rural' livelihoods in southern Africa, however strong their involvement with CBNRM, very often have non-local components, too. These usually depend upon migrant work and social networks elsewhere in the country, or even in other countries. CBNRM in this region cannot be understood or usefully supported unless these non-local elements of livelihoods are understood, too.

Formal CBNRM programmes also usually have strong links to the core institutional structures and processes of rural communities. Although new committees and resource governance systems tend to be introduced for the management of a conservancy or local fisheries (examples from Namibia and Malawi in Chapters 12 and 13), these are normally linked to, and influenced by, existing institutions, such as the chieftaincy or the local council. Chapter 16's case studies of the Richtersveld and the Makuleke in South Africa give further examples of such linkages and show how the success of formal CBNRM ventures can be influenced by the configuration and attitude of existing local institutions.

Institutions, in the sustainable livelihoods terminology, can be regarded as processes that mediate relations between livelihood assets and livelihood strategies. Societal norms and beliefs, and the power relations and modes of social status prevailing in a community, are other types of process. With their strong links to core local governance structures, CBNRM initiatives are influenced by, and in turn can alter, these social processes. The case studies in Chapters 18 and 19 from Zimbabwe are examples of the multiple dimensions that such linkages can take. From Namibia, Nott and Jacobsohn (Chapter 13) report that social empowerment is the driving force of conservancy formation, which is the leading kind of CBNRM initiative in that country. Gender roles in resource access, use and governance are a central determinant of intra- and inter-household livelihood differentials, and are commonly influenced by CBNRM initiatives. Women tend to be most heavily involved in, and dependent upon, small-scale, subsistence-oriented, wild resource collection. When this resource collection is commercialized, as for example when wild plants or timber find lucrative urban or overseas markets, men tend to take over the activity. External support for CBNRM initiatives has often pushed for more gender equity in traditionally male-dominated resource governance (an example is German support in the Richtersveld and Makuleke cases in Chapter 16).

Because of its intimate relationship with core community structures and processes, CBNRM may thus be an arena for strengthening entitlements and support networks. On the other hand, it may be an arena for conflict and exploitation in which disputes between livelihood interests are fought or negotiated, potentially enriching some livelihoods and impoverishing others. Case studies from Botswana, Malawi and Namibia in Chapters 10, 12 and 13 offer examples of these trends and tensions. Variously structured social elites are capturing many of the benefits from CBNRM. For example, from the Okavango, Madzwamuse and Fabricius report that the commercialization of wild resources is leading to domination by richer outsiders (see Chapter 10).

CBNRM typically provides the platform and the opportunity for a variety of human resources (knowledge, skills and capabilities) to be developed and applied, potentially enriching the social, economic and political dimensions of livelihoods. In addition to its material benefits, the successful performance of CBNRM enhances livelihoods by developing the sense of dignity and worth at the individual, household and community levels.

Despite its importance to southern African livelihoods, the role of CBNRM in those livelihoods is commonly misunderstood. The most evident misunderstanding concerns the economic dimension of that role. But this chapter also emphasizes the less tangible importance that many rural southern Africans ascribe to natural resources and their governance by the community.

ASSESSING THE ROLE OF CBNRM IN LIVELIHOODS

Much work has been done in recent years to emphasize the role that CBNRM can play in livelihoods. Largely, though not entirely, the emphasis has been placed on the economic contribution that CBNRM can make. But in learning from these debates and the data they have presented, it is important to be clear about the concepts of resources, tenure and management in CBNRM.

The focus of the debate and analysis is usually 'communal areas', which are areas assumed to be under 'community' ownership and management. In other words, we are concerned here with rural areas outside the sector of private or 'freehold' ownership, and outside specialized zones of state ownership like national parks. Technically, these 'communal' areas are actually state property or held in trust by the state in many southern African countries. Although the state is often conspicuous by its absence as manager of the natural resources, its legal ownership of the land may still cause complications for CBNRM arrangements that seek to assert local management authority. As the case study by Reid and Turner in Chapter 16 shows, this has been an issue in the Richtersveld National Park, which although 'community owned', has so far legally remained the property of the South African Minister of Land Affairs.

It is also important to recognize that much of the recent analysis concerns the value of the natural resources in communal areas, rather than the value of the management of these resources. Strictly speaking, this analysis helps us to establish the role of natural resources and natural resource use in livelihoods. It is a further step to assess what role the community-based management of the resources can play in livelihoods. I return to this issue below.

An analysis of the value of natural resources in 'communal' areas may serve three purposes. Firstly, it may affirm the economic contribution of resource-use practices in these areas, in support of arguments that more technical attention and extension support should be given to such practices and those who undertake them. Secondly, proving the value of such resources can help to emphasize the need to understand and enhance CBNRM. Thirdly, these arguments about the true total value of benefits from the natural resource base under 'communal' tenure can help to affirm the validity of this mode of tenure, and to discredit policies aimed at converting all rural land to private or 'freehold' ownership. This has been the theme of a number of recent publications on the true value of the natural resource base in the former 'homelands' of South Africa, including the case study in Chapter 8 (see also Shackleton et al, 2000a; 2000b).

The value of CBNRM

The value of the natural resource base in these 'communal' settings is now usually assessed under three headings:

1   The direct-use value concerns benefit streams from resources that are consumed or marketed, such as fuelwood, medicinal plants, livestock and crops.
2   Indirect-use value accrues from the environmental functions of natural resources in the system – for example, swamps and forests that help to regulate river regimes, or the ecological role of uncultivated areas in cycling nutrients to cultivated lands.

3 Passive or non-use values are socially determined without reference to economic use. They include the cultural, religious and aesthetic values that local people may attribute to resources or landscapes. They are often more important than outsiders think in local decision-making about potential economic uses of natural resources.

In 'modern' or 'Western' settings, the same three types of resource valuation can also be identified and applied. But there are two key differences with the 'communal' situation that prevails in southern Africa. First, the 'modern' or 'Western' world – which typically includes the world of policy-making – is generally able to apply its perceptions of resource value to the 'communal' setting, often distorting resource use, valuation and management in the latter areas. For example, most governments in southern Africa give higher priority and ascribe higher development value to production under freehold or state tenure than they do to production in communal areas. As Shackleton and Shackleton argue in Chapter 8, they tend to undervalue the latter and give it correspondingly little policy or investment support. Secondly, 'modern' or 'Western' socio-economic systems blur the distinction between direct use and passive or non-use values. People in these systems ascribe aesthetic (sometimes cultural or sacred) value to natural resources and are prepared to link this to an economic valuation. They are willing to pay to preserve or observe nature for the sake of nature. This kind of valuation gives rise to non-consumptive tourism by outsiders in natural resource settings in 'communal' areas to which these outsiders ascribe aesthetic or other intangible value. Such activities represent direct use without consumption. They create an economic value and significant economic benefit streams that can be sustained indefinitely under appropriate management.

Recent analysis of the direct-use value of natural resources (such as that by Shackleton et al, 2000a; 2000b) tends to distinguish three kinds of resource use in communal areas, each of which adds value to livelihoods. In all three cases, conventional analysis and policy tend to underestimate the economic contributions that these uses make:

1 The harvesting of wild resources is often the least visible and most underestimated economic activity in 'communal' areas. It includes such activities as the harvesting of medicinal plants, the harvesting of timber and non-timber forest products and the harvesting of wildlife (see, for example, the case study by Nel and Illgner in Chapter 7). These 'everyday or informal resource' uses, as our case study by Shackleton and Shackleton in Chapter 8 calls them, are often livelihood mainstays for the very poorest rural people. But the harvesting of wild resources can also generate significant income streams if these commodities are marketed further afield. Such income streams may accrue to more prosperous members of local society (and often to their outside collaborators). Or, if community-based management and marketing structures are in place, wild resource harvesting (such as licensed trophy hunting) may generate revenues that

are distributed (directly or indirectly) to all members of the local owner-user group. Non-consumptive tourism also constitutes a form of wild resource harvesting, although such externally inspired forms of economic activity are not usually included in calculations of the total value of natural resource systems in 'communal' areas.

2   Livestock production is an important element of resource use and livelihoods in many southern African 'communal' areas. It has a range of impacts on the natural resource base, and many social and institutional implications. As such, it is often at the heart of indigenous and informal resource use arrangements. Efforts to revive or enhance community-based range management have been prominent among CBNRM project interventions in the region over the last quarter century (see the Lesotho case study in Chapter 11). A steadily growing body of literature – now being challenged in some quarters (Cowling, 2000) – has argued that 'communal' area livelihood production systems are more economically rational, profitable and ecologically sustainable than conventional analysis had concluded. This literature (for example, Abel, 1993; Behnke and Kerven, 1994) argues that livestock production in 'communal' tenure and management systems can be a viable, profitable and sustainable alternative to the fenced 'freehold' ranch model that much southern African policy has advocated.

3   Crop production is the third key direct-use sector in 'communal' areas resource use. Again, recent analysis has shown that the productivity of cropping systems in places such as the former South African 'homelands' is significantly higher than previous studies and policy had assumed (McAllister, 2000). Once more, the implications are that 'communal' tenure systems are not incompatible with high levels of agricultural productivity, and that CBNRM arrangements that can frame and enhance this kind of farming deserve support.

The income streams that these three types of direct resource use generate are often substantial and, as I have pointed out, typically underestimated. Quoting 12 resource valuation studies undertaken in South Africa over the last three years, Shackleton and Shackleton (see Chapter 8) estimate average values of direct consumptive use of 'everyday' woodland resources as 3435 rand (almost US$450 at contemporary exchange rates) per household per year. They indicate that figures from Zimbabwe are comparable, though somewhat lower. These are gross values that exclude labour costs, whose calculation is a vexed issue for such typically labour-abundant situations. Some households would clearly be making much more than these annual averages. Shackleton and Shackleton also estimate that the total gross direct-use value of these 'everyday resources' to the South African economy is 6 billion rand (about US$800 million) per year. As they point out, these incomes are much higher at the national and the average household levels than those accruing from 'CBNRM' schemes such as South Africa's various 'people and parks' initiatives. Further data on the value of timber use in the communal areas of South Africa are shown in Table 2.1.

Table 2.1 *Annual, gross direct-use values (in South African rand) per household of timber use by rural households from various sites*

Province	Site	Fuelwood	Housing timber	Fence/ kraal timber	Total
Eastern Cape	Pikoli	1596	156	132	1884
	Kat River	1145	1	22	1168
KwaZulu-Natal	KwaJobe	726	54	154	934
	Hlabisa	212	6	15	233
Limpopo Province	Mogano	1736	0	5	1741
	Mametja	706	3	17	726
	Hagondo	1569	2	106	1677
	Bushbuckridge	465	62	156	683
Mean		**1019**	**36**	**76**	**1131**

Note: 1 rand = US$0.13 in July 2003.

Arntzen (1998) argues that the value of rangelands is usually underestimated because of analysts' bias towards a sectoral approach (focusing on livestock); their bias towards one marketed product, which is usually meat or livestock; and their limitation of data to use values. Reviewing the value of Botswana rangelands, he argues that there is a considerable 'hidden harvest' from these resources, both within the livestock sector and in wildlife and gathering activities.

Using admittedly rough estimates, Adams et al (2000) calculate the total value per 'communal' area household of cropping, livestock production and natural resource harvesting to be 5535 rand per year in South Africa (US$809 at 2000 exchange rates). They convert this to an estimated total national value of 13.28 billion rand (US$1.94 billion) for this production in the 'communal' areas of that country.

There is, thus, plenty of evidence that direct natural resource use in 'communal' settings generates substantial livelihood benefits. The indirect and non-use values of the natural resource base are much harder to calculate but are increasingly recognized in policy. For example, the new water management policy and legislation in South Africa provide for an ecological reserve that must always be set aside and protected because of the crucial environmental and economic role that it plays.

Given the major contribution that natural resources make to rural livelihoods, how much extra value does the community-based management of these resources generate? Outside the project setting, in the framework of informal CBNRM, this question is hard to answer with any degree of accuracy. One convincing argument is that very few of the types of resource use outlined above take place in situations of completely open access. Although many southern Africans currently lament the decay of previous controls over grazing, timber use, medicinal plant collection and other resource uses, there are not as many cases of a complete free-for-all as these laments might suggest. Nor is there much convincing state control of resource use in the 'communal' areas of southern Africa at present. This implies that some kind of general community-based management, however decayed or inefficient, is continuing to provide at least part of an enabling framework for the majority of livelihood benefits that accrue from the natural resource base in 'communal' settings. In other words, the economic value of informal resource management in southern Africa is a substantial part of the economic value of natural resource use in the 'communal' areas of the region. Without any management, in a state of total open access, the total economic value of this resource use would presumably be considerably less. That difference, although it cannot be quantified, is significant. It corresponds to the value that resource management adds to the economies of communal areas in southern Africa. Given that so many of the informal resource use and management systems around the region are now in tatters, it can also be argued that the renovation and reinforcement of such systems could significantly increase the economic output of natural resource-based production, with corresponding benefits for rural livelihoods.

Rural–urban relationship

How rural are rural livelihoods? It is essential in any livelihood analysis in southern Africa, and therefore in any strategy for CBNRM, to understand that many 'rural' people are urban people, too. Many of them migrate to, or depend upon, work opportunities in town. Households in country areas may draw more of their livelihoods from these urban revenues, or from state benefits such as pensions, than they do from rural income generation by natural resource use or any other means (Sechaba Consultants, 2000; Turner et al, 2001; Ntshona, 2002; see also Hara's case study in Chapter 12, which shows how shrinking opportunities in the national economy of Malawi are increasing the pressure on local fisheries).

The overall economic composition of 'rural' southern African livelihoods obviously varies enormously from place to place, from rich to poor and sometimes from season to season; but it is safe to say that there are typically four components. Two make major contributions and two make smaller contributions. The two major components are, firstly, crops, livestock and everyday resources and, secondly, urban and migrant income. Of the two minor components, one is probably universal across southern Africa: it spans the range of rural, non-agricultural income-generating activities in which people increasingly engage – such as brewing, building, clothes-making and petty trading. The second is much less widespread: it comprises the state benefits that some governments in the region pay to their citizens. State pensions are only paid in Botswana, Namibia and South Africa. In South Africa, their increased availability and benefits for the elderly (and their relatives) in communal areas are introducing major changes to livelihoods.

A fifth livelihood component – namely, formal CBNRM – is far more localized. Very occasionally, as perhaps in the Torra Conservancy described by Nott, Davis and Roman (see Chapter 14) or in some of the Okavango

CBNRM projects in Botswana (see Chapter 9), formal CBNRM may be generating more than half of some households' revenues. More usually, formal CBNRM initiatives, even at those comparatively few localities in the region's communal areas where they occur, generate less revenue than agriculture and other activities dependent upon informal CBNRM. In Chapter 18, Sibanda points to the limited material benefits that the Communal Areas Management Programme for Indigenous Resources (CAMPFIRE) delivers to people in most participating communities in Zimbabwe.

Regardless of the accuracy of our conjectures about how rural people perceive the potential livelihood benefits of conserving and managing their natural resources, there is clearly a basic difference between the kinds of benefits currently accruing from the two types of CBNRM – informal resource use and management, and formal CBNRM. It dovetails with the distinction suggested earlier between tangible and intangible livelihood benefits.

Informal resource use and management yield substantial direct tangible benefits from the household resource use that community institutions govern. In much of southern Africa, as I have acknowledged, this kind of indigenous resource management is patchy and weak. But open access is not yet the norm. Most people in most settings are still subject to some sort of management of their use of at least some of the resources upon which their livelihoods depend. Meanwhile, however, and partly because of the parlous state of informal management systems, the indirect livelihood benefits are few. No revenue flows from the remnants of these institutions and procedures to fund community infrastructure. Occasionally, certain qualities or practices within what is left of indigenous resource use systems may still help to hold the social and cultural fabric of rural life together. This appears to be the case among some of the Tonga reviewed in Zimbabwe by Sibanda (Chapter 18) and among the users of the Mafungautsi State Forest, also in Zimbabwe (Chapter 19). More rarely, CBNRM institutions are still integral to a largely indigenous polity. This is arguably true of a single sector (range management) in Lesotho (see Chapter 11) and of a rich spectrum of indigenous resource management methods prevalent among the Barotse people of Western Province, Zambia (Munalula, 2000).

Formal CBNRM, on the other hand, has so far yielded comparatively few direct livelihood benefits. There are some lucrative exceptions; but in most cases only a fraction of the revenues reaches household level directly. Most of the benefits are appropriated outside of the communities, reinvested or realized indirectly. Furthermore, the formal CBNRM experience has been strongly empowering for many (though certainly not all) of the communities who have engaged in it. Many rural southern Africans can hold their heads higher because of what they have achieved through CBNRM projects. This empowerment is an important livelihood benefit. But it is an indirect one. It does not put money in people's pockets, although there is some evidence that this may not be the highest priority of everyone who engages in formal CBNRM.

ENHANCING LIVELIHOODS THROUGH CBNRM
PROJECTS AND PROGRAMMES

Keeping in mind the crude distinction made above between 'informal' and 'formal' CBNRM, we can identify two broad types of intervention being made by development and conservation agencies in southern African CBNRM.

In a few cases, projects try to help rural people revitalize or upgrade their informal CBNRM. These are broad interventions to enhance CBNRM and/or biodiversity conservation across the whole local landscape – with varying degrees of emphasis on enhancing livelihoods, too. These projects – in such fields as land-use planning and catchment management – often have a stronger institutional emphasis and may address both subsistence and commercial resource users.

A more common recent scenario is the intervention that aims to work with rural people to build some kind of formal CBNRM. These are the interventions with which much of this book is concerned. Often, they are commodity-focused projects – for example, in range management or social forestry – that seek to enhance CBNRM and livelihood benefits in one particular sector of the local environment and economy. Such projects may focus on particular groups within rural society (and may or may not make provision for gender issues). They may emphasize the management of subsistence or market-oriented resource use, often trying to promote a sustainable transition from the former to the latter. Some projects aim to achieve multiple livelihood benefits through the development, management and marketing to outsiders of a range of natural resources and the benefit streams that they can yield. Ambitiously, this kind of intervention may aim at central management of all these processes, including central receipt of the revenues generated and direct or indirect disbursement of net benefits by the central community agency to all community members. This is an increasingly common scenario in community-based nature conservation and nature tourism.

MOTIVES AND BENEFITS IN CBNRM PROGRAMMES

There are two kinds of reasons why external agencies promote CBNRM through their many interventions in the sector. One motive is the conservation of natural resources. The other is the enhancement of the livelihoods of rural people who live among and use those resources. These rationales often overlap, and are increasingly integrated.

The overriding concern of most external interventions in the sector used to be conservation. But decades of mostly unsuccessful colonial and immediately post-colonial experience in southern Africa and elsewhere showed that rural people were largely unmoved by exhortations to engage in conservation for conservation's sake. Conservation was integral to the rationale of these people's indigenous resource management systems; but colonialists and the early generations of development 'experts' generally considered such systems irrelevant, irresponsible or ineffective – if they knew about them at all. Deciding that local resource users had somehow to be convinced that resource conservation and associated management initiatives were in their own best interest, project designers began to link conservation work with agricultural development measures. In these 'conservation through production' initiatives, external agencies hoped to achieve environmental protection by the stimulation of economically profitable resource use and management. Farmers participating in soil conservation work would be given incentives of high-yielding, marketable crop varieties. Range management projects would introduce high-quality breeding stock and marketing programmes alongside pasture conservation. One soil conservation expert referred to such approaches as 'conservation by stealth': Shaxson, 1989, p39). A host of community-based wildlife management projects in southern Africa have linked nature conservation to the prospect of new revenues from nature tourism. This is the 'economic instrumentalism' identified by Jones and Murphree (2001, p43) and central to what, according to Johnson (see Chapter 15), has been one of the most fundamental arguments supporting the introduction of CBNRM in southern African countries over the last decade.

Current projects and programmes tend to emphasize the 'win–win' opportunity of enhancing livelihoods sustainably, and thus protecting the natural resource base while improving users' standard of living. In the agricultural sector, the current emphasis – in keeping with development agencies' poverty concerns and prevailing livelihood paradigm – is production through conservation, rather than the other way round. But how effectively are these initiatives in the formal CBNRM sector managing to achieve tangible benefits for rural people, alongside the conservation of the environment? And how accurate is this concept of 'economic instrumentalism' as a guide to communities' motives and priorities in CBNRM? Are they in it for the money? Are they making any money?

In a few community-based wildlife management initiatives, formal CBNRM is making large amounts of money for rather small communities. The case studies by Boggs (Chapter 9) and by Madzwamuse and Fabricius (Chapter 10) describe the high incomes being earned by the Khwai and Sankuyo communities in the Okavango Delta of Botswana. Sankuyo, with some 350 residents, earned over 4 million pula during 1996 to 2000 (US$1 million at contemporary exchange rates). Khwai earned 1.7 million pula (US$0.34 million) in 2000 alone from its hunting concessions. In Namibia, the Torra Conservancy, with 300 members and a total population of about 1000 people, has earned some 800,000 Namibia dollars (US$133,224 at contemporary rates) in dividends from its joint eco-tourism ventures, 800,000 Namibia dollars in wages, and additional income from activities such as firewood sales and laundry services. It also earns some 120,000 Namibia dollars a year (US$14,473 at 2001 rates) from trophy hunting (Chapter 14) (see Table 2.2). See Magome and Fabricius (Chapter 5) for additional discussion of this topic.

Table 2.2 *Quantum and per household direct financial benefits from CBNRM*

Initiative/project	Quantum benefit (US$)	Number of households	Benefit per household (US$)
Lupande, Zambia (see Chapter 17)	Direct revenue: 220,000		
	wages: 150,000	10,000	37.00
CAMPFIRE, Zimbabwe (see Chapter 18)	450,000	>100,000	4.50
Sankuyo, Botswana (see Chapter 9)	1,043,000	23	45,391.00
Kunene, Namibia (see Chapter 14)	40,000	150	267.00
Richtersveld, South Africa (see Chapter 16)	57,000	1200	47.50

Most formal CBNRM initiatives have so far yielded unimpressive dividends per household. There are few cases where resource values are as high, and owner populations as small, as at Sankuyo, Khwai and Torra. Fabricius et al (2001) argue that where resources have a high unitary value (for example, mega-herbivores and large carnivores) and communities are small (less than 100 households), the income per household from community-based wildlife management can be high. However, they point out, conservation and development agencies often quote the total benefits earned by a community rather than the benefits per household because the amounts per household are often embarrassingly small.

Community-based wildlife management is the most charismatic CBNRM subsector; but Barnes (2001) points out that the returns from wildlife in different parts of Botswana vary significantly. Sibanda's case study in Chapter 18 points out some of the common conclusions arising from analysis of Zimbabwe's CAMPFIRE programme. Households in wards that participate in the programme mostly receive limited material benefits and earn much larger livelihood benefit streams from agriculture, other rural resource uses and migrant labour. Sibanda quotes estimates of annual household income from CAMPFIRE as 99 Zimbabwe dollars in 1990 (US$30 at 1990 rates) and 44 Zimbabwe dollars in 1996 (US$4.44 at 1996 rates). Bond (2001, p235) says that 'in 1990, 1992 and 1993, the median of wildlife benefit as percentage of gross agricultural income was less than 10 per cent'. Significantly, Sibanda's research in CAMPFIRE communities suggests that only 10 per cent of respondents thought that the programme was about sharing benefits from natural resources, while 53 per cent thought it was about nature conservation.

In the two South African 'people and parks' cases reviewed in this volume by Reid and Turner (Chapter 16), the material benefit streams accruing to households from formal CBNRM initiatives are low so far. In the niche nature tourism sector occupied by the Richtersveld National Park, these benefits are never likely to be high, even if co-management is more efficient and tourism more profitable than has been the case in the park's first decade. The Makuleke, who own part of the Kruger National Park, have already amassed a large bank balance from trophy hunting revenues, lodge concessions and government grants. But they are ploughing all of the money back into more eco-tourism projects and various infrastructural investments for the community. A limited number of permanent jobs will become available once lodges are operating. Some 16 Richtersvelders have jobs in their park. For the rest, the real or promised material benefits are indirect, in the form of community facilities.

Ashley (2000) and Emerton (2001) both stress how important it is to consider the costs of CBNRM initiatives, as well as the benefits. Too often, analysis and promotion of CBNRM imply that it is some sort of add-on to existing uses of natural and human resources. In fact, it is vital to consider the opportunity costs of entering into new, formal CBNRM initiatives. How much revenue will be lost if land is converted from existing uses to those proposed for a CBNRM initiative (Barnes, 2001), and if labour is diverted from existing productive activities to those required by the new CBNRM activity? Will current access to some resources be curtailed? How, as Ashley (2000) puts it, will CBNRM activities 'fit' into existing livelihoods in the economic, institutional and cultural senses? What are the institutional transaction costs of engaging in CBNRM? To succeed, the long-term material and intangible benefits from a CBNRM initiative must clearly be greater than the material and intangible opportunity costs that the initiative imposes.

The advantage of applying livelihoods frameworks to these questions is that it permits a more holistic and integrated appraisal of the many potential costs and benefits that any particular strategy poses. A typical question that arises on the economic side of the equation is whether, if people commit themselves to wildlife conservation and nature tourism, they will be able to sustain the costs – such as crop damage and livestock losses – associated with the wildlife that is meant to be delivering livelihood benefits to them (IUCN, 2002). Or will the nature conservation and related resource uses proposed under 'formal' CBNRM physically displace agriculture? The answers to these questions are highly variable; but there is clearly more scope for tension and conflict in better-watered crop-growing areas than in low-rainfall areas where existing land use is more extensive and largely limited to small stock production (Norton-Griffiths and Southey, 1993). Tensions between wildlife and agriculture can thus be serious in areas of Zimbabwe and northern Botswana where formal CBNRM is promoting their coexistence. In arid Namibia and in the Richtersveld National Park in South Africa, it is easier to resolve the conflicts. In the latter case, regulated grazing of local people's small stock in the park is permitted.

CBNRM AND POVERTY

Another important question – central to the current concerns of many development agencies – is what CBNRM does to alleviate poverty. We must try to answer this question with reference to the two types of CBNRM identified in this chapter, and also at two levels of 'poverty'.

At the first level, it is not hard to argue that formal CBNRM initiatives generally take place among the poorer sections of rural society in southern Africa (Hulme and Murphree, 2001, p289). The communities involved are typically to be found on the rural periphery, enduring standards of living that are below the national, and probably below the rural, average. To the extent that CBNRM achieves economic benefits for such communities, it is reasonable to infer that it significantly alleviates poverty there.

But it is more useful to move to a second level and ask what such initiatives do to the livelihoods of the poorest people in participating communities. Here, again, there are two levels at which to answer the question. Firstly, it is not surprising that the poorest are worst equipped to capture many of the benefits of formal CBNRM. They are less likely to compete successfully for jobs in nature tourism, or to benefit from expanded institutional functions and leadership opportunities in CBNRM. Secondly, most such CBNRM initiatives entail tighter regulation of local resource harvesting. The very poor are likely to be disproportionately dependent upon hunting or gathering such resources. Formal CBNRM may divert benefit streams away from these people to less poor elites who are able to capture the new sort of revenues that such projects generate. I point out below that when such CBNRM projects pay cash dividends directly to all households (as sometimes occurs in Zimbabwe's CAMPFIRE), this can make a significant difference to the livelihoods of the very poor. But I also show that such payments are less common than arrangements to distribute the benefits indirectly, reinvest them or keep them in the bank.

What does informal community-based resource management do to alleviate poverty? In their increasingly rare, functional state, indigenous systems reflect the socio-economic structure of rural society (see case studies in Chapters 6, 11 and 18). They often allocate special resource harvests and benefits to elites (for the Lesotho case, see Sheddick, 1954); but they also provide an enabling, regulatory framework for the collection of 'everyday resources' upon which the poorest people depend most heavily. Even in their more typical, dilapidated state, the contemporary remnants of these systems do not usually obstruct the resource use of the very poor.

Perhaps the most important contribution that these landscape-wide resource management systems make to alleviating poverty – or at least to providing a safety net for the very poor – is that they help sustain communal resource tenure. As such systems fall into disrepair, informal privatization prospers and enriches elites at the expense of the poor. This is happening now in southern African countries such as Botswana, Namibia and South Africa. As conventional wisdom conflates communal tenure and common property resource management with open access, the political credibility of CBNRM and the economic prospects of the very poor are endangered. Urgent questions are currently being asked about the motives of planned tenure reform for South Africa's communal areas, and what they will mean for the rural poor of that country. The challenge to pro-poor analysis and policy in the region is to identify ways in which communal tenure and CBNRM can be reaffirmed and rebuilt in order to achieve macro-economic benefits and enhance the livelihoods of all sectors of rural society. In Lesotho, the challenge is to show, through land reform and local government reform, that communal tenure and indigenous resource management systems have a role to play in ensuring and reinforcing the livelihoods of the rural poor.

THE IMPACT OF FORMAL CBNRM REVENUES
ON LIVELIHOODS

Even when the net dividends per household of formal CBNRM are high, and even more so in the usual case of low dividends, a key question is what happens to the money. There are several, often overlapping, scenarios:

- Official stakeholders in the CBNRM process (such as the state or local government bodies) extract a significant part of the revenue: one of many examples is the Tchumo Tchato case reported by Johnson in Chapter 15.
- Community authorities use substantial amounts for project operating expenses (in Chapter 10, Madzwamuse and Fabricius describe how this happens in the Okavango).
- Community authorities invest the revenue in community projects, such as eco-tourism infrastructure that is intended to generate future revenue, or community projects for public welfare, such as clinics, schools or markets. The Makuleke, described by Reid and Turner in Chapter 16, are a case in point.
- Community authorities hold the revenue in the bank. They may be unsure how to spend it, or unwilling to confront the controversy that may arise from any particular spending decision. This is happening in several Namibian conservancies (see Chapter 14).
- Part or all of the revenue (after deduction of official levies and project overheads) may be paid out in cash to member households (Sibanda describes in Chapter 18 the limited extent to which this has been done in Zimbabwe's CAMPFIRE programme).

What do these scenarios tell us? First and foremost, they show that substantial portions of the total potential livelihood benefit stream accruing from formal CBNRM do not enter household livelihoods at all. Emerton (2001) argues that the main issue is not what the total economic value of wildlife is, but rather what proportion of benefits from wildlife actually reaches local people's livelihoods. She points out that there has been surprisingly little analysis of this.

CAMPFIRE is the classic example of the diversion of benefits by official stakeholders in the CBNRM process. Programme revenues accrue to rural district councils (RDCs) who are then not obliged but are encouraged, 'in the spirit of CAMPFIRE', to pass money on to the ward or community level. Of the US$9.3 million earned by RDCs from CAMPFIRE between 1989 and 1996, 53 per cent was passed on to ward level; 22 per cent was used by the RDCs for wildlife management purposes; 13 per cent was kept as a council levy; 2 per cent was for 'other uses'; and 10 per cent was 'unallocated', which probably means that it was used for non-CAMPFIRE purposes (Bond, 2001). Also in Zimbabwe, the Mafungautsi State Forest, discussed by Sithole in Chapter 19, is a co-management case where the government retains ownership but professes to intend sharing management and benefits with local people. In fact, the forest authority tells local resource management committees what projects to spend the money on; the RDC seeks to appropriate the role and revenues of the resource management committees; and the state retains all revenue from high-value forest products. In the Mozambican case of Tchumo Tchato (see Chapter 15), 'the community's perception of the project has become increasingly negative, as financial benefits have been appropriated to enhance the law enforcement capacity and facilities of the conservation officials resident in the area, where these benefits are now being used to introduce punitive sanctions on the community and its use of their natural resources'. In Namibia, on the other hand, there has so far been little diversion of CBNRM benefits by local authorities, although the idea has certainly been discussed in the Caprivi region.

Secondly, we can see that, of the benefits that do reach household livelihoods, the indirect type is more common than the direct type. The payment of direct cash dividends to community members is comparatively rare, although some CAMPFIRE projects, and the Luangwa Integrated Rural Development Project in Zambia, have done it. Where these payments are made, they make a real difference to many recipients' cash income streams. The 200 Zimbabwe dollars (about US$60 at contemporary rates) received from CAMPFIRE by each household in Masoka District in 1989 was a 56 per cent increase on household income from cotton (Murphree 1998, cited in Fabricius et al, 2001). Direct payments in kind – for example, community consumption of game meat from trophy hunting – are more common, but are not a significant livelihood benefit. It is more usual for community CBNRM authorities to invest revenue in expanding the CBNRM initiative – investing in new nature tourism facilities, for example – or in building community infrastructure. The latter can certainly generate indirect livelihood benefits for households – for example, if their journeys to town become easier or the quality of their schools or clinics is improved. The former makes no immediate difference to people's standard of living. It implies a request by the community project authorities to trust that deferred gratification will lead to greater long-term benefits. For the community authorities, it is the least problematic sort of decision to make. The money is simply ploughed back into the expanding project enterprise.

Thirdly, then, we can see that community project authorities are soon faced with the same intractable challenges that have frustrated their government and donor counterparts for so long. They are not going to find sustainable rural development any easier than the last few decades of civil servants and consultants. As continuing deep rural poverty in parts of Botswana attests, money does not automatically unlock rural development. What it can be used for, as Botswana again shows clearly from several decades of responsible investment, is infrastructure. Investing money to achieve sustainable increases in rural people's own earned income is much more problematic, and millions of dollars have been wasted across southern Africa in projects that have mostly just provided income for their designers and administrators. There are signs that similar symptoms may emerge in some community management of CBNRM revenues. The amounts creamed off for operating costs and overheads are sometimes substantial, as Boggs shows in the case of Sankuyo, Botswana (Chapter 9). The flip side of this gross inefficiency in the use of development budgets has been the irreverent argument that it would be much simpler just to hand the money out to the rural poor, rather than spending it on projects that go nowhere. The development industry has never taken that argument seriously. In some cases, as I have shown, direct cash payments are being made to households participating in CBNRM projects. But this is hardly a popular option among these projects' community managers.

Fourthly, however, there is clearly a strong feeling of caution in many community project authorities about using the new money that they are harvesting from formal CBNRM. As Nott and Jacobsohn point out in their case study of conservancies in Namibia (Chapter 13), the profits of CBNRM are proving difficult to spend. This reluctance to spend on development activities is not simply a preference for lavish office overheads and four-by-four vehicles for community officials. Two more genuine factors are at work:

1   Many community managers are responsible and prudent. They know how hard it is to ensure that infrastructure projects are built well and operated professionally. They realize how many commercial investments fail. They recognize that they mostly lack experience in these fields, and they want to avoid mistakes.

2   As community members, community managers know how divisive the use of public funds can be. Every spending decision they make can cause controversy and dissent. Purely as custodians of community money, these managers are exposed to allegations of fraud and embezzlement. While such allegations are not always unfounded, the safest course of action for the most upright of community leaders may seem to be just to keep the money in the bank.

RURAL PEOPLE'S MOTIVES IN CBNRM

A final suggestion from these scenarios is that rural people and their community authorities may not see financial revenue and direct livelihood dividends as the strongest reason for engaging in this formal kind of CBNRM. They may believe that other livelihood benefits that flow from the process are more important. This is what Sibanda (Chapter 18) argues from his review of CAMPFIRE in Zimbabwe. He believes that proponents of the programme have overplayed the role of cash incentives in motivating people to participate, and calls for a much broader interpretation of the interface between nature and livelihoods. At the same time, he finds that CAMPFIRE 'has no capacity to internalize indigenous concepts, ideas, beliefs and practices'.

Perhaps, therefore, 'economic instrumentalism' does not always dominate community motives for engaging in formal CBNRM. Johnson (Chapter 15) quotes Barrow and Murphree's argument that conservation has to pay in more than economic terms. It has to achieve broader livelihood benefits. In their case study from Namibia, Nott and Jacobsohn (Chapter 13) say that the driving force of conservancy formation is the social empowerment that the devolution of rights over resources entails. Also from Namibia comes the story of a conservancy that decided not to issue a lucrative hunting concession for a rhinoceros. They preferred to keep the rhino in their landscape and livelihoods than to have the money that they could get from losing the animal (Garth Owen Smith, pers comm). Just as in informal systems, rural people clearly recognize the economic benefits of sustainable natural resource use within a management framework; but they situate this rationale within a broader value system that sees a wider range of livelihood benefits accruing from care for nature. Rural southern Africans' relations with the natural environment are not the single tree of formal CBNRM. They are more like a forest or grassland, with myriad roots in every aspect of nature.

This makes the current disconnection between the formal CBNRM of projects and the more indigenous or traditional resource management systems of the real rural world in southern Africa all the more unfortunate. The latter potentially have roots, purposes and benefits across the whole spectrum of the natural environment and the full range of livelihood motives and needs. Yet it is the formal kind of CBNRM that is receiving the bulk of the external support.

An emphasis on formal CBNRM can also be economically short sighted. Rural development analysis in southern Africa was crippled for decades by its failure to recognize the multiple nature of regional livelihood strategies. Formal CBNRM initiatives often fall into the trap of assuming that rural livelihoods depend only upon rural economic activity, or into the deeper error of supposing that the resource use upon which the project focuses forms the central livelihood strategy of participating households (see above). As Hara points out in his case study of fisheries on Lake Malombe, Malawi (Chapter 12), the broader state of the economy and of livelihood opportunities within it can determine whether a formal CBNRM initiative has any chance of success. In the Lake Malombe case, opportunities in the broader Malawi economy have been shrinking. People's dependence upon the fisheries has therefore been increasing, and so has their reluctance to apply natural resource management (NRM) measures that would restrict catches and incomes.

CONCLUSION

In rural people's livelihoods, informal resource management systems and formal CBNRM initiatives (if any) should fit fruitfully together. But in the worlds of analysis and policy, the two types are passing each other by, like ships in the night. If these two ships could meet, they would have much cargo to exchange. They might even be able to sail off together in the same, more profitable, direction. The potential livelihood profits are enormous. Evidence presented in this chapter and elsewhere in this volume shows how the value of natural resource extraction under informal resource management regimes (or what is left of them) dwarfs the performance or potential of formal CBNRM projects. If some of the energy and ideas currently devoted to the formal CBNRM sector could be diverted to the landscapes where most rural people in the region make their living, we might really see the African renaissance to which some of our leaders aspire. The political, economic and institutional challenges are correspondingly huge. It is no coincidence that most development effort addresses the easier agendas of formal, localized CBNRM projects. But until the challenges of enhancing informal resource management systems are tackled, the livelihood benefits that CBNRM initiatives achieve for this region will be limited.

The evidence suggests a further, deeper conclusion and a further challenge. It is not enough for us to weigh up the direct and indirect benefits. It is not even enough to recognize the importance of qualitative livelihood motives such as institution-building and empowerment in rural people's decision-making about CBNRM, as I have tried to do above. The further challenge is to recognize that people do not only think about their assets and their capabilities when they weigh up and engage in various types of resource management. They also think about nature. Although the links defy definition and explanation, there are clear signs that nature has a deeper cultural and ethical meaning in rural southern African livelihoods, beyond its economic meaning as a source of sustenance and its political meaning as an arena of exploitation or empowerment. Pure conservation motives are not alien to livelihoods and CBNRM in this region. The ultimate fusion between external and local resource management motives will be achieved when the two sides go beyond economic and institutional instrumentalism and integrate their respective visions of nature for nature's sake.

REFERENCES

Abel, N (1993) 'Carrying capacity, rangeland degradation and livestock development policy for the communal rangelands of Botswana', *ODI Pastoral Development Network Papers* 35c. Overseas Development Institute, London

Adams, M, Cousins, B and Manona, S (2000) 'Land tenure and economic development in rural South Africa: Constraints and opportunities', in Cousins, B (ed) *At the Crossroads: Land and Agrarian Reform in South Africa into the 21st century*. Programme for Land and Agrarian Studies, University of the Western Cape, and National Land Committee, Cape Town and Johannesburg, pp111–128

Arntzen, J W (1998) 'Economic valuation of range lands in Botswana: A case study', *CREED Working Paper* 17. International Institute for Environment and Development, London

Ashley, C (2000) 'Applying livelihood approaches to natural resource management initiatives: Experiences in Namibia and Kenya', *Overseas Development Institute Working Paper* 134, London

Barnes, J I (2001) 'Economic returns and allocation of resources in the wildlife sector of Botswana', *South African Journal of Wildlife Research* 31: 141–153

Behnke, R and Kerven, C (1994) 'Redesigning for risk: Tracking and buffering environmental variability in Africa's rangelands', *ODI Natural Resource Perspectives* 1. Overseas Development Institute, London

Bond, I (2001) 'CAMPFIRE and the incentives for institutional change', in Hulme, D and Murphree, M W (eds) *African Wildlife and Livelihoods: The Promise and Performance of Community Conservation*. James Currey, Oxford, pp247–243

Carney, D, Drinkwater, M, Rusinow, T, Neefjes, K, Wanmali, S and Singh, N (1999) *Livelihoods Approaches Compared*. Department for International Development, London

Cowling, R M (2000) 'Challenges to the "new" rangeland science', *Trends in Ecology and Evolution* 15: 303–304

DFID (undated) www.livelihoods.org/info/info_guidancesheets.html

Emerton, L (2001) 'The nature of benefits and the benefits of nature: Why wildlife conservation has not economically benefited communities in Africa', in Hulme, D and Murphree, M W (eds) *African Wildlife and Livelihoods: The Promise and Performance of Community Conservation*. James Currey, Oxford, pp208–226

Fabricius, C, Koch E and Magome H (2001) 'Community wildlife management in southern Africa: Challenging the assumptions of Eden', *Evaluating Eden Series* No 6. International Institute for Environment and Development, London

Hulme, D and Murphree, M W (2001) 'Community conservation as policy: Promise and performance', in Hulme, D and Murphree, M W (eds) *African Wildlife and Livelihoods: The Promise and Performance of Community Conservation*. James Currey, Oxford, pp280–297

IUCN Species Survival Commission African Elephant Specialist Group (2002) *Human-Elephant Conflict Working Group*. www.iucn.org/themes/ssc/sgs/afesg/hectf/

Jones, B and Murphree, M W (2001) 'The evolution of policy on community conservation in Namibia and Zimbabwe', in Hulme, D and Murphree, M W (eds) *African Wildlife and Livelihoods: The Promise and Performance of Community Conservation*. James Currey, Oxford, pp38–58

McAllister, P (2000) 'Maize yields in the Transkei: How productive is subsistence cultivation?' *Land Reform and Agrarian Change in Southern Africa* 14. Programme for Land and Agrarian Studies, University of the Western Cape, Cape Town

Munalula, C L (2000) 'Community-based natural resource management (CBNRM): Experiences of the Western Province of Zambia – Understanding the role of traditional authorities'. Paper presented to annual regional meeting of CASS/PLAAS programme on CBNRM in southern Africa, University of the Western Cape, October

Norton-Griffiths, M and Southey, C (1993) *The Opportunity Costs of Biodiversity Conservation in Kenya*. Centre for Social and Economic Research on the Global Environment, London

Ntshona, Z M (2002) *The Contribution of Communal Rangelands to Rural People's Livelihoods in the Maluti District*, MPhil thesis, University of the Western Cape, Cape Town

Sechaba Consultants (2000) *Poverty and livelihoods in Lesotho, 2000*. Sechaba Consultants, Maseru

Shackleton, S E, Shackleton, C C and Cousins, B (2000a) 'The economic value of land and natural resources to rural livelihoods: Case studies from South Africa', in Cousins, B (ed) *At the Crossroads: Land and Agrarian Reform in South Africa into the 21st Century*, pp35–67. Programme for Land and Agrarian Studies, University of the Western Cape, and National Land Committee, Cape Town and Johannesburg

Shackleton, S E, Shackleton C C and Cousins, B (2000b) 'Re-valuing the communal lands of southern Africa: New understandings of rural livelihoods', *Natural Resource Perspectives* 62. Overseas Development Institute, London

Shaxson, T F (1989) *Land Husbandry: Lesotho – Land Husbandry Principles for Conservation Farming through People's Participation*. Ministry of Agriculture, Maseru, Cooperatives and Marketing and Food and Agriculture Organization of the United Nations. AG: TCP/LES/6755: Field Document 5

Sheddick, V G J, (1954) *Land Tenure in Basutoland*. Her Majesty's Stationery Office, London

Turner, S D with Calder, R, Gay, J, Hall, D, Iredale, J, Mbizule, C and Mohatla, M (2001) *Livelihoods in Lesotho*. CARE Lesotho, Maseru

Chapter 3

Political economy, governance and community-based natural resource management

Eddie Koch

This chapter looks at the broader political forces that shape people's lives, and examines the effect of national politics and economics and 'macro' forces on the many variables that shape the outcome of community-based natural resource management (CBNRM) in southern Africa. A number of case studies in Part 2 indicate how CBNRM programmes, generally highly decentralized and localized, are shaped by forces that derive from a broader political economy that operates from outside the context in which CBNRM occurs, and over which local people have no or little control. In fact, southern Africa's resource base – its wildlife populations, forests, water resources, protected areas and landscapes – has historically been shaped and scarred by war and conflict.

This chapter describes briefly how this happened, primarily during the period of instability and armed conflict that characterized the region during the 1970s and 1980s. It argues that the emergence of CBNRM during the late 1980s and 1990s as a powerful force for rural development in southern Africa was, in many ways, a manifestation of the peace dividend that derived from an end to apartheid destabilization in the region. Many CBNRM projects were implemented as national governments sought to reconstruct rural economies that were directly or indirectly underdeveloped because of war and armed conflict (Steiner, 1993). Thus, the CBNRM movement in southern Africa probably owes its existence to a set of new national and regional power alignments during the 1990s. Yet, the literature and discourse on CBNRM – probably because of the programme's stress and reliance on the devolution of rights to local citizens – frequently ignore the pressures that derive from the broader political economy in which these rural development projects operate. This chapter attempts to address the gap. It describes the impact of forces that derive from the local and national political economy on southern Africa's wild resource base, on the governance of these resources, and on the ability of CBNRM programmes to achieve their objectives. And in so doing, it makes some practical suggestions about how practitioners of CBNRM can deal with the bigger political forces that shape their work.

Warfare and Eco-conflict in Southern Africa: Impacts on Natural Resource Management

An extensive literature is emerging about the role that military conflict plays in shaping the natural resource base and how, in turn, conflicts over soil, water, fauna, flora, land and forests can lead to or escalate political and armed conflicts. Suliman, for example, describes how environmental degradation and conflict over diminishing natural resources played a central role in igniting the devastating recent conflicts in the Horn of Africa and in central Africa:

> *To continue treating conflicts in Africa as purely ethnic, tribal or religious, ignoring, in the process, the growing impact of restricting or denying access to resources and the growing ecological degradation and depletion of the renewable resource base could, ultimately, lead to a distorted understanding of the real situation and, consequently, limit the possibility of a genuine conflict resolution* (Suliman 1999, p27).

Baechler (1999) describes succinctly how a degraded environment can lead to political and armed conflict, and, in turn, how the natural resource and attempts to use and manage that base can become the casualty of wider conflicts. Baechler describes the above dynamic by showing how 'in a remote village somewhere in South Asia, someone's cow ate someone else's crop' and how this, in turn, led to a national conflict that took the form of an ethnic and religious struggle between Hindus and Muslims (Roy, 1994, cited in Baechler, 1999).

Westing (1992) has noted that militarization, either in the form of armed conflict or extensive expenditure on armed forces, can have a range of negative impacts on wildlife conservation and protected areas. Direct damage can take the form of site destruction, through the use of explosive and chemical devices, or it can be directed at specific components of the flora and fauna through activities such as illegal logging and hunting of wildlife. Damage to the infrastructure of a protected area, as well as the personnel responsible for administering the park, can also take place. Indirect damage can result from disruption of tourism and the revenues it brings to park authorities. Wartime privation can cause armies, as well as civilians, to undertake excessive exploitation of the natural resources inside a protected area. Even where there is no actual conflict, the presence of military operations in and near parks can be disruptive. This can exacerbate hostility on the part of local people, and training activities inside parks can damage forests and other vegetation.

Southern Africa has been no stranger to eco-conflicts of this nature. Since 1960, there have been violent struggles against colonial rule in Mozambique, Angola, Namibia and what was then white-ruled Rhodesia. In the post-colonial period, mainly from the late 1960s onwards, civil war afflicted Mozambique and Angola, as well as South Africa. Lesotho, Zimbabwe and Botswana were exposed to aggression and covert military operations launched from South Africa (Steiner, 1993). Many of these wars had their origins in the South African government's 'total strategy' of the 1980s – an effort to destroy bases of the African National Congress and the Pan Africanist Congress, South Africa's main liberation movements, and to destabilize the Frontline states that hosted these organizations by fomenting internal armed conflicts. The financial cost of South African-sponsored wars of destabilization in these countries – Angola, Malawi, Mozambique, Namibia, Zambia and Zimbabwe – was estimated during the early 1990s as being between US$45 billion and US$60 billion since 1980 (Steiner, 1993).

The environmental impacts of these conflicts have been well documented. The use of ivory by rebels in Mozambique and Angola caused heavy damage to elephant herds in those countries (Huntley and Matos, 1992; Ellis, 1994). The use of bushmeat from buffalo and other mammals to feed soldiers from many different armies involved in the wars of destabilization and liberation decimated other species of wildlife in some of the countries involved. And subsistence hunting by local citizens driven to desperation by the impacts of war had major negative impacts on fauna and flora of the subregion. In Angola, for example, the status of large mammals in the country's protected areas declined by up to 90 per cent during the 1970s and 1980s – especially rare species such as the black rhino and giant sable (Simon Anstey, pers comm). Huntley and Matos (1992) suggest that war reduced the wildlife populations of all national parks to 10 per cent of their original numbers.

The way in which Mozambique's natural resource base was devastated by decades of civil war in that country – ivory poaching, slaughter of buffalo and other mammals, deforestation caused by massive dislocation of local populations – has been extensively described. Mozambique's country report for the United Nations Conference on Environment and Development in 1992, for example, lists four species in a 'desperate situation' because of war (roan antelope, tsessebe, black rhino and sitatunga), while another four are categorized 'endangered' (ostrich, giraffe, cheetah and the marine dugong). The survival of various species of marine turtles that breed on beaches along the coast is mentioned as cause for concern (UNCED, 1992).

Zimbabwe's wildlife and natural resources were also seriously affected during this period. The Gonarezhou National Park, for example, experienced heavy poaching by soldiers and officers from at least three armies in the 1980s – Renamo, Frelimo and the Zimbabwean army.

South Africa's game parks and wildlife were not exempt. There was evidence of extensive military activity in game reserves near the border between northern Natal and Mozambique. And the South African Defence Force used the Kruger National Park to provide support for Renamo bases across the border during the 1980s and were involved in the smuggling of ivory through these routes (Ellis, 1994).

THE PEACE DIVIDEND, CONSERVATION REFORM AND THE PROLIFERATION OF CBNRM IN SOUTHERN AFRICA

During the early 1990s, peace broke out all over southern Africa. The civil war ended in Mozambique in 1992. The destabilizing effects of this war in parts of Zimbabwe that border on Mozambique declined. South Africa experienced a transition from white-minority rule to democracy in 1994, putting an end to the wars of destabilization that devastated the region's resource base, and creating a peace dividend that accelerated a range of policy reforms designed to strengthen various forms of integrated nature conservation and development (Steiner, 1993).

These reforms expanded dramatically during the 1990s. Inspired by a number of innovative projects in which rural groups were able to improve their livelihoods through the use of wildlife – most notably, the Communal Areas Management Programme for Indigenous Resources (CAMPFIRE) in Zimbabwe – government officials and non-governmental organizations (NGOs) began to realize that biodiversity resources play an important role in the lives of impoverished rural people, and that the productive use of plant and animal resources could play a role in rural development (Matzke and Nabane, 1996). Throughout southern Africa and the rest of the world, authorities began experimenting with new approaches to managing natural resources. During the mid 1980s, examples of good private-sector wildlife management and forestry practices outside of protected areas were noticed and documented. Governments and parastatals in east Africa, Zimbabwe, Zambia, Botswana, Namibia, South Africa and Mozambique switched to new approaches.

Apart from the enabling conditions created by the end of political and armed conflict, there were a number of other factors that fuelled these policy reforms and experiments in CBNRM. An analysis of these forces has been made elsewhere (Fabricius et al, 2001). They include a desire by governments and conservation agencies to capitalize on the new conditions of peace by encouraging forms of rural development that made use of, but also further conserved, those natural resources that survived the ravages of war. This was coupled with an emerging strategy and need to diversify the economy and move away from an agriculture-reliant system to tourism and natural resource use, a move that was encouraged by a serious cycle of droughts and floods that afflicted southern Africa during the early 1990s. Other macro-factors influencing the proliferation of CBNRM included a lack of resources for law enforcement inside protected areas and the desire to conserve wildlife populations outside protected areas, as well as strong bottom-up pressures from rural people who, in the new atmosphere of democracy, began pushing for rights to use and regain ownership over natural resources that had been expropriated from them during the colonial period. There was also, clearly, an element of political expediency and a recognition by governments that rural voters are important. For example, in Zimbabwe the government soon started claiming responsibility for the successes of CAMPFIRE and simultaneously gave its district councils an increasingly controlling role in the programme (Hasler, 1999). In Zambia, the Luangwa Integrated Rural Development Project (LIRDP) gained the acceptance of President Kenneth Kaunda on the basis of its political benefits (Dalal-Clayton and Child, pers comm; Richard Bell, pers comm). More recently the Makuleke land claim, by which a portion of land inside the Kruger National Park was transferred to a community, shows how national politics played an important role in expediting this case (see Chapter 16). The minister of land affairs wanted to demonstrate that the pace of land reform was not as slow as was claimed at the time. Broadly speaking, the reforms that were initiated in these and other countries due to some combination of the above factors included most of the basic principles of CBNRM.

NEW POLITICAL FORCES THAT UNDERMINE CITIZENS' RIGHTS TO MANAGE THEIR RESOURCES

Paradoxically, though, although these reforms had their origins in the broad political economy of the southern Africa region, the discourse and practice of CBNRM came to emphasize the need to work at local level. The emphasis in CBNRM on devolution of proprietorship and use rights to the smallest level of local organization, to the direct and primary users of natural resources, relied on the apparent willingness of governments to make policy and legislative changes that allowed for this democratization of environmental rights. Paradoxically, this focus on decentralization and local-level politics led to a relative neglect of the broader political forces that shape the resource base and the way in which it is managed. Many of the chapters in this book show that while the dramatic politics of the 1980s and early 1990s have given way to relative peace, the political economy in which CBNRM programmes are located continues to exercise its hold (see Chapters 9, 11, 15, 17 and 18).

Land reform and land invasions in Zimbabwe are a classic example of how a national political crisis can affect the natural resource base and the CBNRM programmes – in this case CAMPFIRE's tourism and hunting projects – that make use of these resources. Chapter 13 notes how instability and armed conflict in the Caprivi strip in Namibia, historically linked to the civil war over the border in Angola and the incursions of Unita-related paramilitaries into the Caprivi, all but shut down the potentially lucrative tourism concessions linked to conservancies in that region. The chapter also shows how that country's political economy – specifically, an informal alliance between some politicians in the ruling party and tourism developers opposed to the new and fair concession fees required by the conservancies for lodge operations – has conspired to undermine and weaken some conservancies, even though official government policy is supportive of these conservancies.

In Chapter 9 we see how national government officials in Botswana frequently rode rough-shod over the rights that have been granted to local residents through official CBNRM policy in that country, threatening to intervene directly or withdraw natural resource rights in cases where fledgling partnerships between communities and the private sector go through phases of conflict and instability. The Makuleke case in South Africa (see Chapters 5 and 16) shows how various departments of the post-apartheid government have frequently tried to curb or withdraw natural resource rights granted to the Makuleke people in terms of that government's own land restitution programme. In particular, elements of the South African state have, in the past, tried to curb the rights of the Makuleke to conduct consumptive use of their natural resources (that is, safari hunts for elephant trophies) primarily because the state was involved at the time in delicate international debates about elephant hunting and culling and the international ban on ivory sales imposed by the Convention on International Trade in Endangered Species of Wild Fauna and Flora (CITES).

In South Africa, probably as a direct result of the transition to democracy, there has been a proliferation of laws, policies and constitutional principles, each of which reinforce the basic principles of CBNRM. However, at the time of writing, there appears to be a lack of capacity in the primary departments concerned with natural resource management – land affairs, agriculture, environment affairs and tourism, mineral affairs and energy, local government and housing – and a clear lack of coordination between them (Fabricius et al, 2002; Njobe et al, 1999). In addition, there was a contested relationship between national government and provincial governments over which level of the state should control, manage and profit from prime wildlife and landscape assets in the country. In 2001 and 2002, serious tensions occurred between the central government and the provincial government of Mpumalanga Province over plans by central government to convert the provincial Blyde River Canyon Nature Reserve (as well as adjacent and threatened indigenous forests) into a national park. A similar set of conflicts between central government and the Eastern Cape provincial government paralysed efforts to create a protected area in a rich and biodiverse region called the Pondoland Centre of Endemism. By the end of 2002, this intra-government conflict remained unresolved and stymied a range of efforts to promote CBNRM programmes in these wild landscapes of South Africa, effectively undermining the government's ability to implement its own pro-CBNRM policies (Geoff de Beer, pers comm)

Many of the chapters in this book, including Chapter 2 on local conflicts, show that there is tremendous stress and strain in the political economy of local government. Chapter 18 demonstrates how Zimbabwe's district councils depend upon and, therefore, intercept the revenues generated by CAMPFIRE's CBNRM programmes, further reducing the already minimal impact that these revenues can have on improving local livelihoods. Chapter 15 demonstrates how national and local government in Mozambique predates on the CBNRM programme Tchumo Tchato, causing massive leakage of the commercial value of that trophy-hunting programme out of the village of Bawa and into the coffers of district and national government. Conflict between traditional authorities and new institutions set up to create democratic forms of natural resource management – as we have seen in Chapter 2 – is an almost axiomatic consequence of CBNRM's attempt to fuse communal and informal systems of tenure over natural resources with new formal institutions of governance that derive from Western and capitalist property regimes.

The greatly varying constellation of power relations in each of the countries in the southern Africa region also explains why – despite being phrased in a common and unifying lexicon – the real conditions on the ground for implementing CBNRM principles differ considerably in each country. The terms 'co-management', 'joint forest management', 'partnerships', 'involvement' and 'shared management' have become part and parcel of the lexicon that has developed alongside the proliferation of CBNRM in the region; but these mask a high degree of difference in the extent to which human and natural resource rights are given to citizens of the countries in the region.

Thus, although many countries on the subcontinent speak of 'devolution', what they actually do on the ground varies from one country to another. For example, while Botswana (Shackleton and Campbell, 2001) and Namibia (Jones, 1999) allow communities to hold secure tenure over natural resources managed communally, Malawi's policy framework retains rights over resources firmly in the state's hands (Shackleton and Campbell, 2001). Furthermore, while Namibia allows for the formation of conservancies as legal entities for common-pool resource management (Jones, 1999), Malawi falls short of providing statutory authority to local organizations. Yet another variable is the level to which the state is willing to devolve power. While the forementioned countries all devolve control to the village level, Zimbabwe and Zambia do so only to the district level (Getz et al, 1999; Shackleton and Campbell, 2001). Thus, the interpretation of what constitutes 'participation' varies from one country to another (PLAAS, 2001), and the extent to which participation takes place and the rights to use natural resources benefit the rural poor is centrally shaped by the extent to which government departments are willing to devolve these rights – a political will that is, in turn shaped by the balance of class and power relations that underpin the state.

Clearly, despite the commonly voiced commitment by most governments of southern Africa to the principles of CBNRM, there are powerful political and economic forces at play that, in many cases, conspire to undermine the ability of CBNRM programmes to realize their objectives. The obvious question that arises, for practitioners, is how to deal with these factors. Are we farting against thunder, some may ask, or are there strategies that can be adopted to deal with these big and powerful forces?

SOME SUGGESTIONS FOR DEALING WITH THE THUNDER

Firstly, the most obvious point to make is that those forces that are threatened by the democratic and equitable implications of CBNRM are not omnipotent in the region. The fact that there has been such a widespread inscription of CBNRM principles within the policies of many governments – along with an attempt to merge communal with private property regimes – in the region is in itself an indication of a surge towards democracy. Many of the chapters in this book suggest that CBNRM could, in fact, be developing into a mass social movement in favour of democratization. In Namibia, conservancies have grouped into a national umbrella organization that presses for the observation of rights contained in that country's legislation. There appears to be a nascent move to create similar national-level organizations of CBNRM 'user communities' in other countries, including Malawi, Botswana and South Africa (although it is notable that the CAMPFIRE association in Zimbabwe has not adopted any strong stance on the way in which human rights have been violated in Zimbabwe by the Mugabe government). Various communities in South Africa, including the Richtersvelders and the Makulekes, have exerted considerable pressure on the South African state to ensure that their devolved rights to use the wild resources on land that has been restored to them are respected. In the case of the Makulekes, there has been a fairly successful merger of traditional power structures with new democratic institutions. In the case of the Richtersveld, there is growing cooperation between the residents' communal property association and the local municipality.

Secondly, CBNRM is developing the ability and the skills to create lasting institutions that can effectively protect the rights of local citizens. In the Luangwa Valley of Zambia, some traditional authorities who were threatened by the CBNRM programme being implemented there have relented and begun to respect new democratic institutions that have been sensitively but diligently created and set up. Child (Chapter 17) points out that this required patient, open and transparent commitment to the principles of equity and popular participation, along with some sensitivity and respect for the dignity of traditional chiefs. All over the region new institutions have emerged – conservancy committees, trusts, communal property associations, beach committees, participatory forest management forums, and fisherfolk associations – that demonstrate and describe the experimentation that is taking place within the social movement that is now being driven by the principles of CBNRM. Training programmes and skills development courses are being implemented in almost all countries of the region (described in PLAAS, 2001) and practitioners are developing the art of creating robust and appropriate institutions for democratic governance at local level. These require a clear understanding of the power relations that shape the resource base – as well as the way in which resources are governed – and then a combination of sensitivity and light-touch facilitation to create appropriate local institutions. Where existing institutions can be utilized or modified to implement the principles of CBNRM, this is probably preferable to the creation of new institutions. Care should be taken not to use blueprint approaches as this has frequently accounted for the proliferation of clashing institutions described in Chapter 2 (CPPP and GTZ, undated).

Thirdly, and linked to the above, it is clear that the CBNRM movement in southern Africa cannot be divorced from the struggle for human rights and just forms of land distribution and ownership:

> *Historically, control over land...has always been vital to the livelihoods of the world's poorest people. Lack of access to land not only denies people the ability to gather their own food: it also excludes them from a source of power. Who controls the land – and how they do so – affects how land is used and to whom the benefits of its use accrue* (Suliman 1999, p15).

Where there is a clear land reform programme and a strong human rights framework, CBNRM has a greater chance of success. Where these base conditions are weak or unclear – as the crisis now in Zimbabwe so powerfully demonstrates – the prospects for progress are uncertain.

Fourthly, there is clearly a need to build alliances and partnerships. In this sense, the move towards the creation of community private–public partnerships (CPPPs) does not only make sense with regard to commercial success and sustainability. These emerging coalitions between business people, government officials and community leaders represent a progressive political bloc that can be used to protect local people's existing rights to use their natural resources from the predations of anti-democratic elements, as well as lobby for the creation of new policies and legislative reforms.

Fifthly, much of the literature and the manuals on how to do effective CBNRM contain a stress on the need for mediation skills (see PLAAS 2001; CPPP and GTZ, undated). This is obviously appropriate in a situation where the creation of new forms of democracy tends to threaten individuals and groups whose power rests in older traditional political institutions. But the focus that this implies on dealing with local-level intra- and inter-community conflicts should not result in a neglect of the political and ecological conditions – the macro-causes – that underlie much of the conflict that surrounds the implementation of CBNRM programmes. 'It is...possible to solve political conflicts through mediation, persuasion and intervention. However, the economic–ecological conflicts which are likely to dominate the African scene in the years to come demand that more attention be given not to perceptions and manifestations of the conflict, but to its root causes' (Suliman, 1999, p43).

Sixthly, there is clearly the need for CBNRM programmes to encourage a diversity of resource-use strategies by local people. Given the fact that these projects inevitably invite political opposition from groups or individuals who are threatened by them, it makes sense not to depend upon one strategy for resource use. If a powerful business tycoon or a government minister is in cahoots with the magnate who manages to obstruct the development of a tourism concession that is owned and controlled by a group of collectively organized citizens, then it would be useful for those citizens to have other ways of ensuring their livelihoods, possibly through harvesting natural resources or conducting trophy hunts. A diversity of resource-use portfolios for citizens can provide resilience, a way to deal with the thunder and survive the storms of eco-conflict.

Finally, there is the ability to effectively use international conventions and treaties to enforce the rights of local people. As Chatty and Colchester (2002, p11) point out: 'The rights of indigenous peoples in conservation concerns have long antecedents and have even found their way, albeit ambiguously, into international law.' The role that global forces play – such as the international trade regime, the behaviour of transnational corporations, leakage from commercial forms of resource use in the developing world to the developed world, and the global animal rights movement – have not been addressed in this book and require separate attention and analysis. Suffice to say here that citizens and the practitioners of CBNRM should be aware of the body of international conventions that they can call upon to defend themselves. These include the various articles adopted by the World Summits on Sustainable Development, such as Article 22 of the Rio Declaration, which states that:

> *Indigenous peoples and their communities and other local communities have a vital role in environmental management and development because of their knowledge and traditional practices. States should recognize and duly support their identity, culture and interests and enable their effective participation in the achievement of sustainable development* (cited in Chatty and Colchester, 2002, p12).

Other international statutes reinforce such rights, including the Convention on Biological Diversity (CBD), the International Labour Organization's Convention on Tribal and Indigenous Peoples, various guidelines adopted by the IUCN–World Conservation Union and the World Wide Fund For Nature (WWF) and the United Nations Declaration on the Rights of Indigenous People.

There is an evolution taking place in international law that gives recognition and potential protection to the collective rights of human groups to maintain their rights to use their natural environment and the resources found there. Around the world, citizens are mobilizing to use the rights conferred on them by these conventions. There is a:

> *...resurgence of indigenous peoples, who have strategically and quite consciously mobilized to occupy political space at national and global levels to claim recognition of their human rights... Historians may look back on this era of growing recognition of indigenous peoples' rights as a sea-change as significant as the anti-slavery movements of 150 years earlier* (Chatty and Colchester, 2002, p13).

Perhaps the best defence against the storm is for the practitioners of CBNRM to realize that they are not alone, and to huddle together in the global movement that is fighting for the rights that underpin CBNRM.

REFERENCES

Baechler, G (1999) 'Environmental degradation and violent conflict: Hypotheses, research agendas and theory-building', in Suliman, M (ed) *Ecology, Politics and Violent Conflict*. Zed Books, London and New York, pp76–115

Chatty, D and Colchester, M (2002) 'Introduction: Conservation and mobile indigenous peoples', in Chatty, D and Colchester, M (eds) *Conservation and Mobile Indigenous Peoples: Displacement, Forced Settlement and Sustainable Development*. Berghahn Books, New York and Oxford, pp1–21

CPPP unit of DTI and GTZ Transform (undated) *Job Creation and Economic Development through the Use of Natural Resources: A Manual for Rural Communities Planning Partnerships with the Government and Private Sector around Tourism, Conservation and other Forms of Natural Resource Use*. CPPP unit, Department of Trade and Industry, South Africa

Ellis, S (1994) 'Of elephants and men: Politics and nature conservation in South Africa', *Journal of Southern African Studies* 20: 53–70

Fabricius, C, Koch, E and Magome, H (2001) 'Towards strengthening collaborative ecosystem management: Lessons from environmental conflict and political change in southern Africa', *Journal of the Royal Society of New Zealand* 31: 831–884

Fabricius, C, Matsiliza, B, and Sisitka, L (2002) *Support for CBNRM Type Programmes in South Africa*. Department of Environmental Science, Rhodes University for the Department of Environment Affairs and Tourism and GTZ Transform, Pretoria

Getz, W M, Fortmann, L, Cumming, D, du Toit, R, Hilty, J, Murphree, M, Owen-Smith, N, Starfield, A and Westphal, M (1999) 'Sustaining natural and human capital: Villagers and scientists', *Science* 283: 1855–1856

Hasler, R (1999) 'An overview of the social, ecological and economic achievements and challenges of Zimbabwe's CAMPFIRE project', *Evaluating Eden Discussion Paper* No 3. International Institute for Environment and Development, London

Huntley, B J and Matos, E (1992) *Biodiversity: Angolan Environmental Status Quo: Assessment Report*, IUCN/Regional Office for Southern Africa, Harare, July

Jones, B T B (1999) 'Rights, revenue and resources: The problems and potential of conservancies as community wildlife management institutions in Namibia', *Evaluating Eden Discussion Paper* No 2. International Institute for Environment and Development, London

Matzke, G E and Nabane, N (1996) 'Outcomes of a community controlled wildlife utilization programme in a Zambezi Valley community', *Human Ecology* 24: 65–86

Njobe, K, Nomtshongwana, N and Stowell, Y (1999) *Promoting Sustainable Livelihoods for Communities Through The Use and Management of Natural Resources: A Strategic Review of Policy and Practice in South Africa*. Unpublished Proceedings of Department of Environmental Affairs and Tourism seminar, 1999

PLAAS (2001) *Governance in Community Based Natural Resource Management*. Report of a five-day course held at the Manor Hotel in Cape Town, September 2001, organized by Programme for Land and Agrarian Studies (PLAAS), Centre for Applied Social Studies (CASS) and the World Conservation Union, Cape Town

Shackleton, S and Campbell, B (2001) *Devolution in Natural Resources Management: Institutional Arrangements and Power Shifts.* A synthesis of case studies from southern Africa. USAID NRM Project No 690-0251, CSIR, Pretoria, South Africa

Steiner, A M (1993) 'The peace dividend in southern Africa: Prospects and potentials for redirecting military resources towards natural resource management'. Paper presented to UNDP Conference on Military and the Environment, Past Mistakes and Future Options, New York

Suliman, M (1999) 'The rationality and irrationality of violence in sub-Saharan Africa', in Suliman, M (ed) *Ecology, Politics and Violent Conflict.* Zed Books, London and New York, pp25–45

UNCED (1992) *Mozambique Country Report.* UNCED, Maputo

Westing, A H (1992) 'Protected areas and the military', *Environmental Conservation,* 19: 343–348

Chapter 4

Putting out fires: Does the 'C' in CBNRM stand for community or centrifuge?

EDDIE KOCH

One of the most enduring issues facing practitioners and students of both formal and informal systems of community-based natural resource management (CBNRM) in southern Africa is the bewildering array of tensions and conflicts that arise, paradoxically, in situations where local economic development is predicated upon an assumption of 'community' cohesion and stability. Indeed, many of the case studies in Part 2 indicate that local conflicts and tensions are the greatest cause for concern, the highest common denominator in debates about whether or not there has been 'success' or 'failure' in formal CBNRM projects.

This chapter sets out to explore what these sources of local conflict and contestation are and whether fracture in the local body politic is the fatal flaw in CBNRM on the subcontinent. Its conclusions begin, tentatively, to answer questions relating to the kinds of measures that may be adopted to resolve, or at least mitigate, the tensions that bedevil the operations of so many CBNRM programmes in southern Africa. The overall suggestion and, hopefully, some source of comfort to practitioners is that CBNRM is like a roller-coaster ride that oscillates between serious conflict and the creation of good governance. But it is heading, certainly not in a linear way, toward a destination where common and private systems of owning property – and managing the things that live in and on that property – are beginning to merge with and support each other.

BACKGROUND

As reported in Chapter 1, groups of citizens throughout southern Africa are increasingly being endowed with both the right and responsibility to secure and manage the natural resources that they live with and often survive on. Many countries in these regions – including South Africa, Botswana, Namibia, Zimbabwe (until recently), Zambia, Mozambique, Uganda and Tanzania – have enacted land and juridical reforms that give local citizens some form of collective ownership or, at least, use rights over land and the resources that exist in and on land (Wily, 2000). This follows a worldwide trend in which more than 50 countries have begun to pursue some form of devolving ownership or use rights over natural resources to groups of citizens organized in some kind of collective way (FAO, 1999, cited in Agrawal, 2001).

But empirical evidence from case studies in this book, and the performance of other projects in southern Africa, indicate a growing concern about the level of fragmentation that tends to accompany many CBNRM programmes. Optimism regarding the capacity and cohesion of local-level institutional structures has increasingly given way to a concern about unstable governance arrangements at local level. And a number of commentators have noted that various types of conflict account for the high degree of variability in the institutional arrangements that underpin CBNRM programmes in different parts of South Africa, even though these programmes have similar objectives and are cloaked in the same discourse and terminology (Campbell et al, 2001; Twyman, 2001).

Indeed, it may be argued that when concepts are used in a bland and static way, then 'community-based management' of natural resources could, like military intelligence, become an oxymoron. Many of the case studies in this collection indicate that conflicts among the citizens who manage a given set of wild resources are the critical flaws that prevent proper achievement of the goals of CBNRM. Information from the field thus begs the question: has the notion of community been romanticized? Is fracture in the body politic the Achilles heel of CBNRM on the subcontinent and, possibly, in the rest of the world, too?

We have argued elsewhere that the evidence from southern Africa suggests that the 'C' in CBNRM is nebulous, fluid and elusive and often a figment of the imagination of project managers and donors seeking quick fixes (Fabricius et al, 2001b). A common belief among donors and project managers is that it saves time to group people together because of the simplicity of working with fewer groups. Our findings suggest the opposite: if the groupings within a community and the differences between groups are not well understood and taken into account, then conflicts emerge that are difficult to heal (Fabricius et al, 2001b). 'Community' may be one of the most enduring concepts in social science. It is also one of the most vaguely defined terms (Murphree, 1999).

The fluidity of the interplay between conflict and cohesion, and the mercurial nature of the balance of these two states within a 'community', also needs to be stressed. The International Institute for Environment and Development (IIED) study, referred to in Fabricius et al (2001b), presented the Makuleke in South Africa as a case for reinserting the 'C'. This group of people was forcibly removed from the far north of the Kruger National Park in 1969 and regained title from the democratic government of South Africa in 1994.

The community had a high degree of internal cohesion and managed to form a legal entity that enabled its members to hold freehold title – something that is normally held by individuals or a company in a capitalist economy – to the restored land in a collective way. The tribe's traditional leaders effectively merged with the elected leadership of the communal property association, and it appeared that the tension between traditional and democratic forms of community governance that negatively affects so many CBNRM programmes was averted. At the time of publication, there were cracks and fissures in Makuleke civil society. The moment that significant revenues from the commercialization of Makuleke land arrived, tensions within the leadership and between the leadership and the rank and file began to emerge. Conflicts arose over who would benefit most from the new revenues.

We stress that this is 'at the time of publication' because in months from this date, things may be different. There are countervailing tendencies and the Makuleke leadership is acutely aware of the dangers posed by these centrifugal tendencies. Serious efforts are being made to remedy the problem. Ordinary members of the Makuleke communal property association are demanding accountability, and it may well be that a stable form of governance and a genuinely collective way of managing the Makuleke region of the Kruger National Park and the wealth that derives from it may have re-established itself.

In order to answer the questions posed at the beginning of this chapter – are local conflicts the factors that will cause the eventual demise of the common property experiment in southern Africa or are the strategies available for mitigating them, and thus for putting commonly managed development programmes back on an even keel – it may be useful to try and unravel the many strands of local conflict in CBNRM.

A TYPOLOGY OF CONFLICTS

Some of the most common categories of conflict and contestation that come from the case studies include competition for scarce benefits that flow from the commercial and other uses of wild resources (especially where populations are large in relation to their resource base); a related tendency for rural elites to intercept these benefits through a myriad of ingenious devices; tensions between traditional authorities and new democratic institutions; conflicts between individual entrepreneurs within a community and members of a collectively organized group; dissonances between social and geographic boundaries; spiritual leaders alienated by formal projects that ignore their role; and gender conflicts.

The list is by no means exhaustive, and practitioners who have been bewildered by the degree of fragmentation in the communities with whom they work will have no problem trebling the list of variants. For now, eight of the most typical forms of intra-community conflict found in our case studies are examined in more detail below.

Conflicts that emerge at the time of success

We have already referred to the patterns at Makuleke where conflict in a relatively cohesive local community broke out when sizeable revenues began to flow into the settlements where members of the tribe now live, even though a relatively stable and formal legal entity was set up in the form of a communal property association. These dynamics are dealt with in the case study in Chapter 16, which describes the experiences of the Makuleke and Richtersveld communities.

In the case study from Botswana, Boggs (Chapter 9) demonstrates that in some of the communal wildlife areas, often described as being among the more successful CBNRM projects in the region, a set of new intra-community conflicts have emerged as civic leaders try to create new wildlife management institutions. She describes, for example, how a small group of people at Sankuyo village in the south-east terminus of the Okavango Delta, with rights to commercialize high-value resources for tourism in a relatively arid area, ended up in a series of complex squabbles.

In the second year of managing a joint venture with a private-sector partner, a partnership that included trophy hunting and photographic tourism, the 'Sankuyo community lost confidence in their board due to allegations of theft and corruption and elected a new board. Unequal distribution of power and benefits resulted in leadership struggles and the formation of factions within the community membership'. The revenue generated in that year was an enormous 1.1 million pula for a community made up of about 350 people.

Boggs says that the Botswana examples demonstrate how an 'elite' (usually kin) group, which can undermine the local legal entity set up to manage the project and interfere with the democratic process, dominates most communities. In Sankuyo, divisions emerged between educated and uneducated and between generations. Elders were forced to give up power to the young and educated, challenging traditional values. Later, unequal division of benefits created new conflicts.

Competing livelihood strategies within communities

Within communities, there exist large differences between different user groups and entities, each relying on different bundles of resources for their livelihoods. In the Mkambati area, Kepe, Cousins and Turner (2000) identified seven communities of interest who earn their livelihoods in different ways. These 'livelihood clusters' had different needs; all the clusters used natural resources in some way or another and there was wide divergence of opinion among the groups about how best to promote development at Mkambati. This diversity of livelihood clusters is likely to be a critical centrifugal force in most resource-dependent communities.

In Chapter 1, we noted that biological diversity – and also a diversity of livelihood strategies – can provide for a good deal of resilience and sustainability. However, a diversity of strategies for survival through the harvesting and use of natural resources can also be the cause of conflict and instability, especially when the use of a strategy by one group within a community implies a constraint or cost to another group. For example, the creation of a nature tourism lodge on communal land would imply restrictions on goats and cattle grazing in the vicinity of the lodge, causing potential conflict between those who favour a tourism strategy and livestock owners. In addition, it should be stressed that these conflicts may not only be framed in terms of use values and the material benefits. As we shall see later, land and its resources have immense symbolic and cultural importance in most rural societies and, as a result, conflicts between competing strategies for the use of resources are often framed in terms of intangible cultural and spiritual perceptions, a factor making such tensions even more difficult to predict.

Tensions between traditional authorities and new entities

The case studies and literature are replete with this kind of conflict. The conservancy movement in Namibia, listed as one of the more successful attempts at implementing the principles of CBNRM, has also frequently had to deal with this type of conflict. Nott and Jacobsohn (Chapter 13) note how many conservancies in Namibia are experiencing opposition from traditional leaders and that conservancy members are insisting on exercising their rights despite this opposition from traditional chiefs.

Brian Child, in his case study (Chapter 17), notes how some traditional chiefs posed a possible threat to the Luangwa Integrated Rural Development Project (LIRDP). His evidence shows that under the conditions that exist in that part of Zambia, it was possible to counter the stranglehold that chiefs exerted over development by insisting on a highly developed form of participatory democracy. Success bred success and residents began to insist on high levels of participation, overruling the hegemony of traditional authority. This is a small but significant demonstration of how ordinary people are beginning to exercise the rights conferred on them by CBNRM policy reform.

In the Makuleke case study (Chapter 16) there is a close synergy between the communal property association – a democratic and legally constituted entity that holds the community's land and manages the dividends it derives from commercial use of the land – and the traditional authority. There has been a deliberate attempt on the part of the citizens' leadership to achieve this. The chief is *ex-officio* chair of the executive committee of the communal property association. All other positions on the executive are elected. The chief derives benefit from his status and has, for example, been given an expensive four-by-four vehicle purchased from the proceeds of trophy hunting in the Makuleke region of the Kruger National Park. But this benefit was approved and supported at a mass meeting of the members of the communal property association. Many of them noted that it was important for them that their chief be able to display a similar status to other chiefs in the area. From this meeting and the debate that took place, it can, in fact, be deduced that the material benefit that went to the chief in the form of a vehicle was a collective intangible for the rest of the community. It bolstered Makuleke identity and signified a sense of pride and achievement – important to the Makuleke citizens as they live in a province in which other chiefs and politicians have often been hostile to them (Lamson Maluleke, pers comm). At the same time, great care is taken by the Makuleke leadership to ensure that other revenues are shared equally by the Makuleke villages, and there is an explicitly social democratic agenda being promoted. There is, thus, a delicate synergy rather than a tension between the role played by the chief and the elected representatives of the community at Makuleke.

Boggs's study describes the opposite syndrome (Chapter 9). At Sankuyo in the Okavango Delta of Botswana, the local chief was deliberately precluded from having a seat on the committee elected to manage citizens' revenues from hunting and photographic tourism lest he use his power and influence to predate upon those revenues. At Kosi Bay in the KwaZulu-Natal province of South Africa, where local people live inside the Kosi Bay Nature Reserve and land and its resources are managed by a traditional local authority, the local headman participated in decisions about how to distribute revenues from tourism. But he also used his influence to secure a favourable site for his own guest house. Here we see, within the same individual, a tension between the benefits that derive from traditionally defined privilege and power and the obligation to ensure an equitable spread of benefit that derives from the principles of community-based management of natural resources (Stephen Turner, pers comm). During the mid 1980s, at the Madikwe Game Reserve in the North-West Province of South Africa, the former conservation authority set up what it called community development organizations (CDOs) in the villages around the park and grouped these together under a single entity called a CDO forum. This was a genuine effort to create a collective body to administer a set of benefits derived from the park for three villages around the park. The CDO model was based on a flawed assumption of 'community' and cohesion, even though the park was artificially created from above and placed geographically into an area between these three villages. What happened, in fact, was that the CDOs helped contribute to fragmentation and lack of cohesion. In each of the villages, they were set up in parallel to the local tribal authorities and earlier-constituted reconstruction and development committees. Sometimes the CDOs operated in tandem with these other organs of local governance; at other times, they were in conflict with them. The studies dealing with beach committees in Malawi and a participatory forest management programme in Zimbabwe also refer to a mixed pattern of tension and synergies between traditional and elected leaders (see Chapters 12 and 19).

Conflict between individual entrepreneurs and the collective

A common type of conflict that appears to accompany the implementation of CBNRM occurs between individual entrepreneurs within a community and members of the entity set up to represent the collective in the enterprise. This variant of tension is evident in some of the Namibian conservancies.

Jones (1999) shows how the Twyfelfontein Conservancy in the Damaraland region of Namibia was, at the time of writing, dominated by one powerful leadership figure and entrepreneur. Many of the business opportunities that derived from a lodge that had been developed in partnership with a private investor were commandeered by this individual, who appears to have had political support at national level. This was related to a breakaway by the Twyfelfontein Conservancy from the larger Dorra/Novas Conservancy, and ongoing tensions between the two entities slowed down formalization of tourism joint ventures and the flow of revenues from these enterprises to local households.

The same type of conflict can be discerned in different guises in other CBNRM projects. During 2000, there was tremendous tension in the Makuleke leadership over the question of whether individuals on the executive committee of the Communal Property Association (CPA), who received a monthly fee for their work, were entitled to take up business opportunities – such as contracts for construction or the manufacture of bricks – related to the lodges that the community was developing in partnership with the private sector in its part of the Kruger National Park.

Local government versus civic organizations

The case study on the Communal Areas Management Programme for Indigenous Resources (CAMPFIRE) (Chapter 18) refers to an extensive literature that describes the many tensions that occurred between village wards and district councils in Zimbabwe over access to CAMPFIRE's hunting dividends. Sithole demonstrates in her case study of resource management committees in the Mafungautsi State Forest Reserve of south-west Zimbabwe (Chapter 19) that these entities, set up to promote community preservation of some forest resources, were, in fact, highly contested by other local organizations such as village development committees, the rural district council and traditional leaders – a major factor contributing to ineffectual community management of the forest resource.

Sometimes this is a variant of the conflict between chiefs and civil society, especially in situations where chiefs still constitute the only form of local government, such as in the Luangwa Valley of Zambia.

In Mozambique, a critical cause of stress in the Tchumo Tchato project was the predatory nature of district government. Johnson notes (Chapter 15) how dividends from safari hunting were considerably diluted because in that country both the national and district levels of government each took a third of these before the remaining amount could be distributed to the residents of Bawa village (the settlement where most of the Tchumo Tchato's beneficiaries live). In addition, although the programme was designed to strengthen the capacity of village residents to manage their resources, as well as to encourage local government officials to support the CBNRM initiative, it appears that the latter ended up dominating the process. This stands in contrast to the original rationale for the Tchumo Tchato project to include the local community in natural resource decision-making.

Fluid communities and rigid geographic boundaries

There is a tendency in some CBNRM projects to define communities along geographic or biophysical lines. But, frequently, local settlements do not conform to geographic and/or ecological boundaries and are spatially organized in ways other than the unit of CBNRM in question. At other times, CBNRM imposes a false geographic boundary.

The managers of the Madikwe Game Reserve in South Africa, for example, assumed that three villages on the borders of the game reserve would have congruent interests simply because of the existence of the game park. There, the provincial parks board formed a single community development forum to address the needs of three communities who differed greatly in their attitudes and socio-economic profiles. The false assumption of the parks board that these villages represented one single homogeneous community with the same social and economic needs contributed significantly to delaying the effective participation of these three villages at Madikwe (Magome et al, 2000). In Namibia, several communities were grouped together into the same conservancy because of the legislative requirement that conservancies should have clearly defined boundaries. A geographic definition of boundaries was used that did not correspond to the local political boundaries. This roused dormant disputes over land, and the ensuing struggle for group membership delayed the development of the conservancy for a long time (Jones, 1999).

Sithole (Chapter 19) shows how the resource management committees set up in the Mafungautsi forest reserve entailed a similarly false assumption of conformity between geographic and social boundaries. Different resource management committees (RMCs) controlled different areas of forest alongside their villages. Although these areas were clearly defined administratively, boundaries were not observed. Differential endowment and accessibility of forest areas has resulted in users criss-crossing boundaries, generating significant intra-community tensions. Murphree (1999) notes in a more generic way that there is a 'generalized dissonance' between the small user units of ideal CBNRM programmes, in which members have personalized communication and the spatially large geographic areas required for sustainable levels of biological diversity.

The hidden power of spiritual leaders

Bernard and Kumalo's study, in Chapter 6, refers to the neglected role of spiritual ecology in CBNRM. They remind us that spiritual leaders in many African localities have great influence over resource management in that they represent the great spirit deities of an 'African earth religion' (Schoffeleers, 1978) and offer powerful constraints over misuse of resources. Throughout the subcontinent, they recur time and time again in the oral histories of the various sub-groups. They are, along with the ancestors, the guardians of the land. Bernard and Kumalo's chapter makes the crucial point that CBNRM's heavy stress on the need to generate tangible revenues from the use of natural resources may conflict with the spiritual ecological principles that govern use of resources in the CBNRM system. Bell (1999) makes the point that informal systems for managing common resources are frequently referred to in African societies as being regulated by the 'laws of the spirits', while formal management of resources is often referred to as the 'laws of the government'.

A collection of papers edited by Schoffeleers (1978) focuses on the widespread territorial cult complexes found in Zambia, Zimbabwe, Malawi, Mozambique and Tanzania. Territorial cults are usually focused around identifiable natural or man-made shrines that are linked to local ancestral, tribal tutelary spirits or the supra-ancestral spirit beings. They are usually governed by a priesthood, spirit mediums or diviner healers in close conjunction with tribal chiefs or headmen. According to Schoffeleers (1978): 'What sets territorial cults apart from other religious institutions is the combination of communal and ecological concerns and the primacy accorded these concerns.' He describes these as 'ritually directed ecosystems' that aim to:

> ...counteract droughts, floods, blights, pests and epidemic diseases afflicting cattle and man... [They] function in respect of the well-being of the community, its field, livestock, fishing, hunting and general economic interests...they also issue and enforce directives with regard to a community's use of its environment...they provide schemas of thought in which myths, rituals and directives for action appear as parts of a coherent worldview (Schoffeleers, 1978, p2).

Where such spiritual leaders are incorporated within formal CBNRM planning, success can be enhanced. At Tchumo Tchato, Johnson (Chapter 15) shows that spirit mediums played an important role in the traditional lives of the Bawa community, influencing social behaviour and guiding the use of natural resources. The project purposefully engaged with these spirit mediums in an attempt to ensure that its objectives were shared by all sectors of the community.

But spiritual power is often hidden from formal organization. Sithole (Chapter 19) shows how the resource management committees of the Mafungautsi State Forest Reserve of south-west Zimbabwe are undermined by the power of a dominant matriarch. She is the most vocal woman in public meetings and gatherings, and popular beliefs that she was a witch generated fear and a reluctance by residents to organize around indications that revenues were being mismanaged.

Bernard and Kumalo (Chapter 6) show how in the Umnga municipal area of the Eastern Cape a local chief endorsed a private development proposal to establish a power plant at a waterfall that has great spiritual significance for the diviners in the region. Interviews with many of the diviners and local people revealed great concern for the plan since this was where the *abantu bamlambo* (people of the river/mermaids) resided. They feared that the power plant would not only disturb the tranquillity of the surroundings preferred by the *abantu bamlambo*, but that the electricity generated would also drive them away from the pools. They believed that this would have led to serious droughts, electrical storms or floods. Furthermore, the healers would no longer have been able to access the pools for their rituals since the area would have been fenced off for their 'safety'.

The effectiveness of spirit mediums in obstructing outside-initiated management and development programmes has been described by Spierenburg (2000), who details the events that took place in the Zambezi Valley in 1992 as a community resisted a land redistribution and development programme. The Mid-Zambezi Rural Development Project was initiated and funded by the Food and Agriculture Organization (FAO) and was largely a top-down intervention initiative. In this particular case, it was the spirit medium, representing a senior tutelary spirit (*mhondoro*), who wielded the ultimate power, the chief having deferred the decision to approve the project to him, as this had to come from the *mhondoros* who were the 'real owners of the land' (Spierenburg, 2000).

Bernard and Kumalo stress:

> *Proponents of CBNRM initiatives in such areas should be aware of the fact that mediums and diviners are drawing on a worldview that is based on a fundamentally different paradigm from that of sustainable development. The former is more concerned with the maintenance of harmony between the social, ecological and spiritual worlds, while the latter embraces the philosophy of progress based on the modern global economic system. It would be a mistake to assume that all members of a community are as committed to development and entering into the market economy as those who promote such initiatives. Development may accentuate social inequalities and the commercializing of natural resources, even if it is ostensibly done for the good of the community involved, and may often directly threaten the spiritual and social integrity of the area.*

Men versus women

In one of the villages adjoining the Madikwe Game Reserve, the integrated conservation and development programme was bedevilled for many years by a conflict between the newly elected local municipality and the traditional authority – a conflict that took on the form of a battle between women and men.

In Molatedi village, where, as noted, the parks board in the early 1990s encouraged the formation of a local community development organization, there was, in fact, a multiplicity of entities created to drive development. These comprised the CDO, an old reconstruction and development forum, a water forum and an electricity forum. The traditional authority continued to function alongside these in a situation of what one may call fragmented power, but was weakened by the fact that the then chief was a genial but ineffectual character who consumed large amounts of alcohol instead of dealing with the forces that were unravelling the fabric of his village.

Development workers involved in the integrated conservation and development programme at Madikwe encouraged the varying structures to disband and the villagers to elect a single entity responsible for development – in line with the new and statutory system of local government that was set up in post-1994 South Africa. Elections duly took place. A new development committee was installed as an official agency of the local municipality and the majority of members were women. The old structures, including men who were appalled at the thought of being outvoted by members of the opposite gender, refused to disband. The old chief died and a new, more dynamic and more assertive, chief was installed. He, along with his councillors, began recalling the days when women would not even be allowed to walk past the tribal office without averting their heads, let alone tell them how to manage the well-being of the village. For more than two years, effort towards development was thwarted by this conflict.

Other case studies in this book are replete with similar examples, although the women's maxim articulated in the 2002 box-office movie *My Big Fat Greek Wedding* that 'the man is the head of the family, but the woman is the neck that moves the head in any direction it wishes' is also evident in some of the studies. Sithole's study (Chapter 19) is just one clear example of the matriarchal power that can be wielded in the gender conflicts that characterize many CBNRM projects.

As noted, the above typology is far from exhaustive and needs to be supplemented by detailed intelligence for each particular case. It should certainly not be applied mechanically by practitioners wishing to avoid or mitigate local conflicts, as the law of catastrophe states that upheaval comes from the most unexpected quarter. However, it is worth referring, at this stage, to the generic factors listed in the Chapter 1 of this book, which can cause conflicts, such as those listed above, to escalate (Anstey, 1999; Deutsch, 1973).

CONCLUSIONS

The typology of conflict – along with the factors that can enhance conflict – listed above serve to highlight at least five other aspects of intra- and inter-community conflict and the impact this has on the performance of CBNRM. Each of these can be used in a preliminary way to presage some of the practical tips for practitioners that are provided in the concluding chapter to this book.

First, the centrifugal tendencies of the 'C' in CBNRM help to generate what we have called 'fluctuating achievements', a phenomenon that bemuses development practitioners because in week 1, community A is doing remarkably well against the accepted benchmarks of CBNRM, while group B is doing really badly and looks to be falling apart, only to find that in week 4 the reverse applies (Fortmann et al, 2001). It is, thus, certainly a mistake to see CBNRM as a linear progression towards a predetermined set of fixed goals, even though this is useful for those project planners to set criteria and measure progress along a spectrum of degrees of accomplishment (see Murphree, 1999). Goals can only be predetermined in a flexible and indeterminate way. There should be a stress on adaptive and cyclical patterns of management, and on learning from experience. But if practitioners are sensitive and subtle, they can hope for some iterative progress towards achieving the goals of CBNRM, including the 'epochal' articulation of common property regimes with formal systems of tenure that the movement is trying to achieve (see Chapter 1 for more detail).

Secondly, even where there is the semblance of community cohesion, this is frequently a defensive dynamic – a group of people organizing to defend their resources against the predations of another group of people. The Makuleke people were uncharacteristically united in their struggle to win their land and wilderness back from those who took it forcibly under apartheid. They began to fragment once they got the land back and started using it for commercial purposes. Many CAMPFIRE projects show remarkable village-level cohesion because the inhabitants are united in their determination to ensure that the government's district councils do not appropriate all of their hunting revenues. The Tchumo Tchato project in Mozambique demonstrated high levels of community cohesion when the villagers of Bawa organized against a white-owned safari-hunting operation that was plundering the wildlife of the area and feeding none of the revenues back into the local economy. There are numerous examples of people protecting their forest resources from plundering by outsiders only to overharvest the same set of resources themselves. Much of the positive evidence suggests that the 'C' in CBNRM is strongest in a phase of struggle, a defensive phase that all too easily gives way after victory to the need for active management of the resource base. Lore M Ruttan has argued that the primary intent behind territory defence and self-regulated use is to maintain the exclusive access to the resource in a cost-effective manner, rather than to conserve the resource *per se*. At present, he notes conservation may be the incidental, if not intentional, product of these efforts (Ruttan, 1998).

Thirdly, what has been identified as traditional cohesion and collective management is frequently the result of small numbers of local people making use of relatively abundant or high-value natural resources:

> If human populations are at a low density relative to the resource base, there may be an appearance of conservation, and yet the same behaviour may not be sustainable (and may lead to conflict over resources) at high population densities (Ruttan, 1998, p46).

Fourthly, another important determinant of relative cohesion may be the fertility of the soil and rainfall levels. Simply put, aridity limits choices and thus conflicts over contending land uses and competing strategies for survival based on resource use. In natural systems where there is more fertility, there is a much greater chance for individuals, groups, government agencies and private-sector interests to collide with each other because there are so many alternative ways to make money from the land. Seen in this perspective, it may be that the relative cohesion found in communities who manage Zimbabwe's influential CAMPFIRE projects (and even here researchers are coming up with evidence of extensive intra-community tensions that are generated by the need for rural polities to manage revenues that derive from trophy hunting in CAMPFIRE areas) derives from a very specific combination of factors: small communities who command a high-value resource (elephant and buffalo trophies) and are defending their interests against the local organs of a predatory government in arid areas where there are few other land uses.

Murphree makes the critical point that the 'C' in CBNRM is linked to the scale of the user group:

> *Small institutions increase the efficiency and willingness to take responsibility and decrease the likelihood for corruption. They enhance a sense of 'collective identity' and make it more practicable to enforce rules... From a social dynamics perspective, scale is an important consideration: large-scale structures tend to be ineffective, increasing the potential for inefficiency, corruption and the evasion of responsibility. Conversely, a communal resource management regime is enhanced if it is small enough (in membership size) for all members to be in occasional face-to-face contact, enforce conformity to rules through peer pressure and has a long-standing collectively identity* (Murphree, 1998, pp9–10).

Finally, it is important to recognize that the 'community' in CBNRM is frequently a social construct imposed by an articulation of the formal sector and the informal sector. Wily notes that the new tenure laws of Uganda, Mozambique and Tanzania operate in accordance with the customs and practices of the community concerned but insist upon the rights of women, children or the disabled. This frequently involves policies and laws in which the constraints of custom are being whittled away. Customary tenure is being given a new lease of life, but is being reconstructed in a way that gives more emphasis to the rights of citizens organized as a community than to traditional leaders. The trend is towards a new system of social democracy (Wily, 2000).

Practitioners should thus accept that communal structure and local cohesion often have to be created. This involves a degree of construction – dare we even say some (very sensitive) social engineering? CBNRM is frequently a highly value-laden programme and it should be recognized as an artefact of the interaction between informal and formal systems (Bell, 1999). Given the inevitable degree of social intervention in CBNRM, the concluding chapter of this book will refer to the need for sensitive and 'light-touch' facilitation, interventions that can help create new and democratic community institutions in ways that limit the potential to antagonize or provoke ruptures in existing power relations.

Practitioners of CBNRM – some of them surprised and bewildered because they may have, at some time in their lives, been persuaded by the romantic convention that rural people in Africa live in a state of noble and stable equilibrium with their natural world – constantly find themselves putting out the fires of social conflict. In so doing, they often find that the lines of fracture are constantly shifting, the alliances perpetually realigning and that when the blaze is put out here it starts to smoulder again over there. The word 'community' in CBNRM is a bit like the description of smoke in the novel *Perfume*: 'Why should smoke possess only the name "smoke" when from minute to minute, second to second, the amalgam of hundreds of odours mixed iridescently as the smoke rose from the fire...or why should earth, landscape, air – each filled at every step and every breath with yet another odour and thus animated with another identity – still be designated by just these three coarse words' (Suskind, 1987, p27).

This elusive and vapour-like nature of social relations and the tendency of civil society to unravel according to its own, often indiscernible and unpredictable, dynamics questions whether it is worth it to identify the varying compounds, to isolate the elements of community, so that the tremendous energy that goes into its making can be channelled in the best direction. There is no harm in doing so, as long as we remember that there is no blueprint for fighting fires, that general guidelines can never substitute for intense and detailed local knowledge of the issues at hand, and even the most reliable and comprehensive intelligence does not guarantee against being taken by surprise.

REFERENCES

Agrawal, A (2001) 'Common property institutions and sustainable governance of resources', *World Development* 29(10): 1649–1672

Anstey, M (1999) '*Managing Change, Negotiating Conflict*. Juta, Cape Town

Bell, R (1999) 'CBNRM and other acronyms: An overview and challenges in southern Africa', CASS/PLAAS Inaugural Meeting on CBNRM in Southern Africa: A Regional Programme of Analysis and Communication, Harare, September 1999

Campbell, B, Mandondo, A, Nemarundwe, N, Sithole, B, De Jong, W, Luckert, M and Matose, F (2001) 'Challenges to the proponents of common property resource systems: Despairing voices from the social forests of Zimbabwe', *World Development* 29(4): 589–600

Deutsch, M (1973) *The Resolution Of Conflict: Constructive and Destructive Processes*. Yale University Press, New Haven

Fabricius, C, Koch, E and Magome, H (2001a) 'Towards strengthening collaborative ecosystems management: Lessons from environmental conflict and political change in South Africa', *Journal of the Royal Society of New Zealand* 31(4): 831–844

Fabricius, C, Koch, E and Magome, H (2001b) 'Community wildlife management in southern Africa: Challenging the assumptions of Eden', *Evaluating Eden Discussion Paper* No 6. International Institute for Environment and Development, London, pp19–39

Fortmann, L, Roe, E and Van Eeten, M (2001) 'At the threshold between governance and management: Community-based natural resource management in southern Africa', *Public Administration and Development* 21: 171–185

Jones, B T B (1999) 'Rights, revenue and resources: The problems and potential of conservancies as community wildlife management institutions in Namibia', *Evaluating Eden Discussion Paper* No 2. International Institute for Environment and Development, London

Kepe, T, Cousins, B and Turner, S (2000) 'Resource tenure and power relations in community wildlife contexts: The case of the Mkambati area on the Wild Coast of South Africa', *Evaluating Eden Discussion Paper* No 16. International Institute for Environment and Development, London

Magome, H, Grossman, D, Fakir, S and Stowell, Y (2000) 'Partnerships in conservation: The state, private sector and the community at Madikwe Game Reserve', *Evaluating Eden Discussion Paper* No 11. International Institute for Environment and Development, London

Murphree, M W (1998) 'Congruent objectives, competing interests and strategic compromise: Concept and process in the evolution of Zimbabwe's CAMPFIRE Programme'. Paper submitted for publication to Community Conservation in Africa Project, Centre for Applied Social Science, University of Zimbabwe and IDPM, University of Manchester

Murphree, M W (1999) Theme presentation on 'Governance and community capacity', CASS/PLAAS Inaugural Meeting on CBNRM in Southern Africa: A Regional Programme of Analysis and Communication, Harare, September 1999

Ruttan, L M (1998) 'Closing the commons: Co-operation for gain or restraint', *Human Ecology* 26: 43

Schoffeleers, J M (ed) (1978) *Guardians of the Land* (2nd ed). Mambo Press, Gweru

Spierenburg, M (2000) 'Social commentaries and the influence of the clientele: The Mhondoro cult in Dande, Zimbabwe', in van Dijk, R, Reis, R and Spierenburg, M (eds) *The Quest for Fruition through Ngoma: Political Aspects of Healing in southern Africa*. David Philip, Cape Town

Suskind, P (1987) *Perfume: The Story of a Murderer*. Penguin, Cape Town

Twyman, C (2001) 'Natural resource use and livelihoods in Botswana's wildlife management areas', *Applied Geography* 21(1): 45–68

Wily, L A (2000) 'Democratising the commonage: The changing legal framework for natural resource management in eastern & southern Africa with particular reference to forests'. Paper presented at the 2nd CASS/PLAAS Regional Meeting, 16–17 October 2000. Workshop theme: Legal Aspects of Governance in CBNRM

Chapter 5

Reconciling biodiversity conservation with rural development: The Holy Grail of CBNRM?

HECTOR MAGOME AND CHRISTO FABRICIUS

INTRODUCTION

Community-based natural resource management (CBNRM) has a strong conservation and social equity agenda (see Chapter 1). It is, to a large extent, driven by the biocentric sentiments of donor agencies, non-governmental organization (NGO) workers, researchers and tax payers in developed countries, and by their sense of social justice. These role players, concerned about global biodiversity loss, see Africa as one of the last Edens, especially for the survival of larger species of mammalian wildlife. They are also aware that poverty in many rural parts of Africa can, if left unattended, have a negative effect on wildlife. However, many of these role players also consider the commercial use of biodiversity, and especially the hunting of charismatic mega-fauna such as elephant, distasteful. Some have raised concerns about the sustainability of consumptive use practices (for example, Patel 1998; Wainwright and Wehrmeyer, 1998). Inevitably, people engaged in CBNRM get confronted, sooner or later, with the constraints of using wild resources with a high international conservation value.

Some of the constraints of using wildlife resources come in the form of international conventions, such as the Convention on International Trade in Endangered Species of Wild Fauna and Flora (CITES), protected area legislation (see Chapter 10; Fabricius, 2002), fishing regulations (see Chapter 12), forestry policy (Nhira et al, 1998), and donor policies that change in response to pressure from Northern tax payers. This inevitably places limits on how local people may use biodiversity resources, especially resources that have endangered status or are perceived to be scarce. Impoverished people living on communal lands have a particular image problem: they are often subjected to stricter conditions than their freehold landowning, affluent counterparts who generally find it much easier to obtain special permission to harvest resources with high commercial value.

In this chapter, we attempt to establish whether CBNRM can be expected to be the panacea for southern Africa's biodiversity conservation challenges. Our starting point is that for CBNRM to meaningfully reduce biodiversity loss, local people must willingly share the responsibility and action for conserving this biodiversity. This will only happen if:

- the amount of time, land and property that they are required to sacrifice in contributing to biodiversity conservation matches the role of wild resources in their livelihoods (relative to that of other livelihood strategies such as agriculture, urban remittances and wage labour); and
- the direct benefits are high enough to exceed the costs to them of participating in efforts to conserve biodiversity.

In this context, the smaller the role of biodiversity in the form of wildlife and other natural resources in people's lives (relative to that of other livelihood strategies), the less likely they are to accept the process of conserving it. Under these conditions, the benefit-cost ratio must be high for people to remain motivated. However, if the bulk of the benefits from biodiversity conservation accrue to outsiders (that is, someone else benefits from the efforts of local people), then other strategies need to be adopted to conserve the resource in question.

We start off by briefly exploring the biodiversity concept. What is this thing called biodiversity and who benefits from it? We examine the benefits to society as a whole, and the direct and indirect benefits of biodiversity to local people. We also discuss the role of biodiversity in rural people's livelihoods relative to that of other livelihood assets. We then address the contribution of CBNRM to biodiversity conservation. Is CBNRM in southern Africa really contributing to biodiversity conservation? Next, we look at the costs of biodiversity conservation to local people. What do they sacrifice in conserving biodiversity and for whom? Finally, we discuss the implications for conservation policy.

WHAT IS THIS THING CALLED 'BIODIVERSITY'?

Scholars define biological diversity, often contracted as biodiversity, as the sum total of all living things on Earth, taking into account their great variety in structure, function and genetic make-up (Wilson, 1988; Swingland, 1993; La Riviere, 1994). Apart from a few semantic differences (Gaston, 1996), this definition expresses the variety and variability among living organisms and the ecological complexes in which they occur. This variability occurs at the genetic, species and ecosystems levels (Gaston and Spicer, 1998).

Nonetheless, the concept of biodiversity remains abstract to laypeople and to the general public. Local people, for instance, often understand the concept of biodiversity as the variety of natural products that they can utilize in order to improve their livelihoods. This includes products to eat, build with, use for fuel, use for medicine, get spiritual renewal from or trade in. It is therefore naive to assume that, whether historically or more recently, rural people in southern Africa deliberately managed ecosystems for biodiversity. On the other hand, it is highly likely that the management systems that traditionally characterized the subregion created conditions that favoured the retention of biodiversity: wildlife that feared and avoided humans; the frequent use of fire; setting aside sacred patches of ecosystems; declaring certain plants and animals taboo; and zoning landscapes in space and time (see Chapters 6, 10 and 18). Later, the zoning of landscapes resulted in restricting wildlife to areas that were considered economically marginal for other land uses, such as agriculture and residential use. It can be posited that local people did not consciously take biodiversity conservation into account as a productive land-use practice because they could neither capitalize it nor convert it into a tradable asset.

For the global community, biodiversity loss is the main motivation behind many conservation efforts (Frankel and Soulé, 1981). The unprecedented loss of biodiversity is often presented as both a battle and a crisis. Some scientists argue that unless we act now, the generations to follow will be helpless to do so (Frankel and Soulé, 1981). Others argue that unless we rapidly acquire knowledge on which to base wise policies of conservation and development for centuries to come (Wilson, 1988; Western, 1989), the battle is lost (Ehrlich, 1988) and the ark is sinking (Myers, 1988; McNeely, 1992). Some believe that it is in our hands to save our planet at the time when much of it is seriously threatened (Myers, 1988). It follows from these views that biodiversity loss is regarded by many informed people as a major calamity facing humanity today. The impression given is that if life on Earth is fundamentally threatened, then our response must be equally dramatic (Myerson and Rydin, 1996). Those calling for a dramatic response on all fronts point out that biodiversity loss is intimately linked to human-induced global climatic changes, habitat degradation and destruction, invasive alien biota, increasing levels of pollution and the overexploitation of species with a high use or commercial value (Lande, 1998). There is, however, no consensus on how we should act, and this continues to cause tension and conflict.

It is argued that unless humanity is suicidal, it should want to preserve, at the minimum, the natural life support systems and processes required to sustain its own existence (Daily, 1997). Indeed, most people believe that biodiversity *per se* is a good thing, that its loss is bad, and therefore that something must be done to maintain it (Gaston, 1996). As a result, from the level of multilateral organizations to grassroots groups, biodiversity has become a buzzword, a funding bandwagon, a growth industry, a global resource, a political slogan and a story around which to construct a social problem (Gaston, 1996; McNeely, 1996; Haila, 1999). Consequently, the agenda whether opaque or explicit, is often that biodiversity conservation should assume top priority and other development paths based on land conversions should receive less priority (Magome, 2000; Swanson, 2001). The key contemporary debate in biodiversity conservation is *who benefits from biodiversity and how?*

The Convention on Biological Diversity

The Convention on Biological Diversity (CBD) was approved in 1992 and, as of 13 June 2003, has been ratified by 186 countries as well as the European Union. The CBD has three core objectives: 'the conservation of biological diversity, the sustainable use of its components, and the fair and equitable sharing of the benefits arising from the utilization of genetic resources'. The CBD requires contracting parties, often biodiversity-rich developing countries, to allow access to their genetic resources for uses by other contracting parties, often developed countries, on mutually agreed terms (UNEP, 1992). The main obligations of the signatories of the CBD are to:

- develop national strategies and action plans to conserve biodiversity by integrating the plans and operations of different sectors;
- identify components of biodiversity that require attention and monitor them;
- monitor activities that are likely to have a negative impact on biodiversity; and
- maintain and organize monitoring data.

The provisions of the CBD, although binding in theory, are broad aspirational goals and policies (Holdgate, 1992). The CBD also recognizes the challenges that countries, particularly developing countries, face in the conservation of their biodiversity and calls for capacity development to assist these countries. Consequently, it has been recommended that the resolutions of the CBD are strengthened to provide a coherent framework for delivering biodiversity incentives efficiently and justly, and for measuring the CBD's effectiveness (Vickerman, 1999). However, there appears to be a contradiction between the objectives of the CBD and those of the WTO (World Trade Organization), which promotes the privatization of biodiversity resources, knowledge and technologies, possibly to the detriment of nation states and local people (Kennedy, 1998). Currently, developed countries appear to be the major beneficiaries of biodiversity conservation efforts, while developing countries are the custodians of these resources.

WHY BIODIVERSITY IS IMPORTANT

The indirect values of biodiversity to society

Biodiversity provides goods and services without which humankind will not be able to survive. These goods and services include food, carbon storage and freshwater production from watersheds. Biodiversity also stores genetic information for future use in, for example, genetic engineering and breeding programmes to improve existing domestic strains and breeds, and in the production of medicines (Koziell, 2001). This 'un-mined richness' (Bass et al, 2001) keeps our options open, and maintains humankind's capacity to adapt to future shocks and surprises (Gunderson and Holling, 2002). The aesthetic value of biodiversity supports the global tourism industry and generates valuable income for national economies, while giving pleasure to visitors from countries that have already lost much of their own biodiversity.

The direct-use values of biodiversity to local people

Tangible benefits from informal, everyday use

Biodiversity plays an important role in the lives of rural people (see Chapter 2). The monetary benefits from ecosystems can be higher than that of individual enterprises (see Chapter 8), and in most instances (except for some of the very lucrative tourism initiatives in Botswana) these benefits are much higher than that from 'formal' biodiversity management (see 'Tangible benefits from "formal" CBNRM'). The benefits of these informal ecosystem services, both tangible and intangible, are consistently underestimated. The dominant form of natural resource management in southern Africa, and the direct use of ecosystem services, is often the greatest livelihood asset to people in rural and peri-urban areas (Chapter 8). Furthermore, the spiritual values that people attach to, and derive from, ecosystems is substantial. Most traditional belief systems are coupled to the land and its resources (Chapter 6).

Wild resources also play an important safety-net role when unexpected events throw the lives of rural people into crisis. Non-timber forest products (NTFPs) play a crucial role in many rural settings and their monetary value frequently exceeds that of rural wages in the subsistence strategies of many families (see Chapter 8). The variety of uses includes the construction of baskets from grass, palm leaves or even climbers; the use of hardwoods to make animal enclosures (*kraals*), and the construction of walls and roofs of houses, using insect-resistant wood such as sneezewood (*Ptaeroxylon obliquum*).

Households increase their food security during droughts by relying on wild resources in times of need or crisis, or by substituting cultivated foods with wild alternatives (Mutangadura and Mukurazita, 1999). Seeds of *Eragrostis* grass are used to make beer and bread during famine years. Seeds and nuts are highly nutritious and play an important role in providing essential nutrients in times of need when money or food is scarce and when other sources of protein and fats are unavailable. While the calabash (*Lagenaria siceraria*) fruits are traditionally used for storage vessels, their young fruits are consumed as emergency foods in times of need (Van Wyk and Gericke, 2000). The fruit and kernels of marula (*Sclerocarya birrea*) are a good source of protein and fat, but are also sold to raise cash for school fees, uniforms, books and stationery (Shackleton et al, 2002).

The roots, bulbs and tubers of some plant species are an important source of starch. The list of plant species uses is extensive, but examples include *Cucumis kalahariensis* and *Solenostemon rotundifolius* that are still important in food security when crops of exotic potato or sweet potato fail, or when there is not enough cash available to purchase these foods. Wild tubers are more drought resistant and have a higher nutritional value than ordinary potatoes (Van Wyk and Gericke, 2000). In addition, many tubers contain large quantities of water and are key to the survival of the San in the Kalahari when water is scarce. The tuber of the succulent *Tylosema esculenta* contains 81 per cent moisture, and its seed is also highly nutritious, containing high concentrations of protein and oil (Van Wyk and Gericke, 2000).

Rural and urban communities in southern Africa make extensive use of medicinal plants in their day-to-day lives. The use of medicinal plants may be escalating because of the AIDs pandemic in southern Africa and increased poverty. In South Africa alone, 3000 plant species (10 per cent of all species) are used for medicinal purposes and more than 1 per cent (some 350 species) is commercially traded. South Africa has 200,000 traditional healers and 60 per cent of the population consults a traditional healer from time to time, to complement modern medical treatment (Mander, 1998).

Alcoholic beverages are also important, both for trading and for social consumption. Sorghum beer is the most common home-brewed beverage; but honey beer, palm wine and beer from berries, such as *Grewia robusta* in Botswana, are also popular. Various roots, fruit and tubers are used as fermenting agents. The importance of insects as a source of protein in rural areas tends to be underestimated. At least 83 species of insects belonging to 35 families and 9 orders are used, and in some rural areas up to 80 per cent of people's protein and fat intake is from insects. There are processing plants for mopane 'worms' (caterpillars of the emperor moth *Gonimbrasia belina*) in Botswana (Brandon, 1987) and South Africa (Dreyer and Wehmeyer, 1982), and the annual sales of the caterpillars, through agricultural co-operative markets alone, is estimated at 1600 tonnes.

Bushmeat is an important source of protein in southern Africa. In Botswana, 46 per cent of households surveyed in one study consumed bushmeat at an average of 18.2 kilograms per month in areas where this is the only affordable animal protein. The trade in wild meat is rife. It is estimated that 50 tonnes is traded in Maputo Province of Mozambique every year. Demand does, of course, vary. Bushmeat is 50 and 30 per cent cheaper than domestic meat in the rural areas of Zimbabwe and Botswana respectively; but the reverse pattern is evident in urban areas, where affluent urbanites are willing to pay 43 per cent more for bushmeat in Zambia and 157 per cent more in Mozambique (Barnett, 2000). The transfer of wildlife ownership to rural people involved in the bushmeat trade could encourage them to manage and produce wildlife for meat. 'Once benefits accrue to land-holders from a resource they own, wildlife can play an important sustainable role in community development and, by doing so, ensure its continued survival' (Barnett, 2000).

Tangible benefits from 'formal' CBNRM

In general, the direct financial benefits from 'formal' CBNRM initiatives in the region are disappointingly low. The average household income from the Communal Areas Management Programme for Indigenous Resources (CAMPFIRE) in Zimbabwe in 1996 was US$4.50 (see Chapter 18). In Namibia, the richest conservancy yielded US$132 per household per annum in 1999 (Sullivan, 2002), while the mean annual household benefit from wildlife in Lupande was US$37 in 2001 (including wages from tourism). At Makuleke, a gross income of US$50,000 from hunting (after a major battle with parks authorities for permission to allow hunting) translated into a benefit of US$10 per household in 2001. The annual household dividend from lease fees at Richtersveld National Park was less than US$50 in 2001 (H Reid, pers comm). However, a number of cases exist in southern Africa where small villages are receiving significant revenues from high-value tourism. In Botswana, for example, the average annual household income from wildlife tourism was US$400 (Rozemeier, 2000). The residents of Sankuyo village received an exceptional high level of donor and institutional support, and the average annual direct benefit to households from wildlife tourism was US$45,000 (Boggs, pers comm), while the household income derived from wildlife tourism at Xaxaba was more than US$18,000 (M Madzwamuse, pers comm).

Intangible benefits

The intangible benefits that accrue to rural people from biodiversity conservation are considerable but difficult, if not impossible, to quantify. Biodiversity enhances the livelihood security of rural households by providing invaluable opportunities for rural livelihood diversification to families who are cash-strapped, hit by periodic drought or dependent upon marginal agricultural land (Koziell, 2001). CBNRM activities enhance food security and stimulate wildlife-related tourism enterprises, which generate income during drought, and thus offset, to some extent at least, the costs associated with agricultural failure (Ashley, 1998). This, in turn, helps many rural people to cope with more gradual change, such as climate change, as well as sudden, more unexpected events, such as drought, floods, pest outbreaks, market collapses and even political upheaval. It is the rural poor, in particular, who benefit the most from wild plants and animals.

The *relative* role of biodiversity in livelihoods

The role of biodiversity in people's livelihoods (*sensu* Carney, 1998) varies from case to case. Project managers are sometimes guilty of overstating the importance of biodiversity resources in the lives of rural people. A participatory rural appraisal (PRA) exercise with user groups involved in participatory forest management (PFM) at Mount Coke State Forest in the Eastern Cape, South Africa, revealed that indigenous woodlands and forests (the focus of PFM) constituted less than 25 per cent of the total complement of land uses around their villages (Cundill, forthcoming).

Even in the most promising wards in CAMPFIRE, the annual income per household from the programme is far less than the value of a single goat (see Chapter 18). Villagers can get more for one poached impala than from the annual household dividend of CAMPFIRE (Campbell et al, 2000). In Namibia, the average income from conservancy revenues was less than that received from an old-age pension of US$160 for the year in 1999 (Sullivan, 2002). In Zambia, while households earned US$37 (including income from wages) from projects aimed at wildlife conservation in 2001 (Child, pers comm), people in the same villages valued a single snared impala at $9.63 in 1995 (Lewis and Phiri, 1998).

THE ROLE OF CBNRM IN BIODIVERSITY CONSERVATION

Rural people can play an important role in biodiversity and, particularly, wildlife conservation. In Namibia, for example, wildlife numbers are increasing rapidly after a community game guard system was introduced (Jones, 2001; see also Chapter 13). In Lupande, Zambia, people have begun to appreciate wildlife, thereby decreasing the incidence of poaching. In South Africa, land claims to protected areas have led to an increase, rather than a decrease, in protected land and numerous other benefits for conservation (Fabricius and de Wet, 2002).

On the whole, however, we would argue that CBNRM, as it is practised in southern Africa at the moment, is not the answer to biodiversity conservation, although it plays a key role in rural livelihoods. Traditional taboos play a limited role in mitigating the impacts of resource harvesting (see Chapters 6 and 18). Traditional healers, generally believed to be the custodians of biodiversity and important institutions in rural communities, are often guilty of overexploiting plants and animals. In South Africa, 31 per cent of the animals used by traditional healers are *Red Data Book* species (Simelane and Kerley, 1998).

There is evidence to suggest that bushmeat collection is having a major negative influence on some species, and serious concerns have been raised about the conservation implications of current bushmeat harvesting levels, as is evident from IUCN–World Conservation Union Resolution 2.64 (Mainka and Trivedi, 2002). The evidence supporting suspicions of overharvesting include a shift towards smaller species being hunted; a steady increase in the price of bushmeat; greater distances being travelled by illegal hunters; a decrease in catch per effort reported by hunters; the disappearance of traditional hunting seasons – that is, a shift towards year-round hunting; and the fact that taboos on certain animals are being discarded (Barnett, 2000). In Lupande, Zambia, snaring near villages has caused trophy hunters to move their operations further away from villages because of the scarcity of wildlife (Lewis and Phiri, 1998). This has affected the livelihoods of local people. The scarcity in bushmeat has caused prices to increase and people have had to substitute animal protein with plant protein (DFID, 2002).

Numerous authors have highlighted the increase in illegal hunting, particularly with snares, in CBNRM projects. Even where local people receive licences to legally hunt wildlife, the licence is much more valuable if sold to a commercial operator who is prepared to pay up to ten times the purchase price to take over local licences (Wainwright and Wehrmeyer, 1998). Villagers sell their licences and continue to snare animals, to the detriment of the safari industry and to their own livelihoods (Lewis and Phiri, 1998). The impact of snaring on wildlife is exceptionally high: it is unselective, and anything from an impala to an elephant can be caught in a snare. Efforts to counter this trend include the training of community guards, as in Lupande (see Chapter 17).

Wildlife populations are variable in southern Africa, and it is unclear whether CBNRM managers would be able to reduce off-take quotas when wildlife numbers are on the decline (Newmark and Hough, 2000). Extended selective hunting may have an impact on trophy quality. In the South Luangwa Valley, park officials claim that the size of trophy male lions is declining (Wainwright and Wehrmeyer, 1998). In woodlands and savanna, the impact of grazing and fuelwood collection by local people varies, depending upon the characteristics of the ecosystem and the choice of indicator. For example, Fabricius et al (2003) recorded a 37 per cent decrease in plant and arthropod biodiversity when they compared a communal area in Xeric Succulent Thicket in the Eastern Cape of South Africa to an adjacent protected area. An opposite pattern was observed with lizard diversity in the same vegetation type: there were more lizard species, and a much higher density of lizards, in the communal area than in the well-vegetated protected area. In lowveld savanna vegetation, Shackleton (2000) found that communal land near Bushbuckridge in Mpumalanga, South Africa, had 11 per cent more vascular plant species than adjacent conserved areas.

Even in villages where people receive significant benefits from CBNRM, space is shrinking because of population increases and immigration from cities due to shrinking urban economies (Wainwright and Wehrmeyer, 1998). In Masoka in Zimbabwe, where people receive the highest revenues from CAMPFIRE, the immigration rate is also highest. Villagers believe that if the human population increases, the village will get a school and a bus route (Murombedzi, 1999). In Zimbabwe, elephant density remains independent of human density up to a point; but elephants disappear altogether when human density exceeds 15.6 people per square kilometre (Hoare and Du Toit, 1999).

For their part, local people are seldom prepared to reinvest the revenues from CBNRM in natural resource management, and use revenues for infrastructure and purchasing assets, such as vehicles for local organizations. Furthermore, in many of the most lucrative initiatives in Botswana, yielding very high direct annual benefits per household, there is little evidence of community law enforcement or any other type of wildlife management (Boggs, 2000). There are some exceptions (see Chapters 13 and 17); but even in these instances it involves game guards who enforce the law because they are paid to do so, rather than a wildlife management technique aimed at consciously investing in the future. Monitoring by communities, frequently highlighted as

Table 5.1 *Conditions for effective CBNRM*

Context	Projects likely to achieve both developmental and conservation objectives	Projects unlikely to achieve both developmental and conservation objectives
Wildlife resource harvest	Yields sustainable revenue	Does not yield sustainable revenue flow
Sustainability of market for wildlife resource	Sustainable	Not sustainable
Adequacy of wildlife resource	Large enough to secure local support for conservation action	Not large enough to secure local support for conservation action
Range of biodiversity upon which economic benefits depend	High	Low
Loss of rights by local people	Outweighed by economic benefits and/or other incentives	Not outweighed by economic benefits or other incentives
Donor investment	Long term	Short term
Influence of integrated conservation and development rhetoric on conservation agency	Ideology and practices of conservation agency change	Ideology and practices of conservation agency do not change
Extent to which expectations are met	Project delivers benefits as planned	Project promises are not delivered upon
Extent to which conservation agency shares power with local people	Genuine power sharing (in terms of tenure security in resource access and/or revenues and decision-making)	Token power-sharing
Non-monetary values of nature	Shared by local people	Not shared by local people

Source: adapted from Adams and Hulme (2001)

essential, in reality only takes place in exceptional circumstances and the reliability of its data is questionable.

Why the lure of CBNRM?

CBNRM offers the promise of a 'win–win' solution to the human–wildlife conflict (Adams and Hulme, 2001) and is often used as a tactic to convince rural people of the value of biodiversity conservation (Fabricius et al, 2001). In extreme cases, local people are expected to tolerate conflict with dangerous species of wildlife, such as crop-destroying elephants and lions that eat their livestock and endanger their lives. In practice, any debate about whether CBNRM works or not depends upon the context under which projects are implemented (see Table 5.1). The reality is that CBNRM projects are dynamic, vary greatly over time and space and are influenced by unpredictable events, such as socio-economic conflicts, history, politics and natural ecosystem dynamics.

Our experience is that it is extremely dangerous to extrapolate from one CBNRM initiative to another. Different role players have different end goals and measure success differently. Indeed, government officials, communities and private investors have different perceptions about the scarcity of natural resources and of human impacts on biodiversity, and this lies at the root of many of the conflicts observed (Fabricius et al, 2001). Most CBNRM projects are some form of 'revivalism' (Agrawal and Gibson, 1999) in that they attempt to revive historical traditions and cultural institutions for managing nature. However, there is no turning back to a state of harmonious balance with nature. The noble savage can no longer become the ecological hero because biodiversity conservation is now a complicated, politicized issue and not one that takes place in blissful isolation from the real world. Different interests seek to own the problem of biodiversity loss and define it in their own terms (Peuhkuri and Jokinen, 1999).

These arguments should of course not be viewed as a vote for a return to already discredited protectionism. Morality and legitimacy are important considerations in biodiversity conservation, and role players need to keep searching for innovative solutions and negotiating rather than advocating a return to outdated models (Brechin et al, 2002). In an earlier, unpublished paper, Brechin et al (2000) list five incomplete arguments frequently used by the 'anti-participation' lobbyists (see Table 5.2).

THE COST OF BIODIVERSITY CONSERVATION TO LOCAL PEOPLE

Living with wildlife comes at a cost to rural people. These include:

- direct costs, due to crop damage, loss of both livestock and human life;
- the cost of not being able to use the land;
- the cost of not being able to freely exploit biodiversity resources; and
- the transaction cost of participation in CBNRM.

The direct cost of living with biodiversity

The main direct cost of biodiversity conservation is damage to crops and livestock from wild animals. At Mount Coke State Forest, for example, people identified the incidence of crop damage by bush-pig as an indicator of forest 'health'. This means that the healthier their forest is (one of the goals of the participatory forest management initiative in which they were partners), the greater the damage to crops and therefore the greater the costs to them. Rural people living adjacent to the Kruger National Park suffer severe livestock losses due to stray lions moving freely in and out from the park and as a result, are anti-conservation. Concerns over damage by wild animals could be one of the reasons why the Makuleke readily accepted a land agreement stipulating that their newly claimed land should remain part of the Kruger National Park

Table 5.2 *Five incomplete arguments in the new protectionist paradigm*

Argument	Counterpoints
1 Protected areas are the last remaining safe havens for biodiversity.	• Ignores wider agro-ecological landscapes. • Strict enforcement mentality ignores histories of domination. • Protected areas significantly alter social and political landscapes.
2 Biodiversity protection is a moral imperative.	• Ignores how different cultural groups/ways of interacting with natural world might contribute to its protection. • Imposes knowledge and cultural practices. • Assumes zero-sum trade-off between human welfare and nature protection.
3 Conservation linked to development does not protect biodiversity.	• Ignores social and political realities (ie pre-existing use rights) to which interventions must adapt. • Lack of protection success could stem from implementation shortfalls. • Ignores impact of intervening variables such as conflict, organization and governance. • Appraisal time frame is inappropriate to measure impact of human development activities.
4 Harmonious, ecologically friendly local communities are myths.	• Implies that no traditional peoples are able to conserve their resources. • Oversimplifies rural communities' motivations and cultural practices. • Ignores how decision-making, organization and governance shape peoples' motivations and abilities to participate.
5 Emergency situations require extreme measures.	• Assumes that governments serve the common good of their citizens. • Relies on long-term social engineering to sacrifice some areas to conventional development (urbanization and industrialization) and thus depopulate other zones around protected areas. • Ignores the possibility that military might use conservation as an excuse for territorial control and ethnic cleansing.

Source: Brechin et al (2000)

(Fabricius and de Wet, 2002). In the Okavango Delta, the San villagers at Xaxaba no longer plant crops because of the severe and consistent damages caused by elephants and other wildlife. More people in the village have been injured by wildlife than before the CBNRM initiative was launched. People also feel that, due to hunting prohibitions, wild animals no longer have respect for humans and that this is the cause of the increase in injuries (see Chapter 10). In Namibia, 74 per cent of residents in the Kwandu area in Caprivi claimed that they had experienced wildlife-related crop damages between 1993 and 1998, while four people were killed by crocodiles in three months during 1998. In 1999, 140 cases of elephants destroying property were recorded in the Kunene region alone, and 450 cases were reported by the Ministry of Environment and Tourism throughout Namibia (Sullivan, 2002).

The cost of not being able to use land for agricultural purposes

The opportunity cost to rural people of land under CBNRM – that is, their inability to use it for other types of land uses such as agriculture or livestock production – can be substantial in high rainfall areas. Recent models suggest that in areas where the mean annual rainfall is higher than 600 millimetres, production systems based on natural biodiversity cannot compete, economically, with agricultural production systems on transformed land (M Norton-Griffiths, pers comm).

A conservative value of Makuleke's 250 square kilometres of land in the Kruger National Park (KNP) is US$5 million, which excludes the value of wildlife. At an average of 10 per cent interest per annum, the Makuleke could at least realize US$500,000 per annum if they were to sell their land and put the money in the bank. This income would then be realized without the struggles to get quotas for harvesting wildlife that they face every year. However, the contract signed by the Makuleke makes it difficult for them to trade or lease their land to realize this income.

The cost of not being able to use biodiversity on conserved land

The cost of controlling hunting and other resource-use activities to communities is also high. For example, the average household income from CAMPFIRE revenues was around US$4.50 in 1996 (Hasler, 1999). In stark contrast, a villager can illegally hunt and sell a single impala for more than that (Campbell et al, 2000). Lewis and Phiri (1998), for example, calculated a unit value of $9.63 for one snared impala in 1995. This means that there have to be other incentives for the majority of the people to participate in, or strong disincentives to prevent people from poaching.

The Makuleke people would like to hunt elephant on their land in the KNP, which has an overpopulation of elephants. They could safely hunt a number of elephant per annum, thereby assisting the KNP in controlling the elephant population. In early 2000, the Makuleke proposed concessions for trophy hunting of two elephant and two buffalo bulls in order to raise US$80,000 for community projects; but this initially met with strong objections from the management of the KNP, who argued that hunting should not take place inside a national park (Magome and Murombedzi, 2003). The Makuleke insisted and, following various interventions, the hunt finally took place. In May 2001, the Makuleke struggled to earn a further US$130,000 from a second hunting quota, and had to justify hunting common antelope such as eland. In stark contrast to this case, some private land partners of the KNP harvest high-value animals for a variety of reasons. There is also the opportunity cost of time: the reality of inflation means that money in the bank now is worth more than the same amount of cash later. Where nature tourism is involved, there is often a time lag and rural people still have to wait before they can derive meaningful tourism-related income (Magome et al, 2000; Magome and Murombedzi, 2003). Thus, people opt to use resources now, for a much smaller cash benefit, rather than waiting for something that may never be theirs anyway.

The cost to people's time

In 'formal' CBNRM, it takes time to negotiate agreements, to attend and organize meetings, to apply for licences, and to administer revenues. Even in areas where the opportunity cost to people's time is low, because of high unemployment, committee members and other people are expected to attend these meetings without compensation, and are sometimes not even provided with meals when they do attend. The paradox is that CBNRM aims to reduce unemployment, which increases the opportunity cost of people's time, resulting in less voluntary participation. Some village committee members now demand payment for attending committee meetings (see Chapter 12), and in many co-management committees there is a high turnover of volunteers.

The transaction cost of biodiversity conservation

The transaction cost of active participation in CBNRM includes the risk of causing conflict when sanctioning people who transgress the rules; negotiating among each other about the sharing of benefits; making decisions about who should receive benefits and who should not; and administering revenues and other assets. Local people often participate passively in order to reduce the transaction cost to themselves. This could be the reason why people in the Richtersveld National Park, South Africa, do not appear to participate in joint management committee meetings (Reid, 2001).

HOW CAN CBNRM CONTRIBUTE TO BIODIVERSITY CONSERVATION?

To summarize our argument thus far:

- The contribution of CBNRM to biodiversity conservation is questionable, and there is little evidence of local people investing resources (time and money) in biodiversity management.
- The direct benefits from formal biodiversity management are negligible in most instances, while the direct benefits from informal resource use are substantial.
- The relative contribution of biodiversity to people's total complement of livelihood strategies is poorly understood, but can be relatively small in some instances.
- The cost of living with biodiversity (in terms of the opportunity cost to land and labour, and the direct costs of damage to property) is high. The transaction costs, in terms of causing conflict and administering initiatives, is also high.

It is therefore not surprising that local people do not generally invest in biodiversity conservation, and that the role of CBNRM in biodiversity conservation is, on the whole, disappointing. The benefits that rural people receive from their informal use of resources generally exceed those from formal biodiversity management, and biodiversity often brings unexpected costs. Donors and project managers should be realistic about what contribution towards biodiversity conservation can realistically be expected from local people. Again, there are notable exceptions (for example, in the Okavango Delta) where a substantial contribution can be expected. Where this does not happen, project managers need to address other CBNRM management aspects, such as the devolution of authority, training and land ownership.

The problem is particularly acute in those instances where biodiversity constitutes a small portion of the total assets that contribute to people's livelihoods, and the amount of effort or sacrifice required by people in conserving biodiversity is high. In these cases, the tangible and intangible benefits that flow from biodiversity conservation must, by a wide margin, exceed the costs to people if they are to make the required contribution. If the benefits from biodiversity are largely external to the local people – for example, if the international community, national citizens or future generations are the main beneficiaries – then national and international tax payers need to make an ongoing and committed contribution to CBRNM.

REFERENCES

Adams, W M and Hulme, D (2001) 'If community conservation is the answer, what is the question?' *Oryx* 35: 193–200

Agrawal, A and Gibson, C C (1999) 'Enchantment and disenchantment: The role of community in natural resource conservation', *World Development* 27: 629–649

Ashley, C (1998) *Intangibles Matter: Non-Financial Dividends of Community-Based Natural Resource Management in Namibia.* Report for the World Wildlife Fund Living in a Finite Environment (LIFE) Programme, Windhoek

Barnett, R (ed) (2000) 'Food for thought: The utilization of wild meat in eastern and southern Africa', TRAFFIC East and Southern Africa, Nairobi

Bass, S, Hughes, C and Hawthorne W (2001) 'Forests, biodiversity and livelihoods: Linking policy and practice', in Koziell, I and Saunders, J (eds) *Living off Biodiversity.* International Institute for Environment and Development, London, pp1–10

Boggs, L P (2000) 'Community power, participation, conflict and development choice: Community wildlife conservation in the Okavango region of Northern Botswana', *Evaluating Eden Discussion Paper* No 17. International Institute for Environment and Development, London

Brandon, H (1987) 'The snack that crawls', *International Wildlife* March/April: 16–21

Brechin, S R, Wilshusen, P R, Fortwangler, C L and West, P C (2000) 'Policy reviews. Reinventing a square wheel: A critique of the new protectionist paradigm in international biodiversity conservation'. Unpublished manuscript, School of Natural Resources and Environment, University of Michigan, Ann Arbor

Brechin, S R, Wilshusen, P R, Fortwangler, C L and West, P C (2002) 'Beyond the square wheel: Toward a more comprehensive understanding of biodiversity conservation as social and political process', *Society and Natural Resources* 15: 41–54

Campbell, B M, Sithole B and Frost, P (2000) 'CAMPFIRE experiences in Zimbabwe', *Science* 287: 42–43

Carney, D (ed) (1998) *Sustainable Rural Livelihoods: What Contribution can we Make?* Department for International Development (DFID), London

Cundill, G (forthcoming) *Institutional Change and Ecosystem Dynamics in the Communal Areas around Mount Coke State Forest, Eastern Cape, South Africa*, MA thesis, Rhodes University, Grahamstown

Daily, G C (1997) *Nature's Services: Societal Dependence on Natural Ecosystems.* Island Press, Washington, DC

DFID (2002) *Wildlife and Poverty Study.* Livestock and Wildlife Advisory Group, Rural Livelihoods Department, Department for International Development, London

Dreyer, J J and Wehmeyer, A S (1982) 'On the nutritive value of mopanie worms', *South African Journal of Science* 78: 33–35

Ehrlich, P R (1988) 'The loss of diversity: Causes and consequences', in Wilson, E O (ed) *Biodiversity.* National Academy Press, London, pp21–27

Fabricius, C (2002) *A Social Ecology Policy for South African National Park.* SANParks and DANCED, Pretoria

Fabricius, C, Burger, M and Hockey, PAR. (2003) 'Comparing biodiversity between protected areas and adjacent rangeland in xeric succulent thicket, South Africa: arthropods and reptiles', *Journal of Applied Ecology* 40: 392–403

Fabricius, C and de Wet, C (2002) 'The influence of forced removals and land restitution on conservation in South Africa', in Chatty, D and Colchester, M (eds) *Conservation and Mobile Indigenous Peoples: Displacement, Forced Resettlement and Conservation.* Berghahn Books, Oxford, pp149–165

Fabricius, C, Koch, E and Magome, H (2001) 'Towards strengthening collaborative ecosystems management: Lessons from environmental conflict and political change in South Africa', *Journal of the Royal Society of New Zealand* 31(4): 831–844

Frankel, O H and Soulé, M E (1981) *Conservation and Evolution.* Cambridge University Press, Cambridge

Gaston, K J (ed) (1996) *Biodiversity: Biology of Numbers and Difference.* Blackwells, Oxford

Gaston, K J and Spicer, J L (1998) *Biodiversity: an Introduction.* Blackwells, Oxford

Gunderson, L H and Holling, C S (2002) *Panarchy: Understanding Transformations in Human and Natural Systems.* Island Press, Washington, DC

Haila, J (1999) 'Biodiversity and the divide between culture and nature', *Biodiversity and Conservation* 8: 165–181

Hasler, R (1999) 'An overview of the social, ecological and economic achievements and challenges of Zimbabwe's CAMPFIRE project', *Evaluating Eden Discussion Paper* No 3. International Institute for Environment and Development, London

Hoare, R E and Du Toit, J T (1999) 'Coexistence between people and elephants in African savannas', *Conservation Biology* 13: 633–639

Holdgate, M (1992) 'Biodiversity conservation after Rio', *Biodiversity and Conservation* 1: 346–347

IUCN (1994) *A Guide to the Convention on Biological Diversity.* Environmental Policy and Law Paper No 30. The World Conservation Union (IUCN), Gland

Jones, B (2001) 'The evolution of a community-based approach to wildlife management at Kunene, Namibia', in Hulme, D and Murphree, M (eds) *African Wildlife and Livelihoods: The Promise and Performance of Community Conservation.* James Currey, Oxford, pp160–176

Kennedy, K (1998) 'The GATT-WTO System: Environmental friend or foe?' *Journal of International Wildlife Law and Policy* 1: 217–259

Kepe, T (2002) *Grassland Vegetation and Rural Livelihoods: A Case Study of Resource Value and Social Dynamics on the Wild Coast of Southern Africa.* PhD thesis, University of the Western Cape, Cape Town

Koziell, I (2001) 'Introduction', in Koziell, I and Saunders, J (eds) *Living off Biodiversity.* International Institute for Environment and Development, London, pp1–10

Lande, R (1998) 'Anthropogenic, ecological and genetic factors in extinction', in Mace, G M, Balmford, A and Ginsberg, J R (eds) *Conservation in a Changing World.* Cambridge University Press, the Zoological Society of London and Conservation International, Cambridge, pp29–52

La Riviere, J W M (1994) 'The role of the International Council of Scientific Unions in biodiversity and global change research', in Solbrig, O T, van Emden, H M and van Oordt, P G W J (eds) *Biodiversity and Global Change.* CAB International, London, pp3–8

Lewis, D M and Phiri, A (1998) 'Wildlife snaring: An indicator of community response to a community based conservation project', *Oryx* 32: 111–120

Magome, H (2000) 'Biodiversity conservation, development and local people: Politics, puzzles and potentials'. Keynote address at Conference Towards Best Practice: Communities and Conservation, 15–19 May 2000, Berg and Dal, Kruger National Park, South Africa, pp14–18

Magome, H, Grossman, D, Fakir, S and Stowell, Y (2000) 'Partnerships in conservation: The state, private sector and the community at Madikwe Game Reserve, North West Province, South Africa', *Evaluating Eden Discussion Paper No 7.* International Institute for Environment and Development, London

Magome, H and Murombedzi, J (2003) 'Sharing South African National Parks: Community land and conservation in a democratic South Africa', in Adams, W M and Mulligan, M (eds) *Decolonizing Nature: Strategies for Conservation in a Post-Colonial Era*, Earthscan, London, pp108–134

Mainka, S and Trivedi, M (eds) (2002) *Link between Biodiversity Conservation, Livelihoods and Food Security: The Sustainable Use of Wild Species for Meat.* Occasional Paper No 24, IUCN Species Survival Commission. IUCN, Gland, Switzerland and Cambridge

Mander, M (1998) *Marketing of Indigenous Medicinal Plants in South Africa: A Case Study in Kwazulu-Natal.* Food and Agriculture Organization of the United Nations (FAO), Rome

McNeely, J A (1992) 'The Sinking Ark: Pollution and the world loss of biodiversity', *Biodiversity and Conservation* 1: 2–18

McNeely, J A (1996) 'Politics and economics', in Spellerberg, I F (ed) *Conservation Biology.* Longman, London, pp38–47

Murombedzi, J (1999) 'Devolution and stewardship in Zimbabwe's CAMPFIRE Programme', *Journal of International Development* 11: 287–293

Mutangadura, G and Mukurazita, D (1999) 'A review of household and community responses to the HIV/AIDS epidemic in the rural areas of sub-Saharan Africa', UNAIDS, www.unaids.org/publications/documents/economics/agriculture/una99e39.pdf

Myers, N (1979) *The Sinking Ark: New Look at the Problem of Disappearing Species.* Pergamon Press, Oxford

Myers, N (1988) 'Tropical forests and other species: Going, going...?', in Wilson, E O (ed) *Biodiversity.* National Academy Press, London, pp28–35

Myerson, G and Rydin, Y (1996) *The Language of the Environment: New Rhetoric.* UCL Press, London

Newmark, W D and Hough, J L (2000) 'Conserving wildlife in Africa: Integrated conservation and development projects and beyond', *BioScience* 50: 585–592

Nhira, C, Baker, Z, Gondo, P, Mangono, J J and Marunda, C (1998) *Contesting Inequality in Access to Forests.* Policy that Works for Forests and People Series No 5. Centre for Applied Social Sciences and Forestry Commission, Harare and International Institute for Environment and Development, London

Patel, H (1998) *Sustainable Utilization and African Wildlife Policy: The Case of Zimbabwe's Communal Areas Management Programme for Indigenous Resources (CAMPFIRE).* Report for the Indigenous Environmental Policy Centre, Cambridge, Massachusetts

Peuhkuri, T and Jokinen, P (1999) 'The role of knowledge and spatial contexts in biodiversity policies: Sociological perspective', *Biodiversity and Conservation* 8: 133–147

Reid, H (2001) 'Contractual national parks and the Makuleke community', *Human Ecology* 29: 135–155

Rhodes University, Unitra and Fort Cox (2001) *A Monitoring System for Community Forestry: Combining Scientific and Local Knowledge in the Eastern Cape.* Report to the Department of Water Affairs and Forestry, DWAF Project RU1/100, Pretoria

Rogerson, C M and Sithole, P M, (2001) 'Rural handicraft production in Mpumalanga, South Africa: Organisation, problems and support needs', *South African Geographic Journal* 83: 149–158

Rozemeier, N (2000) (ed) *Community Based Tourism in Botswana (The SNV Experience in Two Community Tourism Projects).* SNV Botswana, Gaborone

Shackleton, C M (2000) 'Comparison of plant diversity in protected and communal lands in the Bushbuckridge lowveld savanna, South Africa', *Biological Conservation* 94: 273–285

Shackleton, S and Steenkamp, C (in press) in Lawes, M, Eeley, H, Shackleton, C and Geach, B (eds) *The Use and Socio-Economic Value of Indigenous Forest and Woodland Resources in South Africa.* University of Natal Press, Durban

Shackleton, S, Shackleton, C, Cunningham, A, Lombard, C, Sullivan, C and Netshiluvi, T (2002) 'Knowledge on *Sclerocarya birrea* subsp *caffra* with emphasis on its importance as a non-timber forest product in South and southern Africa: A summary. Part 1: Taxonomy, ecology and role in rural livelihoods', *Southern African Forestry Journal* 194: 27–41

Simelane, T S and Kerley, G I H (1998) 'Conservation implications of the use of vertebrates by Xhosa traditional healers in South Africa', *South African Journal of Wildlife Research* 28: 121–126

Soulé, M E (1985) 'What is conservation biology?' *Bioscience* 35: 727–734

Soulé, M E (ed) (1986) *Conservation Biology: the Science of Scarcity and Diversity.* Sinauer Associates, Sunderland, Massachusetts

Soulé, M E (ed) (1987) *Viable Populations for Conservation.* Cambridge University Press, Cambridge

Sullivan, S (2002) 'How sustainable is the communalizing discourse of "New Conservation"? The masking of difference, inequality and aspiration in the fledgling "conservancies" of Namibia', in Chatty, D and Colchester, M (eds) *Conservation and Mobile Indigenous Peoples: Displacement, Forced Resettlement and Conservation.* Berghahn Books, Oxford, pp158–187

Swanson, T (2001) 'Conserving global biological diversity through alternative development paths', in Koziell, I and Saunders, J (eds) *Living off Biodiversity*. International Institute for Environment and Development, London, pp11–22

Swingland, I R (1993) 'Tropical forests and biodiversity conservation: New ecological imperative', in Barbier, E B (ed) *Economics and Ecology: New Frontiers and Sustainable Development*. Chapman and Hall, London, pp118–145

UNEP (1992) *The Convention on Biological Diversity*. United Nations Environmental Programme, Nairobi

Van Wyk, B E and Gericke, N (2000) *Peoples Plants*. Briza publications, Pretoria

Vickerman, S (1999) 'A state model for implementing stewardship incentives to conserve biodiversity and endangered species', *The Science of the Total Environment* 240: 41–50

Wainwright, C and Wehrmeyer, W (1998) 'Success in integrating conservation and development? A study from Zambia', *World Development* 26: 933–944

Western, D (1989) 'Conservation without parks: Wildlife in the rural landscape', in Western, D and Pearl, M (eds) *Conservation for the Twenty-First Century*. Oxford University Press, New York, pp158–165

Wilson, E O (ed) (1988) *Biodiversity*. National Academy Press, London

Part 2

Case studies

Chapter 6

Community-based natural resource management, traditional governance and spiritual ecology in southern Africa: The case of chiefs, diviners and spirit mediums

PENNY BERNARD AND SIBONGISENI KUMALO

INTRODUCTION

The iKhamanzi, a tributary of the Mvoti River, nestles in a relatively biodiversity-rich valley of KwaZulu-Natal (KZN). The valley of iKhamanzi is under the custodianship of the Zondi chieftaincy. The boundaries of this traditional administrative area, like many others in the region, begin where the optimum conditions for extensive agricultural cultivation declines – that is, at the edge of the escarpment as it drops into the valley. Small hamlets dot the valley slopes and floor, surrounded by patches of indigenous forests and grasslands containing a diverse range of medicinal and other useful plants. Patches of cultivation take place near the homesteads or along the valley floor, interspersed between the dense valley bushveld. But, on the whole, the integrity of the environment still appears to be relatively good, with few signs of soil erosion or loss of plant diversity.

In order to reach these small havens of diversity, one has to drive through hundreds of square kilometres of biodiverse-poor, privately owned, commercial farmland dedicated to either sugar cane or fast-growing timber plantations (wattle, gum and pine) that have replaced well over 90 per cent of the indigenous grasslands and forests in the region. One could be forgiven, therefore, for wondering why the focus for externally initiated conservation management programmes has been on indigenous communities who have, in many cases – and despite all odds with land appropriation, population pressure and institutionalized inequities – still managed to preserve environments rich in biodiversity. Is it more about the control of the powerful over the weak, a new form of paternalistic colonialism and yet another way of tapping into their resources? Should the emphasis not be more on the real threats to biodiversity, that of uncontrolled commercial agriculture and development? Another question to ask is: what helps to contribute, despite the high population pressure, to the relatively biodiverse environments under the control of traditional chieftaincies like these?

BELIEF SYSTEMS AND RESOURCE MANAGEMENT

Part of the answer to these questions lies in the belief systems and spiritual links between southern Africa's rural people and their natural resources. The following two accounts might help to elucidate this. The first is a composite story, told with remarkable consistency by many people in the iKhamanzi valley.

Inkosazana

It was in this valley some time ago that old MaZuma was tending her vegetables in her garden, when a young woman approached her with a plea that she knew she could not ignore. The woman was *Inkosazana*, 'the lady', the princess of heaven, the giver of life and fertility, she who can manifest sometimes as a beautiful young woman, sometimes as an old hag dressed in ragged clothes. *Inkosazana* can also transform herself into soft life-giving rain, a snake, a mermaid, the rainbow or even a small animal. She is also sometimes referred to as *Nomkhubulwane* and her dwelling place is in the rivers and the forests that surround them. MaZuma knew how important *Inkosazana* was to the life of her people, the amaZulu, because as an *isangoma*, or diviner, she had heard a lot about her during her training. She had probably seen her in her dreams and she had participated in rituals for her and the ancestors at the river pools and in the deep forests.

Inkosazana requested the old diviner to go tell the people her important message: 'My children are *NoMgqibelo* (Saturday) and *NoMsombuluku* (Monday). These are special days when we like to wash in the rivers. On these days no one must draw water from the rivers, wash their dirty clothes in it or till their fields. They must be left quiet for my children and I to enjoy.' MaZuma knew that she had to relay this message as soon as possible to the headman of her area, Mr Gabela. He would take it to the chief who would then instruct the people. The chief, on hearing the news, knew that this was a very important message, for it had come from one 'who could not lie', an old woman who was also an *isangoma*. There was more to this message than the request to respect *usuku LweNkosazana*, the days of rest for *Inkosazana*. Her manifestation was also a reminder that the people had been neglecting her in other ways. The old people remembered the time, before the white missionaries had come and told them that these beliefs were 'things of the darkness and the devil', when their forefathers would always conduct annual rituals for *Inkosazana*. These rituals were done to ensure harmony and respect between people and the environment, and would give fertility to the women, the crops and the livestock.

On the instructions of the chief, these observances were to be reintroduced. The rivers were to be respected and left in peace on the days requested, and in the beginning of spring each year the ritual hoeing and planting of *Inkosazana*'s field would take place, followed by the ritual slaughter of the goat where the gall would be sprinkled into the river and then onto the field in the forest, symbolically unifying them. All of these rituals are now performed annually and are officiated over by the women under the direction of the chief's wife and the elderly women in the area. It is expected that every household should contribute a portion of their seeds to be planted in *Inkosazana*'s garden. This is to ensure that all the people will be blessed with rain and good harvests. Those households failing to contribute risk being fined by the chief.

Even though many of the people are now vague as to who *Inkosazana* is, the majority are happy to do these things for her as these are 'the ways of the ancestors and a part of our *isiko* (culture)'. There is general consensus that it is the chief's responsibility to ensure that all adhere to the instructions, as some, especially those who are 'born again' Christians, refuse to participate. Some women still tend their fields on the taboo days; but this is partly because the agricultural extension officers come on the Monday to give advice.

Inkosi the python

The following account is an extract from Sibongiseni Kumalo's fieldnotes while he was conducting research in the same valley.

On one of the sunny days as we were climbing down the mountain, we were accompanied by a middle-aged man. He told me not to look around but to look at the path. I wasn't supposed to shake the trees as we were passing them. In my mind I just took this for granted and didn't question why I should not do so. On our way back, it was still the three of us. At the same spot this man ordered Nathi (the guide) and I to walk faster. He told us that we would rest on the top of the mountain. I walked behind them so that I could rest when I had to. When we got to the top of the mountain we sat down under the tree. It was then that I questioned him on why I should not touch the trees or look around. He reminded me of a place on the path on the mountain. This was a flatter place with tall, soft grass. The grass showed signs of some animals having walked over it, crossing the path. He told me that people don't frequently use the path and that *inkosi* stays there. Literally, *inkosi* is a king or a chief and it can also refer to God. I asked him further what he meant by this. Apparently, the term is a euphemism for a python. Out of respect, people around here don't refer to it by its name. Almost everyone I have spoken to knows it stays there; but the amazing thing is that people don't talk about it unless you ask them. Still they call it *inkosi*. I was interested in the link between *inkosi* the animal and *inkosi* a traditional leader (S Kumalo, fieldnotes, 24 January 2002).

Discussion

These two accounts are significant for a number of reasons. Firstly, they are connected to a complex of beliefs, containing key symbols that are to be found throughout southern and central Africa. The symbols of the python *inkosi* and the mermaid *Inkosanzana* are intimately linked not only to fertility, rain and pools, but also to healing and divinatory power (Bernard, 2000). They also have great influence over resource management in that they represent the great spirit deities of an 'African earth religion' (Schoffeleers, 1978), and act as powerful constraints to the misuse of resources. Throughout the subcontinent they recur time and time again in the oral histories of the various sub-groups. They are, along with the ancestors, the guardians of the land. The python is regarded by the Zulu as the representation of the great ancestors and is often likened to God. In particular, it is frequently believed to be the guardian of key features of the landscape, particularly sacred mountains (De Beer, 1999) and pools (Bernard, 2000).

The second significant feature of these two accounts is the implicit recognition given to the authority of the chief. What was demonstrated in both of these accounts was the great respect accorded to the spirit forces that exist within the natural environment and expressed through the medium of the diviner and the chief. These and a host of other anecdotes provide evidence that a complex spiritual ecology still exists among segments of the diverse and mainly rural communities of the southern African region. However, it cannot be denied that the impacts of Western education, religion, politics and economics have led to the erosion of much of this spiritual ecology among large sections of the population.

The importance of spiritual ecology, a term used to denote how concepts of the supernatural and spirit world influences a group's management and use of an ecological resource, is becoming increasingly well recognized worldwide (Posey, 1999). Community-based natural resource management (CBNRM) programmes need to be particularly sensitive to the role of spiritual ecology to many rural people in southern Africa, especially regarding the ways in which it influences their perception and use of certain resources and features of the landscape.

HEREDITARY CHIEFTAINSHIP AND NATURAL RESOURCE MANAGEMENT

More significant is the association of spiritual ecology with hereditary chieftainship, and traditional healing practitioners, such as diviners and spirit mediums. One of the principle functions of traditional leadership is in regulating access to natural resources, and it can be argued that, through the chiefs, effective natural resource management has been present in African societies for centuries. In a general anthropological text on the Nguni-speaking peoples of southern Africa, Basil Sansom emphasized this ecological role of traditional leadership: 'In southern Africa, the chief regulated public access to the means of production...against feckless and selfish use of resources the chief set boundaries in both time and space, using his authority to enforce them' (Sansom, 1974, p137). Although, to some extent, the colonialist intrusion in Africa eroded the power and credibility of traditional authority structures, it was largely the legitimacy of the incumbent rather than the institution itself that rural people questioned.

Ironically, the greatest threat to the institution of traditional leadership has arisen in the post-independent democratic state (Oomen, 2000; Peires, 2000), as new players struggle to attain leadership roles hitherto denied them. Some observers have argued that traditional leaders are no longer significant players in the field of local governance; but recent evidence disputes this view (De Beer, 1999; Oomen, 2000; Peires, 2000).

In those mainly rural areas where traditional structures still have public support and influence, the legitimacy and authority of traditional incumbents, such as kings, chiefs and headmen, usually depend upon hereditary links to founding lineages within an area. This legitimacy usually arises from consensus within the community through a historical memory that is integrally connected with the landscape, both in time and space. Furthermore, much of their authority derives from spiritual sanction and, in some areas, they may be seen as representatives of the great ancestral spirits themselves. The ancestors not only validate traditional governance, but also provide the foundation for the creation and maintenance of a particular identity that is similarly connected to key features of the landscape. When dealing with issues of land and resource use, it is imperative that we understand this more complex notion of landscape, which embraces a wide range of social, spiritual, political, ontological and historical meanings.

While recent CBNRM discourse is beginning to realize the need to accommodate the role and the influence of chiefs and headmen (Anon, 2001), the relationship between chiefs and spirit mediums (diviners) in ecological management has received relatively little attention. Anstey and de Sousa (2001) have, however, revealed some interesting insights into the issues of traditional leadership, spiritual sanction and resource management in the Chimanimani district of central Mozambique. With reference to CBNRM and some unspecified groups in Zimbabwe, Mamimine and Chinhoyi have argued that 'In essence, a chiefdom had most of the features of a modern state, that is, a legislature constituted primarily of spirit mediums, chiefs and headmen, an executive, composed of chiefs, headmen, village heads and the councillors and a judiciary system with *dare* or courts encompassing all community members at large' (Mamimine and Chinhoyi, 2001, p7). Significantly, they emphasize that it was 'the spirit mediums that conferred legitimacy on the chief designate', a finding also affirmed by other scholars of southern African ethnography (Lan, 1985; Daneel, 1970; Schoffeleers, 1978).

The ethnographic literature of central and southern Africa is replete with examples of the connection between traditional governance, religious complexes and their functionaries, on the one hand, and resource use and management, on the other. In particular, ethnographers have emphasized the complex interrelationship that exists between these institutions. Much of this ethnographic focus preceded the more recent global concerns with sustainable development, which have emerged over the last two decades or so. Although the primary concern of many of these ethnographic studies was the explanation and analysis of social forms, rather than ecological issues, much of what was written is still directly relevant to contemporary issues of CBNRM and sustainable development today.

GUARDIANS OF THE LAND

A case in point is the collection of papers edited by Schoffeleers (1978) and appropriately entitled *Guardians of the Land*. The focus of this edition is on the widespread territorial cult complexes found in Zambia, Zimbabwe, Malawi, Mozambique and Tanzania. These complexes are ecologically based politico-religious structures that are governed by what Schoffeleers describes as the 'African philosophy of the earth'. Territorial cults are usually focused around identifiable natural or man-made shrines that are linked to local and tribal ancestral spirits, or the supra-ancestral spirit beings. They are usually governed by a priesthood, spirit mediums or diviner-healers, in close conjunction with tribal chiefs or headmen.

These cults vary in levels of hierarchy and range of influence, and have been classified as local, state, tribal or federative (Scoffeleers, 1978). A member's allegiance to a cult is primarily through residence in a territory, rather than through claims to ethnic or lineage membership. The cults of Chikang'ombe, Chisumphi, Mbona, Mwari, and Dzivaguru, for instance, serve a number of groups straddling Malawi, Mozambique, Zimbabwe and South Africa, and are significant in that they centre around the symbols of the sacred pool and the python. According to Schoffeleers: 'What sets territorial cults apart from other religious institutions is the combination of communal and ecological concerns and the primacy accorded these concerns' (Schoffeleers, 1978, p2). Using a phrase coined by Rappaport (1969), Schoffeleers describes them as 'ritually directed ecosystems' that aim to counteract droughts, floods, blights, pests and epidemic diseases afflicting cattle and man. He notes that they are geared towards the well-being of the community, its fields, livestock, fishing, hunting and general economic interests. He draws attention to the way in which these territorial cults issue and enforce directives with regard to the use of local environments, and how they provide schemas of thought that make apparently discrete myths, rituals and directives for action appear to be parts of a coherent worldview. This explanation of territorial cults is highly suggestive of their importance to conservation-oriented initiatives, and to any proposed systems of co-management, in particular. Generally, they should always be consulted on any programmes that involve utilization of the resources as they are seen to have supernatural sanction to stop any unwanted intrusions of the land and resources in question.

THE CONTEMPORARY POWER OF SPIRITUAL BELIEF SYSTEMS

Bedevilling the Mid-Zambezi Rural Development Project

The effectiveness of spiritual belief systems in obstructing outside-initiated management and development programmes has been described in a paper by Spierenburg (2000), who details the events that took place in the Zambezi Valley in 1992 when a community resisted a land redistribution and development programme. The Mid-Zambezi Rural Development Project was initiated and funded by the European Economic Community (EEC) and the Food and Agriculture Organization (FAO), and was largely a top-down intervention. In this particular case, it was the spirit medium, representing a senior tribal spirit (*mhondoro*), who wielded the ultimate power, the chief having deferred the decision to approve the project to him, as this had to come from the *mhondoros* who were believed to be the real owners of the land. Significantly, the *mhondoro* received public support for his resistance against the project; but his popularity and credibility as a true *mhondoro* medium began to wane as soon as it was noted that the developers were trying their best to change his stance through financial incentives (for example, by building him a nice house).

Perhaps it was no coincidence that the events that Spierenburg describes transpired at the time of a severe drought in Zimbabwe. The drought of 1992 to 1993 served as a potent symbol and weapon that strengthened the medium and the community's resolve to obstruct the externally imposed project. It provided the *mhondoro* mediums with the opportunity to offer powerful social commentaries against the intrusive and repressive modern state and unwanted foreign intervention on their land. A point to note here is that droughts, floods and blights/disease are seen as the ultimate expression of ancestral displeasure over the activities of the living, and are intimately linked to the python/ mermaid water spirit complex in southern Africa.

Proponents of CBNRM initiatives in such areas should be made aware of the fact that mediums and diviners are drawing upon a worldview that is based on a fundamentally different paradigm from that of sustainable development. The former is more concerned with maintaining a harmonious balance between the social, ecological and spiritual worlds, while the latter embraces a philosophy of progress based on the modern global economic system. It would be a mistake to assume that all members of a community are as committed to development and entering the market economy as are those who promote such initiatives. Development often accentuates social inequalities, such as between young and old, male and female, those with formal education and those with none, between those with the control over and access to financial and political resources and those without. The commercializing of natural resources, even if it is ostensibly done for the good of the community involved, may often directly threaten the spiritual and social integrity of the area. This is because it alters concepts of ownership and exchange of resources that, in turn, govern the nature of these spiritual and social relationships.

The *Ambuya Juliana* movement

An example of such community resistance to global economic forces was evident in the south-eastern part of Zimbabwe during the same drought of 1992. Mawere and Wilson (1995) have given a detailed account of the *Ambuya Juliana* movement that emerged in the Mberengwa region with the appearance of a medium/diviner by the name of Juliana. She claimed that she had spent four years under water with the *njuzu*, or mermaids, and had been sent back with a message from them to give to the people. She attributed the drought to the breakdown of respect that the people had for the land and the Earth's resources, the lack of social harmony, the abandonment of traditional practices and beliefs, and the failure of the government to acknowledge the role of the spirit world in the war of independence. She instituted a set of harsh taboos that the community had to observe should they wish to break the drought and to facilitate the return of the *njuzu*, who would bring rain and rejuvenate springs and rivers. It is worth listing some of these taboos (see Mawere and Wilson, 1995) in more detail, particularly as they relate to some of the previous cases described in this chapter and are relevant to broader CBNRM issues:

- The need to institute the days of rest: There was to be a complete ban on normal work activities on *chisi* days (Sundays and Wednesdays). No water was to be drawn from the rivers, nor was washing to be done. Fetching firewood, sweeping yards and making handles and yokes (from wood) were all prohibited on those days.
- People were forbidden to collect wild plants for sale or to kill wild animals as these plants and animals attract the rain.
- There was a ban on using borehole water as the drilling of boreholes frightens away the spirits.
- There was a ban on referring to mice and baboons by their Karanga names.
- They opposed a grazing plan scheme 'on the grounds that the spirits do not want to be enclosed by wire fences'.

The thousands of people who responded to Juliana's pronouncements, and adhered to the taboos and restrictions, are proof of the great respect many people still hold for the water spirit complex in the region, as well as their collective rejection of the less palatable aspects of capitalism, modern methods of agriculture and resource use.

TRADITIONAL LEADERSHIP WALKS A TIGHTROPE

Although one can argue that traditional leadership has long been involved in community-based natural resource management, there is a fundamental difference between this indigenous system of resource management and the formal systems of CBNRM today. The latter, which are largely initiated and orchestrated external to the communities in question, are clearly oriented towards wider state interests based on global environmental–economic conservation and development paradigms. The principles that govern CBNRM, such as the application of commodity values to natural resources, may conflict with the spiritual ecological principles that govern use of resources in indigenous resource management systems.

We support the argument that traditional systems of resource management were concerned more with sustainable use, while CBNRM tends more towards sustainable development. Contemporary traditional leaders, however, now have to negotiate a delicate balance between these two principles, which are often conflicting, to accommodate the variety of needs in their diverse communities. On the one hand, they are required to maintain the social and ecological balance by preventing conflicts, punishing wrongdoers and ensuring fair allocation and the wise use of resources. On the other hand, they have to be seen to address the new aspirations and needs of their communities, such as the provision of services and the promotion of income-generating projects. This latter role was never a part of their traditional duties. Their dilemmas have increased since they now have to compete with democratically elected local councils, and so it is more imperative now that they are seen to address the problems of poverty in the rural areas (Peires, 2000). However, many of them do this at their own peril since they risk losing support if they appear to ignore the spiritual ecology of their area.

Some traditional leaders may even fall prey to unscrupulous developers who come in with promises and incentives, and bargain on their lack of sophisticated knowledge about accepted requirements and procedures regarding impact assessments and the like. If they fail to consult with the full range of their community, they risk becoming unpopular, and suspicions of bribery become rife. Serious divisions may arise within the community if broad consultation is not implemented. In the Umnga municipal area of the Eastern Cape, for instance, a local chief has recently endorsed a private development proposal to establish a hydropower plant at a waterfall that has great spiritual significance for the diviners in the region. None of them have been consulted about the proposed development. Interviews with many of the healers and local people have revealed great concern for the plan since this is where the *abantu bamlambo* or people of the river/mermaids reside. The hydropower plant will not only disturb the tranquillity of the surroundings preferred by the *abantu bamlambo*, but the electricity being generated will drive them away from the pools. This could lead to serious droughts, electrical storms or floods. Furthermore, the healers will no longer be able to access the pools to perform their rituals since the whole area will be fenced off for their 'safety'.

Despite the fact that colonial and post-colonial structures of governance at the local, regional, national and international level have now profoundly affected traditional management structures – and, in some cases, have divorced the traditional leaders from their spiritual advisers – it is striking how in many rural areas in southern Africa communities still indicate a preference for traditional systems of control. In interviews with 36 individuals in the iKhamanzi valley, there was 100 per cent endorsement for the institution of traditional leadership from those whom we interviewed, with most individuals indicating that it was because it connected them with their culture. Oomen found a similarly high number of respondents (73 per cent) in the Mamone region who claimed to support the local chief. The most important reasons for this were that it connected them to their culture and their identity (Oomen, 2000). One cannot assume, however, that this support of traditional authorities is universal: there are areas in South Africa where chiefs and headmen are resented and sidelined, largely as a result of their past abuse of powers and complicity with colonial and apartheid political structures (Manona, 1997; Fatman, 2001).

CONCLUSIONS

In order to get a deeper understanding of the intricacies of resource management in southern Africa, we have to alter our rather shallow perceptions of what the landscape and the resources within it mean to the communities inhabiting these landscapes. Scientifically informed and Western notions of landscape are more concerned with its ecological, functional or aesthetic use values, rather than its more complex relational (spiritual, political and social) representations within a historical framework that are of major concern to many of the indigenous inhabitants. Tilley has observed that 'The landscape is the fundamental reference system in which individual consciousness of the world and social identities are anchored' (Tilley, 1994, p40). Landscapes anchor people not only in the present but also link them with the past. Traditional leadership is embedded in the landscape and thus helps to connect the people with the past through relational memories. In other words, through their ability to condense time, landscape and traditional leadership act as a powerful mnemonic device. By maintaining a connection with the past and affirming a strong identity with the land, a sense of stability arises. With regard to resource management, indigenous systems (through traditional governance) are more enduring and often have greater continuity with the past than CBNRM systems, which are more sensitive to the vagaries of unpredictable market and political forces. Although the former are not necessarily immune from the effects of such forces, the latter are more heavily impacted by the highly fluid state of emerging democracies, global economic systems, local regional and national power struggles and competition for wealth. These highly volatile factors often leave the programmes in tatters (Oates, 1999) and the communities divided and worse off.

REFERENCES

Anon (2001) *Commons Southern Africa*, 3(2). Newsletter of joint CBNRM programme, Centre for Applied Social Sciences, University of Zimbabwe, and the Programme for Land and Agrarian Studies, University of the Western Cape, Harare and Cape Town

Anstey, S and de Sousa, C (2001) 'Old ways and new challenges: Traditional resource management systems in the Chimanimani mountains, Mozambique', in Hulme, D and Murphree, M (eds) *African Wildlife and Livelihoods: The Promises and Performance of Community Conservation*. David Philip, Cape Town, pp195–207

Bernard, P (2000) 'Water spirits. Indigenous Peoples' Knowledge Programme: The relevance of indigenous beliefs for river health and wetland conservation in southern Africa', *Wetlands Newsletter* 11: 12–16

Daneel, M (1970) *The God of the Matopos Hills: An Essay on the Mwari Cult in Rhodesia*. Mouton, The Hague and Paris

De Beer, F (1999) 'Mountains as cultural resources: Values and management issues', *South African Journal of Ethnology* 22(1): 20–25

Fatman, Z (2001) *The Influence of Social Dynamics on Resource Management in Machibi Village*. BSc thesis, Rhodes University, Grahamstown

Lan, D (1985) *Guns and Rain: Guerillas and Spirit Mediums in Zimbabwe*. Zimbabwe Publishing House, Harare

Mamimine, P and Chinhoyi, C (2001) 'Sub-theme: Traditional authorities, governance and CBNRM', *Commons Southern Africa* 3(2): 7–8

Manona, C (1997) 'The collapse of the "Tribal Authority" system and the rise of civic associations', in de Wet, C and Whisson, M (eds) *From Reserve to Region: Apartheid and Social Change in the Keiskammahoek District of (Former) Ciskei: 1950–1990*. Institute of Social and Economic Research, Grahamstown, pp49–68

Mawere, A and Wilson, K (1995) 'Socio-religious movements, the state and community change: Some reflections on the Ambuya Juliana cult of southern Zimbabwe', *Journal of Religion in Africa* 25(3): 252–287

Oates, J (1999) *Myth and Reality in the Rain Forest: How Conservation Strategies are Failing in West Africa*. University of California Press, Berkeley

Oomen, B (2000) '"We must now go back to our history": Re-traditionalisation in a Northern Province chieftaincy', *African Studies*, 59(1): 71–95

Peires, J (2000) 'Traditional leaders in purgatory. Local government in Tsolo, Qumbu and Port St Johns, 1900–2000', *African Studies* 59(1): 97–114

Posey, D (1999) *Cultural and Spiritual Values of Biodiversity*. United Nations Environmental Programme. Intermediate Technology Publications, London

Rappaport, R (1969) 'Regulation of environmental relations among a New Guinea people', in Vayda, A (ed) *Environment and Cultural Behaviour*. The Natural History Press, New York, pp181–201

Sansom, B (1974) 'Traditional economic systems', in Hammond-Tooke, W (ed) *The Bantu-Speaking Peoples of Southern Africa* (2nd ed). Routledge and Kegan Paul, London and Boston, pp135–176

Schoffeleers, J (ed) (1978) 'Introduction', in *Guardians of the Land* (2nd ed). Mambo Press, Gweru, pp1–46

Spierenburg, M (2000) 'Social commentaries and the influence of the clientele: The Mhondoro cult in Dande, Zimbabwe', in van Dijk, R, Reis, R and Spierenburg, M (eds) *The Quest for Fruition through Ngoma: Political Aspects of Healing in Southern Africa*. David Philip, Cape Town, pp76–98

Tilley, C (1994) *A Phenomenology of Landscape: Places, Paths and Monuments.* Berg, Oxford and Providence

Chapter 7

The contribution of bees to livelihoods in southern Africa

ETIENNE NEL AND PETE ILLGNER

INTRODUCTION

Traditional beekeeping in southern Africa is a good example of rural people's complex and diverse relationships with their social, economic, cultural and natural landscapes. Beekeeping is a livelihood and way of life that is intricately connected with the health of the forests that sustain and nourish the honey- and wax-producing wild bee populations. In the first part of this chapter, we explore the importance of honey-hunting and beekeeping as an ecologically sound and economically appropriate livelihood option in rural southern Africa. We argue that beekeeping is a valuable, yet overlooked, component of community-based natural resource management (CBNRM) in southern Africa.

Important in a number of other ways, beekeeping is often a commercial activity that generates a cash income supplementary to that which rural people derive from subsistence farming and fishing occupations (Quong, 1993). In the second part of the chapter, we review some of the recent attempts by certain government and aid agencies to enhance the productivity of more commercial beekeeping.

Interest in the interface between people and the environment has, traditionally, focused upon charismatic mega-fauna and flora, often overshadowing the less obvious invertebrate fauna, such as insects, spiders and other arthropods. With few exceptions, the value of insects, including bees, to rural people has seldom been assessed. When viewed from a utilitarian perspective, it is apparent that the honeybee is among the most widely used and valuable insects to humankind. Honey is utilized by communities throughout the world and is a key environmental product available to, and used by, people in rural Africa.

Although recorded evidence of traditional beekeeping in southern Africa dates back to the 16th century in Angola, and David Livingstone noted the presence of log and bark hives in the upper Zambezi area in the 1850s (Clauss, 1992), honey has been collected in southern Africa since ancient times. Techniques of beekeeping and honey collection are handed down through the generations and it is apparent that traditional beekeeping has always been part of the lifestyles of a high proportion of families throughout southern Africa (Clauss, 1992). Contemporary beekeeping clearly reveals the persistence of traditional methods of hive construction, and of smoking bees prior to honey collection and production (for example, of beer), which have been developed and perfected for hundreds of years.

THE VALUE OF TRADITIONAL HONEY-HUNTING AND BEEKEEPING IN SOUTHERN AFRICA

While honey-hunting from naturally occurring honeybee nests is widely practised across southern Africa, traditional beekeeping has been particularly prominent in the northern savanna regions of the subcontinent (Ntenga and Mugongo, 1991). Traditional beekeeping differs from honey-hunting in that the colony of honeybees is not destroyed, but managed in such a way that honey is extracted without eliminating the honeybees. In this way, the resource is protected and repeated harvests can be made from the same colony.

Traditional beekeeping in southern Africa is most widespread in Zambia, Zimbabwe, Tanzania and Mozambique, where the honeybees are kept in traditionally designed 'bark hives'. The bark hives are made by ring-barking (cutting the desired length of bark from a large tree). The two ends of the hive are then plugged with woven grass leaving a small hole as an entrance. The hives are then hung in trees, out of the reach of children, pests and predators.

Traditional beekeeping, although normally carried out on a small scale or as a supplement to other activity, can range in scale from an individual with less than 10 hives to beekeepers who possess up to 1000 hives (Ntenga and Mugongo, 1991; Clauss, 1992).

Honeybees and their products are an important part of the rural economy in many parts of southern Africa as a food source, an ingredient in traditional medicine and as an additive in the brewing of honey-beer, while beeswax is used by local craftsmen for a variety of purposes. This is over and above the vitally important role that bees play in terms of the pollination of crops. In some areas, honey also plays an important role in traditional rituals such as initiation ceremonies (Ntenga and Mugongo, 1991). Evidence from Zambia suggests that more than 50 per cent of honey produced by traditional methods is sold or bartered locally within tribal groups in order to meet these non-market requirements (Clauss, 1992).

From a livelihood perspective, the region has enormous beekeeping potential because of three considerations:

1   the presence of vast numbers of diverse honeybee colonies that are adapted
    to the environmentally diverse conditions of southern Africa;
2   the presence of large numbers of traditional beekeepers; and
3   'the presence in abundance of a great variety of flora whose nectar and
    pollen are readily available to bees' (Kihwele, 1989, p391).

Currently, one of the major occurrences of beekeeping in the southern African
region is in the *Brachystegia–Julbernardia* woodlands of southern
Mozambique. The mainstream, contemporary relevance of beekeeping can
also be seen in the Babati District of Tanzania, where there are some 6000
productive bee colonies producing between 60 and 90 tonnes of honey a year
(Ntenga and Mugongo, 1991). The key role that beekeeping plays as a source
of employment in rural areas is clearly indicated by the fact that, of the
approximately 400,000 people in the North-Western Province of Zambia,
nearly 15,000 are beekeepers (Clauss, 1992). In the districts of Tabora,
Urambo and Nzega in Tanzania, over 60 per cent of the population are
involved in beekeeping in some fashion (Quong, 1993).

The growing importance of honey-based self-reliance strategies is also
reflected in a doubling in the number of rural beekeeping clubs in Malawi
from 42 to 92 during the early 1990s (Mensing, 1993). The attractiveness of
beekeeping has to do with the role it plays in promoting overall rural self-
reliance. Beekeeping relies on indigenous skills and interests, uses locally
available resources and has a positive effect on other forms of farming and
the environment, more generally, through the pollination of cultivated crops
and the natural vegetation. At its best, contemporary beekeeping is a valuable
illustration of how informal CBNRM can be ecologically sound, promote
sustainable livelihoods in marginal areas and be an important vehicle for the
empowerment of women.

A recent study undertaken in a rural community living next to the Machibi
State Forest, near King William's Town in South Africa, highlights the richness
of community-based knowledge, the reliance on traditional skills in working
with honeybees and the overall significance of honey supplies to the livelihoods
of people in the region (Rhodes University et al, 2001). In terms of ecosystem
biodiversity, this study also identified the important role of honey guide birds
(*Indicator indicator*) in guiding collectors to sources of honey, and the fact
that local honey collectors used variability in the abundance of locally
available honey as an indicator of the state of local forest health.

BEEKEEPING AND CBNRM

Beekeeping is notable for its widespread occurrence throughout large parts of
southern Africa. In many parts of central Africa, beekeeping families constitute
an important component of rural village economies. Even though beekeeping
tends to be an individual and often family-based activity, it nonetheless has
important community-wide implications. This is evidenced by the use of honey

in traditional village celebrations, the reality that beekeeping 'clubs' collaborate on issues such as hive construction and controlling access to forested areas, and the role of tribal decision-making powers over access to resources.

In terms of more generalized CBNRM, beekeeping is of particular importance. Maintaining hives clearly facilitates crop and plant pollination, thus helping to ensure ecological diversity and sustainability. Although there is a cost to the environment in that hive construction through ring-barking can permanently damage trees, at the broader level, honey production provides a nutritious, natural product for human consumption. Beekeeping has been noted for encouraging plant and natural vegetation growth in places such as Malawi, where community access to nature reserves has been encouraged with this objective in mind (Clauss, 1992; Quong, 1993). Beekeeping thus encourages the environmental conservation of local habitats as it is clearly in the interests of beekeepers to conserve local nectar- and pollen-producing vegetation (Ntenga and Mugongo, 1991). Beekeeping is a passive form of agriculture since it does not require the clearing of indigenous vegetation to make way for the planting of crops. Beekeepers also discourage the use of pesticides on crops, which could kill their honeybees. In some cases, beekeepers may actively protect conservation areas, as studies in northern Malawi have documented (Mensing, 1993).

BEEKEEPING AS A SIGNIFICANT COMPONENT OF THE 'HIDDEN HARVEST'

It is a truism that for rural communities living in close interaction with their local environments, ecological and socio-economic issues are closely intertwined. It is not surprising, then, that something like crop pollination by bees has both ecological and economic implications. While beekeeping is unlikely to be the sole source of income for rural people, its significance lies in its valuable contribution as an additional source of food and as a secondary source of income and employment.

Beekeeping promotes rural economic diversification, and has become an activity that, owing to its relatively low physical demands and its low input costs, is increasingly pursued by women (Clauss, 1992). This value is particularly apparent in areas where there is pressure on land resources owing to population growth and the associated subdivision of land. The flexible nature of beekeeping allows the beekeeper to undertake this activity in her spare time. Besides routine maintenance, honey extraction and hive construction, the labour requirement is generally very low.

Beekeeping allows owners to minimize the risks associated with farming by diversifying their sources of income and by providing a high-value product. This is of particular importance in times of economic crisis or drought. Honey and beeswax are both sought-after products that can be stored for considerable lengths of time and do not require specialized facilities for their refining, storage or transport.

At its most basic level, beekeeping may be practised with relatively little financial investment, compared with many cash crops that require the purchase of plants or seedlings, pesticides and fertilizers (Mensing, 1993). A subsistence-level farmer who keeps honeybees does not have to purchase land and can construct hives from locally available material. Bees can be obtained by placing empty, baited hives in trees, with the expectation that these will be occupied by wild swarms. In southern Africa, a particular advantage is that beekeeping can even be carried out in areas with a low agricultural potential, where little or no arable land exists or where rainfall is unreliable. People are able to draw on their traditional knowledge in hive construction, honey collection and the processing of hive products.

Beekeeping is a culturally accepted practice in most of the region since virtually all population groups in southern Africa have some knowledge of honeybees and honey collection. This makes it widely accessible. Increasingly, women household heads have begun to keep bees because of the economic benefits that this promises. In Zimbabwe, both the chairperson and treasurer of the successful Bondolfi Beekeepers' Association are women. In the Kasempa District of Zambia, honey-hunting has traditionally been a male-dominated activity; but in recent years, women household heads have begun to show an interest in beekeeping. Clauss (1992) quotes examples from Zambia where women producers are harvesting up to 500 kilograms of honey each and, as a result, are able to pay for their children's education.

Value-adding activities such as beekeeping can help to address the livelihood challenges that are compounded by a growing population and increasing rural landlessness (Ntenga and Mugongo, 1991). Employment opportunities also exist for those craftsmen in the manufacturing of hives, smokers, gloves and other beekeeping equipment. For example, some participants in a beekeeping project in Mpumalanga Province in South Africa have started earning additional income by manufacturing hives for newcomers to beekeeping (Lundall-Magnuson, 1997).

THREATS TO RURAL BEEKEEPING

Rural beekeeping, like all livelihood activities, faces certain threats. Some of the most apparent ones include the following:

- Inadequate hive management may lead to the spread of bee diseases and pests.
- Vandalism, theft and damage to hives caused by animals and bush fires can be a problem. The inability to enforce spatial boundaries of control on a low-intensity activity of this kind makes the practice vulnerable to abuse by other people.
- Marketing is a challenge given that the product has both traditional and commercial value, and, as such, existing and new marketing structures need to coexist.

- If honey is not marketed or consumed, it will eventually start to ferment.
- Tropical honeybees are known to be very aggressive, which ideally requires beekeepers to take precautions, such as wearing protective equipment and placing colonies away from their dwellings or animals.
- Beekeeping has environmental costs. Bush fires can be started inadvertently when hives are smoked for honey collection. The construction of bark hives can result in the loss of a tree and, sometimes, of valuable bee-foraging plants.

Overexploitation of trees has been noted in parts of Tanzania, where a shortage of traditional materials could oblige some beekeepers to abandon traditional beekeeping altogether (Ntenga and Mugongo, 1991). The members of the Bondolfi Beekeepers' Association in Zimbabwe found that the construction of bark hives has led to the depletion of certain trees. As a result, where bark hives are constructed they now tend to be made from fallen branches (Nel et al, 2000).

ENHANCING THE POTENTIAL OF TRADITIONAL BEEKEEPING

The contribution of traditional beekeeping to rural livelihoods has been recognized by numerous organizations, including the Food and Agriculture Organization (FAO) (Lim, 1994). Through appropriate interventions, attempts have been made to improve the production and sale of honey. Critical in terms of the support provided by organizations, such as the Zambian Forest Service and the Kenyan and Tanzanian governments, was the recognition that traditional bark-stripping techniques used to make hives were environmentally destructive. These traditional hives are inefficient in terms of honey yield and reuse is problematic.

To address this problem, a modification to traditional hive construction techniques has been introduced through the borrowing of ideas from Kenya and other countries. The principles that have been applied have built on the reality first identified in Kenya – namely, that 'with beekeeping, as with other agricultural inputs, the question...is not one of seeking new knowledge only, but rather one of improving and implementing what exists already' (Kigatiira, 1976). The adapted hive design known as the Kenyan Top Bar Hive is appropriate for use by most rural beekeepers. It consists of a wooden box covered by a series of removable wooden slats on which the honeycombs are built by the bees. Promotion of these hives and support for the marketing of honey has been the key form of intervention pursued in terms of beekeeping since the 1970s in southern Africa (Ntenga and Mugongo, 1991; Clauss, 1992).

Critical to the success of such endeavours has been the recognition that new technologies should not be imposed upon rural communities. Instead, only limited and appropriate changes drawing upon and using local resources, skills and knowledge should be used to promote more efficient beekeeping. In so doing, indigenous ownership and control are retained. Furthermore, and in common with many other rural development initiatives, the 'successful development of...beekeeping often requires an intimate understanding of the society within which it is to take place – [and] of its systems of values' (Swanson, 1976). While such support mechanisms are clearly having an impact, they should, wherever possible, be grafted on to what already exists to avoid the risk of destabilizing and marginalizing participants and to draw optimally on traditional knowledge and institutional structures.

Some of the most innovative programmes designed to offer guidance, training and improvements to beekeepers have been initiated by the Deutsche Gesellschaft für Technische Zusammenarbeit (GTZ) in Zambia, Malawi and Mozambique (Mensing, 1993). In northern Malawi, GTZ has assisted with setting up nearly 100 beekeeping clubs. Advice on improvements to hives, new techniques and assistance with the marketing of honey has increased honey production and associated income by as much as 500 per cent (Mensing, 1993). Equipment has often been provided in return for a portion of the yields from the hives over the first three years (Mensing, 1993). The new hives that were introduced have the potential to increase honey yields from 6 kilograms to 40 kilograms per annum. In addition, annual production in the GTZ project areas has increased from 1.4 tonnes during 1990 to 1991 to 5.5 tonnes during 1992 to 1993, an increase which is largely attributable to the project intervention. Evidence of improved lifestyles resulting from adaptations to traditional beekeeping can be found in the Nhkalanga beekeeping club in the village of Karonga in northern Malawi where income derived from honey sales has increased fivefold in the space of just five years (Mensing, 1993).

An interesting initiative in Zimbabwe – where traditional beekeeping was enhanced through limited, but appropriate, external support – is to be found in the Bondolfi area. The economic hardship experienced in the area during the early 1990s prompted a local church, with the aid of a United Nations programme, to attempt to enhance honey production and marketing. Support took the form of training and technical assistance with the setting up of local enterprises to make improved hives and honey-collecting equipment. Assistance was also provided with the marketing of honey (Nel et al, 2000). Beekeepers now support nearly 7 per cent of households in the area and derive an income nearly 20 times higher than the standard Zimbabwe rural income.

CONCLUSION

In conclusion, it is apparent that both traditional beekeeping and the environmentally and culturally appropriate enhancements that have been introduced have minimal negative ecological impact. Beekeeping has an important role to play in addressing issues of rural poverty, in building rural self-reliance and in diversifying income sources in order to better enable communities to cope with periods of climatic and economic uncertainty (Gooneratne and Mbilinyi, 1992). Moreover, beekeeping can enhance the position and income of women. Beekeeping relies upon indigenous skills and interests, uses locally available resources and has a positive effect on other forms of farming through the increased pollination of cultivated crops.

External and donor agencies, through appropriate technology and carefully targeted support, can clearly help to ensure community and ecological sustainability. As a source of food and income or through the vital role that it plays in plant pollination, and as an indicator of environmental health, beekeeping is an important component of community-based natural resource use and management.

REFERENCES

Clauss, B (1992) *Bees and Beekeeping in the North Western Province of Zambia.* Forestry Department, Ndola

Gooneratne, W and Mbilinyi, M (eds) (1992) *Reviving Local Self-Reliance: People's Responses to Economic Crisis in Eastern and Southern Africa.* United Nations Centre for Regional Development, Nagoya

Kigatiira, K (1976) 'Beekeeping Development Programmes in Kenya', in Crane, E (ed) *Apiculture in Tropical Climates.* International Bee Research Association, London, pp143–146

Kihwele, D (1989) 'The African Honeybees and their potential for commercial beekeeping', in Crane, E (ed) *Proceedings of the Fourth International Conference on Apiculture in Tropical Climates.* International Bee Research Association, London, pp182–188

Lim, J (1994) 'Beekeeping development activities supported by the Food and Agriculture Organization of the United Nations', in *Proceedings of the Fifth International Conference on Apiculture in Tropical Climates.* International Bee Research Association, Cardiff, pp145–148

Lundall-Magnuson, E (1997) 'Developmental beekeeping', *Plant Protection News* 47: 5–6, Plant Protection Research Institute, Pretoria

Mensing, F (1993) *Beekeeping in Malawi: New Chances for Smallholders.* Deutsche Gesellschaft für Technische Zusammenarbeit (GTZ), Eschborn

Nel, E, Illgner, P, Wilkins, K and Robertson, M (2000) 'Rural self-reliance in Bondolfi, Zimbabwe: The role of beekeeping', *The Geographical Journal* 166(1): 26–34

Ntenga, G and Mugongo, B (1991) *Honey Hunters and Beekeepers: A Study of Traditional Beekeeping in Babati District, Tanzania.* Swedish University of Agricultural Sciences, Uppsala

Quong, A (1993) *The Implications for Traditional Beekeeping in Tabora Region, Tanzania for Miombo Woodland Conservation.* School of International Training, Dar es Salaam

Rhodes University, Fort Cox and Unitra (2001) *A Monitoring System for Community Forestry: Combining Scientific and Local Knowledge in the Eastern Cape.* Department of Water Affairs and Forestry (DWAF) Research Report RU 01/100, Environmental Science Programme, Rhodes University, Grahamstown

Swanson, R (1976) 'The case for beekeeping development in west Africa', in Crane, E (ed) *Apiculture in Tropical Climates.* International Bee Research Association, London, pp191–197

Chapter 8

Everyday resources are valuable enough for community-based natural resource management programme support: Evidence from South Africa

SHEONA SHACKLETON AND CHARLIE SHACKLETON

INTRODUCTION

The term non-timber forest products (NTFPs) is one with which many of us are familiar, although coined only a decade or so ago. It was introduced to draw attention to the fact that indigenous forests and woodlands produce a range of important natural products besides merchantable timber. The concept of the 'hidden harvest' was similarly used to highlight the importance of non-agricultural resources for rural households. Many NTFPs are key to rural dwellers' livelihoods and have considerable commercial potential. It is this potential of NTFPs as a source of income for rural communities and as an incentive for natural resource management and conservation that has been researched and developed in many countries. Access to, and use of, such resources is frequently the foundation for formal community-based natural resource management (CBNRM) or 'people and parks' programmes in South and southern Africa.

While it is apparent that the increasingly common use of the concept of NTFPs has done much to raise the profile of a complex of natural resource products and uses that previously received little recognition or support, we argue that there is a group of NTFPs that continues to be neglected in both policy and practice. These are the ordinary resources depended upon by millions of households to meet their daily domestic requirements. The importance of these rather inconspicuous and generally unremarkable 'everyday' resources for rural welfare is seldom appreciated, and their value and role in society is consistently underestimated by resource managers, conservation officers, decision-makers and rural institutions. One reason for this is that, taken individually, many of these resources appear relatively insignificant and of low value, with only a few entering formal markets (although they may be traded within communities). Indeed, it is only when the entire portfolio of resources and their intensity of use is considered that it is possible to build a meaningful picture of their considerable contribution to the household, local and national economies.

This chapter aims to build this picture by drawing primarily upon case studies from South Africa, although acknowledging the excellent work done in neighbouring countries, especially Zimbabwe, Botswana and Namibia. In addition, we explore why this sector has been neglected by policy-makers and practitioners. We provide arguments as to why CBNRM programmes should take greater cognizance of everyday resources and seek ways to assist users to better manage these resources for use by future generations.

THE ESSENTIAL NATURE OF EVERYDAY RESOURCES FOR RURAL LIVELIHOODS

A number of recent studies in southern Africa have highlighted just how essential everyday resources are for the livelihood security of rural dwellers (Cavendish, 1999; Dovie, 2001; Shackleton et al, 2001; 2002). Fuelwood, wild foods, medicines, honey, building and fencing wood, and materials for household implements and tools are all used on a regular basis by a majority of households. Many of these NTFPs also contribute to other livelihood sectors (for example, tools for agriculture, fencing, fodder and medicines for livestock, and mulch for crops). Some are exchanged for purchased goods or traded in local markets for cash (see Figure 8.1). Children consume wild foods on a frequent basis as they play, collect water or herd livestock in the surrounding rangelands, obtaining much needed protein and vitamins. Many households have limited access to substitutes for locally procured products, and even where such products are available, they may be unaffordable. This increases dependency on locally available natural resources. A number of products also have a role to play in tradition and culture (for example, consumption of wild foods; the tradition of sitting around an open fire; use of local materials in traditional building styles; and maintenance of cattle *kraals* by Xhosa men even when they do not possess livestock). Other resources have less tangible, more spiritual significance and may be used in rituals, such as burial and initiation ceremonies and healing rites (for instance, certain plants may be scattered around a home to protect it from witchcraft or other harmful influences).

In addition to these benefits, recent research has revealed that poorer households and those headed by women are often more dependent upon everyday resources than more well-off households or those headed by men (Cavendish, 1999). This points to an important social welfare function

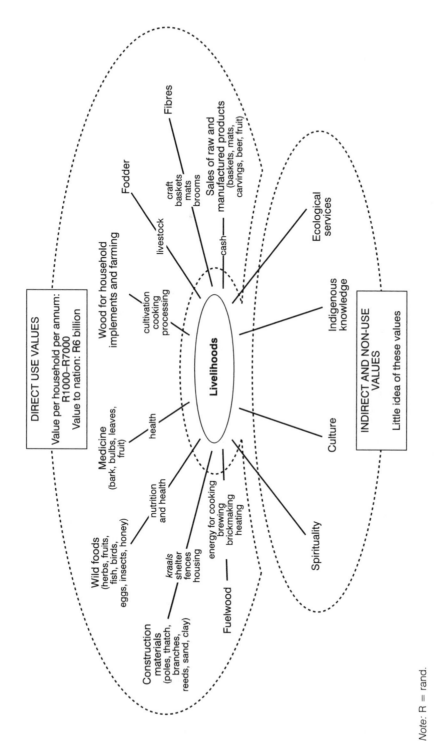

Figure 8.1 *Contribution of woodland products to rural livelihoods*

Note: R = rand.

associated with NTFPs that is not often recognized. Indeed, having access to a diversity of NTFPs provides opportunities for livelihood diversification and helps to reduce risk and vulnerability. In extraordinary circumstances, the natural resource base also often forms a 'safety net of last resort' for households experiencing severe economic difficulties, a death in the family or the loss of a job. During a survey in the Kat River area of the Eastern Cape, one woman mentioned that she had moved to the area 'to struggle better for life' after losing her job in the nearby town of Fort Beaufort.

Everyday resources are procured primarily from communal lands and are typically common pool resources (CPRs). In the past, many rural communities would have managed these resources through their traditional leadership, with chiefs being recognized as the custodians of the resource base. Customs, beliefs, norms and regulations all contributed to controlling the use of important species. Today, however, many of these customary management systems have come under severe pressure. Population growth, increasing commercialization, widely differentiated communities with varying incentives to manage resources and the erosion of the authority of hereditary leaders – through both their co-option by colonial/apartheid regimes and the decentralization policies of subsequent democratic governments – have resulted in a situation akin to 'open access' in many areas. The institutional gap formed in this process has not been adequately filled by alternative institutions and, as a result, natural resource use is being pushed beyond sustainable limits in many parts of the region.

Rural households typically use several different types of natural resources to meet their daily needs for food, fuel, shelter, and medicine (see Box 8.1). The range and number of NTFPs that are drawn upon differ between households and communities in response to a myriad of local and external contextual factors, including resource endowment, availability of substitutes, availability of labour to collect, local prices, proximity to urban centres, education and disposable income. Studies from South Africa that report on complete inventories of NTFPs used per household reveal that the most commonly used products are wild spinaches, fuelwood, wooden utensils, grass brooms, edible fruits and twig brooms – typical everyday resources (Shackleton et al, 2001). All of these resources were used by 85 per cent or more of the households surveyed. More than half of households also made use of all or some of the following: edible insects, wood for fences or *kraals*, bushmeat, wild honey and reeds for weaving. It is probable that the proportion admitting to the use of bushmeat and medicinal plants has been under-recorded due to people's fear of religious or legal sanction in some areas.

THE ECONOMIC VALUE OF EVERYDAY RESOURCES: RESULTS FROM CASE STUDIES

Over the past three years, 12 different resource valuation studies, covering approximately 800 households, have been conducted across the woodland regions of South Africa from the Northern Province to KwaZulu-Natal and the Eastern Cape (Shackleton and Shackleton, in press). In this section we draw on these studies to demonstrate the significant value of everyday resources to rural communities in South Africa.

Annual direct-use value to households

Gross direct-use values are determined as the product of the amount of a resource used and the local, or farm-gate, price. Where prices are not available locally, prices at the closest point to the target community or replacement values are used. The range in gross annual direct-use values of everyday resources averaged across the studies is large, ranging from less than US$100 per household per year, to over US$700. This is a reflection of differences in both the quantities consumed and the unit prices. The range in unit price of commonly used resources was often larger than that of the quantities consumed, and thus price had a significant influence on the relative direct-use values. The mean gross direct-use value across the 12 South African studies is almost US$450 per household per year (1 rand = US$0.13). This is higher than comparable figures from Zimbabwe. It is also markedly greater than incomes derived from most formal CBNRM schemes based on high-value species (typically wildlife), or from 'people and parks' projects. For example, annual dividends per household through Zimbabwe's renowned Communal Areas Management Programme for Indigenous Resources (CAMPFIRE) are less than US$10. Similarly, the annual value of resources, such as thatch or wood, which rural people are permitted to harvest in protected areas in KwaZulu-Natal and the Eastern Cape, is typically less than US$10 to US$40 (Roe et al, 2000).

Most of the current resource valuation data reflect gross annual values, since there is limited information available on costs. But in most situations, capital input costs are low with tools, which have a long lifespan, shared across more than one livelihood sector. Other inputs include time and, in some instances, transport.

It is debatable whether or not the time factor, representing an opportunity cost of labour, should be deducted in areas of high unemployment (locally and regionally) where very low daily wages are paid for the few scarce jobs. In any event, opportunity costs of labour across the studies ranged between 9 per cent and 61 per cent of gross value. In fact, it is not unusual for the deduction of opportunity costs of labour to result in negative values, indicating that the time spent harvesting resources is potentially worth more than the value of the supposed benefits obtained. This suggests that either rural households are not economically rational in how they exploit everyday resources, or that the application of conventional resource economic methods is inappropriate in rural settings with poorly developed markets.

Alternatively, it could indicate that the total benefits accruing from the use of everyday NTFPs have not been adequately accounted for. For example, the social and cultural benefits of harvesting activities with relatives and neighbours in terms of kinship ties also need to be taken into account. Why else would women in the Bushbuckridge lowveld be prepared to spend the entire day at the roadside selling marula beer during season, earning as little as US$0.50 to US$1.00? When this question was put to them, they replied that this was for 'bread and chicken feet' that they could not otherwise have afforded. Similarly, an old man at Pikoli in the Peddie District, Eastern Cape, admitted to only receiving 30 rand for a pile of sneezewood poles that took him three days to collect. When asked why he was willing to accept so little, he said: 'There is no work in this place [and] I'm still five years from my pension' (Christo Fabricius, pers comm).

The gender implications of opportunity cost calculations also require examination. It is common in the rural areas of southern Africa for men to become migrant workers in regional and national urban centres. Women typically remain at home to mind the children and the rural homestead. For these women, the opportunity to engage in other employment is limited, because such employment is rarely available within the immediate vicinity and compatible with household responsibilities. Another factor could be that households often simply do not have the cash to purchase alternatives to resources that they can collect 'free', or they have more important uses for this cash. Under such circumstances, natural resource harvesting appears to be a rational option.

Value to the national economy

Scaling-up from the household to national level is fraught with difficulties; but despite the pitfalls, it is useful to illustrate the potential magnitude of the value of everyday resources to the country as a whole. This would be indicative of the potential costs if such resources were no longer available. With 2.4 million rural households, 76 per cent of which reside in woodland areas, and a mean gross annual direct-use value of nearly US$450 per household, the gross direct-use value of woodland resources to the economy is in the region of US$800 million per annum. This is an order of magnitude greater than the tourism income derived from South Africa's national parks.

This economic value of everyday resources not only represents a cash saving for rural communities, but also a saving to national expenditure. The various roles of these resources in energy provision, housing, health care and social security helps to alleviate some of the costs that the government would incur in providing these services. Continued overharvesting or loss of resources through land transformation means that the local or national economy would have to supply goods and services somewhere in the region of US$800 million annually, at current monetary values. Hence, the need to address the sustainable management of everyday resources is not simply an environmental concern and responsibility, but the responsibility of a far wider section of society and government.

Value relative to other livelihood sources

Relatively few studies have considered the financial value of everyday resources within the total livelihoods of rural households. Moreover, this value differs within and between communities, in relation to numerous factors, such as availability of employment, education levels, gender, wealth status and biophysical setting. Cavendish (1999) found that wild resources contributed, on average, 40 per cent of total household income for poorer households, but closer to 29 per cent for wealthy households. Such resources also provided proportionally more cash income to poor households (20 per cent of total) than better-off households (5 per cent). Similarly, Dovie (2001) found that the value contributed by woodland NTFPs to households decreased as the amount of income from formal sources increased. In this case, the mean income share by NTFPs was 28 per cent across all households.

NEGLECT OF EVERYDAY RESOURCES: BLINKERED OFFICIALS AND DEVELOPMENT WORKERS

Given the situation set out above, the question needs to be asked: why are these resources not being given the attention they deserve and their value recognized? We explore this from the perspectives of those concerned primarily with CBNRM and those working in the rural development sector.

The rural development perspective

Sectoral foci and a lack of multidisciplinary research are two factors that have obscured the linkages between rural development, livelihoods and the natural resource base. The extensive research on the use of indigenous resources in southern Africa has been undertaken primarily by natural scientists outside of the mainstream rural development debates. Social scientists, on the other hand, have been more concerned with factors relating to migrancy, farming livelihoods and formal earnings than the contribution of locally available natural resources to household income and livelihood (Cavendish, 1999). Until recently, most writings on rural livelihoods in South Africa made only passing mention of woodland and forest resources (for example, Lipton et al, 1996). In short, there has been a lack of a holistic approach that recognizes and embraces the full diversity, complexity and multidimensional nature of rural livelihoods.

In many cases, development workers have continued to focus on traditional rural development sectors, such as service delivery, livestock production and agriculture, with the promotion of small-scale commercial farmers particularly receiving attention. Social forestry interventions have concentrated on tree planting (invariably exotics) with individuals and small groups rather than the management of communal lands – the primary source of everyday resources. Certainly, in terms of visible impact, it is easier to plant trees than to amend policies, build local capacity and create incentives, especially given the complexity that exists on the ground. Land reform in South Africa has tended to focus on administrative aspects of land transfer and commercially oriented business plans, with little attention to the sustainable management of useful resources on the newly acquired land. Thus, in South Africa in particular, the overwhelming impression, to date, is that the role of everyday resources has been largely overlooked by those involved with rural welfare and development. Furthermore, role players in this sphere still tend to see resource management issues as the responsibility of the conservation rather than the development sector. This is clearly evidenced in the complete neglect of indigenous resources as a rural development concern in South Africa's new rural development strategy.

The natural resource management perspective

Other chapters in this book reveal that in southern Africa the policy emphasis for CBNRM has been on wild game (for example, Zimbabwe, Namibia and Botswana). There are various ways in which to interpret this. Some might argue that this is the resource with the greatest potential for generating revenue (Boyd, 2001); but this approach fails to consider the dividends relative to the value of everyday resources to households. Others feel that the situation is a reflection of the high-profile nature of wildlife, and its value to stakeholders other than the affected rural communities, especially international animal welfare organizations and conservation non-governmental organizations (NGOs). It is also perceived that the driving agenda for CBNRM is usually the promotion of biodiversity conservation rather than rural livelihoods. This factor is particularly significant. Timber and other financially valuable forest resources also retain high focus in some southern African countries – for example, in Mozambique (Boyd, 2001).

This policy emphasis on wild resources of national or international value has meant that scant attention has been paid to those resources with high local value and significance for the rural poor. This is of particular concern in South Africa where the densely populated communal areas lack the game and timber resources found elsewhere in the region. In these areas, there is little evidence of commitment by government to improving the management of everyday communal resources. What exists tends to be piecemeal and scattered (for example, selected 'Landcare' projects and catchment management projects) or driven through NGOs with donor support.

If CBNRM aims to target the rural poor, then it is imperative that this policy bias is addressed and greater attention is paid to the management of resources upon which people's livelihoods depend. Their value and importance demonstrate that such investment by government and donors makes economic and social sense, as well as conservation sense in the long run. Decision-makers can no longer use a lack of understanding of the importance of wild resources for direct household provisioning as an excuse for inaction.

EVERYDAY RESOURCES AND SUSTAINABLE MANAGEMENT: THE WAY FORWARD

Given the considerable importance of everyday resources to the majority of rural households, it is crucial that the state develops policies and strategies to address the management of these resources in order to enhance sustainable development and poverty alleviation in the rural areas of southern Africa. This requires shifts in both CBNRM and rural development approaches to accommodate this new emphasis. Some of these shifts, both conceptual and practical, are discussed below.

Firstly, resource management interventions need to focus on the role of all natural resources in local livelihoods, both for direct provisioning and income – not just high-value or flagship resources. The aim of CBNRM should thus be to contribute to enhanced management of complete ecosystems and not just individual species or species guilds (this is not incompatible with the conservation agenda). Such an approach will help to ensure that the CBNRM agenda is led by local priorities, rather than conservationist paradigms and concerns. Conservation will follow. Furthermore, if CBNRM initiatives paid more attention to gender equity issues, then everyday resources, which are primarily the domain of women, may receive more attention. Certainly, women need to begin to have greater say in natural resource management decisions.

Secondly, in some countries – for example, South Africa – there needs to be a more substantive move away from investment in state-owned protected areas towards investment in the communal areas. Communal areas have plainly not received the same attention and, in South Africa, continue to be neglected. These areas are the primary source of everyday resources.

Thirdly, greater synergy with the agricultural and rural development sectors is required to move towards a paradigm of land care, support for diverse and complementary livelihood activities and sustainable development. The need for the management of everyday resources must be embraced by the state through allocation of appropriate resources and the provision of competent extension services to match those provided for arable agriculture and animal husbandry.

Lastly, the value of everyday resources and the importance of conserving them – for example, in livelihoods and ecosystem functioning – should be shared with resource users themselves. Rural people need to understand what the costs will be to them should resources continue to degrade. It is essential that users take responsibility for the management of these resources because they recognize that they are important to them in their lives and not because they may deliver any cash rewards (in contrast to many other CBNRM initiatives). Some observers argue from a purely economic perspective that the returns may be too low and the transaction costs too high for this to happen. But we feel that the importance of non-use values and the supposed economic irrationalities in the use of labour and resources must be considered more rigorously, rather than being dismissed as not fitting with conventional wisdom and economic theory. Our experience is that there are many concerned rural people who, for many reasons, do not want to see their resources disappear. Given this sentiment and the right type of support, it should be possible to institute some system of natural resource management.

However, we recognize that there is no easy way forward. Systems for managing the whole spectrum of natural resources within communal areas

---

**BOX 8.1 THE STORY OF EVERYDAY RESOURCES IN AN
ORDINARY RURAL LIFE**

Every morning Lettie Mathebula wakes up at 5:00 am to prepare the morning porridge for her family of four. She cooks on an open fire using fuelwood that she collects twice per week. She uses, on average, 290 kilograms of wood per month or 3.4 tonnes over the year. If she had to buy this it would cost her just over US$100, or approximately $0.30 per day. She is concerned about dwindling supplies as she must walk further and further to find suitable slow-burning wood. It takes her approximately ten hours per week to collect wood. She knows that she would battle to afford electricity or paraffin, or to purchase wood from a vendor.

At 7:00 am the children leave for school, stopping to pick handfuls of fruit from the large sour plum (*Ximenia caffra*) bush by the gate to eat on the way. Mrs Mathebula then releases the goats and cattle from their *kraals* for the herder to take to the communal lands. She notices a gap in the thorn fence of the goat *kraal* and makes a mental note to collect some branches later in the day. Her *kraals* have about three cubic metres of wood in them, and she replaces about 185 poles and branches every year. Since Mrs Mathebula is widowed, she usually buys the large poles from her neighbour at a cost of US$0.80 per pole.

The next task is to prepare the *morogo* (wild spinaches), collected the night before, for lunch. Lettie's family is lucky if they eat meat once per month. Most of their meals consist of *pap* (maize porridge) and *morogo* and cultivated vegetables such as tomatoes, ground nuts, beans and cabbage. During summer they eat *morogo* twice per day, consuming approximately 58 kilograms over the year. The annual market value of this is about US$190. It is marula season, and time to make marula beer. Mrs Mathebula's daughters collected an 80 kilogram sack of fruit the evening before. Although the family doesn't drink beer, Mrs Mathebula always makes some and invites her neighbours around to share it. As a single mother, she needs to maintain good relations with her neighbours because she often requires favours from them. Sometimes she sells the beer in the local town. Once the beer is fermenting, she goes out to collect her fencing material and along the way procures some medicine for her son who has a stomach-ache. She regularly self-medicates with some of the more popular herbal medicines. On returning, Mrs Mathebula sets to work on the reed mat she is making. She sells two or three of these a month at the monthly pension markets or to neighbours who buy them as wedding gifts. She earns US$5 to US$10 per mat depending upon the size and degree of decoration. Towards early evening, Mrs Mathebula again lights her fire and cooks the dinner, pap with wild spinach relish and peanuts.

---

will be complex, far more so than developing strategies for the joint management of similar resources on state land. Some scholars are, indeed, sceptical of the possibility of a community-based approach at all, given the pressures and complexities that exist in communal systems today (Ainslie, 1999; Campbell et al, 2001). This complexity derives from a host of factors, including the following:

- Traditional management systems for everyday NTFPs have all but broken down and communities have become accustomed to free use of these resources.
- Institutional confusion and competition exists regarding who is or should be responsible for this resource manager role. Although the questionable legitimacy and poor downward accountability of many of the existing local institutions is problematic, ordinary people in rural communities, local government, traditional leaders or new combinations of these must all find a role in resource management.
- The general absence of an identifiable collective entity that one might call a 'community' is a challenge. Communities are highly differentiated along social, economic and political lines, with different households and individuals having widely varying interests and incentives for resource management.
- Intense competition exists for the use of both resources and land by diverse groups or specific individuals within, or even outside of, communities.
- The lack of clarity regarding tenure rights in communal areas is a major stumbling block and indicates the lack of government commitment to these areas.
- The scale of support, facilitation and capacity-building needed is high; consequently, resources are required.
- There is a high and increasing demand for everyday resources, and the inability of the poor to substantially curtail use is problematic.

There are, thus, considerable challenges ahead for those providing CBNRM support for everyday resources (CIFOR, 2000). However, we should not allow complexity to stall progress because if action is not taken soon, some of the poorest people in South Africa and the region will be further impoverished and their means of livelihood will be threatened as resources continue to decline.

REFERENCES

Ainslie, A (1999) 'When "community" is not enough: Managing common property natural resources in rural South Africa', *Development Southern Africa* 16(3): 375–401

Boyd, C with Jones, B T B (Botswana and Namibia), Anstey, S (Mozambique), Shackleton, S and Fabricius, C (South Africa) (2001) 'Wild resource theme paper', SLSA Working Paper 5. Sustainable Livelihoods in Southern Africa: Institutions, governance and policy processes, www.ids.ac.uk/ids/env/PDFs/SLSA5

Campbell, B, de Jong, W, Luckert, M, Madondo, A, Matose, F, Nemarundwe, N and Sithole, B (2001) 'Challenges to proponents of common pool resource systems: Despairing voices from the social forests of Zimbabwe', *World Development* 29(4): 589–600

Cavendish, W (1999) 'Empirical regularities in the poverty–environment relationship of African rural households', Working Paper WPS 99-21. Centre for the Study of African Economics, University of Oxford

CIFOR (2000) *Managing Common Property Resources in Catchments: Are There Any Ways Forward?* Policy Brief. Centre for International Forestry Research (CIFOR), Bogor

Dovie, B (2001) *Woodland Resource Utilisation, Valuation and Rural Livelihoods in the Lowveld, South Africa.* MSc thesis, University of the Witwatersrand, Johannesburg

Lipton, M, Ellis, F and Lipton, M (eds) (1996) *Land, Labour and Livelihoods in Rural South Africa. Volume Two: KwaZulu-Natal and Northern Province.* Indicator Press, Durban

Roe, D, Mayers, J, Greig-Gran, M, Kothari, A, Fabricius, C and Hughes, R (2000) *Evaluating Eden: Exploring the Myths and Realities of Community-Based Wildlife Management.* International Institute for Environment and Development, London

Shackleton, C and Shackleton, S (in press) 'Use of wild resources for direct household provisioning', in Laws, M, Healy, H and Shackleton, C (eds) *Use and Value of Forest and Woodland Resources in South Africa.* University of Natal Press, Pietermaritzburg

Shackleton, C, Shackleton, S and Cousins, B (2001) 'The role of land-based strategies in rural livelihoods: The contribution of arable production, animal husbandry and natural resource harvesting in communal areas in South Africa', *Development Southern Africa* 18(5): 581–604

Shackleton, S, Shackleton, C, Netshiluvhi, T, Geach, B and Balance, A (2002) 'Use patterns and values of savanna resources in three rural villages in South Africa', *Economic Botany* 56(2): 130–146

Chapter 9

Community-based natural resource management in the Okavango Delta

LESLEY BOGGS

INTRODUCTION

The Botswana community-based natural resource management (CBNRM) programme has often been regarded as one of the most successful and most progressive of its kind in the region. It is based on a model in which the management of key natural resources undergoes devolution of power from state to local communities. As it is a conservation-based *development programme*, the economic component is paramount. A monetary infusion from natural resources, which are valued on their income-earning potential, is aimed at encouraging communities to diversify local economic activities, increase the value of natural resources and produce long-term community-based economic models.

It is anticipated that by returning the authority over wildlife and natural resources to rural communities and benefits derivable from them, communities will regain the incentive toward sustainable management of the resources (Government of Botswana, 1997). Botswana's CBNRM programme differs from other regional programmes, such as Zimbabwe's Communal Areas Management Programme for Indigenous Resources (CAMPFIRE) and Zambia's Administrative Management Design for Game Management Areas (ADMADE), primarily in that most revenue is returned to the community. In Zimbabwe and Zambia, on the other hand, most funds end up being controlled by the state (Taylor, 2000).

Although the CBNRM programme has made many advances, and may still become the landmark for other programmes in the region, it is not yet there. This chapter begins with a brief background of CBNRM in Botswana. It follows this with a review of two case studies. Questions are raised about the assumption that benefits from wildlife equate to change and the assertion is made that flaws in the original theoretical framework are central to contemporary CBNRM problems. The chapter concludes with a discussion of the key issues and lessons emerging from these case studies for CBNRM practices more generally.

BACKGROUND TO CBNRM IN BOTSWANA

Starting in the late 19th century, a number of events have occurred in the Okavango Delta with respect to natural resources and the human uses of them that have, ultimately, given rise to the current CBNRM programme. These events or trends (Bell, 1997) can be summarized as follows:

- Decreasing annual rainfall has reduced the annual regular seasonal flooding area of the Okavango Delta (McCarthy et al, 1986–1994).
- A progressive recovery of the elephant population (following its decimation during the late 19th century) has led to increasing conflicts with people.
- The designation, after independence in 1966, of 18 per cent of the land for national parks and game reserves has involved changing the management jurisdiction to the central government, the eviction of many rural inhabitants, and reduced legal access to wildlife.
- The widespread regulation of hunting stripped many rural dwellers of their special game licences and what most Batswana considered to be their birthright.
- A government-sponsored livestock development programme, including a massive investment in boreholes, encouraged the commercial and rural cattle industry to expand northward.
- Since the 1950s, a network of veterinary cordon fences, designed to separate wildlife from cattle, were constructed. These fences contributed to the collapse of migratory wildlife populations of the Kalahari, although some argue that the fences now protect wildlife by maintaining cattle-free areas within the Okavango Delta.

Since the early 1970s, the country has been transforming from poor to rich, primarily as a result of the exploitation of diamonds and a European Union-subsidized commercial cattle industry. Under the subsequent rural development scheme, the Okavango region benefited from the increase in national wealth. Borehole construction and cattle subsidies brought livestock owners to the region. A tarred road from Francistown provided easy access to the natural resources of the Okavango. New communications infrastructure linked the central delta town of Maun, schools and clinics were built, and a new market economy replaced the subsistence lifestyles of many local inhabitants. Coincident with this, a flourishing hunting and photographic safari tourism industry developed. The population of the once frontier town of Maun grew from 14,925 during the late 1970s to 26,569 during the late 1980s (Okavango

Community Consultants, 1995). By 2000, Maun had become a bustling administrative hub and home to approximately 40,000 people.

During the late 1980s, the threat to the region was characterized by declines in the wildlife populations and increased competition from other forms of land use – most importantly, livestock husbandry. Commissioned anthropological research during this time demonstrated pronounced and widespread utilitarian attitudes toward wildlife and perceptions that individuals were powerless against nature (Mordi, 1991). Research also revealed strong antagonistic feelings among rural people who complained that new government hunting regulations made people feel as though they no longer had direct ties to wildlife. The 1990 Land-Use Plan was the impetus for the launching of the United States Agency for International Development (USAID)-supported Natural Resources Management Project (NRMP), while the Wildlife Conservation and National Parks Act of 1992 gave rise to the Botswana CBNRM programme.

THE NATURAL RESOURCES MANAGEMENT PROJECT (NRMP)

The goals of the NRMP were to:

- increase rural economic activity through natural resource management; and
- improve attitudes on the part of the communities towards wildlife through associating conservation with increased incomes, thereby improving both the status of wildlife and conservation (Rihoy, 1995).

The early mandate of the CBNRM programme was to 'provide the legal, institutional and economic frameworks for communities to become co-managers of wildlife resources and possibly other resources' (Government of Botswana, 1997).

The founding assumption, therefore, of CBNRM in Botswana is that financial benefit derived from wildlife will accrue directly to the community members and will change attitudes and improve wildlife management practices.

Between 1990 and 1997, the programme was funded by USAID and managed jointly by USAID and the Botswana Department of Wildlife and National Parks (DWNP). Between 1990 and 1993, when the CBNRM programme was designed, the NRMP team was staffed primarily by natural scientists and economists.

BOTSWANA'S CBNRM CONCEPT

Between 1993 and 2002, community management areas (CMAs) were assigned across the country within previously designated wildlife management areas (WMAs). All were zoned as multiple-use areas, specifically allocated for consumptive and non-consumptive wildlife and natural resource utilization. An area-specific management plan was produced for each CMA (Okavango Community Consultants, 1995). All of these CMAs were granted between 1993 and 2002.

Once allocated, the first step was to identify the recipient community. Consultations were undertaken and, typically, the existing residents (or closest neighbours outside the area) became 'the community'. Specific guidelines were established whereby the community was required to elect a representative community council or board, submit a constitution, establish a 'representative and accountable legal entity' (RALE), and register this as a 'trust' or community-based organization (CBO). Once completed, the community would apply to DWNP for a wildlife-hunting quota that would be held and managed by the RALE.

Once registered, the RALE was also given a 'header lease' on the CMA by the land board. A further process of entering into a joint venture agreement (JVA) with commercial operators for consumptive and non-consumptive resource use was strongly encouraged. Under this strategy, communities would enter into a 15-year lease with an existing safari operator to manage the photographic or hunting operation. This would enable immediate revenue generation, capacity-building and transfer of skills to the local community. It was anticipated that in 15 years, the communities would own and operate successful companies.

Logistically, companies would tender for leases, and a government-based technical committee would review and present the community with the shortlist of acceptable partners from which to choose. Leases were theoretically for 15 years, but were broken down into contracts of 1, 1, 3, 5 and 5 years, with provision made for probationary reviews between these discrete periods. The purpose of this was to protect inexperienced communities from a long-term relationship with an unsuitable operator, or to provide an opportunity for change pending unforeseen conflicts.

As predicted, it has been difficult to create a single programme that adequately accommodates the diversity among the communities involved. Communities across Botswana vary dramatically in numerous ways, which include ethnic background; historical land-use practices (such as hunter-gatherers, agriculturists and pastoralists); age of the community itself; and consequent cohesion of members; size (some are small single communities numbering as few as 300 individuals; others incorporate several communities numbering in the thousands); wildlife populations resident in the area; tenure on the land; historical ties to the land they currently lived on; attachment to the cattle industry; cultural beliefs and spiritual systems regarding their interaction with wildlife; and, finally, their influence by, and acceptance of, a market economy.

CASE STUDIES

As it is impossible to discuss all manifestations of the variations listed above, the following is a brief case study of two CMAs that demonstrate some of the key critical issues facing CBNRM in Botswana today.

Sankuyo – Ngamiland Area 34

Sankuyo village is primarily a Bayei community of about 350 residents. The village was founded through the government villagization programme during the 1970s. Prior to this, families were predominately agro-pastoralists, although some subsistence hunting and gathering did take place. Before the introduction of CBNRM, there was no means of formal employment in the village and residents either left to find work or subsisted through cottage industry, agriculture or state-funded welfare programmes. The community was awarded approximately 860 square kilometres called Ngamiland Area 34 (or NG34) in March 1996 (Government of Botswana, 1991, p80).

The area, situated on the south-eastern terminus of the Okavango Delta, is dry mixed scrub and broken woodland. Traditionally, utilized natural resources include wildlife, thatch grass and reeds. Wildlife populations in the area have been relatively healthy, although regular surveys conducted between 1989 and 2001 by the Botswana Wild Dog Research Project show a significant decline in impala densities for the period of 1998 to 2001. Figures between 1990 and 1998 consistently showed the impala population to be 16.2 per square kilometre. Between 1998 and 2001, however, the population declined to an estimated 5.2 per square kilometre (McNutt, 2001). This 65 per cent decrease may be an important figure as impala represent the most numerous herbivore in this area. They are a predominant prey species for all large predators, and are historically a primary meat animal for local human off-take.

Following the advice of the NRMP team, and a decision to capitalize on benefits, Sankuyo opted to immediately enter into a joint venture agreement. The first year went well, with few conflicts within the community and between the community and the joint venture partner. The second year, however, was difficult. The Sankuyo community lost confidence in their council due to allegations of theft and corruption and elected a new council. Unequal distribution of power and benefits resulted in leadership struggles and the formation of factions within the community. In addition, the relationship between the photographic safari operator and staff was not good. The USAID-funded project was coming to an end, and project managers were eager to build as much capacity within the community as possible, in anticipation of their withdrawal from the project.

At the end of the second year, the Sankuyo community's contract with their partner was terminated for a second time. Although the community council provided no explanation, no legal action was taken by the partner and the area was put out to tender again. Tangible financial benefits over these two years amounted to approximately US$220,000, or about US$10,000 per household. Most of this money stayed within the community trust account (apart from one household dividend disbursement), leaving many community members uncertain of the benefits of CBNRM.

In 1998, a new partner, who had been peripherally involved in year one, was chosen for the three-year contract. What soon became clear was that community expectations were vastly different from those of the commercial operator, who expected the community to act as a business partner willing to take responsibility and incur risk. The community, anticipating a development programme, expected training, financial benefit and social upliftment. In the process, natural resource management was neglected and the government focused primarily on conflict resolution rather than proactive management. Within the community, internal struggles persisted; the council was replaced once more and legal action was taken against at least one member for embezzling funds. By the end of the three-year lease, the relationship had broken down and the community once again decided to terminate the lease. During this tenure, US$576,400 accrued directly to the community. An estimated US$317,000 of these funds were spent on a community vehicle, salaries, transport, operating expenses, a community campsite project and household toilets (which, unfortunately, lasted less than one year owing to substandard construction).

In 2001, again without any legal dispute, the area went out to re-tender. Only two companies were presented to the community. One was the previous hunting partner and the other was unknown to the community. Interestingly, the financial bid of the 'unknown' company was significantly higher; but the 'known' company was voted in. Allegations, too complex to list here, of improper conduct during the tender by members of the community followed. The government became involved and a long legal battle ensued. At the time of writing, the 'unknown' company had secured a legal lease with the community, but had frozen investments pending the outcome of a lawsuit instigated by the 'known' company against the government for interfering with the tender process.

Amid all of this, in 1999, an independent non-governmental organization (NGO) approached the community to help start a community campsite and cultural village. It was anticipated that these enterprises would provide an alternative to the joint venture model that was showing some signs of dysfunction. The initiative was met with enthusiasm by some in the community and disdain by others. It went forward, was staffed by a membership of some 40 villagers and, by 2001, had become a financially successful enterprise. However, by the end of 2001, it was on the verge of collapse purportedly following concerted efforts by some village members (who were not receiving benefits) to close it down.

Revenue stream

Although exact figures are unavailable, the primary expenditures of the trust since 1996 include community vehicle, household toilets, campsite and cultural

Table 9.1 *Direct financial benefits from the joint venture to Sankuyo,*
1996–2000 (US$)

Type of financial benefit	1996	1997	1998	1999	2000
Lease payment and land rental	125,545	16,090	35,000	41,800	49,400
Wages/rations/uniforms	45,454	93,636	80,000	90,000	90,000
Community development fund	3636	7273	17,000	18,600	20,400
Game quota fee	27,727	60,909	40,600	44,600	49,000
Financial benefits/year	206,364	318,636	172,600	195,000	208,800
Total financial benefits/1996–2000					**1,101,400**

Source: Management Plans for NG34 1996 and 1998 (on file with the Tawana Land Board, PO Box 134, Maun, Botswana)

village, operating expenses (30 per cent of income), and wages for a community staff of 12. Offices and radio for the trust were paid for by the third joint venture partner (JVP).

Khwai – Ngamiland Area 18

Khwai village lies to the north of the protected Moremi Game Reserve on the permanently flowing Khwai River. It is situated in the middle of one of the primary game and tourist areas of the Delta region. Wildlife populations also appear healthy in this area and other veld products such as thatch and reeds are abundant. Khwai is almost exclusively a Basarwa (San) community with a hunter/forager history. Hunting remains of primary importance as a form of social cohesion. Khwai village is the result of the resettlement of various smaller family groups out of what is now the Moremi Game Reserve at the time of its designation during the early 1960s. Many residents now make a living through employment at one of the three adjacent tourist lodges. Khwai was awarded an 1815 square kilometre area called Ngamiland Area 18 (NG18) in March 1996 (Government of Botswana, 1991).

In the months following the designation of Khwai as a community area, conflict between the DWNP/USAID–NRMP team and the community resulted in the breakdown of their relationship. An alternative adviser, who is not a member of the community or of Basarwa heritage, was chosen by the community and became a main 'power broker', responsible for many decisions relating to community management. Under his guidance, the community was reluctant to enter into any joint venture agreement. Fear of losing power and distrust of commercial operators is prevalent among the majority of community members. The philosophy that has become paramount is that 'self-management is critical to successful long-term management'.

A legal RALE was not registered at the deeds office until 2000, four years after being awarded the area. Their delay was due to intense internal tensions, and differences between the government and the community, over whether they should go into partnership with the private sector or whether the community should manage its own enterprises.

At this time, another adviser, who counselled the residents to auction their quota through a public and transparent process, replaced the original adviser. This would allow the residents to maintain control, while still reaping financial benefits. The idea was to divide the quota up into blocks, selling each one individually to several different operators. The resultant auction in 2000 raised US$240,000. Most of the money generated in this way was used to build a hunting camp that would provide additional incentive for bidders the following year. The 2001 auction came on the heels of increased government licence fees, officials removing lion from the hunting quota, and general dissension about the previous year's auction. People came to realize that the auction had been controlled by a syndicate and that all blocks were controlled by one operator. The 2001 auction raised only US$120,000.

By 2002, many operators expressed their apprehension, citing high costs and poor management of the area. In previous years, hunters complained that the 'overbearing community presence' in the area and in the camp detracted from the exclusivity that clients expected and were paying for. A single offer of US$320,000 for the whole 2002 quota was accepted. At the time of writing, this operator was reported to be setting up a camp, independent of the designated community hunting camp. There was no official exploitation of the photographic tourism potential of the area, although plans were presented to develop rental campsites for mobile safari operators. Other important benefits to community members came in the form of thatch grass and reeds, which were cut and sold, and meat from the hunting quota, as well as subsistence fishing.

KEY ISSUES: WHAT WORKS IN THE CBNRM PROGRAMME AND WHAT DOES NOT?

Joint venture partnerships

The fact that there is an operating CBNRM programme in Botswana can, in itself, be considered a success. The joint venture system is in place and once it begins to function as a true partnership, it will build capacity and empower local citizens to own and operate successful tourist enterprises. All three members of the tripartite agreement (government, communities and private enterprise) are, at least on paper, committed to making CBNRM work. One could argue that the groundwork has been laid, and although many initial conflicts were anticipated, the current shuffling of responsibilities and relationships are necessary lessons on the road to success.

However, there is work to be done. What was intended as a true partnership resulted in a management contract where communities have had little to do with the management, monitoring or any practicalities of running a business. They became the labourers and landlords – quickly learning that money can flow regardless of participation or performance. This resulted in a situation where raised expectations were linked to passive participation and strong disincentives to work. Moreover, the third member of the agreement, the government, has taken a backseat role. DWNP staff are often ill equipped to deal with community issues, having no or limited background in social science, conflict resolution or common property management schemes. Private-sector partners complain that they get no support from the government. They are also expected to maintain good relations with their community colleagues in these difficult situations, while they have to keep the money flowing in. Essentially, they are being relied upon to keep the entire CBNRM programme afloat.

The result has been the breakdown of relationships between all three parties. It has provided a disincentive to the local people to actively manage their areas and has led to fear among safari operators to become involved in CBNRM. Common property theory argues clearly that rural resource users need to be empowered to make decisions, enforce rules, and actively own and operate enterprises in order to realize change and be successful (Oström, 1990; Peters, 1994). Unless these CBNRM schemes are restructured into a true partnership system, it is likely that some of the key objectives of CBNRM will not be met.

Lease arrangements

The lease arrangements discussed in the above case studies were intended to provide an opportunity for change. Residents of communal areas, it was thought, would benefit from a long-term relationship with a close working partner who would empower them and build capacity. Leases were structured according to a set formula that was designed to protect the communities from being bound to unacceptable joint venture partners. On the one hand, the lease arrangement has allowed community members to slowly adjust to a changing land tenure system and to the responsibility of being curators of the country's natural resources. On the other hand, it has led to development stagnation and unhealthy power relations by allowing individuals and communities to exercise a type of extortion over their joint venture partners. The system has also opened up opportunities for other interested but unsuccessful bidders to undermine the existing operators' relationship with the local people by promising them more. Because there was no guarantee of renewal beyond the first probationary year, and because a continued agreement was based on 'tangible development', joint venture partners were predictably reluctant to invest, yet needed to produce jobs and infrastructure in order to gain the support of the local people. This produced an environment ripe for corruption.

For these and other reasons, the government has reviewed the issue of lease tenure. As of 2002, first leases can be offered for five-year periods.

Financial benefits, changing attitudes and natural resource management

On the positive side, massive financial benefits are being realized. In fact, as a result of CBNRM, the two case study communities are among the richest in Botswana. Furthermore, people are compelled to make the adjustment to a representative governing system that is difficult and slow, but ongoing. The next step is to translate these benefits into improved attitudes and resource management practices.

Providing benefits as a means to 'improve natural resource management through improved attitudes to wildlife' continues to be a primary objective of the NRMP/CBNRM programme. In reality, many community members perceive CBNRM as a development programme, without taking cognizance of the NRM aspect of CBNRM. Studies conducted in Khwai and Sankuyo in 1998 (Boggs, 2000) suggested that benefits were not automatically associated with natural resources and their conservation. More than 60 per cent of individuals in both communities did not understand the relationship between benefits and wildlife resources. Although new data is needed to quantify changing attitudes, the focus on development rather than the linkage between social empowerment and wildlife has not encouraged a change in attitudes. There is also very little data available to quantify or demonstrate improved natural resource management. Wildlife population figures (cited earlier from the Botswana Wild Dog Research Project; see McNutt, 2001) are the best available. These data show an increase in most wildlife populations, but a worrying decline in impala. Wildlife populations should be more intensively monitored and factored into any assessment of CBNRM success. The resource conservation aspect of CBNRM is integral to its long-term success. It has been sidelined and needs to get back to centre stage.

Monitoring, enforcement and indicators of success

From the inception of the CBNRM programme, a number of different agencies and groups were identified as monitoring bodies of CBNRM. These include NRMP, DWNP, the Botswana Defence Force, land boards, the Botswana Ministry of Agriculture, the Botswana Department of Water Affairs, district authorities, NGOs, private operators and the community-based organizations. Attempts were made in the early stages to include a monitoring component as part of the responsibilities of the CBOs and partners. But the process of setting up these programmes, and having DWNP staff train local guides, was riven with tensions.

Attempts to set up a monitoring system were also bedevilled by the fact that the USAID funding term had come to an end. Members of the DWNP were unwilling to accept data collected by the local people as scientifically significant, providing a disincentive for communities to continue. Bell's conclusions following his review of these early CBNRM monitoring and evaluation systems were that 'Monitoring of CBNRM in Botswana is largely irrelevant...and is not co-ordinated between the various agencies and interested parties. There is no significant basis for evaluation of the programme' (Bell, 1997). Without a clearly defined set of indicators of success – which should include the status of the resource base, living standards in the community and measures comparing CBNRM to the theoretical principles of common property management – it is difficult to take the provisional assessments of CBNRM in Botswana further.

Other concerns

Three further concerns that are related to these four key issues deserve mention:

1 *Questionable support for the programme by the central government:* Central government has been reluctant to invest its own money in CBNRM, and has been slow to formulate policy. There have also been threats that the district councils would take over the financial management of community organizations in some of the problematic CBNRM areas, although it was soon realized that this was impossible and unconstitutional. This threat has publicly called into question the state's full support for CBNRM.

2 *Community cohesion and collective identity:* It has been widely documented in the common property literature that community managed commons often break down as a result of conflict between community members (Peters, 1994). The Botswana case is no exception. An elite, often kin-related, group that can undermine the board and interfere with the democratic process dominates most communities. In Sankuyo, for example, elders were forced to give up power to the young and educated, interrupting generational and cultural hierarchies. Later, unequal division of benefits created new layers of privilege in the community, again causing conflict. Finally, most members were ill equipped to manage the vast resources accruing to the community, corruption occurred and this resulted in a deepening of mistrust and severing of ties between community members. In Khwai, the inability to reach community consensus on a management strategy resulted in the loss of over four years of financial benefits. Many communities are now hiring external advisers and counsellors, having realized that internal conflicts often require external mediation. Providing that the advisers are well trained, this must be viewed as a positive development.

3 *Global dimension of community tourism:* Finally, the important ties to a larger system cannot be overlooked. Firstly, both the money and the incentive for the programme were tied to USAID, which is no longer involved. Most CBNRM programmes are not viable without external funding, making the entire system vulnerable to a changing global economy. We should also be aware that the forces of globalization are alive and well in local rural communities. The CBNRM programme is based on the ideal that community members wish to remain in rural areas, living out lifestyles based on the sustainable use of natural resources. Evidenced by what community members spend their money on – namely, satellite television, cell phones, clothes and expensive vehicles – a rural life is not what many aspire to. It must be acknowledged that cultures are dynamic and fluctuating. In order to succeed, the CBNRM model must incorporate mechanisms for change that allow it to adapt to changing environments.

On a final and positive note, an important evolution has been the formation of a national forum on CBNRM in Botswana. This not only shows the depth of support for success of the programme, but allows a functional medium where the private sector, communities, government and practitioners can discuss and resolve these important issues.

CONCLUSIONS AND RECOMMENDATIONS

Although it would be misguided and premature to attach labels of 'success' or 'failure' to the CBNRM programme in Botswana, it is imperative that progress is monitored and actions altered where necessary. The following provisional conclusions and recommendations help to chart the way forward.

The most important conclusion is that the underlying assumption of CBNRM in Botswana – that economic benefits alone automatically translate into improved wildlife management – is not well founded. A more direct and proactive method of accomplishing this objective might achieve better results. For example, lease payments to local people could be made dependent upon the fulfilment of predefined obligations to fulfil the aims of CBNRM.

The second important conclusion is that CBNRM, as implemented in the two case study areas, had not (at the time of writing) accomplished the goals of capacity-building or empowerment. To achieve these aims, communities should become participants in full and effective joint venture partnerships, and this implies that they must share financial risk, investment and management.

In effect, the design itself of the short-term lease periods sets the stage for a difficult relationship between local people and any potential joint venture partner. Furthermore, it is clear that the short lease periods do not fit with the aspirations of all stakeholders. Changes are in progress to address this problem.

Finally, the importance of monitoring and evaluation has been overlooked. If there is no measure by which to assess the programme, then there is no way to answer the question of whether it is working or not. A clear set of measures of success needs to be established and used for both the development of rural communities and the management of their natural resources. This is an ideal opportunity for the DWNP and local government to change from passive observers to active participants in order to help direct the future of the CBNRM programme in Botswana.

REFERENCES

Bell, R (1997) *Monitoring and Evaluation for CBNRM Botswana*. Unpublished manuscript presented at the Savegame Workshop March 2001, Save Conservancy, Zimbabwe

Boggs, L (2000) 'Community power, participation, conflict and development choice: Community wildlife conservation in the Okavango region of Northern Botswana',

Evaluating Eden Discussion Paper No 17. International Institute for Environment and Development, London

Government of Botswana: Ministry of Local Government and Lands, Ngamiland District Land Use Planning Unit (DLUPU) (1991) 'Land Use and Development Plan, Kwando and Okavango Wildlife Management Areas', DLUPU/Tawana Land Board, PO Box 134, Maun, Botswana

Government of Botswana (1997) ' Community based natural resource management policy: A paper on the promotion of natural resource utilization, preservation and management', Discussion Draft of 24 June 1997, Gaborone

McCarthy, T, Ellery, K S, McIver, J R, Rogers K H, Grobicki, T S, Stanistreet, I S, Oeloffse, R, Walker, B H, Metcalfe, J, Ellery, W N, Green, R W and Franey, N J (1986–1994) 'Okavango Research Group Papers', University of Witwatersrand, Johannesburg

McNutt, J (2001) *Quarterly Report from the Botswana Wild Dog Research Project.* Submitted to the Department of Wildlife and National Parks (DWNP), December 2001, DWNP Office, Gaborone

Mordi, A (1991) *Attitudes Toward Wildlife in Botswana.* Garland Publishing, New York and London

Okavango Community Consultants (1995) 'Management Plans for Controlled Hunting Areas allocated to communities in Ngamiland WMAs', Okavango Community Consultants, Maun

Oström, E (1990) *Governing the Commons.* Cambridge University Press, Cambridge

Peters, P (1994) *Dividing the Commons: Politics, Policy and Culture in Botswana.* University Press of Virginia, Charlottesville and London

Rihoy, E (ed) (1995) *The Commons without the Tragedy? Strategies for Community Based Natural Resources Management in Southern Africa: Proceedings of the Regional Natural Resources Management Programme Annual Conference, Kasane, Botswana.* Southern African Development Community, Lilongwe

Taylor, R (2000) *Life, Land and Power: Contesting Development in Northern Botswana.* PhD thesis, University of Edinburgh, Edinburgh

Local ecological knowledge and the Basarwa in the Okavango Delta: The case of Xaxaba, Ngamiland District

MASEGO MADZWAMUSE AND CHRISTO FABRICIUS

INTRODUCTION

The Okavango Delta changes constantly. Fire, flooding, droughts, animal migration and seasonal fluxes in the abundance and availability of plant and animal products characterize this dynamic ecosystem. It requires exceptional knowledge and adaptations for humans to subsist here permanently. The Basarwa people have evolved a body of knowledge and practices about ecosystems and their function to enable them to deal with constant change in ecosystems. These include a nomadic lifestyle, flexible livelihood strategies, a heavy reliance on social capital, such as customs and traditional institutions, and adaptive ecosystem management, such as the deliberate use of fire to enhance wildlife habitat, selective and opportunistic harvesting methods, and lifestyles that are independent of financial capital. The Basarwa's nomadic lifestyles have more recently been replaced by sedentary lifestyles in rural settlements, under government-sponsored betterment schemes and land and conservation policies that undermined their traditional ways. This has placed considerable constraints on their ability to cope with social and ecological change.

The adaptive renewal cycle (Gunderson and Holling, 2002; Figure 10.1) can be used as a framework to better understand the current predicament of the Basarwa and the processes leading up to it. This model, first proposed to explain change in non-equilibrium ecosystems, was adapted by Gunderson, Holling and Light (1995), Berkes and Folke (1998) and Gunderson and Holling (2002) to explain changes in integrated social ecological systems (that is, people living in and using ecosystems). The model suggests that

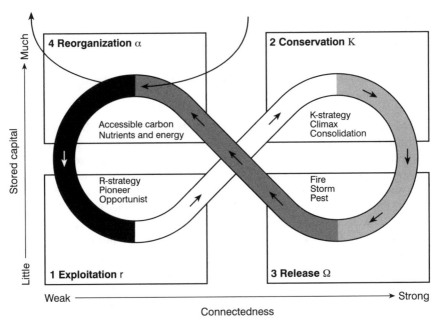

Notes: The adaptive renewal cycle is an abstraction of any living system (ie social or ecological). The main features of the model are that the system is dynamic and changes all of the time; the system can be abstracted in two dimensions; the first axis represents 'connectedness' – for example, the number of species or trophic levels in an ecosystem, or the institutional complexity in a social system; the y axis represents 'stored capital' – for example, the amount of accumulated biomass in an ecosystem or the amount of financial capital (for instance, money in the bank) or social capital (for instance, population density) in a social system; at some point in the cycle the system can undergo a 'flip' – that is, change its basic properties or become driven by a different set of factors; and arrows spaced close together indicate fast change, whereas arrows further apart indicate slow rates of change.

Source: Gunderson and Holling (2002)

Figure 10.1 *The adaptive renewal cycle*

social–ecological systems go through cycles of adaptive renewal, characterized by a build-up of capital (for example, tangible assets and biomass) and connectedness (for example, the complexity of organizational hierarchies and species richness), to a point of climax ('K' in Figure 10.1), whereafter they inevitably release their built-up capital. The release phase could be triggered by a surprise event such as a fire, or drastic political change. The predictability of the cycle varies: whereas one can be fairly certain that 'release' (Ω) will invariably follow 'conservation' (K), the timing between phases is largely unpredictable. The events that trigger a shift from one phase to the next vary in their predictability. The knock-on effect of events at higher spatial scales (for example, a major shift in policy or regional climatic change) on local-level processes is also unpredictable and poorly understood. The release phase is often followed by a phase of reorganization (α), firstly, to rebuild stored capital and, secondly, to build up connectivity.

A major shock may cause the systems to 'flip' into a different phase of organization – for example, when an ecosystem changes from woodland to grassland and is maintained in that state by fire and animals, or when a human population changes from being mobile to sedentary.

The Basarwa in Ngamiland have gone through several stages in the adaptive renewal cycle:

- *The mobile and flexible phase (pre-1910):* This was their traditional lifestyle, which was extremely resilient and adaptable. Legal title to the lands of the Basarwa and other minority tribes such as the Bakgalagadi were passed to the state under the 1910 Order in Council, which redefined crown lands in the protectorate as all other land that was not part of the Tati District, native reserves and Barolong farms (Ngo'ngo'la, 1997). This period was characterized by short periods of being sedentary and aggregation, followed by rapid social reorganization and mobility. Groups disbanded and aggregated in response to fine-grained changes in the ecosystem. Traditional ecological knowledge, which acted as the memory of the system, and which had evolved over many generations, enabled them to anticipate and predict periods of shortages and abundance and to respond before a crisis took place. The Basarwa rapidly and proactively moved between K and other phases of the adaptive cycle in response to change. Renewal cycles were extremely short, and traditional ecological knowledge, natural resources and social capital played a major role in their lives.
- *The restricted and sedentary phase (1968–1992):* Major policy shifts caused their loss of territorial space, loss of wildlife resources, loss of mobility and outcompetition by other ethnic groups. This hamstrung their ability to make use of their traditional knowledge and management systems. Events and processes occurred at much coarser-grained scales than they were used to: national policies and macro-economics were governing their lives. They were locked into the release phase (Ω) and were incapable of responding to challenges and change.
- *The reorganized and beleaguered phase (1992–present):* The Basarwa underwent a 'flip' (α) and have moved into a new stable state from which they are unlikely to escape in the near future. This change, from an adaptive society that relied almost exclusively on natural capital to a sedentary one that relies on multiple sources of income, mainly from tourism and government grants, is leaving the Basarwa at a competitive disadvantage relative to other groups in Ngamiland. They are also at the mercy of processes over which they have no control, and have little room for proactive decision-making and strategizing. This situation is unlikely to change under the current global and national political dispensation.

STUDY AREA

Xaxaba is a remote settlement in the Ngamiland District – an area of about 109 square kilometres in the north-west corner of Botswana: 18° 30'–20° 00'S; 23° 15'–24° 30'E, bordering Moremi Game Reserve. This district is endowed with rich natural resources such as the Okavango Delta, which is best known as a tourism destination because of the wildlife it sustains and its scenic beauty. 60 per cent (around 13,500 individuals) of working people in Ngamiland are employed in the tourism industry. Tourism is a major and growing component of the national economy, contributing about 5 per cent of the gross domestic product (GDP) (Scott Wilson Resource Consultants, 2001).

The Okavango Delta experiences large variations in the flooding of permanent, seasonal and seasonally intermittent wetlands. This results in big fluctuations in plant and animal resources in space and over time. The Okavango system is also a biodiversity 'hot spot' (Scudder et al, 1993). It is important for terrestrial and water bird species, and contains high densities of large species, particularly elephant, which migrate between Namibia's Caprivi strip, Chobe Game Reserve and Hwange National Park in Zimbabwe. It is also the habitat of one of the largest remaining populations of African wild dog and a stronghold for the sitatunga antelope and the Nile crocodile.

It is less well known that the Delta has, for many centuries, sustained the livelihoods of its nomadic Basarwa (Bushman) inhabitants, who have adopted a lifestyle that was in tune with the ever-changing Okavango ecosystem.

The people and their history

Some 20 per cent of Botswana's Basarwa population live in Ngamiland. These are the so-called River Bushmen comprising the Bugakhwe and the Xhanikhwe. Although San populations are becoming increasingly concentrated, historic records show that they were scattered over all parts of what is now Ngamiland (Cassidy, 1999). The River Bushmen (referred to in Setswana as *Banoka*) who lived and fished along the fringes of the Okavango Delta were the earliest inhabitants of the area. They learned to use canoes (*mekoro*) and fishing skills from later immigrants, the Bantu-speaking Bayei and the Hambukushu from latter-day Zambia. Over the next century, a fifth ethnic group, the Batawana, arrived in Ngamiland (Taylor, 2000), contributing political institutions, laws, language and pastoralism. This melting pot of cultures, skills and knowledge led to the development of a people with a diverse portfolio of livelihood strategies, belief systems and natural resource management tactics that has evolved in response to the highly variable natural environment.

MOBILE AND FLEXIBLE: THE TRADITIONAL LIFESTYLE OF THE BASARWA

The Basarwa had evolved an extremely diverse portfolio of livelihood strategies before being forced to become sedentary. They used a combination of hunting and gathering, and a form of social organization that allowed them to flexibly use large territories, adjusted to seasonal changes. Key adaptations that enabled the Basarwa to cope with drought and periodic shortages of resources were:

- mobility and flexibility in the use of resources;
- flexibility in group size;
- flexible leadership structures;
- detailed knowledge of the local ecological system and appropriate skills to capitalize on this knowledge; and
- sharing networks (Hitchcock et al, 1989).

The traditional Basarwa rapidly and naturally accommodated cycles of ecosystem reorganization and release by reorganizing their own lifestyles in response to fine-grained and subtle changes in the ecosystem (Saugestad, 1998). Basarwa's main strategy to cope with changes in climate and weather patterns and the availability of local resources was to aggregate, disaggregate and be mobile. A second coping strategy was territoriality, which varied depending upon the productivity of the land. The size of territories was negatively correlated with rainfall (Barnard, 1992). Tenurial rights were obtained through birth, marriage and residence (Cashdan, 1983). In areas with an abundance of food and water, bands would typically have access rights to more than one territory. Outsiders had to seek permission from a band in order to gain access to resources within their territory, not only from the band leader, but also from the ancestors.

The Basarwa also had (and still have) traditional ethics, norms and rules to govern the use of natural resources (Spinage, 1991). For example among the G/wi, animals are *kx'oxudzi* (things to be eaten), but they are also *N!adima*'s (God's) creatures. They may be killed in self-defence or for food. Greedy hunting is not allowed, fearing that it will displease *N!adima* and they will suffer the consequences. Primarily ageing animals are hunted; pregnant females are left alone, and during the mating season, male animals are spared. Taboos, which may not have been aimed directly at conservation, often have the effect of relieving the pressure on scarce resources. For example, the first fruits of the season may be eaten only by the elderly, relieving pressure on wild fruits at a time when resources are still limited. In some cases, a total prohibition of harvesting on certain totem species is imposed. A woman in Xaxaba who was badly scarred on her face said that she had had a skin reaction after merely eating from a pot in which her husband had earlier cooked her totem: elephant meat. Other Xaxaba people, such as Mma Monjwa and Rra Monjwa, on the other hand, claimed that they ate their totem animals, suggesting that this taboo is flexibly applied.

RESTRICTED AND SEDENTARY: COLLAPSE AND VULNERABILITY OF THE BASARWA

Life is lot more difficult now; if you go into any of these homes you will not find a single household which is well off. No one can claim to be coping and comfortable; this is experienced through all the different age groups, the young and the elderly. Re a Sheta, we are struggling (Rra Kgalalelo, Xaxaba).

Between 1968 (the year marking the beginning of a post-independence land reform process) and 1992, a number of policies and acts were promulgated that virtually negated the Basarwa's adaptive livelihood strategies. The 1968 Tribal Land Act had catastrophic consequences for the Basarwa's resilience. This act defines land rights and use in agro-pastoral terms at the expense of hunter-gatherers (Ngo'ngo'la, 1997). The Tribal Grazing Land Policy (TGLP) of 1975 and the 1991 Agricultural Policy aggravated the problem of overgrazing in communal areas due to maintenance of dual grazing rights by ranch owners. Population growth and the development of deep boreholes in the western Kalahari and eradication of the tsetse fly around the Okavango Delta prompted the opening of new areas to cattle and human settlement (Neme, 1995), causing many Basarwa and poor farmers to be displaced and to lose their traditional use rights.

The government responded with 'betterment schemes': the setting-up of villages of up to 750 people (referred to as remote-area dweller settlements), consisting of aggregations of families from different clans and ethnic groups. This sedentarization was unfamiliar and incompatible with the Basarwa's traditional social organization, causing them to rapidly lose social capital. Alcoholism became rife, teenage pregnancies increased, and conflicts within and between clans escalated. One of the major problems faced by these betterment schemes was forging coherence among various social groups. One such example is of an incident in Diphuduhudu where one Basarwa clan refused to accept a Mosarwa who came from a different clan as a headman of the settlement (Mazonde, 1994). Such lack of social cohesion means that social development – which, under current circumstances, depends upon successful clusters of settlement around villages – cannot take place (Mazonde, 1994). The residents of Khwai alluded to the fact that management of natural resources has become difficult because the present communities are comprised of people from different areas with different norms, values and practices. As Alcorn and Toledo (1998) argue, the successful implementation of community-wide decisions depends upon widely shared values that strengthen social capital. Mazonde (1994) further notes that most remote-area dwellers who settle in these betterment schemes experience a deterioration in their standard of living. When settlements grow too big, available game and veld products within reasonable reach rapidly diminish, which sets a limit to the number of people who can engage in sustainable livelihood strategies (Saugestad, 1998).

The erection of cordon fences to control the spread of foot-and-mouth disease further reduced the Basarwa's access to land and natural resources. The cordon fences also trapped wildlife during their migrations, confining them to the northern part of the country where Ngamiland is situated. The effect of this concentration of wildlife in the north had both negative and positive effects on the Basarwa. While, on the one hand, the wildlife encroached into human settlements, destroying crops and posing a threat to human life, the Basarwa communities in Ngamiland stood to benefit from the growing wildlife-based tourism industry.

The Herbage Preservation (Prevention of Fires) Act of 1978 (Chapter 38:02 of Botswana law) prevented traditional Basarwa practices, such as fire, to open up blocked river channels, control wildlife movement patterns, improve feeding habitat for wildlife and clear areas for better visibility. New conservation laws (for example, the 1992 Wildlife Conservation and National Parks Act) reduced their access to traditional territories. Communities were not (and still are not) allowed to gather wild resources within Moremi Game Reserve. The Basarwa of Xaxaba and Khwai found themselves trapped within increasingly smaller areas of land that could not accommodate their traditional livelihood strategies. Hunting regulations criminalized one of the central markers of Basarwa identity, affecting their sense of pride and identity. The introduction of compulsory hunting licences, which the Basarwa could not afford, controlled hunting area regulations, the Fauna Conservation Act of 1977 and the Unified Hunting Regulations of 1977 all affected the Basarwa's ability to practice their traditional hunting-and-gathering lifestyles.

The Basarwa were never politically influential; but their extreme political weakness resulting from these events resulted in them being economically outcompeted by non-Basarwa. While trading in veld products, such as thatch, reeds and game products, could bring cash income for the Basarwa, most collection seemed to be done by rich Batawana with vehicles (Cassidy, 1999).

The Basarwa gradually became more vulnerable, marginalized and were finding it increasingly difficult to cope in a political and economic environment where their traditional adaptations were ineffective. Their social system had undergone a 'flip', from being mobile, flexible and in control of their own destiny, to being sedentary and controlled by external (mainly government and private-sector) forces.

REORGANIZED BUT BELEAGUERED: MAKING THE MOST OF NEW POLICIES

New policies and strategies in Botswana are, however, beginning to recognize the importance of community involvement and participation in the management of natural resources. The community-based natural resource management (CBNRM) draft policy (Government of Botswana, 2001) is an example of this new move towards community participation in resource management. CBNRM in Botswana has been accepted as a rural development and conservation strategy. The ultimate aim is to improve the living conditions of the people who reside alongside natural resources, to the point that they see the value of conserving their environment for future generations (Government of Botswana, 2001). A wide range of CBNRM activities, such as commercial hunting, photographic tourism, eco-tourism, craft production, basketry, the processing of veld products and game skin tanning, are managed by community-based organizations (CBOs) with the assistance of government and international donors.

CBNRM is based on the ideals of equality, natural resource conservation and social development. This policy is designed to:

- provide for broad stakeholder coordination at district and national level;
- give communities incentives to engage in sustained development and conservation activities;
- establish clear links between the reception of community benefits and the existence of natural resources;
- encourage the investment of community benefits gained from natural resources into activities that will not adversely affect those resources or otherwise hinder the viability of ecological systems;
- enhance community autonomy through programmes directed towards community self-reliance and where participation uses democratic and transparent mechanisms; and
- ensure respect for the needs of all members of society.

In order to qualify for government support for CBNRM, a community has to form a representative, accountable and legal entity called a CBO, also referred to as a village trust committee (VTC). The CBO must be managed using a participatory process sanctioned by district authorities. Communities in controlled hunting areas (CHAs) are then granted resource leases over wildlife and tourism on their land for a period of up to 15 years. Although CBNRM permits communities to enjoy increased and direct management of resources, the government retains the ultimate authority to protect species and ecological systems and continues to regulate the use of these valuable resources (Government of Botswana, 2001). The people of Xaxaba and Khwai have adapted to the new political status quo by engaging in a diversity of new livelihood strategies and sometimes combining these with traditional strategies.

New financial capital and livelihood diversification

To cope with the vulnerabilities due to global and local economics, the residents of Khwai and Xaxaba engage in a cash economy and wage labour to supplement other livelihood options. They earn a lot of money through employment in the tourism industry and leases from their joint venture partners. According to Government of Botswana (2001), CBNRM activities in the Ngamiland District earn the highest income in the country. The dry season, when there is not much in the veld, coincides with the peak season in the tourism industry. Part-time tourist guides can make up to 700 pula (US$116) in a good month. Primarily, men are employed in this industry as dug-out canoe (*Mokoro*) polers, guides and trackers. Almost 50 per cent of the 15 households sampled in Xaxaba rely on remittances from family members employed in tourism.

In 2000, 1.1 million pula (US$180,000) was received by the Kopano Mokoro CBO in Ngamiland Area 32 (NG32) (which Xaxaba is a part of). Xaxaba received a share of 150,000 pula (US$25,000). This money was used to build and stock a tuck shop, managed by the VTC chair and its treasurer. The remainder of their profits from CBNRM for that year was used to buy a vehicle and a boat. The Xaxaba community treasurer believes that by investing in tangible goods, the community's confidence in CBNRM has been boosted. On the contrary, though, a group of elderly women who were interviewed questioned the rationale for buying a vehicle and a boat when some members of the community were struggling to meet such basic needs as food and clothing.

The women continue to engage in gathering food from the veld, making crafts and brewing traditional beer. The baskets they make are sold to tourists for 150 pula to 250 pula (US$25–US$42). 73 per cent of the households in Xaxaba stated that basket-weaving is one of their livelihood options and 50 per cent of the households in Khwai relied on basket-weaving as one of their livelihood options. Women also collect thatch grass and reeds, which they sell to the safari lodges in their areas and to buyers from Maun and other villages. 64 per cent of the households in Khwai and 54 per cent in Xaxaba engage in collecting thatch grass and selling it to the lodges and buyers from Maun. The builders in the community charge 400 pula (US$66) for a complete wooden frame for a hut. Some men earn income from making and selling *Mokoro* at 1200 pula (US$200) a piece to tourism operators.

In fact, 62 per cent of the livelihood options listed in Table 10.1 are based on a cash economy. It is important, however, to bear in mind that this financial income is seasonal and is thus not steadily available throughout the year.

New institutions

Although there have been major changes in the traditional institutions of the Basarwa, they have adopted new institutions for monitoring and regulating natural resource use. Apart from the village trust committees for CBNRM initiatives, the residents of Khwai have formed resource committees, such as the committee that monitors the collection of thatch grass. The rule is that grass is only cut between June and September when it is mature enough and after seeds have been dropped. People who are caught cutting grass are sanctioned before a public meeting and given a warning. If they are caught doing it again, the punishment will be stiffer. Generally, those who do not obey the rules are treated as outcasts and hence do not get to benefit from the

Table 10.1 *Livelihood options in Xaxaba and Khwai*

Source of livelihood	Number of households	
	Xaxaba (n = 15 households)	*Khwai (n = 14 households)*
Fishing	15	9
Basket-making	11	7
Arable farming	0	8
Mokoro safaris	4	0
Hunting	2	0
Formal employment	5	3
Remittance	7	5
Sale of reeds	15	8
Sale of grass	8	9
Drought relief and food ration	0	3
Traditional building material	9	4
Wild fruits and vegetables	13	4
Other CBNRM	4	0

safety nets of being part of a larger community. They are kept out of any decision-making at community level, which is, anyhow, a traditional practice.

The Basarwa adopted the *Kgotla* system, a Tswana traditional forum for decision-making and discussion, to cope with their new sedentary status. The VTCs linked to CBNRM have, however, become the most important formal institutions at local level. VTCs draw the largest crowds to the *Kgotla* for meetings.

Keeping traditional knowledge alive

The use of the traditional *Mokoro* has become central to the modern livelihoods of the Basarwa. The tracking skills of the men are honed when they play the role of hunting guides, and there is a lot of inter-generational transfer of knowledge when young men work alongside older men. Female children accompany women on gathering trips where they participate and observe their parents collecting wild fruits, cutting grass or collecting reeds. They are also shown how to collect these in a sustainable manner and are taught essential skills for gathering and processing wild foods. The traditional skill of basket-making is transferred in the same way. Young women work side by side with the older women, preparing palm for making baskets and weaving these. A general observation was that the Bayei women made baskets of a better quality than the Basarwa women. A, perhaps obvious, explanation is that the art of basket-making was introduced to the Basarwa by the Bayei.

IS CBNRM THE NEW PANACEA?

Despite the existence of the CBNRM programme, the people of Xaxaba and Khwai remain concerned that their access to natural resources was reduced without giving them a suitable alternative means of making a living. Many of the older residents spoke of their traditional territories with a sense of longing and loss. The Xaxaba elders constantly reminisced about a better life in Tsobaoro, the centre of their traditional territory, referring to it as *matota abo ntate* (our ancestors' ruins). They argue that CBNRM has replaced subsistence hunting, which not merely *fitted* their traditional lifestyles; it was their lifestyle, and only they and their God were in control. CBNRM, they argue, means depending upon government for handouts (food, clothes), pensions for the elderly and employment through the government's drought relief programme. Their dependence upon tourism means being at the mercy of events over which they have no control, such as being dictated to by joint venture partners and government officials, as well as market fluctuations. The eco-tourism industry in Botswana is affected by political events in neighbouring Zimbabwe, the opening up of new markets in Namibia and South Africa, the price of fuel and global peace.

Their complaints are well founded: the commercial safari operators still give preference to non-community members for employment, and have no legal obligation to improve the livelihoods of the Basarwa. Of 15 safari lodges or camps surveyed, only one operator mentioned the local population or culture in its brochures (Damm et al, 1997). The Basarwa settlements therefore do not benefit as much as they could from tourism in the delta, where the safari operators generally regard them as an obstruction to a place marketed as a 'pristine wilderness'.

In addition, modern institutions have created conflict with the traditional institutions. In Xaxaba, for instance, the establishment of VTCs has resulted in a conflict between the villagers and Chief Thogotona, who now spends most of his time away from the village. Says Thogotona:

> *I am spending a lot of time in Maun attending to my own business interests. What is the point of being here and serving the community when they seem to have forgotten everything that I did for them for the past 17 years? All they are interested in now is the VTCs because it generates money and brings money into the community. Nothing else seems to be of equal importance.*

It is difficult for the pluralistic CBO (the larger body to whom the VTC answers) to achieve acceptable levels of participation in governance, management and in the necessary flow of benefits (DWNP and PACT, 2000). Community members in the six villages feel that management issues, including benefits, are controlled by the board of trustees. The board of trustees is so remote from the population that trustees are unknown to the majority of the general membership. Furthermore, there is mistrust between the southern communities and the northern communities of the CBO, with both sides accusing each other of dominating and controlling the CBO Okavango Kopano Mokoro Trust (OKMCT). The NG32 VTC is often accused of misappropriating funds. In 1999, 25,000 pula were recorded missing.

According to villagers attending the 2001 NG32 annual meeting, this mistrust is fuelled by outsiders such as government officials – for example, officials in the Department of Wildlife and National Parks (DWNP) and Partnership Agencies Collaborating Together (PACT) – and certain non-governmental organizations (NGOs).

Although the Basarwa people of Khwai and Xaxaba have adopted new institutions for natural resource management, conflict at community level is seen as a stumbling block for the success of these institutions. It would be difficult, today, for the Khwai community to collectively manage the natural resources in their wildlife management area because of conflicts over community membership. This explains why the constitution for the trust in Khwai, until 2001, had a clause excluding the non-Basarwa residents from being committee members although some of them have been living in Khwai for more than 20 years. While conflicts around institutions and membership are characteristic of 'new' societies, the dissatisfaction of the Basarwa with CBNRM is more deep rooted and needs to be addressed in policies and programmes.

GENERAL DISCUSSION

In this chapter, we have attempted to demonstrate how highly adaptive, mobile societies can 'flip' into a new type of social organization, which requires different livelihood strategies. Societies that rely on mobility and flexibility to build resilience in response to fine-scale change in their environment are often at the mercy of coarser-scale shocks, such as policy change and globalization, over which they have little control and with which they have never had to contend (Gunderson and Holling, 2002). These coarse-scale processes can negate the traditional resilience-enhancing strategies of mobile people. This leaves them extremely vulnerable to competition from other groups who are able to respond to higher-level changes at the macro level. Mobile people are only, to a limited extent, able to use their age-old adaptive strategies to cope with new challenges.

Uncertainty is inevitable for communities who rely directly upon natural resources for their livelihoods. It therefore remains important that a diverse and flexible range of livelihood strategies is maintained. Through CBNRM, the government intended to give communities the responsibility to manage natural resources, but not necessarily the authority to make this possible. It is thus important for communities to be given the authority to use and manage their natural resources through their local and traditional institutions. CBNRM also has to take into account temporal fluctuations in livelihood assets. Income from CBNRM needs to fill a gap at times when alternative resources are at their scarcest, rather than usurping all other strategies.

Hitchcock et al (1989) argue that one of the reasons for the adaptive success of Kalahari hunter-gatherers was their knowledge of the local environment and their efficient means of exploiting it. Local knowledge and inter-generational transfer of this knowledge is important in order to adapt to the climatic shocks that characterize the Okavango Delta. To cope with droughts, the Basarwa communities draw on their human capital, such as hunting skills, knowledge of alternative foods and other survival skills. In seasonal shortages and famines, people broaden their definition of food (Shipton, 1990) and elders remember emergency food repertoires and pass them along as oral history. Famine sufferers often break food taboos, suggesting that food taboos may function to conserve resources for emergencies (Shipton, 1990). Current conservation and land policies in Botswana do not permit the optimal use of these strategies. The sustainability of CBNRM initiatives depends upon the continued strengthening and maintenance of local ecological knowledge and the traditional coping systems of the Basarwa communities.

Hunting and gathering, although limited and restricted by government regulations, remain of symbolic importance to the Basarwa (Twyman, 2000). Hunting regulations have not eliminated subsistence hunting; instead, they have transformed it into a hidden practice promoting mismanagement of resources (Taylor, 2000). To avoid this, CBNRM benefits have to be felt at household level instead of only at the community level. People question the rationale of having large sums of community money in the bank while the members of the communities remain poverty stricken.

In the final analysis, land remains a major determinant of the natural, physical and financial capital available to the Basarwa. The loss of their traditional lands is the most immediate threat to their resilience, their identity and their ecological knowledge. Extensive use (in the form of access to large territories of land) is a prerequisite for adaptive management by the Basarwa. Appropriate CBNRM should therefore ensure the people's access to some of the lands within the parks – for example, through co-management agreements.

REFERENCES

Alcorn, J B and Toledo, V M (1998) 'Resilient resource management in Mexico's forest ecosystems: The contributions of property rights', in Berkes, F and Folke, C (eds) *Linking Social and Ecological Systems: Management Practices and Social Mechanisms for Building Resilience.* Cambridge University Press, Cambridge, pp216–249

Barnard, A (1992) 'Social and spatial boundary maintenance among southern African hunter gatherers', in Casimir, M J and Rao, A (eds) *Mobility and Territoriality: Social and Spatial Boundaries among Foragers, Fishers, Pastoralists and Peripatetics.* Berg, New York, pp137–151

Berkes, F and Folke, C (eds) (1998) *Linking Social and Ecological Systems: Management Practices and Social Mechanisms for Building Resilience.* Cambridge University Press, Cambridge

Cassidy, L (1999) *EU Regional Assessment of the Situation of San in Southern Africa – Botswana Component: A General Review and Socio-Economic Baseline Data.* European Union, Brussels

Cashdan, E A (1983) 'Territoriality among human foragers: Ecological models and an application to four Bushman Groups', *Current Anthropology*, 24: 47–56

Damm, C, Lane, P and Bolaane, M (1998) 'Bridging the River Khwai: Archaeology, tourism and cultural identity in Eastern Ngamiland, Botswana', in Bank, A, (ed) *The Proceedings of Khoisan Identities and Cultural Heritage Conference, South African Museum, Cape Town, 12–16 July 1997*. Institute for Historical Research, University of the Western Cape

DWNP and PACT (2000) *Enabling Recommendations by the NG32 Strategic Planning Coordinating Team*. Government of Botswana, Gaborone

Government of Botswana (2001) *CBNRM Draft Policy*. Government Printers, Gaborone

Gunderson, L H and Holling, C S (2002) *Panarchy: Understanding Transformations in Human and Natural Systems*. Island Press, Washington, DC

Gunderson, L H, Holling, C S and Light, S (1995) *Barriers and Bridges to Renewal of Ecosystems and Institutions*. Columbia University Press, New York

Hitchcock, R K, Ebert, J D, and Morgan, R G (1989) 'Drought, drought relief, and dependency among the Basarwa of Botswana', in Huss-Ashmore, R and Katz, S H (eds) *African Food Systems in Crisis: Part One – Micro Perspectives*. Gordon and Breach, New York

Mazonde, I N (1994) 'Community studies', in Saugestad, S and Tsonope, J (eds) *Developing Basarwa Research and Research for Basarwa Development: Workshop Report, 17–18 September 1993*. University of Botswana, Gaborone, pp50–52

Neme, L A (1995) *The Political Dynamics of Environmental Decision Making: A Case Study of Botswana's Bureaucracy*. PhD thesis, Priceton University

Ngo'ngo'la, C (1997) 'Land rights for marginalized ethnic groups in Botswana, with special reference to the Basarwa', *Journal of African Law* 41: 1–26

Saugestad, S (1998) *The Inconvenient Indigenous: Remote Area Development in Botswana, Donor Assistance and the First People of the Kalahari*. University of Tromso, Norway

Scott Wilson Resource Consultants (2001) 'Environmental impact assessment of tsetse eradication programme in Ngamiland: Final report'. Prepared for Department of Animal Health, Govenment of Botswana, Gaborone

Scudder, T, Manley, R E, Coley, R W, Davis, R K, Green, S, Howard, G W, Lawry, S W, Martz, D, Rogers, P P, Taylor, A R D, Turner, S D, White, G F and Wright, E P (1993) *The IUCN Review of the Southern Okavango Integrated Water Development Project*. IUCN, Gland

Shipton, P (1990) 'African famines and food security: Anthropological perspectives', *Annual Review of Anthropology*, 19: 353–394

Spinage, C (1991) *History and the Evolution of the Fauna and Conservation Laws of Botswana*. The Botswana Society, Gaborone

Taylor, M (2000) *Life, Land and Power: Contesting Development in Northern Botswana*. PhD thesis, University of Edinburgh, Edinburgh

Twyman, C (2000) 'Livelihood opportunity and diversity in Kalahari wildlife management areas, Botswana: Rethinking community resource management', *Journal of Southern African Studies* 26: 806–807

Chapter 11

A land without fences: Range management in Lesotho

Stephen Turner

Informal community-based natural resource management: The national norm

Lesotho differs from all other southern African countries in never having had a settler population. Outside the towns, land rights and land management continue to be framed by a communal system still strongly influenced by traditional authorities and practices. Apart from residential and commercial property, there is no fully individual title to rural land or resources. Although enclosure of residential sites and home gardens is becoming more common, the mountain kingdom is still rightly described as a land without fences.

Informal systems of community-based natural resource management (CBNRM) are thus the norm in rural Lesotho. Indigenous systems for the governance of farmland, rangeland and other resources such as trees have evolved through a succession of relatively gentle adjustments introduced by the British administration and the independent government, which relied heavily upon the Laws of Lerotholi (a codification of indigenous law first promulgated in 1903). These systems remain community based, as a matter of course. This case study focuses on the management of rangeland within Lesotho's local systems of resource management. But other resources, such as fields and forests, are governed in the same institutional framework.

Traditionally, Lesotho's resource management framework was administered by the chief (sometimes a woman), sitting in council with senior advisers from the community. From 1992, chiefs shared range management tasks with Village Development Councils (VDCs), on which they served as *ex-officio* members. However, VDCs did not take over chiefs' powers of setting aside reserved grazing areas and impounding livestock (Ntlhoki, undated). Chiefs will lose their *ex-officio* position when VDCs are replaced by new

Community Councils, following elections that were due to be held in 2002. Interim councils are currently being established following the end of the term of office of the VDCs, and for the time being the range management functions of the VDCs have been handed back to the chiefs.

It should be clear that chiefs retain a central role in range management. Indeed, throughout the years of the VDCs, some chiefs have retained virtually complete *de facto* authority over range management and other land matters in their communities. The traditional gathering of the chief and senior men remains the core management mechanism for rangelands and other resources in many parts of the country, although this varies with local politics and is affected by the personality and ability of the chief. Women chiefs normally hold office as widows of former chiefs, or replace husbands who prove to be too incompetent to do the job. Like stock-keeping, range management is traditionally seen as a male preserve, and women chiefs normally delegate it to male councillors. Quite how far or fast range management roles will change after the introduction of the new Community Councils remains to be seen.

COMMUNITY-BASED RANGE MANAGEMENT: PRACTICE AND PROJECTS

Basotho and outsiders have long shared the view that range management is an environmental necessity. The pressures of colonialism and apartheid meant that the Basotho were forced to raise their livestock, which form a key part of their livelihood, in a small and rugged country. It was apparent to all that their grazing resources needed to be carefully managed, and that this could be done primarily by using these resources in rotation through the landscape and the seasons. Generations of chiefs and subjects have followed a system in which pastures and fields (after harvest) are declared open or closed to grazing by specified types of stock. Linked to this is the long-standing practice of transhumance. Stock owners in the strip of lowlands and foothills along the north and western edges of Lesotho typically send their animals to high pastures in the more extensive mountain areas for the summer, bringing them back down for the winter.

The British authorities became seriously concerned about soil erosion in the territory during the 1930s, when it was also becoming a major issue in South Africa and other parts of the world. Concern about the state of rangelands and their management only emerged after independence in 1966. From the 1970s to the 1990s, a succession of US-funded programmes pursued agricultural soil conservation, but also sought to contain perceived rangeland degradation through enhanced management strategies. These programmes proceeded from the assumption that the kingdom of Lesotho was heavily overstocked and overgrazed. In fact, studies of pasture condition and livestock numbers concluded that the country's rangelands were some 200 to 300 per cent overstocked (Weaver, undated). Over the quarter century since such programmes were launched in Lesotho, there has been much international debate about notions of overgrazing and appropriate stocking rates, and it is clear that the initial estimates of overstocking in the kingdom were exaggerated. For one thing, they failed to consider the role of crop residues in the annual cycle of livestock nutrition. More recent work suggests that Lesotho is 17 per cent overstocked (AGRER, 1999). Nevertheless, few would dispute the continuing decline in ground cover and pasture productivity across much of Lesotho's rangeland during recent decades. Whether this trend will continue depends upon the shifts in Lesotho livelihoods that will be discussed later.

The range management programmes of the last quarter century have achieved some local successes in making resource management more effective. Based on the principle that effective common property resource management requires clear and agreed boundaries between management areas, the government has worked hard to adjudicate and define the borders of chiefs' areas of jurisdiction. It was hoped that this would reduce the number of disputes over who could graze their livestock where, making systems of rotational range management easier to apply. These matters are complicated in Lesotho by the complex geography of chiefly jurisdictions. Local chiefs owe allegiance to principal chiefs, who, in turn, owe allegiance to the king. Because Basotho originally lived only in the lowlands and the foothills, using the mountains for summer grazing, most of the mountains fell directly under the principal chiefs, who had authority over range management there. Although the mountains are now more densely populated, local chiefs there often report to principal chiefs far away in the lowlands. Principal chiefs remain responsible for most of the very high mountain pastures, where there is no human habitation, and reserve some grazing areas for their exclusive personal use. Meanwhile, expanding settlements have encroached on mountain grazing areas.

Partly because of these trends, government policy now discourages transhumance between lowlands and mountains. Principal chiefs were meant to discontinue the issue of cattle post permits to people not resident in the mountains. This was intended to give the now numerous mountain residents sole access to mountain pastures (AGRER, 1999). However, this policy was facilitated by the decline in transhumance that was already taking place in response to stock theft and the shortage of herders. It accords with the government strategy of promoting more intensive, partly stall-fed, livestock production in the lowlands.

More locally, donor-funded government programmes have tried to codify and structure community-based range management in the mountains so that groups of villages and residents have a tighter and clearer affinity with a defined local territory. Range management areas (RMAs) of 10,000 to 35,000 hectares have been set up in exhaustive consultation with village and principal chiefs and local populations, who have formed grazing associations (GAs) to manage them. Usually, these initiatives have been linked to efforts to increase the value of livestock production – for example, through breeding and marketing programmes. This, it was hoped, would strengthen the incentive for effective range management by producing healthier and better-quality livestock that would generate higher returns from wool, mohair and meat.

As in the kingdom's extensive soil conservation efforts, the range management focus during recent decades has thus been on increased production through conservation. In Lesotho, few have contested the argument that resources can be used while they are being conserved. The country has had little scope for dedicating precious land and resources solely to biodiversity conservation. The small Sehlabathebe National Park, established in 1970, was, until recently, the single exception. There was little consultation with local people about its creation. People's livestock were denied access to grazing resources in the park. Thirty years on, this loss of land is still deeply resented. Livestock are often taken into the park, whose management has always suffered from its remote location and the vagaries of donor funding.

Broader and cruder efforts to reduce perceived overstocking have had less success. The Basotho have been as reluctant as other southern Africans to reduce livestock numbers in the name of the environment. The 1992 imposition by a military regime of grazing fees met such opposition that it was withdrawn in 1993 by a subsequent elected government. Various other donor-funded livestock and range management initiatives were similarly unsuccessful (Ferguson, 1994).

A more focused rationale for the introduction of RMAs and GAs emerged with the construction of the first two dams of the Lesotho Highlands Water Project (LHWP) over the last ten years. There is comparatively little soil cover on the high mountain catchments of the Katse and Mohale reservoirs, and both have large dead storage capacity below their off-takes. However, project authorities were concerned to enhance range management in these catchments in order to reduce the reservoir sedimentation risk. They have, therefore, stimulated the formation of more RMAs and GAs in these areas.

The RMA/GA concept has had only modest success. In 2000, there were nine RMAs and eight GAs, although two of the GAs were reported dormant in 1999 (Ntsokoane and Rasello, 2000; AGRER, 1999, Annex 1). It has achieved some reinforcement of CBNRM objectives in at least some of the areas where it has been applied; but the existing RMAs and GAs have experienced many operational difficulties in recent years. The concept currently needs review and overhaul. Moreover, the areas covered by functioning RMAs and GAs do not exceed 10 per cent of the national rangelands. In the rest of the country, range management has continued to be practised to a greater or lesser extent by the gradually evolving, or gradually decaying, local institutions that were outlined above.

Meanwhile, the context for CBNRM, livestock production and range management in Lesotho is changing significantly. Most important are the trends currently transforming Basotho livelihoods. Of course, trends in the priorities and strategies of development agencies are also significant. The rest of this case study considers the implications of these changes for community-based range management in the kingdom.

Changing livelihoods

A century ago, some Basotho were prosperous farmers, engaged in profitable export of crops and livestock to South Africa. More recently, much development strategy for Lesotho has foundered on the misapprehension that rural Basotho have rural livelihoods, and that they depend upon crops and livestock for a living. This has been untrue for several generations, during which time migrant Basotho have been employed in building the South African economy: working in its mines, farms and factories. Nevertheless, the often sub-subsistence wages paid to migrant workers meant that livestock production and the use of rangelands were critical components of Basotho's multiple livelihood strategies.

Over the past decade, migrant labour opportunities for Basotho in South Africa have steadily dwindled. While a spell on the South African mines used to be a standard part of a Mosotho man's career, only the fortunate few have jobs in South Africa these days. Despite the doubling of the population of Lesotho since independence in 1966, agricultural intensification has not occurred. Instead, the urban and peri-urban economies within Lesotho have been growing fast. More and more Basotho are making a living through new combinations of livelihood strategies that increasingly involve in-country employment or operating small enterprises away from the land. Indeed, the remoter mountain areas that used to depend most heavily upon livestock production are experiencing diminishing populations as people migrate to more accessible places. The proportion of households owning livestock is dwindling, and the practice of annual transhumance of livestock to and from the mountains is becoming less common. Dependence upon the range is becoming polarized between the richest and poorest groups in rural society. Livestock ownership is increasingly concentrated among better-off rural households. Very poor households are disproportionately dependent upon collecting wild resources, such as fuelwood and wild vegetables, from grazing areas.

Ironically, given the numerous government initiatives and donor projects, the governance of rural society is weaker than before. Partly as a result of these government initiatives, chiefs generally do not command the respect or exert the authority that their forebears did. With minimal resources and very little training, the modern village institutions that were meant to be the backbone of local government in recent decades have proved to be an ineffective replacement. In range management, as in other fields of governance, the result is weaker administration and widespread transgression of whatever rules may still exist. Some strong chiefs do still govern the range effectively, and this management shows in the condition of the resource. But many Basotho complain that open access now prevails on their rangeland. This is one manifestation of growing lawlessness in rural Lesotho. A more dramatic symptom of the same trend is the steady increase in stock theft, both within the country and across the Lesotho–South Africa border. Stock theft now ruins many rural livelihoods each year. Herds that have taken a decade or longer to build up disappear overnight and are seldom retrieved. Stock theft has become a powerful disincentive to livestock ownership. It has also affected patterns of transhumance, which are now subject to stringent stock movement regulations that are meant to counter the theft of livestock. People fear that their herds will be easier targets at remote mountain cattle posts. While this may increase pressure on lowland pastures, the broader result is decreased use of Lesotho's rangeland because more and more people feel that livestock ownership is not worthwhile. Indeed, some pastures, in areas where stock theft is most rampant, are in the best condition for many years because nobody dares to use them any more.

A third livelihood trend affects livestock production and range management. In a land without fences, the sector has always depended upon herd boys to keep animals grazing in the permitted locations within the range management system. Government has started to introduce free primary education and now more and more boys go to school. Herding labour has become a major constraint on livestock production, partly because people fear the penalties that unherded stock will attract when they wander, but mainly because of the fear of theft. Unlike some residents of neighbouring areas of the former Transkei, in South Africa, who call for the reconstruction of fences to paddock the rangeland, Basotho do not regard fencing as the answer. Options that they are starting to adopt include the combination of households' livestock into larger groups for herding purposes, the use of more adult herders, and the establishment of village anti-stock-theft committees. All of these are community initiatives in which the state is playing, at most, a background role.

Although it is still unfashionable to say so, there is a growing prospect that the perceived overstocking and degradation of Lesotho's rangelands may resolve themselves. These livelihood trends point towards a smaller number of animals (owned by a minority of the rural population) and a significantly reduced grazing pressure. But the mountains of Lesotho will always be good stock country. Livestock production will certainly continue. Range management and the control of stock theft will continue to be necessary. Basotho reject both open access and privately owned, fenced ranches as future scenarios. They still see community-based systems as their future mode of governance. But there is a long way to go before such systems can be achieved across the country. While the environmental problems may diminish, the social and institutional ones remain.

CHANGING GOVERNMENT AND DONOR STRATEGIES

After several decades spent grappling with community-based range management in Lesotho, the strategies and performance of government and donors seem to be shifting. There are three phenomena at work here. Firstly, for a number of reasons, the Lesotho government has suffered a decline in its recurrent budgets, its human resources and its capacity to implement. Secondly, there has been a general decline in donor support for Lesotho in recent times. Thirdly, we see the focus of government and donor interest shifting to include new approaches and issues with respect to the Lesotho rangelands. New players are involved. While old supporters such as the US Agency for International Development (USAID) no longer have programmes in Lesotho, the Global Environment Facility (GEF) now makes resources available, as does the United Nations Development Programme (UNDP). South Africa, formerly an all-powerful enemy, is now an all-powerful friend, interested in joint projects along the Maloti–Drakensberg border ranges, as well as in the LHWP.

While the concern with environmental well-being and human livelihoods persists in these evolving approaches to the Lesotho rangelands, there is a clear shift in their character. New projects place greater emphasis on conserving biodiversity. These include UNDP/GEF's Conserving Mountain Biodiversity in Lesotho, the Maloti–Drakensberg Conservation and Development Project and the new Maloti–Drakensberg Transfontier Conservation Area. Livestock production and range management are still significant components of some of these projects. However, there is a new emphasis on tourism as a way of generating wealth from these wild environments, while also conserving them.

Although its CBNRM experience has greatly differed from that of most other parts of the region, Lesotho may thus, ultimately, be edging closer to the mainstream. The conservation of wild resources, and associated initiatives for community-based nature tourism and natural resource management, are at the core of the region's experience with CBNRM as a development concept. They remain very much in vogue in donor and development circles. They are, at last, becoming significant rural development strategies for Lesotho's rangelands, even though older questions about community-based range management in the kingdom have not yet been adequately answered.

Some Basotho chiefs and communities are aware of these trends and opportunities. For example, in moves that would have been unthinkable just a decade ago, the chiefs and people of the Bokong and Tsehlanyane areas have dedicated thousands of hectares of rangeland to new community-based nature conservation and nature tourism initiatives. In collaboration with the Lesotho Highlands Development Authority (which is responsible for the LHWP), they have banned all grazing in these areas and aim to develop income-generating nature tourism there. There could be no clearer sign that shifting livelihood and development strategies are changing people's approaches to CBNRM on the rangelands of Lesotho.

ACKNOWLEDGEMENTS

Thanks to Thuso Green, Rapelang Ramoea and Leonia Thulo for information and comments, and to John Bruce for supplying recent documents from Lesotho. The author remains responsible for any inaccuracies.

REFERENCES

AGRER (1999) *National Livestock Development Study. Phase I Report. Technical Report A: Range Management.* SA AGRER NV report for Government of Lesotho and African Development Fund, Brussels

Ferguson, J (1994) *The Anti-politics Machine. 'Development', Depoliticization and Bureaucratic Power in Lesotho.* University of Minnesota Press, Minneapolis and London

Ntlhoki, M (undated) 'Legal aspects of the Range Management Area/Grazing Association programme'. Presentation to a Community Natural Resources Management Project, short-term training workshop, Maseru

Ntsokoane, K and Rasello, S (2000) 'Range Management Area/Grazing Association Section'. Paper presented to Livestock Seminar, 26 October 2000, Maseru

Weaver, L C (undated) 'Planning for Grazing Associations in Lesotho'. Paper written for seminar on Grazing Associations, January 1986, Maseru

Chapter 12

Beach Village Committees as a vehicle for community participation: Lake Malombe/Upper Shire River Participatory Programme

MAFANISO HARA

INTRODUCTION

Malawi is endowed with a sizeable capture fisheries resource (between 50,000 and 70,000 tonnes are landed annually) through possession of Lakes Malawi, Chilwa, Malombe and Chiuta, and other aquatic systems. The fish that come from these resources provide valuable protein (over 50 per cent of the nation's animal protein intake), income and employment. During recent years, there has been growing concern that these resources are being overexploited. A case in point is that of the Lake Malombe fishery.

In 1993, the Food and Agriculture Organization (FAO) of the United Nations reported that, based on 1991–1992 data, the chambo (*Orechromis* spp) stocks in Lake Malombe had collapsed and that fishermen had switched to the less valuable but still abundant kambuzi (*Lethonops* spp) fishery (FAO, 1993). Worse, fishermen had also started reducing the mesh size of the kambuzi seine nets from the legal size of 32.5 millimetres, meaning that the kambuzi stocks were also in danger of becoming overfished. By 1995, there were clear signs that even the kambuzi stocks were in decline (see Figure 12.1). Three main causes were suggested for the decline and collapse of the stocks: overcapitalization, increased use of illegal fishing gear and methods, and the inability of government to enforce the existing regulations effectively.

Several recommendations emanated from the FAO report to the Malawi government. In general, these recommendations were aimed at the biological recovery of the fishery through the restoration of fish habitats, protection of juveniles and breeding fish and a reduction of fishing effort. While these

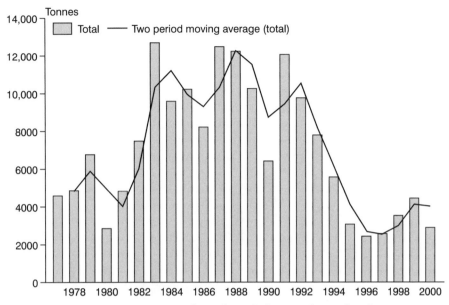

Figure 12.1 *Estimated total catch from Lake Malombe*

recommendations had a sound biological basis, it was realized that, in the past, this alone had not been enough to ensure successful implementation of such recommendations in the form of regulations or restrictive controls. One of the major constraints was recognized as budgetary shortages (Fisheries Department, 1993). In addition, the Fisheries Department (FD) was faced with increasing defiance and open resistance to compliance with regulations from fishermen (Hara, 2001). In fact, by the early 1990s, incidents of violence against fisheries inspectors who were out on patrol duties had become common. To implement the new and more stringent regulations as recommended by the FAO report, the Malawi government would have needed even greater resources and enforcement capability. At a time when government was streamlining its activities and cutting down its budget under the structural adjustment programme, this approach was a non-starter. The government had to search for an alternative regime. It was decided that the regime that seemed most practical, and which promised the best chance for success, was to involve a certain amount of self-regulation by the user communities.

In view of the foregoing, the Malawi government decided, in 1993, to launch a pilot project for user participation in the management of capture fisheries, the Lake Malombe/Upper Shire River Participatory Fisheries Management Programme (PFMP). The programme started in 1993 with a consultancy by Bell and Donda that drew up the proposed programme of activities and institutional set-up (Bell and Donda, 1993). While the immediate objective of the project was the recovery of the fishery, the long-term objective was to develop a management regime that would require minimum inputs from the FD, while at the same time ensuring sustainability and economic

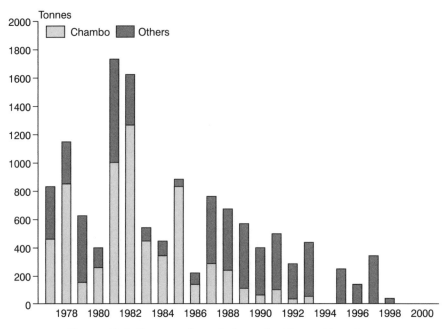

Figure 12.2 *Estimated catch from the Upper Shire River*

viability of the resource for the fishing communities (Fisheries Department, 1993). This project was made possible through the assistance of several donors, including the United Nations Development Programme (UNDP), the FAO, the Deutsche Gesellschaft für Technische Zusammenarbeit (German government agency for international cooperation – GTZ), the UK Overseas Development Administration (ODA) and the World Bank.

The institutional arrangement for the PFMP is that the Mangochi District Fisheries Office is the lead government agent in this co-management arrangement. It was assumed that the fisher communities did not have an adequate institutional set-up to enable them to play an effective role in the new management regime (Bell and Donda, 1993). Thus, the Fisheries Department facilitated the creation and training of community-level institutions called Beach Village Committees (BVCs) (Hara, 1996). In theory, BVCs are democratically elected community-level committees that represent the fishing communities in the co-management arrangement. The village headmen are *ex-officio* members of the committees in their areas of jurisdiction.

After seven years of implementation (1993 to 1999), there did not seem to be real positive recovery of the fish stocks. Figures 12.1 and 12.2 show the official statistics available to date. Interviews with FD field staff and fishers indicate that, as of 2001, there had not been any real evidence of the fishery recovering. The question is why has the new regime failed to have a positive impact during that time?

A number of factors, such as ineffectiveness of the revised regulations, the continued violation of the regulations by the fishers, the delayed start of some of the programme activities and ecological effects, could have contributed to the lack of recovery. However, Hara et al (2002) argue that the main reasons can be attributed to institutional problems. This study will explore the most probable reasons for the lack of positive impact on the fishery by the co-management regime as implemented through the use of BVCs.

Probable reasons for the PFMP's
lack of positive impact

The constitution of the BVCs

The role of the Fisheries Department as facilitator in initiating and mobilizing communities for participation in the new management regime has been problematic. There was a general feeling within the communities that the elections and nominations for BVC members were not fair and that those elected did not get their positions on merit or with the support of the majority of the fisher community. It was felt that most of the people elected were friends or acquaintances of the FD personnel or the village headmen. Given this responsibility in the past, the FD has continued with the facilitation of training newly elected members because the impression had been created that one cannot become a qualified BVC member unless one has had training. As a result, there have been cases when elections for new BVCs had to be postponed because government did not have money to train the new BVC members. The new BVC members also demanded training because of the allowances they got during training.

Stakeholder objectives for co-management

The FD's objectives for adopting co-management were to stop and reverse the decline of the fishery through improved compliance to regulations, reduction of fishing effort and improved legitimacy for a regime that had grown increasingly alien from the user communities (Fisheries Department, 1993). Another important reason for introducing co-management was the belief that some amount of self-regulation would result in a reduction in transaction costs to the state. For the user communities, the motivation for agreeing to participate in the management of the fishery was to stem the decline of the fishery and effect its recovery in order to continue deriving socio-economic benefits from the resource (Bell and Donda, 1993).

In the main, therefore, the objectives of the Fisheries Department were oriented toward conservation. The existing regulations were duly reformulated under the direction of government, only this time with the supposed participation and support of fishermen under more 'democratic' and 'transparent' arrangements. The FD presented the proposed regulations to fishermen for discussion, stating that 'in the event of strong negative reaction to the regulations, the Fisheries Department may be prepared to compromise slightly', (Fisheries Department, 1993) and that government would, initially, retain decision-making power concerning the objectives and regulations of the programme. What should be noted is that the regulations drawn up under the co-management regime are still seen by fishers as emanating from the Fisheries Department rather than having been jointly formulated with the fisher community.

International donors are clearly also stakeholders in initiatives of this sort. They want to achieve the best possible use for their funds, with positive social and economic outcomes for the intended beneficiaries. By influencing the adoption of co-management, donors seem to believe that the subsidiarity principle being commonly applied elsewhere should also be applied in developing countries such as Malawi. Donors further believe that political empowerment of user communities in the resource management process will result in sustainable resource exploitation practices and thus have positive economic effects on user communities. Whether Western-style democracy and advocacy can work and be of benefit to the management of fisheries on Lake Malombe remains an open question. In this regard, it is important to note that most decisions in the fishing communities are taken either by consensus or by the autocratic authority of traditional leaders rather than through a formal, 'winner-takes-all' democratic process (Donda, 2001; Hara et al, 2002).

Organizational structure, participation of vested interests and incentives for participation

The problem of the active participation of vested interests in the BVCs is an important factor. This relates to gear ownership and the organizational structure of the fishing units. The majority of gear owners employ crews to fish on their behalf. Thus, the operational decisions out on the lake are taken by the crewmembers. In terms of the Fisheries Act, it is the gear owner, not the crewmember, who is legally responsible for any infringement of regulations. The benefit-sharing systems are based on a ratio of 45 per cent of the catch or catch sales for the gear owner and 55 per cent for the crewmembers (Hara, 2001). Crewmembers' security of tenure in a fishing unit depends upon their performance. As the fishery has deteriorated and gears have increasingly been retired from the fishery, the turnover of crewmembers has increased. It has also become common to find two or three crews operating one set of gear in turns. All of these factors mean that there is great pressure on crewmembers to increase catches in any way possible. In general, the sharing schemes and the lack of long-term tenure within fishing units make crewmembers prone to operational decisions that stem from short-term economic maximization strategies and therefore encourage illegal fishing activities. In addition, because crewmembers lack legal responsibility for their actions, there are few deterrents to infringing upon regulations (Hara et al, 2002).

Donda (2001) points out that only 30 per cent of the BVC members were active fishers up to 1998. Most of these 30 per cent were gear owners rather than crewmembers. As a result, most fishers shunned or boycotted meetings called by the BVCs and, to a large extent, ignored the resolutions that were passed by the BVCs. They complained that the BVCs were taking decisions on fishing issues that they had little knowledge about. Some fishers went so far as to say that they felt that the BVCs took decisions that were meant to punish fishers. One effect of the high percentage of non-fishers on BVCs was that members felt strongly that they should be paid for their services since they did not benefit directly from the fishery (Hara, 1996).

The government's main incentives for co-management are a reduction of transaction costs and improving the legitimacy of the management system. For members of BVCs, the main incentives seemed to be monetary, through their attendance at meetings and workshops. This divergence in incentives for co-management remains, and since the number of meetings and workshops has declined after the initial implementation stages, people are reluctant to take up positions as BVC members, arguing that it is *thangata* (work without pay). The decline in local people's willingness to take up voluntary positions of responsibility is attributable, in part, to the political change in Malawi from a dictatorship to democracy. Whereas people could be forced to do self-help work under the former dispensation, more and more people now demand that they be paid for any work that they do.

The composition of BVCs is important to the legitimacy and, thus, the success of the PFMP. What are perceived as incentives for membership is crucial for the viability of BVCs. The greater the membership of vested interests, the greater the possibility of creating effective management bodies. The involvement of crewmembers, who make operational decisions out on the lake, is particularly important if BVCs are to function effectively as management institutions.

Power struggles: Their effect on legitimacy and representivity

The model of BVCs as fisher-community representative bodies envisaged them as strong independent bodies that could eventually assume delegated management responsibilities from government. The model gave village headmen honorary positions on the BVCs as *ex-officio* members. In a typical African village setting, decision-making and authority have historically been dominated by the village headman (Mamdani, 1996). While issues may be discussed in an open forum or by a council of elders and consensus reached, the village headman retains the ultimate authority for making the final decision. Village headmen can even issue authoritative decrees without consultation (Donda, 2001). Thus, village headmen have been prone to ignoring the authority of BVCs since by historical tradition they hold ultimate authority. The institution of BVCs brought about contestation for power between BVCs and village headmen since BVCs viewed themselves as independent power brokers within the villages.

By custom, and through historical tradition, village headmen derive privileges from the fishery through their positions. For example, when a migrant fisherman comes to the village, he normally has to seek permission from the village headman to stay; he also has to pay something to the village headman as a token of his gratitude. In addition, all fishers landing their fish in his area are supposed to give him a weekly honorarium – that is, a specified amount of fish called *mawe*. Under the co-management arrangement, incoming migrant fishermen have to seek permission from both the village headman and BVC. This directly infringes upon the privileges of village headmen. In some cases, gear owners saw the new arrangement as a chance to cut out the customary practices, such as the giving of *mawe*, by encouraging BVCs to challenge these.

The challenge to their powers and privileges led some village headmen to try to curb the powers of BVCs. In this context, some village headmen disbanded the elected BVCs and put in place BVCs that they could control. In other instances, village headmen forced the replacement of specific members whom they did not like with BVC members whom they favoured. Where the BVCs have resisted being taken over by village headmen and have established some semblance of independent authority, fishers have often been confronted with dual authority as village headmen have continued to exercise their traditional authority on their own (Hara et al, 2002). In some cases, communities felt that BVCs largely represented the interests of the village headmen rather than their own.

While there is a need to have reasonably independent BVCs, it also appears necessary to ensure that their powers and authority are complementary to those of the village headmen. It is likely that the traditional and customary system of justice under the village headmen will play a role in administering justice and sanctions in the co-management regime, since village headmen preside over traditional courts and informal systems of justice in their areas of jurisdiction (Hara, 2001). Thus, village headmen cannot be excluded from such a regime. Finding ways in which the powers of BVCs and village headmen can accommodate and complement each other remains one of the main challenges to the success of co-management.

As bodies elected by the fisher community to represent their interests, BVCs were supposed to derive their power from the fisher community. Instead, most BVC members feel that they derive their powers from government (Hara et al, 2002). Since BVCs assumed Fisheries Department enforcement and licensing duties, this perception has been further strengthened. Because of these roles and duties, BVCs also saw themselves as doing the dirty work of the FD. For these reasons, most BVC members felt that they should be remunerated for the tasks that they carried out. Concurrently, fisher communities view BVCs as representing the FD, rather than as bodies representing them. Due to the confrontational nature of their tasks, there was growing animosity towards BVCs from fishermen. The result was that most BVCs appeared to have alienated themselves from the fisher communities on whose behalf they were supposed to be acting. Improving the representivity of BVCs to their constituency is, thus, a crucial aspect of increasing the legitimacy of the regime in the eyes of the fishers.

Enabling legislation

The 1997 Fisheries Act (Government of Malawi, 1997) contained four particular changes essential for the promotion and facilitation of the participatory management regime:

1   the introduction of flexibility to allow for a regular review of policy and regulations;
2   the transfer of property rights over specified fish resources to communities;
3   permission to allow part of the revenue obtained from gear licensing to be ploughed back into local-level institutions to cover administrative costs and incentives; and
4   provision for the transfer of management responsibility to local institutions when appropriate.

While the revised Act seems to provide adequately for some of these changes, there are still aspects in which it falls short. Two of these are the real transfer of property rights and the ability of local managerial institutions to prosecute offenders and apply sanctions. The legal transfer of property rights is particularly important for limiting entry and access in order to reduce fishing capacity and effort.

Changes to the powers of various courts under the revised 1995 Courts Act (Government of Malawi, 1995) have the potential to hamper the ability of traditional courts to prosecute and apply sanctions (Hara, 2001). Under the new system, criminal offences can only be heard in a magistrate's court, while traditional authorities can only hear civil cases. In this context, it is not clear how traditional authorities can adjudicate over fisheries offences, which are criminal in nature (Hara, 2001). Furthermore, village headmen cannot impose cash fines under the new system. Such ambiguities could adversely affect the implementation of the co-management regime. These shortfalls suggest that the revised 1997 Fisheries Act might still be inadequate in providing all of the provisions that local-level institutions might require in order to carry out their assigned tasks efficiently and effectively under the co-management regime.

The main problem with the revised 1997 Fisheries Act, though, remains that of implementation. Two years after it had been passed, most of its provisions remained unimplemented. This affected the legal authority of BVCs, the legality of enforcing the revised regulations and the legality of ploughing back a part of licensing revenues to communities.

Short-term external (donor) support

The introduction of co-management was implemented as a multi-donor funded programme (Hara, 2001). Problems that come with differences in donor policies, disbursement and control of funds, and different time frames could not be avoided completely. By 1997, all of the projects but one had phased out. This has prompted the usual concerns surrounding donor-funded programmes, such as the dependency syndrome and the sustainability of activities once projects are phased out. Already, the programme has been severely affected as most of the projects were phased out before the management regime could be firmly entrenched (Donda, 2001; Hara, 2001). In addition, the impression seems to have been created that co-management is a donor-funded government project of limited duration, rather than a long-term partnership that should move towards sustainability. The question is, how long will outside assistance continue to be required before the two partners, government and local people, can take over full financial responsibility? Can the programme be sustained without outside assistance? In the short term, this seems rather doubtful.

The effects of prevailing socio-economic conditions

Mangochi District, where Lake Malombe lies, is characterized by adverse socio-economic indicators, such as high unemployment and population growth, inadequate land-size holdings, low agricultural productivity, high rates of illiteracy, low self-help ethic or voluntary spirit and weak micro-enterprises (Hara, 2001). In 1996, an estimated 75 per cent of the people in the economically productive age bracket did not have formal full-time employment (Hara, 2001). The inability of seasonal agriculture and the formal sector to absorb most of the economically active population means that most people derive their livelihoods from the fishery. The fact that the number of crewmembers continues to increase, even though the number of fishing units has been declining during most of the 1990s, is a clear indicator of this trend. This absorptive role that the fishing industry has to play is placing the fisheries under ever-increasing pressure.

During the 1990s, the structural adjustment programme and greater globalization resulted in the collapse of many local manufacturing industries and the shrinking of the manufacturing sector (National Economic Council, 1998). Unable to find work in the formal sector, most people are being forced to derive livelihoods from natural resource-based activities, such as farming, fishing and selling firewood. With an average population growth rate of over 3 per cent per annum (Government of Malawi/UNDP, 1998), this pressure can only increase as the balance between population growth and natural resources becomes increasingly skewed.

One of the underlying reasons for the introduction of co-management was that this could facilitate the introduction of measures to limit access and entry into the fishery, thereby reducing overall fishing effort. For the fisher community, such measures were seen as desirable in principle, but unpalatable in practice due to the economic hardship and possible social disruption that they could bring about (Bell and Donda, 1993). In addition, there are moral and strategic dilemmas for fishers as far as proposals to limiting access are concerned. Fishers are not keen on the proposal to introduce limited access because it implies the 'privatization' of a common pool resource in which everyone has historically been free to fish (Hara, 1996). In addition, such measures would imply denying others in similarly desperate economic circumstances the chance of deriving a livelihood from the fishery.

The rural setting of the Lake Malombe fishing community, its assumed homogeneity, kinship social structures and traditional authority systems of governance appeared, at first, to provide favourable conditions for co-management. In reality, though, the communities are greatly influenced by the market economy due to their link to the urban economies of cities, such as Blantyre, Zomba and Lilongwe, which act as the main fish markets.

The success of measures aimed at limiting access depends upon the ability of the general economy to act as a sink for excess labour from the fishing communities. As long as employment opportunities in the other sectors of the economy remain low and the fishery continues to act as the main source of livelihoods, such measures are likely to be viewed unfavourably within the fishing communities. In this context, it is doubtful whether co-management alone without other support or complementary measures can influence fishers to adopt sustainable patterns of exploitation.

CONCLUSION

What can be deduced from this case study is that one of the most critical aspects in the introduction of co-management is the tension between two organizational aspects. The first problem concerns the struggle for authority and power between the BVCs and the traditional authorities. The second source of tension can be attributed to the source of initiative and drive for co-management – whether this is top-down from government or bottom-up from the fisher communities (Hara et al, 2002). In order for the co-management regime to be seen as legitimate and representative, the fishing community must feel that they own the management process and its organs in terms of representation, the balance of power and the election of BVCs. Too much influence from the Fisheries Department or village headmen results in a process where BVCs are seen as alien to the constituency whom they are intended to represent.

As a focus for fisher community participation in the co-management partnership, the BVC is located among three groupings: the Fisheries Department, village headmen and the fisher community, each seemingly straining for control and influence of the BVC. In such a position, BVCs have to achieve a balancing act in terms of influence and derivation of power and authority. The government's main aim seems to be that BVCs should act as a vehicle for implementing and achieving its conservation objectives. At the same time, the BVCs must contend with the traditional powers and authority of village headmen. While trying to balance between these two forces, the BVCs must try to fulfil their obligations of representing the interests of their constituency – the fishing community – even if these might not be in line with the objectives of the Fisheries Department or the interests of village headmen.

It would appear that for an effective co-management regime, the influence of fishers on BVCs should be greater than the influence of the FD and/or village headmen. Thus, how the powers and authority of the BVCs are related to those of the FD and village headmen is one of the main challenges to comanagement on Lake Malombe. In setting up BVCs sufficiently independently in order to command the respect and confidence of fishers, it is necessary that, firstly, village headmen are not rivalled or antagonized and, secondly, that the objectives of the fisher community are not in contradiction with the aims and objectives of government.

The issue of objectives raises the question of what the short- to medium-term objective of the PFMP ought to be. Should it be institution-building or the recovery of the fishery? If co-management is seen as holding the best promise for improved management and recovery of the fishery, then institution-building for co-management should be taken as the short- to medium-term objective in the hope that recovery of the fishery will follow as a result of successful reform of the regime. After all, if the present prioritization of objectives does not seem to be achieving recovery of the fishery, it would be prudent, first, to try concentrating on the reform of the regime and see what results this brings.

Finally, the effects of external factors such as the economy have a bearing on the effectiveness and thus the success of the new regime. Probably, the external factors pose the biggest challenge to sustainable recovery of the fishery and to moving towards sustainable exploitation. Economic livelihood realities mean that the prospects for effective co-management are bound to be poor.

REFERENCES

Bell, R and Donda, S (1993) *Community Participation Consultancy Report, volume 1.* Fisheries Department, Lilongwe

Donda, S (2001) *Theoretical Advancement and Institutional Analysis of Fisheries Co-management in Malawi: Experiences from Lakes Malombe and Chiuta.* PhD thesis, University of Aalborg, Aalborg

FAO (1993) *Fisheries Management of the Southeast Lake Malawi, the Upper Shire River and Lake Malombe.* FAO CIFA Technical Paper no 21, FAO, Rome

Fisheries Department (Government of Malawi) (1993) *Artisanal Fisheries Management Plan.* Fisheries Department, Lilongwe

Fisheries Department (1998) *A Guide to the Fisheries Conservation and Management Act 1997.* Fisheries Department, Lilongwe

Government of Malawi (1995) *Courts Acts Miscellaneous Amendments of Statute Law No 19.* Ministry of Justice, Lilongwe

Government of Malawi (1997) *The Fisheries Conservation and Management Act.* Government Printer, Zomba

Government of Malawi/United Nations Development Programme (1998) *Management for Development Programme: Revised Mangochi Socio-Economic Profile.* Mangochi, Malawi

Hara, M (1996) *Problems of Introducing Community Participation in Fisheries Management: Lessons from Lake Malombe and Upper Shire River (Malawi) Participatory Fisheries Management Programme.* Southern African Perspectives No 59, Centre for African Studies, School of Government, University of Western Cape, Bellville

Hara, M (2001) *Could Co-Management Provide a Solution to the Problems of Artisanal Fisheries Management on the Southeast Arm of Lake Malawi?* PhD thesis, University of the Western Cape, Cape Town

Hara, M, Donda, J and Njaya, F (2002) 'Lessons from Malawi's experience with fisheries co-management initiatives', in Geheb, K and Sarch, M-T (eds) *Africa's Inland Fisheries: The Management Challenge.* Fountain Publishers, Kampala, pp31–48

Mamdani, M (1996) *Citizen and Subject: Contemporary Africa and the Legacy of Late Colonialism.* Princeton University Press, New Jersey

National Economic Council (1998) *Malawi Government Economic Report 1998.* Budget Document No 4, Government Printer, Zomba

Chapter 13

Key issues in Namibia's communal conservancy movement

COLIN NOTT AND MARGARET JACOBSOHN

Namibia's national community-based natural resource management (CBNRM) programme aims to link democracy and social and economic development to the conservation and management of natural resources. The focus of the Namibian programme on both participatory development and democracy-building promotes the economic upliftment of the majority of residents, and seeks to avoid the usual skewed pattern whereby a minority elite captures rights over, and benefits from, common property resources, so common in Africa (Adams and Hulme, 2001). Namibia's CBNRM philosophy also attempts to weave together best practices from free enterprise and common property management to support the long-term economic, social and environmental sustainability of rural Namibia. Two of the key features of the Namibian experience have thus been the growth of grassroots democracy and new opportunities for biodiversity conservation.

BACKGROUND

Namibia has three types of land tenure: state land (including national parks), commercially owned land and communal land. Although about 40 per cent of the country is communal land, more than 60 per cent of the population live there. Today's communal areas are the former 'homelands' created by the old South African apartheid system under which Namibia was ruled until its independence in 1990. Ethnic groups were allocated land in different parts of the country and the policies of the day served the interests of the ruling elite while limiting livelihood improvement strategies in communal areas.

Despite the hostile political environment under South African hegemony, community-based initiatives addressing environmental issues in the communal areas were started before independence. These have now grown into a national movement. Namibia's CBNRM and conservancy programme could be described as the largest grassroots movement since the struggle for independence.

THE ROOTS OF THE PROGRAMME

During the early 1980s, wildlife was being decimated in many parts of Africa. The spectacular, arid north-west of Namibia, today known as the Kunene and Erongo regions, was no exception. A crisis situation had developed as a result of severe drought and extensive illegal hunting, and it seemed inevitable that wildlife, including desert rhino and elephant, would be virtually exterminated from this area.

The political system of the day, however, rendered local people virtually powerless to take action against massive illegal hunting of almost all species. From the 1980s, a process of building mutual trust between community leaders and conservationists began, and from this grew a shared vision of a future with wildlife. Discussions resulted in traditional leaders appointing their own community game guards. Local leadership and, later, communities shifted from being the biggest threat to the continued survival of wildlife to being the key ally.

THE POST-INDEPENDENCE ERA AND LEGISLATIVE REFORM

Lessons learned from conservancies on privately owned land in Namibia suggested that if the right to manage and benefit from wildlife was not devolved to the farm level, then wildlife numbers would steadily decline. Visits to and from Zimbabwe's Communal Areas Management Programme for Indigenous Resources (CAMPFIRE) suggested that the appropriate level for the devolution of authority should be the community itself. Thus, after independence, conservation laws were amended so that communal area farmers had similar rights as those already enjoyed by farmers on privately owned land (Jones, 1999). The resulting legislation afforded communities who organized themselves into a conservancy the right to utilize wildlife for consumptive and non-consumptive use, as long as use remained sustainable. Finally approved in 1996, the legal system has been embraced as an opportunity by communities across the country. By the beginning of 2002, 15 communal area conservancies were registered in Namibia, with more than 30 emerging during the past five years. CBNRM and the conservancy process has thus become a national movement, representing more than 100,000 people, most of whom are remote rural residents, and covering an area in excess of 8 million hectares.

Key issues related to the programme

Natural resource management and biodiversity

Impressive increases in wildlife numbers, including black rhino, elephant, plains game and predators, have occurred in many conservancy areas. Wildlife has been re-introduced in other areas where it previously occurred and also re-established within adjacent areas, resulting in wildlife corridors emerging between major parks. Many conservancies have employed staff and run offices, while new robust systems are being established by conservancies for wildlife monitoring and management. Land-use zoning of conservancies is being conducted by committees and members of conservancies for wildlife, tourism and agricultural activities. A solid foundation has thus been established for securing wildlife on communal land over the long term (Child, 2001).

The resultant impact of problem animals on people's lives, however, has become a significant threat to the long-term future of certain species on communal land. Proactive decision-making is required to manage problem animals in such a way as to maintain a positive cost-benefit analysis from the point of view of the farmer. Creative solutions to challenges are being investigated and implemented. There is a need to compensate individual losses incurred by farmers from high-value species and this is being addressed by an innovative compensation/insurance/trust fund scheme, which is to be tested in three Kunene and four Caprivi conservancies. While the viability of the scheme requires a uniform policy for all conservancies, flexibility will allow individual conservancies to select options of premium payment. For example, conservancies can decide whether conservancy members should pay premiums individually or from conservancy funds (Child, 2001).

Issues related to income generation

By 2002, communities had begun to earn considerable income through consumptive and non-consumptive use of wildlife. At the time of writing, five conservancies had signed trophy-hunting agreements, with nine others preparing to do so. Four conservancies have 'own use' quotas to harvest game for local consumption. Three conservancies have entered into joint venture agreements for high-earning lodges, with many more in progress. There are numerous smaller campsites and other income-generating activities.

Notable has been the conservancy emphasis in joint venture agreements around long-term conservancy ownership, job opportunities and training for local members and joint management responsibilities. Secondary to this has been the financial deals concluded. During 2001, more than US$600,000 in benefits were generated by conservancies. This amounts to a more than 230 per cent increase over the previous year and this trend is expected to continue. Had tourism not collapsed in East and West Caprivi in early 2000 – as a result of a number of local and regional conflicts – the conservancy earnings for 2001 would have been considerably more.

Two conservancies are now financially independent, employing their own staff, paying their own management costs and still making a profit for their members. One conservancy, Torra, had about US$80,000 in its bank account during late 2001.

Currently, however, an important area of conflict regarding tourism revenues is the right of individual entrepreneurs versus those of the collective membership of a conservancy. Conservancies encourage individually owned tourism businesses but require the owner to enter into some form of legal agreement with the conservancy as the body responsible for the management and conservation of the common property natural resources. The entrepreneur may be required to pay a levy from tourism revenues and is expected to comply with tourism standards and codes of operation. This has led to severe conflict in some cases between the conservancy and local business people – essentially, a clash between collective and capitalist styles of operating. The Ministry of Environment and Tourism is currently drawing up codes and guidelines for mediating and merging these two systems of using wild resources through the conservancy movement.

Issues related to institution-building

The conservancy legislation does not take adequate account of the roles played by traditional authorities in conservancies, although they have played key and supportive roles in a number of places. It is intended that this should be addressed by investigating mechanisms to ensure an appropriate level of jurisdiction in relation to the conservancy by these local authorities (IRDNC, 2002). In some areas, where traditional authorities are strongly supported by conservancy members, the chief or headman has appointed one or more councillors to the conservancy committee, with the chief acting as conservancy 'patron'. Where support for a particular traditional authority is weak or split, the traditional authority has tended to perceive the conservancy as a threat. In at least one case, this perception has proved to be correct as the enhanced capacity and organization of ordinary people facilitated by conservancy development has enabled such people to voice their dissatisfaction with an established but unpopular headman.

The establishment of conservancies has built upon the need for local, representative and transparent social structures. The vehicle for this under the conservancy legislation is the conservancy committee. These committees have formed the basis for joint planning and communication and have sustained partnerships with communities, government, non-governmental organizations (NGOs) and the private sector. Conservancies are required to operate as membership organizations while dealing with issues such as staff management, budgeting, book-keeping and administration, and with institutions such as government, donors and the private sector.

While committees face the challenges of management, new institutions have been established for lobbying and advocacy. The first of these was the formation of the Namibian Community-Based Tourism Association (NACOBTA). This is a membership-based organization for communal tourism entrepreneurs established to deal with the integration of tourism on communal land within mainstream tourism activities. NACOBTA has become a key player in lobbying for communal tourism rights and in bringing community-based tourism into the market-place.

Another forum, the Communal Conservancy Association for North-West Namibia was, at the time of writing, in the process of being established. In different regions, conservancies have been meeting quarterly to plan, learn and share experiences, as well as to assist and evaluate one another's progress. The interest in such meetings has grown to the point where a joint forum to represent the collective interests, needs and issues of conservancies in north-western Namibia was established. In response to conflicts that have inevitably arisen with the establishment of conservancies, a conflict resolution group was formed. Comprised of leaders from most registered or emerging conservancies in the north-west, the group has taken the initiative to mediate conflicts between communities.

Support organizations have also gathered themselves into a national collaborative body – the Namibian Association of CBNRM Support Organizations (NACSO) – and, through a number of working groups, cooperation is taking place. Given the well-known tendency of NGOs to fight among themselves and with government, the smooth running of NACSO is an achievement within the CBNRM programme. These institutions are, for the first time, providing a legally constituted framework for communities to be taken seriously at a local, regional and national level.

THE WAY FORWARD

Namibia has made great strides in achieving community conservation in the wildlife sector; but it still has to develop a holistic approach to managing all resources by government and other support agencies. Communal area conservancies and their traditional authorities are developing such a vision – one in which the local users of resources will manage and coordinate inputs from government, NGOs and the private sector, as clients and partners. It is a vision of true empowerment that could revolutionize rural development in Namibia, alleviating poverty while, at the same time, maintaining a healthy and diverse resource base.

REFERENCES

Adams, W and Hulme, D (2001) 'Changing narratives, policies and practices in African conservation', in Hulme, D and Murphree, M (eds) *African Wildlife and Livelihoods: The Promise and Performance of Community Conservation*. James Curry, London, pp9–23

Child, B (2001) *Mid-Term Review of LIFE-II and An Assessment of the Namibia National CBNRM Programme*. Prepared for USAID, Windhoek

IRDNC (2002) *CBNRM in Kunene: Five-Year Proposal, July 2002 to June 2007.* Integrated Rural Development and Nature Conservation, internal document prepared for WWF-UK, Windhoek

Jones, B T B (1999) 'Rights, revenue and resources: The problems and potential of conservancies as community wildlife management institutions in Namibia', *Evaluating Eden Discussion Paper* No 2. International Institute for Environment and Development, London

Chapter 14

The Torra Conservancy in Namibia

Colin Nott, Anna Davis and Bernard Roman

As we look to the future, we continue to value the beauty of our natural environment and the peaceful rural character of Torra Conservancy. We envision sustainable use of natural resources contributing to social upliftment and appropriate economic development (IRDNC, 2002).

BACKGROUND

Torra Conservancy, one of Namibia's 15 legally registered communal area conservancies (Davis, 1998), is situated on remote communal land in north-western Namibia. It is sparsely populated (less than one person per square kilometre) and has an average rainfall of less than 150 millimetres per annum. Torra Conservancy is situated in the Kunene region and covers an area of 3522 square kilometres with 300 registered members and a total estimated population of approximately 1000, including children. The residents of Torra Conservancy are made up largely of Riemvasmaak residents who were forcibly removed and relocated from South Africa during the 1970s and indigenous Damara-Nama groups, most of whom are small-stock farmers. The area consists of a numbers of 'farms', based on the originally white-owned land, and one main settlement, Bergsig, which accommodates a police station, clinic, primary school, several government offices, shops and a conservancy office. The conservancy is characterized by spectacular arid scenery and a wide range of wildlife, including desert-adapted elephant, black rhino and, occasionally, lions.

Before 1990, the conditions in this area were extremely adverse, including poor accessibility, limited water and immense problems with predators. Indicative of the extent of this problem was the loss by one farmer of 90 sheep and goats to a pride of 13 lions in one night during the early 1980s at the height of a severe drought (Davis, 1998). Conflict with the then Department of Wildlife was inevitable and illegal hunting was the order of the day. When hunting in the region shifted from subsistence to commercial gain, the rhino and elephant populations were in danger of being exterminated.

This has changed over a number of years to the current situation where a conservancy has been registered, wildlife numbers have increased dramatically and sustainable natural resource-use practices are in place. A long-term tourism joint venture contract has been entered into, delivering considerable direct and indirect benefits. In addition, a trophy-hunting contract has been signed with an external operator. This resulted in financial independence for the conservancy within a very short period of time. It is able to meet its own operational costs, as well as make a profit of several hundred thousand Namibia dollars for its members (Child, 2001).

Many organizations have contributed to Torra's success, to date. A strong partnership between the Ministry of Environment and Tourism (MET), the non-governmental organization (NGO) Integrated Rural Development and Nature Conservation (IRDNC), the Save the Rhino Trust and pioneering private-sector partners (Wilderness Safaris Namibia and Savanna Safaris) have provided the field base for the success achieved (Jones, 2001). Additional, vital support has been obtained from centrally based organizations, including the Namibian Community-Based Tourism Association, Rossing Foundation and the Legal Assistance Centre. However, Torra Conservancy still faces many challenges, which include institutional development, vital administration and management issues, and a holistic approach to resource management, including a focus on biodiversity conservation to ensure long-term economic prosperity and social stability. This chapter outlines some of the milestones of the Torra Conservancy, how they were achieved, important lessons learned and some of the challenges ahead.

WILDLIFE: A LOCAL COMMITMENT TO CONSERVATION

Because of the widespread illegal hunting in north-west Namibia during the early 1990s (Jones, 2001), local conservationists realized that the battle to save wildlife, including desert rhino and elephant, would be lost if local people remained hostile to conservation. This, coupled with the knowledge that the majority of residents and their leadership did not support the illegal hunting, but felt unable to stop it, laid the basis for a new approach. This included improving relations with the local leadership and developing mutual trust and respect, as well as directly involving local people in conservation through a community game guard network. Suspected poachers were treated with dignity, their family commitments respected and, where possible, cases were handled together with the traditional authority.

From this, a shared vision based on a future with wildlife was developed and supported by local communities in partnership with government, NGOs and community leaders. Today, the majority of residents actively support

Table 14.1 *Estimated game numbers for Kunene region and Torra Conservancy*

Animal	1982 Kunene region (70,000 km²)	2001 Kunene region (70,000 km²)	2001 Torra Conservancy (3522 km²)
Springbok	650	74,575	5000
Oryx	400	15,364	1500
Zebra	450	12,593	560
Elephant	250	561	40
Giraffe	220	1075	110
Black rhinoceros	Confidential data	Population doubled	Population increased

Note: The 1982 census was aerial.
Source: data taken from joint MET, Torra Conservancy and NGO vehicle census

conservation. Typically, there are exceptions and isolated cases of illegal game hunting still occur. Save the Rhino Trust, although not primarily involved in community development, has played a key role in monitoring rhino populations over the years, together with IRDNC and community game guards.

Under the legislation inherited from South Africa, wildlife belonged to the state and virtually no rights to manage and benefit from it were available to local people. The new conservancy legislation passed in 1996 addressed this by linking the right to utilize and benefit from wildlife to its sustainable management. Torra met the rigorous requirements of government and was registered as a conservancy in 1998. The partnership in conservation and the formation of the conservancy has sustained growth in wildlife populations in the Torra area and the north-west, in general (see Table 14.1).

This increase in wildlife has created many opportunities for the region, in general, to diversify economies beyond farming. Opportunities for tourism and the live sale of game are considerable in Torra.

FRUSTRATIONS: REALIZING THE RIGHTS OF CONSERVANCIES

Despite clear signs of progress, Torra has experienced frustrations that are centred around the incomplete implementation of legislation and policy. When applying the legislation, communal conservancies are often subject to far more stringent rules and regulations than their counterparts on freehold land or in parks. For example, Torra has been obliged to acquire permits for all hunting and was initially required to have a MET staff member accompany every hunt. The MET staff insisted on this, although MET had no legal basis to do so, and MET staff were frequently unable to meet their own requirements as a result of logistic limitations. As a result, hunts have been delayed and the conservancy committee and trophy hunter left frustrated.

Considerable delays in obtaining hunting quotas from MET have also adversely affected planning. Torra has struggled and finally succeeded in obtaining a three-year trophy-hunting quota, allowing better contracts and training to be negotiated. Delays in quota approval have also reduced the time needed to prepare and evaluate tenders. This has considerably reduced the bargaining power of the conservancy and has limited marketing by the operator.

MANAGING THE CONFLICTS BETWEEN RESIDENTS AND WILDLIFE

More serious are the inevitable consequences of higher wildlife numbers, with lion and cheetah, in particular, causing stock losses to farmers. In Torra, lion are expanding their range from within an adjacent communal area tourist concession beyond areas zoned by Torra for wildlife and tourism and into areas zoned for livestock farming. The lack of a proactive process to deal with the ensuing conflict has resulted in stock losses, lions being shot by farmers and friction between Torra residents, government and their tourism partners. However, in 2001, Torra obtained permission from MET to sell one of three problem lions in the area as a trophy, and although only US$1000 were obtained in this manner, the realization that lions have a value has made a considerable impact on members and may, in the long term, secure a future for lions in the conservancy. Torra put the income from the lion hunt into a separate bank account to be used to compensate farmers from losing stock to lion.

A new initiative is being investigated where livestock will be insured against losses from particular species, including lion, leopard and cheetah. This involves a combination of insurance and a trust fund and is possible only in legally registered conservancies, where members are listed. While predators and elephants pose the greatest threat, competition for grazing between livestock and wildlife is becoming an increasingly important issue.

PLANNING FOR IMPROVED NATURAL RESOURCE MANAGEMENT

An additional requirement of communal area conservancies is a management plan. Considerable progress has been made in developing a local wildlife monitoring programme to aid both conservancy and government decision-making. Already, this data has been used together with that of the MET to set annual quotas for the conservancy. Conservancies have also conducted local land-use planning activities, resulting in the allocation of areas for tourism, wildlife and farming, or combinations of these land uses. The MET has initiated a Tourism Option Planning exercise. As part of this, Torra Conservancy is willing to allocate exclusive-access tourism areas, which will form the basis of securing wildlife in the greater conservancy area.

GENERATING BENEFITS FROM WILDLIFE AND TOURISM

Torra Conservancy has been engaged in a long process to build an organization with legal status, the mandate to represent all members, the capacity to negotiate with the private sector, and the ability to effectively manage the conservancy. This process began with two local village development committees. These institutions had a village focus and did not afford the legal status required to enter into binding contracts with the private sector. Consequently, a residents association and trust were established for the whole Torra area. This was set up to enable conversion into a conservancy at a later stage. This was the first of its kind in Namibia and the process took three years to reach completion.

JOINT VENTURE LODGE AGREEMENT

At the time of writing, Torra has gained extensive experience in negotiating with the private sector. Negotiations have included four major components: community consultation, legal considerations, contractual components and mutual learning between the private sector and conservancy.

As the first conservancy in Namibia to negotiate a tourism joint venture contract with the private sector, the process was long but paved the way for future agreements. During the negotiations, extensive household-level consultation was conducted, legal advice was sought and environmental economists provided recommendations for negotiating an equitable deal. Independent brokers, from the IRDNC, maintained close contact between parties to enable the venture to be understood from different viewpoints. This resulted in the signing of a 15-year contract between Torra Conservancy and a private tourism company, Wilderness Safaris Namibia (WSN). The contract is characterized by its emphasis on joint management, benefit-sharing and enhanced opportunity and focus on local conservancy residents.

With several investment options, Torra opted to go into partnership with WSN based on a number of critical factors, many of which are reflected in the contract. The most important components of this contract include that staff must be recruited from within the conservancy. Only where skills were not available within the conservancy would external staff be hired, with the aim of training local residents to do these jobs. No additional tourism ventures in the concession area would be approved by the conservancy without the consent of the tour operator and a ten-year contract, with an option for the conservancy to buy WSN out or extend for a further five years, after which the ownership would revert to the conservancy. A joint management committee made up of representatives of the Torra Conservancy Committee and WSN was established to deal with the successful implementation of the contract. WSN is responsible for tourism-related decision-making and marketing. Other developments could only be undertaken with the consent of the Torra Conservancy Committee.

The venture, Damaraland Camp, is a luxury, upmarket tented camp. With a capacity to house 18 guests, occupancy rates increased from 33 per cent to more than 50 per cent between 1997 and 2000. Torra receives a 10 per cent levy per bed night, as well as a nominal annual rental of the development site. Nineteen members of the community are employed by the camp and have been trained as guides, chefs, waiters and assistant managers. The commitment of WSN to train local staff and to the transfer of ownership, once the contract has expired, was more keenly negotiated than an increase in revenue share. A local woman, having received training at other WSN lodges, formally took over general management of the camp in February 2002. This contact with a national operator has also resulted in numerous other job opportunities for Torra residents in other tourism camps throughout Namibia. WSN has, for instance, specifically recruited staff from Torra for its lodges in Sossusvlei and Ongava (bordering Etosha National Park). A further lodge at Cape Cross on the Skeleton Coast has also recruited staff from Torra.

Since the joint venture began, both parties have experienced and resolved various problems caused primarily by a lack of experience and poor communication on both sides. While the conservancy committee has not always adhered to strict business principles, causing frustration for WSN staff, the conservancy has had to deal with a high turnover of WSN management staff based on WSN's rotation system. New managers are not always aware of the background and nature of the agreement, causing unnecessary tension. This has recently been addressed in a joint management meeting where both parties agreed to draft a document describing the intent and history of the venture for new managers.

Since the lodge began operation in 1996, Torra Conservancy has earned more than US$80,000 in dividends, and a further US$80,000 in wages, as well as income through associated activities such as firewood sales and laundry services. Remarkably, this single joint venture has enabled the conservancy to wean itself off donor start-up support and meet its own management costs, as well as make a profit. This bodes well for the economic sustainability of other conservancies throughout the country. WSN recognizes that entire ownership of the camp will accrue to Torra Conservancy, according to the signed agreement. It does, however, envision the partnership between the parties extending beyond this time period and that it will continue to market and operate under a mutually acceptable contract.

WILDLIFE UTILIZATION

Through a tender process, the Torra Conservancy has leased out a trophy-hunting concession in the area. A contract was signed with Savanna Safaris and has been renewed annually for three years. This venture has gone well, with the hunter obtaining extremely good-quality trophies and the conservancy being equitably compensated, earning an average of US$12,000 a year (at the time of writing). The contract is quoted in US dollars and the hunter is required to take a conservancy game guard on every hunt. The pitfalls experienced are largely those of poor communication and the need for Torra to improve its institutional structure. The operator has had to develop new ways of working with the conservancy. With a three-year quota now approved, it is hoped that Savanna Safaris, the original operator, will go on to train conservancy appointees as hunting guides. In addition to the cash income, local skinners and butchers are hired and meat is distributed to local residents.

The tourism joint venture, surrounding tourism operators and species protectionist organizations are concerned about trophy hunting in the conservancy, even though the quota approved by the MET is sustainable. Perspectives on this issue vary; but meetings between the parties have created a better understanding of different points of view. WSN would like to see no hunting in the conservancy and have suggested the possibility of buying the trophy quota from the conservancy in order to ensure this. At this stage, the committee has declined the offer, which is regarded as a mechanism to halt all consumptive use. Considering the increase in wildlife numbers and the attendant competition for resources, such a move could severely threaten the mainstay of people's livelihoods: their domestic stock. It is proposed that in the tourism planning process, consumptive and non-consumptive use will compete on a tender basis, which will probably result in the designation of consumptive use to areas of lower tourism potential. A short-term solution has been arrived at which aims to ensure that hunting will be conducted as far away from the tourism concession area as possible. WSN feels strongly that if hunting does take place, it should be in a non-tourism area with a well-defined buffer zone, and no hunting should take place along public roads.

TOURISM PLANNING

Torra Conservancy holds considerable potential for further sustainable tourism development, while maintaining the wilderness feel of the area. Torra is one of 12 conservancies in the north-west developing tourism option plans together with the Namibian Community-Based Tourism Association (NACOBTA), the private sector and MET. The biggest hindrance, at present, to the conservancy legislation is that it is ambiguous about conservancy rights over tourism. Until addressed, uncontrolled tourism will continue and income may continue to accrue to largely white tourism operators from the cities. Moreover, uncontrolled access will negatively impact upon the wilderness appeal of the area.

At the time of writing, Torra was considering a further two high-income joint ventures in the area over the short term and has begun to make income from the live sale of game. In 2001, the conservancy sold a small number of springbok and earned more than US$3000. The production of crafts has started, as have ideas for developing secondary industry and the informal sector. There are several new investors interested in the area; but the conservancy has opted to wait until the tourism option planning process with the MET and NACOBTA is complete.

Table 14.2 *Income and expenditure from commercial tourism and wildlife activities in Torra Conservancy (US$)*

	Joint venture lodge (photographic tourism)	Trophy hunting	Live sale of game	Interest earned	Operational costs	Development projects
2000	22,321	7525	–	2225	11,482	699
2001	21,465	13,606	3750	3322	13,642	396

Note: Figures cover Torra Conservancy fiscal year ending 30 June 2001.

Table 14.2 gives a summary of revenue earned by Torra from different commercial activities within the conservancy.

THE DILEMMA OF USING CONSERVANCY FUNDS

Torra Conservancy is required to have an equitable distribution plan to deal with its income. Expenditure, to date, has primarily covered the running costs of the conservancy (approximately US$14,000 per annum) and other selected minor amounts, such as school improvements and independence day celebrations. Extensive consultations have been undertaken at a community level in order to ascertain how residents would like to utilize these funds. It has been agreed that funds should be used for establishing other income-generating enterprises that focus, in particular, upon providing jobs for local youth.

Earning income from wildlife has been a hard-won battle. Spending income over and above running costs has proven to be equally difficult. There are a number of reasons for this. One important factor has been the executive committee's lack of time – several members of which were in full-time employment elsewhere – to dedicate to the process of deciding how funds should be used. Lack of confidence and inexperience by both the committee and conservancy members to handle this complex issue further hindered the process.

The lack of action has, in effect, been a very responsible approach to dealing with conservancy income. The development of small- and medium-sized enterprises is complex, particularly in remote, sparsely populated areas, and in this case where there are few easy opportunities for income generation outside of the wildlife and tourism industry. It is hoped that, with the appointment of a local full-time conservancy manager, new impetus will allow this process to move forward.

Torra, together with other conservancies, has suggested that a fee be paid to the regional council. The traditional authority and regional council are major stakeholders at a local and regional level. Without their active support, the long-term future of conservancies could be an uphill battle. With their full support and cooperation, created through the clarification of roles and responsibilities, a co-operative arrangement could be reached between the conservancy and local authorities, replacing the current, often competitive, one. This has been welcomed by the governor of the Kunene region who requested that structures and systems should first be put in place before such a scheme commences.

INSTITUTION-BUILDING: ESTABLISHING A ROBUST MANAGEMENT UNIT

Torra Conservancy is a legally constituted body. The conservancy has agreed boundaries with its neighbours, as well as a defined membership who elect a committee to run the conservancy on its behalf. The constitution and policies give guidance to the committee in carrying out this function. Local NGOs have provided significant support to Torra Conservancy, with the main facilitation and support from its close partner, the IRDNC. Committee members are re-elected every two years, some of whom have permanent jobs that limit their input. Committee members are not paid but receive a small sitting allowance. However, they are expected to keep two large joint venture contracts operational, manage a staff of seven people, ensure that the residents are kept informed and consulted, that vehicles are maintained and that administration and financial accountability are in order. Ultimately, they are accountable for the social, environmental and economic sustainability of the Torra Conservancy.

An important lesson learned by both conservancy and support organizations is that financial viability does not mean that a conservancy is ready to go it alone. One of the first actions of the new Torra Committee was to call a meeting with IRDNC to request more technical support. The committee, having completed its visioning exercise, is seeking support to design the strategic plan for the conservancy, based on the key areas that emerged from the visioning exercise. This is likely to include aspects such as the conservancy's communication strategy and problem animal strategy. Although it is now independent, Torra still takes part in the IRDNC quarterly evaluation and planning meetings and uses this forum to keep abreast of opportunities provided by support organizations, as well as to network with other conservancies and support agencies in the region.

The appointment of a conservancy manager will greatly help the overburdened situation; but a revision of the institutional decision-making frameworks, policies, activities and duties across all aspects will be necessary to accommodate and make best use of the new structure.

CONCLUSION

In working towards success, the Torra Conservancy has identified several critical issues that require attention. Torra's members need to become more actively involved in ensuring that committee members are accountable to them. In turn, the committee needs to be restructured in order to function as both a business and as a membership organization. The roles of the traditional authority and regional council within conservancies needs to be clarified and an environment created that ensures their active and long-term support. For its part, the MET will need to review CBNRM policy and legislation, through active consultation with producer communities, to ensure that future government frameworks build on the enabling environment currently in place. In tandem with these concerns, appropriate management systems that enable biodiversity conservation should be examined and developed.

Conservancies are young community-based organizations and, as such, they face major challenges in institutional development, local governance, income generation and equitable benefit distribution, as well as all of the critical issues around sustainable natural resource management. Torra and several other Namibian conservancies have already demonstrated that they have the potential to meet such challenges, given sufficient time and technical support. Torra has proved that CBNRM can work through the conservancy approach. While far from perfect, the progress made to date under the current constraints has been considerable. Building on existing partnerships and meeting the key challenges ahead, the residents of Torra Conservancy hold great potential to realize their conservancy vision.

REFERENCES

Child, B (2001) *Mid-Term Review of LIFE-II and an Assessment of the Namibia National CBNRM Programme*. Prepared for USAID, Windhoek

Davis, A (1998) 'Community experience of partnerships. The Namibian experience: A case study'. Presentation to the regional workshop on community tourism in southern Africa, ART and SADC, NRMP, Windhoek

IRDNC (2002) *CBNRM in Kunene: Five-Year Proposal, July 2002 to June 2007*. Integrated Rural Development and Nature Conservation, internal document prepared for WWF UK, Windhoek

Jones, B T B (2001) 'The evolution of a community-based approach to wildlife management at Kunene, Namibia', in Hulme, D and Murphree, M (eds) *African Wildlife and Livelihoods: The Promise and Performance of Community Conservation*. James Curry, London, pp160–176

Chapter 15

The Tchumo Tchato project in Mozambique: Community-based natural resource management in transition

STEVE JOHNSON

It should be kept in mind that customary institutions have no intrinsic linkage to popular legitimacy or decentralization: they have been used as a means to increase state control over rural populations by authoritarian regimes not only in colonial Africa... but also in the post-colonial context (Virtanen, 1999, p2).

We are now citizens who own or at least have control over our land and the benefits that come from using it. Government is becoming a partner in our development and officials in our area are starting to feel that they should work for our benefit. The company that hunts in our area is also becoming our partner. And all of this means that in the eyes of our neighbours in Zimbabwe and Zambia we are no longer refugees, poor cousins whose land is no man's land where anyone can do as they want. We are also now people in our own right (community Bawa member, cited in Anstey and Chonguica, 1998)

INTRODUCTION

As most people working in rural contexts in Africa and elsewhere now acknowledge, the term 'community' does not necessarily imply homogeneity, cohesiveness, or shared norms among people in a single locality. In this chapter, the term is used to include the resident peoples of the Magoe District in the Tete Province of Mozambique and, more specifically, those resident in the Bawa area of that district. The Tchumo Tchato initiative, based in the Bawa community of north-western Mozambique, is an interesting case study of community-based natural resource management (CBNRM) in transition. The initiative involves a deeply rural community dealing with a confused past that has been complicated by influences of colonialism and remoteness, and, more recently, by the effects of military conflict, ideological contests, the disruption of institutional structures, and a need to adjust to rapid social change.

The CBNRM project at Tchumo Tchato is aimed at giving the residents of Bawa a future in which the community's rights over the use and management of natural resources will be clarified and strengthened. Through this, it is hoped that the community will be able to secure its livelihood needs and achieve its socio-economic aspirations.

This initiative, a pioneering one in the context of Mozambique, already has numerous accomplishments. This includes reduced conflict between the community, the government and a safari operator working in the Bawa area; increased benefits from the use of natural resources; the introduction of democratically elected institutions for the localized management of the Bawa people's natural resources; and the development of a model that has convinced central government in Mozambique that CBNRM is a viable and complementary development option that can supplement agriculture as a strategy in alleviating poverty in many rural areas.

Despite the positive aspects, the Tchumo Tchato project has experienced influences and actions that have raised false expectations about the potential benefits that could be derived. These influences have resulted in greater tension between some stakeholders and greater confusion over proprietorship and access rights than existed previously. It may therefore be valuable to explore some of these issues more closely, especially the following:

- communities' needs to receive tangible benefits, particularly revenues from the use of natural resources, to ensure long-term support for the conservation of these resources;
- internal divisions that can arise within communities because of raised expectations and the delivery of lower-than-expected revenues or benefits;
- complex differences in worldviews between local residents and external actors – specifically regarding peoples' relations to, and rights to use, natural resources;
- the role of donor agencies in promoting dependency or sustainability;
- the question of whether partnerships with the private-sector agency can promote sustainable tourism projects; and
- the interference and interception of benefits by local and national elites.

This chapter explores the ways in which the above issues have played themselves out at Tchumo Tchato.

THE CONTEXT OF TCHUMO TCHATO

The story of Tchumo Tchato centres around the remote village of Bawa in the Magoe District of Tete Province in the north-west corner of Mozambique, where the country's border interfaces with those of Zimbabwe and Zambia on the Zambezi River. Due to its remoteness, the area was largely marginalized under Portuguese colonial rule and relied upon its links with Zimbabwe and Zambia to meet its socio-economic needs. During the civil war in Mozambique, spanning nearly 30 years from the mid 1960s to 1992, the area was even further isolated and had to endure an almost complete lack of infrastructure, such as roads, telecommunications, electricity and health and education facilities.

In particular, the people of Bawa had to contend with the vagaries of ineffective governance systems, coupled with the occasional 'interference' from the centralist and socialist government operating from the capital, Maputo, nearly 2000 kilometres away. They were thus forced to rely upon many different uses of their natural resources as a means of survival. Their traditional authority structures and processes played a major role in managing the use of these resources, particularly those that provided vital protein needs or impacted significantly upon their agricultural practices. Fishing and the harvesting of wild animals (especially elephant, buffalo and antelope species) were important livelihood strategies.

EMERGING COMPETITION FOR CONTROL OVER NATURAL RESOURCES

In 1983, the government, using existing legislation that designated ownership of, and control over, wildlife and forestry resources to the state, allocated a hunting concession to a Zimbabwean safari operator. By imposing this concession on the community, it restricted the Bawa peoples' customary access to wildlife resources upon which they had historically relied for their livelihood and cultural needs, while giving the safari operator the impression that he had the protection of the central government. However, members of the local administration were deeply involved in the illegal hunting of wildlife for meat and ivory, thus reducing their credibility as managers of the natural resources. Due to the remoteness of the situation, and in the absence of any credible form of law and order, the safari operator assumed the role of law enforcer. This created a hostile and volatile relationship between himself and the local people, who, in response, adopted an open-access approach to the natural resources. This led to bitter conflict between the community and the safari operator, and the eventual suspension of hunting operations by the governor of the province pending an official inquiry (Anstey and Chonguica, 1998; Mugabe and Murphree, 2000).

As this was one of the few operative hunting concessions in the country, the government attempted, in 1993, to resolve the conflict between the hunting safari and the community by using CBNRM principles that had evolved from Zimbabwe's Communal Areas Management Programme for Indigenous Resources (CAMPFIRE). The two Mozambican wildlife officers based at Bawa at the time used the CAMPFIRE project that had been developed just across the border at Masoka as a model, and negotiated a deal that ensured that the Bawa community receive a share of the benefits from the hunting operation. A donor agency, the Ford Foundation, agreed to assist the wildlife officers in developing the scheme into a more formal CBNRM project as a two-year pilot programme. The agency was looking at mechanisms for building institutional capacity in Mozambique and the Bawa project was designed 'to develop institutional capacity within the forestry and wildlife service' (Mugabe and Murphree, 2000).

Murphree (pers comm), however, argues that the project was not presented to the community in this light, but rather as a means of resolving conflict and increasing the community's control over the safari hunting operations. The project was also introduced as a programme that would improve local livelihoods through various benefits received from the sustainable use of natural resources via the safari-hunting process. Furthermore, it was argued that the initiative would enhance residents' control over natural resource management processes through the formation of a community-based management institution to which the state would devolve certain levels of authority.

It would appear that in the early stages, the project successfully resolved many of the issues of conflict with the safari operator and facilitated the receipt of some economic benefits for the community. These benefits included a reduction in damage to their crops by wildlife and the construction of a tourist camp that promised to provide employment and income. But recent evaluations of the project indicate that various tensions and divisions had arisen within the groupings involved in this initiative. Some of the factors influencing these dynamics are analysed in the next section.

THE ROLE-PLAYERS IN TCHUMO TCHATO

The main actors involved in the development of the Tchumo Tchato project between 1993 and 1995 were a traditional authority structure; the community itself, which comprised a number of villages; the two young wildlife officers mentioned above who represented an emerging central government presence in the area; and the safari operator who had central government's sanction to harvest wildlife in the Bawa communal area (Anstey and Chonguica, 1998). Another major player in the process was the Ford Foundation – the international donor organization based in the capital, Maputo, which advised central government on the development of CBNRM processes in the country. It was largely due to the Ford Foundation's influence that the project took root and developed along the lines that it did. The provision of funding through central government played a key role in establishing the power relationships that eventually emerged within the process.

Overlaying this set of actors were Mozambique's two main political parties (Frelimo and Renamo); two religious-cum-cultural structures representing the church and the traditional spirit-medium system; and a democratically elected community council. The two political parties, based upon rather different ideologies, both had supporters within the area despite the fact that peace had been restored after the civil war and a new government elected. The charismatic and powerful spirit mediums, who lived among the people, were an important influence over the community's decision-making processes. These mediums, working through trances and ceremony, invoked the presence of various spirits representing natural elements, such as land, wildlife (in the form of lions, baboons, fish, leopards and other species) and sacred areas. These mediums channelled the wisdom inherent in the particular spirit represented – for example, *Sekwati*, the Spirit of the Land – and provided guidance in the form of instructions or comment about how the land should be used or managed. The lion spirit was particularly influential, given the community's reliance upon wild animals as a source of bushmeat and other products.

The two government conservation officials who were placed in the area to work with the community on issues of natural resources management also played a significant role in guiding the process. Young graduates with a missionary zeal, the two officials attempted to introduce innovative CBNRM ideas within the Bawa community.

DYNAMICS THAT INFLUENCED THE TCHUMO TCHATO INITIATIVE

The Tchumo Tchato initiative initially showed many signs of success in terms of proving that CBNRM can accelerate development processes and enhance the livelihoods of rural people. At the time of writing, however, it appeared to have been suffering from many of the weaknesses that other such initiatives in southern Africa have displayed at various stages of development. A number of dynamics began to emerge that hampered the ability of the project to carry out its development agenda and enhance the livelihoods of the members of the Bawa community.

Some of these dynamics included:

- a struggle for power for control over access to, and management of, the local natural resources;
- changes in perception about the benefits generated by the project; and
- the influence of donor support on the overall process.

Each of these is discussed in the following sections.

COMMUNITIES REQUIRE TANGIBLE BENEFITS IN ORDER TO ACCEPT THE NEED FOR CONSERVATION

The need for communities to receive tangible benefits in order to support conservation has been one of the most fundamental arguments endorsing the introduction of CBNRM in southern African countries over the last decade (Jones and Murphree, 2001). Seen as 'economic instrumentalism' by Jones and Murphree (2001), it has, in many ways, driven the adoption of CBNRM in the subcontinent. A key argument in this regard has been that benefits, of whatever nature, have to outweigh the costs of conservation on rural land for the users of this land. In this context, a significant argument can be made that local-level economic benefits are crucial to the acceptance, or otherwise, of conservation as a component of land use (Barrow and Murphree, 1998).

In the early stages of the Tchumo Tchato project, an electric fence was constructed around the Bawa village and its fields, preventing elephants from raiding the community's crops. The protection of their crops as a key economic livelihood component convinced many community members of the benefits of developing and adopting a CBNRM programme in the area. The receipt of a US$12,000 dividend from the proceeds of the local safari concession fee in 1996, and the receipt of other amounts in subsequent years, further enhanced the image of the project among the people of Bawa.

Where such benefits are misappropriated or inequitably distributed, however, they may, in fact, have the opposite effect and cause conflict and tension. In the case of Tchumo Tchato, the community's perception of the project became increasingly negative as financial benefits were appropriated by the government conservation agents based within the community. Some of these intercepted revenues were used to enhance their law enforcement capacity and provide accommodation for the conservation officials resident in the area. As a result, a perception grew in the community that the benefits were now being used to introduce punitive sanctions on the community and its use of their natural resources.

As in Zimbabwe and Zambia, the Mozambican government effectively still taxes the use of wildlife resources by retaining significant proportions of any fees obtained through licences for hunting trophies and hunting concessions. In the case of CAMPFIRE in Zimbabwe, a large percentage of revenue earned from wildlife is, in some form or another, retained within central and local government structures, and communities, in general, receive less than 50 per cent of the revenues earned (CAMPFIRE, 2001). In the case of Zambia there is a legislated disbursement of revenue accrued. There, 40 per cent of revenue is to support wildlife management activities; 35 per cent goes to local communities; and 25 per cent to the Zambia Wildlife Authority (ZAWA) to support administrative costs of the project. However, the actual disbursement of these funds has often been held up because of institutional problems (Nyambe and Nkhata, 2001).

Although the reliance upon economic instrumentalism has been a predominant paradigm in the region's CBNRM programmes, Barrow and Murphree (1998, p22) contend that:

> For community conservation to be successful, there has to be a sense of responsibility and ownership, or proprietorship devolution at the community and resource-user level. Without this, incentives for conservation become marginal and ad hoc.

However, it is now being increasingly accepted that the cause-and-effect relationships inherent in sustainable use are much more dynamic and complex than economic instrumentalism on its own (Pearce 1996; Barrow and Murphree, 1998). A number of other less tangible benefits exist that communities perceive to be important and that play a role in the level of acceptance of the need for conservation or not. Barrow and Murphree (1998) indicate that for conservation to pay, it has to be seen not only in financial terms, but also in terms of more qualitative cultural values. Examples of such less tangible benefits include the restoration of land and resource rights; increased access rights; in some cases, restoration of communal 'pride'; the attainment of greater levels of decision-making powers over the use and management of natural resources; and the development of greater cohesion within the community.

Other social-political factors may come into play with the attainment or fulfilment of traditional needs and communal aspirations through CBNRM processes. In the context of Tchumo Tchato, a number of these were achieved or addressed:

- *Social institutions such as spirit mediums were recognized, reinforced or supported:* Spirit mediums still play an important role in the traditional lives of the Bawa community, influencing social behaviour and guiding the use of natural resources. The project purposefully engaged with these spirit mediums in an attempt to ensure that its objectives were shared by all sectors of the community.
- *Recovery of limited levels of tenurial and access rights over land and natural resources:* The acceptance of the project by central government enhanced the community's level of decision-making over the local wildlife natural resources and secured increased levels of benefits over the previous situation (Anstey and Chonguica, 1998). This was attained by developing a democratic institutional structure in the community and convincing central government to allocate a portion of benefits obtained from the safari-hunting concession to the community. The latter was largely achieved by trebling the trophy fees paid by the local safari concession, which satisfied central government by maintaining its level of financial return, while also allowing for the channelling of a significant level of funds to the community and apportioning an amount to the local government administration.

- *Democratic approaches were introduced:* By 1995, the community had developed a democratic, representative institutional structure through an open electoral process. This process introduced a participatory and transparent element within the decision-making processes, which included representation from the main actors in the community – the traditional authority, the two political parties (Frelimo and Renamo), and the two religious and cultural structures (the church and the spirit mediums). These community councils were crucial in that they evolved to meet local democratic agendas and were able to change the dynamic from a passive community status to an empowered one in relation to the state and the private sector.
- *Recovery of community identity and 'self-image':* An important outcome of the introduction of the project was the regeneration of pride as a communal group of people and the recognition that the Bawa community had the capacity to manage its own affairs – or as one community member expressed it: 'We are now also people in our own right.' The level of government acceptance was indicated by a visit to Bawa by the Mozambican president, government ministers and the governor of the province. It also showed an acceptance of a bottom-up grassroots process that was a change from the former top-down ideology of the previous government.

INTERNAL DIVISIONS CAN ARISE WITHIN COMMUNITIES

The nature of a 'community' may be seen as the sum of the needs, aspirations and roles of the individuals within it. These needs, aspirations and roles are dynamic and change in response to changes in the overall environment, and may conflict with those of other individuals. In the context of Tchumo Tchato, community members were recruited as game guards and represented 'community management and control' of natural resources. When these game guards were brought under the control of the local wildlife officer and they were required to begin enforcing laws on fellow community members, division and dissent began to grow within the community.

During the various eras of civil war and conflict, the Bawa community was, in many ways, divorced from the actual governance processes in place at the time, and largely managed the local natural resources on its own, through traditional authority mechanisms. Residents thus had a long history of *de facto* access to resources. However, with the adoption of the Tchumo Tchato project, and the introduction of *de jure* control over access to resources and management over them, the community experienced a loss of decision-making power and control. Local people perceived a lower level of benefits accruing to them. Thus, community structures, which were elected as management institutions in the early stages of the project development, became increasingly sidelined. This so-called 'aborted devolution', as Murphree (pers comm) terms it, resulted in the Bawa people becoming disillusioned with the project and its initial promises of increased benefits and tenure. Internal tension grew, causing divisions within the community. Levels of wildlife 'poaching' increased, while a feeling of apathy and silent resistance developed towards the project. Mugabe and Murphree (2000) comment that the wildlife service camp that was built on a hill near Bawa village, initially viewed as a sign of development by the community, had become a symbol of state control at the time of writing.

DIFFERENCES IN WORLDVIEWS EXIST BETWEEN LOCAL RESIDENTS AND EXTERNAL ACTORS

The actual livelihood needs of many rural communities are usually very basic and simple, and generally relate to water, food and human security. Although their livelihood needs may be construed as simple, their worldviews may, in many ways, be rich and dynamic. They are also influenced by levels of education, as well as varying degrees of exposure to national politics, governance and ideology, and economic processes. Worldviews often determine the livelihood strategies of communities, including attitudes towards CBNRM. In the case of Tchumo Tchato, given its marginalized and remote situation, it would appear that CBNRM strategies became inextricably linked to local religious, social and traditional institutions and processes (Anstey and Chonguica, 1998). Prior to the introduction of the safari-hunting concession and the development of the Tchumo Tchato project, most of the natural resource management functions were adequately governed and controlled by traditional practices, largely through the guidance of the spirit mediums.

As with many development processes, the external actors with a stake in the initiative are multiple and the issues they bring are often complex. Donors have their own agendas; governments attempt to propagate their own ideologies; local governments and the individuals within them reflect parochial aspirations; various agencies promote their goals and objectives; and local officials introduce their own personal aspirations and power plays. Tchumo Tchato has, clearly, been no different in this regard.

During the early 1990s, when the government imposed its safari-hunting concession on the Bawa community, the differences in worldview between the three parties (government, community and hunting operator) caused conflict over access to natural resources and the receipt of benefits. The introduction of the Tchumo Tchato project as an attempt to resolve the conflict merely introduced a number of new worldview variables into the equation, with the personal development perspectives of the change agents on the ground, and the organizational objectives of the donor agency – the Ford Foundation – coming into play. Commenting on the overall process, Mugabe and Murphree (2000) found that:

> *The Bawa project was in [the government's] opinion still primarily a vehicle for developing institutional capacity within the bureaucracy. The result was an increase in state and local*

> *bureaucratic intervention in a management and decision-making process that the community expected to make itself... [The government] also assumed that communities could only really manage natural resources under state direction and control.*

This contrasts with the original concept of including the local community in the management and use of the natural resource decision-making processes, as envisioned by the two original, locally based, conservation officials.

DONORS, DEPENDENCY AND SUSTAINABILITY

Most development projects have a need for some kick-start or seed funding. In the case of the donor agency supporting Tchumo Tchato, it would appear that, at times, it may have inadvertently attempted to meet its own thematic and institutional objectives, while also attempting to fit into national government policy – rather than supporting the real needs of the Bawa community. Although these were not original objectives of the project, it would appear that important feedback, evaluating and monitoring processes were not in place to ensure that community needs and aspirations were being addressed. In doing so, it appears that the donor agency continued to fund a process that increasingly marginalized the community in favour of enhancing central government control in the area, effectively counteracting the principle of devolution that is seen to be crucial in making CBNRM processes succeed.

In channelling funds toward developing the government's conservation capacity in the area, and not toward enhancing the community's capacity to use the initiative to strengthen evolving community institutions, the project missed important opportunities to ensure its own economic viability. By promoting individual or communal enterprise, the possibility of introducing some form of levy for use or access rights could have contributed to the wages of a small management or enforcement unit.

Development of the official conservation capacity in the area has seen a growth in the size of the unit and the number of officers employed, as well as the infrastructure and equipment needed to support these officials. The annual funding requirements are now huge, and with little funding from central government, conservancies are almost totally reliant on donor funding. A crisis was reached in 2001 when the donor indicated that its funding would cease, leaving the unit on the brink of collapse.

In addition, by focusing support on the local central government presence, the community's participation in key decisions about natural resource management was reduced. This created apathy and disillusionment, effectively making sustainability an all-but-impossible goal to achieve.

PRIVATE-SECTOR PARTNERSHIPS

It is possible that the Tchumo Tchato process may not have emerged had the Bawa community managed to develop an effective partnership with the first safari-hunting operator in their area. However, conflict arose when the safari concession was imposed upon the community, and the operator chose to depend upon the authority assigned to him by central government, rather than attempting to negotiate some level of access rights with the community. It would appear that a true partnership with this concessionaire has never really emerged, although the community received a portion of the revenue paid by the hunting operation to central government. Various other partnerships were explored in the initial stages of the project, although none of these have materialized. A number of tourist camp operations were discussed using the conservation officers' camp as a base; but the remoteness, lack of infrastructure and bureaucracy excited little private-sector interest in the area. Apart from the hunting concession, there is almost no private-sector involvement, and it would seem that the Tchumo Tchato project had not demonstrated a taking on board of the lessons learned from Zimbabwe, Botswana or Namibia about how to structure more equitable joint venture partnerships.

This is in spite of the fact that Mozambique's 1999 Forestry and Wildlife Act indicates that communities must be allowed free access to private-sector concessions and to continue using resources for subsistence purposes, and that they may negotiate other benefits from the concessionaire.

INTERFERENCE AND INTERCEPTION OF BENEFITS BY LOCAL AND NATIONAL ELITES

The administrative capacity of the Mozambique government to implement policy and legislation over wild natural resources has, historically, been weak, and has given rise to many situations where *de facto* rights over resources are more significant than *de jure* rights. Anstey and Boyd (2000) report that access to wild resources is generally not governed by state laws; rather, it is governed by local or traditional rules. Factors such as whether individuals have the time or capacity to exploit certain resources, and whether subsistence or commercial markets exist and provide incentives and benefits, also play a role.

Operators may legally exploit wild resources on delimited land without community consultation through a government-issued licence. Communities are entitled to a percentage of taxes arising from the exploitation of forestry and wildlife resources by private enterprises, set at 20 per cent in the draft regulations. However, as in much of the new legislation being developed at the time of writing, communities were not aware of any proposed benefits and, therefore, are unable to claim these rights.

However, as new capacity is developed within the central and provincial government processes, or as new non-governmental organization (NGO)-driven CBNRM initiatives are developed in certain areas, *de facto* access rights are gradually being eroded. Anstey and Boyd (2000) argue that such changes are undermining functioning traditional and local management systems that have previously ensured sustainable levels of resource use.

CONCLUSION

The Tchumo Tchato project was developed with the honest intention of assisting the community in managing and benefiting from the use of local natural resources. The case study, however, shows how such initiatives can easily become distorted if adequate monitoring and evaluation processes are not in place and used in an adaptive management process by the parties involved.

In the first place, the development of the Tchumo Tchato CBNRM process has highlighted the importance of communities receiving equitable benefits from the use of their natural resources if they are to adopt a feeling of ownership or custodianship towards them. If they perceive that they are not being treated fairly in terms of returns on any use, they will withdraw from the management process and invoke various forms of sanctions – refusing responsibility for consequences of non-involvement, boycotting management processes, or even actively sabotaging attempts by other stakeholders to manage the resources. These forms of protest undermine the long-term viability of the CBNRM process, placing the burden of management on government or on donor agencies.

The case study also points out the dangers of not developing consensus around the purpose and objectives of such initiatives, both in the initial stages and as the project progresses. It would appear that, although this was attempted in the beginning, various parties may not have been clear about their reasons for being involved in the process, leading to confusion and disillusionment. A key lesson from the initiative is that such processes demand an enormous amount of effort in ensuring that, on an ongoing basis, systems are in place to guarantee that all parties involved maintain a common vision and sense of purpose about the eventual outcomes.

A further lesson is that – in order to ensure proper devolution – donors and funding agencies should have mechanisms in place to monitor their efforts in achieving the programme's objectives. It is also important that these agencies are conscious of not imposing their own agendas on the recipients.

Note should also be taken of the loss of opportunity suffered by the Bawa community in not having been able to form viable long-term partnerships with the private sector. The formation of such entrepreneurial partnerships plays a major role in moving such initiatives towards some level of financial and institutional sustainability. Many other examples and case studies mentioned in this book provide insights into how such relationships often facilitate the provision of a wider range of benefits than the intended economic ones. Private-sector partners frequently initiate the introduction of benefits such as access to telecommunications, electricity and potable water, as well as improved road and health services.

A significant achievement of this project in Mozambique, however, is that it has served as a catalyst to create awareness of CBNRM in the country and has resulted in the central government accepting CBNRM as a significant development option alongside agriculture, commerce and industry. A number of other such initiatives are being developed and implemented in the country, and legislation has been modified to enhance the ability of communities to enter into such processes.

Despite it deficiencies, the project was, at the time of writing, undergoing rigorous evaluation. Hopefully, many of the negative aspects outlined above will be taken into consideration and rectified.

REFERENCES

Anstey, S and Boyd, C (2000) *Access to Wild Resources: Mozambique*. Draft report produced for the Institute for Development Studies, University of Sussex, Brighton

Anstey, S and Chonguica, E (1998) *A Review of Community Wildlife/Natural Resource Management Initiatives in Mozambique*. Report produced for the International Institute for Environment and Development, Evaluating Eden: Assessing the Impact of Community Wildlife Management Research Programme (first phase), IUCN Mozambique, Maputo

Barrow, E and Murphree, M W (1998) *Community Conservation from Concept to Practice: A Practical Framework*. Research Paper No 8 in the series Community Conservation Research in Africa: Principles and Comparative Practice, Institute for Development Policy and Management, University of Manchester, Manchester

CAMPFIRE (2001) *CAMPFIRE Association of Zimbabwe: Determination of Proceeds*. Report on the study of revenue and allocation of proceeds, CAMPFIRE Association, Harare

Jones, B and Murphree, M W (2001) 'The evolution of policy on community conservation', in Hulme, D and Murphree, M W (eds) *African Wildlife and Livelihoods: The Promise and Performance of Community Conservation*. James Currey, Oxford, pp38–58

Mugabe, P and Murphree, M J (2000) 'Building the capacity of communities to handle CBRNM issues'. Paper presented at Constituting the Commons, the Eighth Annual Conference of the International Association for the Study of Common Property, Bloomington, Indiana, 31 May–4 June

Nyambe, N and Nkhata, A (2001) 'CBNRM benefits and cost sharing: A case study of the Chiawa District', in Richardson, G and Johnson, S (eds) *Challenges to Developing CBNRM and Effective Participatory Environmental Policy Processes in Zambia*. IUCN Zambia, Lusaka, pp51–66

Pearce, D (1996) 'An economic overview of wildlife and alternative landuses', in ODA (1996) *African Wildlife Policy Consultation: Final Report of the Consultation*. Overseas Development Administration, Berkshire

Virtanen, P (1999) 'Community in context: Chiefs and councils in Mozambique'. Paper presented at the Seminar on Governance, Property Rights and Rules for Woodlands and Wildlife Management in Southern Africa, WWF-SARPO, Harare

Chapter 16

The Richtersveld and Makuleke contractual parks in South Africa: Win–win for communities and conservation?

HANNAH REID AND STEPHEN TURNER

INTRODUCTION

For many decades, tourists have enjoyed their visits to South Africa's impressive network of national parks. Since the advent of democracy in the country, much has changed for the better with regard to access to these precious conservation resources and the way in which they are managed. But the tourist who enters the rugged desolation of the Richtersveld National Park, or admires the unique beauty of the Makuleke region of the Kruger National Park, is unlikely to realize one other key change. These conservation areas are not owned by South African National Parks (SANParks). Instead, they belong to communities of rural people who live nearby. These are contractual parks, in which an unconventional kind of community-based natural resource management (CBNRM) is evolving. It has the potential to be a kind of win–win CBNRM that profits both the community owners and the conservation agency.

In various countries around the world (including Australia and Canada), contractual parks have emerged as a new way of sharing conservation responsibilities and benefits between official conservation agencies and rural landowners. In conventional national parks and nature reserves, the state or the official conservation agency owns the land. In contractual parks, they do not. Instead, the conservation agency collaborates with the landowners in some sort of joint management of the area, its natural resources, the conservation function and possibly other activities such as tourism.

The landowners who enter into such arrangements fall into two broad categories. Both categories can be found in South African contractual parks. Firstly, there are private and corporate landowners who choose to dedicate their farm or ranchland to the protection of nature, in collaboration with the conservation authorities. Secondly, and more interestingly from the CBNRM perspective, communities of the rural poor with clear land rights may decide to go into contractual park arrangements. This is what the Makuleke and the people of the Richtersveld have done.

Clearly, these contractual arrangements are not a purely community-based kind of CBNRM. But they certainly can be considered as one form of CBNRM since they are meant to involve communities managing natural resources for their own benefit, in collaboration with conservation agencies. The question for this case study is how promising a kind of CBNRM they are for people whose livelihoods are affected by nature conservation, and for the nature conservation sector itself. (Around Africa and beyond, various other forms of co-management are developing in such sectors as forestry, fisheries and range.) Can this kind of CBNRM achieve the threefold target of sustainability at the economic, social and ecological levels?

In theory, contractual parks can be a win–win situation. From the point of view of the conservation authorities, they can increase the size of the national conservation estate beyond what it is economically or politically possible for them to own themselves. They can enhance the political credibility of these authorities, and of nature conservation, by putting responsibility and benefit in the hands of the rural poor. They ought to be able to achieve conservation at lower cost for the authorities since the community owners of contractual parks shoulder some of the management load. From the perspective of the rural poor, engaging in these contracts with conservation authorities may entrench their ownership rights in situations where these rights might otherwise be vulnerable. Communities may achieve significant social and institutional empowerment from their role in these co-management arrangements. Lastly, but potentially most important, poor rural people may achieve higher economic benefits from a contractual park than they could from alternative land uses or management arrangements.

This case study outlines the experience of the Makuleke and Richtersveld people and their co-management partners in their respective contractual parks in order to establish whether they have attained this potential win–win CBNRM yet.

CONTRACTUAL PARKS IN SOUTH AFRICA

The contractual park model began to appear attractive in South Africa during the 1980s. White landowners in certain areas knew that the then National Parks Board had the legal right to expropriate their property if it wanted to create new parks. A conservation contract would enable them to retain their ownership. The National Parks Board, on the other hand, was finding it more difficult to acquire the land that it wanted to convert to conservation because of conflict with existing or potential land users such as mining companies. The contractual park model would enable the Board to extend conservation to important new areas, while accommodating these other users. During the 1990s, the model gained new significance for the renamed South African National Parks (SANP), more recently abbreviated as SANParks. It was seen as a way of addressing land claims by people who had been driven off their property to make way for parks created or expanded during the apartheid era. Such people might regain their land rights, but might also agree to keep the land under conservation as part of a contractual park.

The first such contractual arrangement in South Africa was declared in 1987, incorporating the privately owned Postberg area into what is now the West Coast National Park. This was done on the basis of a 1983 amendment to the National Parks Act that allows for national parks to be established on land that remains private property. This amendment was revised in 1986. The National Parks Act is currently undergoing a complete revision; but the new legislation will, presumably, continue to provide for the contractual park model.

In South Africa, contractual national parks are managed in terms of a joint agreement that specifies the rights and responsibilities of SANParks and the landowners. In the simplest case, all management work is assigned to SANParks. In other contractual national parks, the owners have certain management responsibilities, too, and the contract may provide for these owner responsibilities to be increased or renegotiated over time. The contract may thus allow for periodic adjustments of the respective roles of owners and SANParks. Some contracts provide for SANParks to pay a ground rent to the owners. In others, no such rent is payable. A joint management board, comprising democratically selected representatives of the owners and officials of SANParks, plays the central management and decision-making role. Some contracts specify procedures and mechanisms for handling disputes between the parties that this board cannot resolve. Contractual parks give formal structure and legal authority to co-management arrangements. In theory, they give the landowners clear rights and a potentially powerful role in managing the area's natural resources. As such, contractual parks should be a more durable and better-resourced form of co-management than some of the other kinds of 'participatory' natural resource management in which conservation authorities and rural people have engaged around Africa. Again, in theory, when contractual parks are owned by rural communities rather than private individuals, this ought to be a 'win–win' form of CBNRM. The natural resource management is not entirely community based; but the contract provides an enabling framework for a potentially strong community role. Meanwhile, provided that the co-management is effective, SANParks's conservation targets are attained, and more of the nation's biodiversity is conserved.

The Richtersveld National Park

Throughout the 1980s, as it began to consider the contractual park model, the then National Parks Board was eager to establish a national park in the Richtersveld, an area of enormous botanical importance. After long and often bitter negotiations, the Richtersveld National Park (RNP) became the nation's second contractual park in 1991.

Located in the Northern Cape on the border with Namibia, the RNP covers 162,445 hectares. It lies in one of the most species-rich arid-land zones in the world and is an area of striking desert beauty. It remains the only one of South Africa's national parks that is wholly contractual: all of the other contracts are for portions of national parks. The contract runs for 24 years, after which the community can give six years' notice of its intention to renew or end it. Under the contract, SANParks pays rent for the park to a community trust, which uses the money for local educational and social purposes. The RNP contract as eventually signed resulted from an extended contest between the then National Parks Board and conservative political elements, on the one side, and more progressive forces, on the other. During the negotiations and the intermittent political crises that surrounded them, the original emphasis on conservation for conservation's sake was diluted. The finally agreed contract was meant to represent a broader commitment to the welfare of Richtersvelders and the Richtersveld, with local people playing a strong role in managing the park. These negotiations took place on the cusp of political change in South Africa, as the African National Congress was unbanned and the prospect of democracy began to seem real. Although its arid, empty landscape might not suggest it, the RNP has deep political roots.

In one of the many continuing quirks of the former apartheid system, the RNP still technically belongs to the minister of land affairs, pending reallocation to community ownership in terms of a 1998 land reform law. But ever since the then National Parks Board began negotiations during the 1980s, it has been considered the property of the people of the Richtersveld, who number about 6000 in total and live in four villages to the south and west of the park. The ancestry of some of these Richtersvelders stretches back hundreds, if not thousands, of years in this area. For countless generations they have herded small stock in what is now the park, and the RNP contract provides for this use to continue. Mining companies were also operating in the park area before the RNP came into being. They continue to do so. There is some evidence that there are too many livestock grazing in the park (H Hendricks, pers comm); but this community land use does not clash with the RNP's conservation objectives in the way that the ongoing mining operations do.

The RNP has made slow progress during its first decade. It is in one of the remotest corners of the country, and its harsh desert scenery is a rather specialist attraction compared with the 'big five' experience that South Africa's mainstream parks offer. Visitor numbers and tourist income are correspondingly low. Facilities are minimal (the park administration operates in borrowed mine buildings), and only some 16 Richtersvelders have jobs there. Local mining and migrant labour are the economic mainstays of the

Richtersveld, not the revenues from any kind of CBNRM. Nevertheless, the park occupies a central place in Richtersvelders' view of their community assets and in their plans for the future, as captured in one of the most thorough Integrated Development Plans that a South African local authority has produced to date (Richtersveld Transitional Council, 2000).

The nature of Richtersveld society and geography has influenced the RNP's experience with co-management. Although external threats (such as the original plans for the park, or recent local government restructuring) can temporarily unite Richtersvelders into something like a 'community', there are many ancient and modern differences that make cooperation between them difficult. Such differences are not surprising when the villages are so small and so far apart (over 100 kilometres in some cases). Ethnic differences between the northern and southern Richtersveld underlie some of the tensions. Party political divides also play a role. The Richtersveld is not the simple sort of 'community' that outsiders often take for granted in constructing models of CBNRM and co-management.

The Makuleke region of the Kruger National Park

Like the Richtersveld National Park, the Makuleke region of the Kruger National Park (KNP) has deep political roots. In 1969, for a combination of conservation and military reasons, the KNP was extended northwards from the Pafuri River to the Limpopo, which forms the border with Zimbabwe. The Makuleke people were forcibly removed from their homes in this area and resettled some distance away outside the KNP at Ntlaveni, where they live to this day. Following the launch of a land restitution programme in 1994 by the new democratic government, the Makuleke laid a claim for their lost land to be returned. This claim succeeded in 1996 in an out-of-court settlement with the then National Parks Board and the government that committed the Makuleke to continuing conservation activities on the land for 99 years. In terms of the land restitution award, there will be no residence or agriculture in the area during this period.

The land that the Makuleke have regained is now known as the Makuleke region of the KNP, and covers some 20,000 hectares (Reid, 2001). It contains the lion's share of the park's biodiversity, as well as important cultural and historical sites, and includes areas of exceptional natural beauty. Its floodplains are under consideration for designation under the Convention on Wetlands of International Importance, negotiated in Ramsar, Iran, in 1971, and its borders with Mozambique and Zimbabwe make it a key component of the proposed Great Limpopo Transfrontier Park.

The Communal Property Associations (CPA) Act of 1996 was intended to create a legal mechanism for communities to own land that was restored or redistributed to them by land reform. The Makuleke set up a CPA to own their newly acquired region of the KNP. This body has taken on a number of other governance and development functions on behalf of the community, and represents it in the contract for the Makuleke region of the KNP that was signed in 1999. The contract leases the region to SANParks for 50 years, although the agreement can be cancelled after 25 years. It establishes a Joint Management Board (JMB) to act on behalf of the CPA and SANParks in carrying out the provisions of the contract. Conservation management responsibility is assigned to SANParks as agent of the JMB; but there are provisions for the Makuleke to play an increasing role in conservation management as they develop capacity for this purpose. SANParks retains full responsibility for law enforcement in the Makuleke region, which remains part of the KNP.

The CPA, on the other hand, has exclusive cultural and commercial rights to the region, although all its decisions and actions in this regard must conform to the conservation and environmental guidelines set out in a master plan approved by the JMB. Although SANParks does not pay rental for the Makuleke region as it does for the Richtersveld National Park, the Makuleke region has much stronger eco-tourism income-earning potential than the Richtersveld. It is more accessible and links into the established infrastructure and tourist markets of the KNP. Since its creation, the Makuleke CPA has moved ahead quickly with planning and tendering procedures for eco-tourist lodges in the region, and has been busy with a training programme for young community members who can develop careers in the local conservation and tourism sectors. While arrangements for the sustainable use of the Richtersveld National Park's grazing resources were specified in detail in that contract, the Makuleke contract only provides a general framework for community use of the region's resources. Apart from some limited and controversial trophy-hunting, progress has been slow in this regard. Nevertheless, although very little revenue has yet flowed into Makuleke livelihoods, there are good prospects that eco-tourism will generate some employment and substantial economic benefits for the community.

EXPERIENCE WITH CO-MANAGEMENT

Contractual parks can provide clarity regarding where management responsibilities lie, particularly where contracts, management plans and effective joint management boards exist. They provide a framework within which it is possible to ensure that the levels at which responsibilities lie correspond to the levels at which benefits are accrued. In the Makuleke region, for example, it is clear that SANParks is responsible to the JMB for all conservation management and that the community has the rights to commercial development. However, such devolution of authority has required a considerable leap of faith by SANParks. It takes time and, often, painful attitudinal changes for an organization that has always been characterized by top-down management to shift into a collaborative approach as part of a JMB.

Successful joint management requires that the conservation authority operate in conjunction with legitimate local institutions. These institutions can be new or old. Makuleke JMB members are chosen from the CPA's executive committee, and joint management benefits derive from the CPA's strength. In the Richtersveld, by contrast, members of the management plan committee (the JMB for this park) were elected independently from any other local institutional process. This may help explain why Management Plan Committee elections and community feedback meetings were notoriously poorly attended. However, members of both JMBs are, generally, genuine in their intentions to represent the landowning community, perhaps because they are accountable to the whole community and feel that SANParks observes their performance critically.

Conflict is resolved at many levels in both contractual areas. JMBs provide an important forum through which conflict is resolved, and both boards meet regularly. Both boards suffer, however, from the fact that their SANParks members have considerable power but little time to devote to the contractual parks. Contracts and management plans help to provide clarity regarding management issues, thus reducing conflict. But some issues remain disputed, such as who should pay for Management Plan Committee members' costs in the Richtersveld. (This will be solved under the forthcoming management plan, which obliges the park to budget for these costs.) Contractual conflict-resolution mechanisms have been of importance at Makuleke, where they enabled quick resolution of a hunting dispute. There are no such conflict-resolution mechanisms in the Richtersveld contract. The strength of community institutions affects their ability to resolve conflict, and other informal mechanisms for conflict resolution, such as external mediators or facilitators, are also sometimes effective.

Makuleke and Richtersveld JMBs make important contributions towards ensuring that genuine and effective consultation occurs. They meet several times each year, and relations on them tend to be good. Despite difficulties, the Richtersveld Management Plan Committee has operated for over ten years, which is impressive when compared to consultative committees established around state-owned protected areas that often collapse shortly after establishment. This suggests that JMBs offer significant incentives for landowners to participate, probably due to the relative power that they can wield to determine how their land is managed and how they will benefit. By contrast, day-to-day consultation with the community has been poor in both contractual areas.

For joint management to be genuinely 'joint' in nature, it is important that neither party is significantly more powerful than the other. Language can alter power balances, and support from external advisers who speak the 'language of conservation' has helped the Makuleke community to meet on equal terms with SANParks. Makuleke capacity has grown, as is, perhaps, illustrated by their increasing dominance of discussions in JMB meetings. Some steps have been taken in the Richtersveld to even out the balance of power, such as a community majority on the Management Plan Committee, meetings of which were chaired by a community member. Despite this, SANParks has dominated meetings, and over the years the issues discussed have been of decreasing relevance to the community. JMB member capacity was problematic in both contractual areas, and capacity-building needs to be an ongoing process due to board member turnover. This may include providing board members with skills or experience, but can also involve simple issues, such as paying the costs of attending meetings.

Despite the apparent power balance that a contract is able to provide, SANParks still retains control over budgets in both contractual areas, and the Makuleke community only had their land returned to them on the condition that it was used for conservation purposes. The Richtersveld National Park has operated for a decade without a fully approved management plan, resulting in SANParks managing the park according to its own criteria rather than acting on the mandate of a jointly determined plan. The Richtersveld contract is also outdated. It contains some inappropriate clauses and others that are no longer adhered to. This de-legitimizes the document. Joint management is a dynamic process requiring updated agreements to ensure that any aspirations to 'joint' park management are not undermined.

Overall, the Richtersveld's progress towards effective co-management has been slow and unconvincing (Isaacs and Mohamed, 2000). Despite various non-governmental organization (NGO) initiatives, developing the capacity of community representatives on the management plan committee has been an uphill struggle, and the effectiveness of these representatives in defending Richtersvelders' interests has often been questioned. The committee's operations have been sporadic, and relations between community and SANParks representatives have sometimes been difficult. Almost ten years of ineffectual debate failed to achieve an approved management plan for the park. Only when a donor-funded project revitalized the issue in 2001 and provided a new planning consultant did the prospect of an approved plan and some effective co-management start to seem real.

The Makuleke, on the other hand, have made much quicker progress. The authority of the JMB as the co-management authority for the region has been quickly asserted, and both parties recognize that SANParks carries out the conservation management of the Makuleke region on behalf of the board. Furthermore, as we have noted, the Makuleke representatives on the board were soon able to assert themselves forcefully. A constructive and mutually respectful atmosphere usually prevails in the board's meetings. Co-management is already a reality in the Makuleke region.

A WIN–WIN KIND OF CBNRM?

Our first step in assessing Richtersveld and Makuleke experience to date should be to decide whether any kind of CBNRM exists in these contractual parks. Is it realistic to say that the conservation management of these parks is, in any sense, community based? In the Richtersveld, despite the community majority on the Management Plan Committee, and despite the fact that local people continue to graze their stock in the park, the answer, so far, has to be negative. Once the new management plan has been approved and a revitalized joint management body begins to implement it, some more genuine elements of community-based management may start to emerge. They should be reinforced by the community formally taking ownership of the land, probably through a CPA in 2003, and by the integration of the park within local development planning and management as the Richtersveld Integrated Development Plan is implemented (Isaacs and Mohamed, 2000).

In the Makuleke region, on the other hand, a special kind of CBNRM already operates. The CPA is widely endorsed as the legitimate and effective representative of the Makuleke community. The CPA has quickly become an effective partner to SANParks in the JMB and, thus, an effective instrument of community authority in the conservation management of the region. In a contractual park, natural resource management can never be wholly community based because of the nature of the partnership with the conservation agency. Nevertheless, by virtue of that contract and its rigid stipulation of rights and roles, it may prove to be a more effective kind of CBNRM than the many other kinds of devolved resource management authority that have been tried in developing countries. All too often, such devolution is more real on paper than in practice (Shackleton et al, 2002).

The core of our assessment is whether this CBNRM model is achieving any of the 'win–win' type of benefits that we suggested might make it attractive to communities and conservation agencies. SANParks is certainly gaining from the expansion of the national conservation estate through one of these contractual parks (the Richtersveld) and has avoided its reduction by the retention of the Makuleke region in the Kruger National Park. (It has made similar gains in its contractual park negotiations with communities in and around the Kalahari Gemsbok National Park.) It is harder to decide what the Richtersveld and Makuleke contractual parks have done for SANParks's political credibility. Locally, both communities are still mostly sceptical about the attitudes and intentions of SANParks, although, on balance, they trust them somewhat better than they used to. Nationally, the political credibility of nature conservation and of SANParks is a broad and complex issue. The most that can be said is that these contractual parks have not harmed SANParks's image, and have provided some evidence that SANParks is prepared to adopt a more progressive stance.

Another gain for the conservation authority in contractual parks, we suggested, could be lower operating costs. SANParks has not achieved this yet in the Makuleke or Richtersveld cases. The Makuleke contract states that SANParks should carry these costs for the first five years. After that, the CPA should contribute 50 per cent of the costs, provided that this contribution does not exceed half of its net profit from commercial operations in the region. Ultimately, SANParks may win budgetary benefits from the Makuleke contractual park. There is much less potential for this in the Richtersveld, where there is no prospect of revenue streams being earned by either party that could significantly reduce the ongoing operational deficit of the park. In both cases, moreover, the co-management obligations of the contractual parks probably mean that the total operating costs of these areas for SANParks are higher than they would be if they were normal national parks. Meetings must be attended, and negotiating positions developed and defended. In some ways, a contractual park is an extra burden for SANParks. But the organization recognizes that, in the longer term, contractual parks are a key way of winning ongoing community and national commitment to nature conservation. SANParks appears to believe that the current costs and difficulties of the contractual process are a worthwhile – or inevitable – price to pay.

How much are the Makuleke and Richtersveld communities winning from these contractual parks? We suggested that these contracts might help entrench their rights to the land in question. This has happened, indirectly, in both cases. The Makuleke were able to shortcut a potentially protracted land restitution claim process by agreeing to commit their land, if they regained it, to continuing conservation for 99 years. Without that conservation commitment, their struggle to regain the land would have been much more difficult. The contractual park concept is not part of this undertaking; but the agreement of the 50-year contract with SANParks has provided a workable way for the Makuleke to effect the conservation management that their commitment required. Their active participation in co-management of the area with SANParks has clearly consolidated their image as undisputed owners and productive users of their regained property.

The gains are more diffuse for the Richtersvelders. When the contractual park was being negotiated, nobody seriously disputed that the land was theirs, although technically it remains the property of the Minister of Land Affairs, to this day. Over a decade later, Richtersvelders' *de facto* 'ownership' of the park, as recognized by the contract, may have new meaning as the transfer of the whole of the former Richtersveld 'coloured' reserve from state to community ownership is debated and negotiated in terms of the 1998 Transformation of Certain Rural Areas Act. Richtersvelders do not trust the new enlarged municipality, of which they now find themselves part. They do not want it to take ownership of their commons, and the park, under the act. Instead, recognition through the contract with SANParks of their rights to the park will strengthen the case that these areas should be transferred to a separate Richtersveld CPA.

These potential gains are clearly linked to the notion that contractual parks help communities to win social and institutional empowerment. Despite the often demoralizing weaknesses of the community representation process in the Richtersveld, the contractual national park has helped the people of the area to gain political, social and institutional confidence. This empowerment has come in fits and starts, centring on processes and events that focused popular attention and brought people together. The original threat of a park created on the then parks board's terms, and the negotiations and court cases that ultimately achieved the current contract, formed the first wave of empowerment for Richtersvelders. Ten years later, the consultation process that led to the Integrated Development Plan was another empowering experience in which the existence and future of the contractual park were central issues. Once again, the park has been central to the debates around local government and land ownership to which we referred above. The likelihood that a Richtersveld CPA will come to own the park further reinforces the identity and confidence of the Richtersvelders.

There is little doubt that the seven years since the Makuleke launched their land claim have been a period of great social and institutional empowerment for the community. The development of a form of CBNRM through the contractual park has been central to that empowerment. Institutions were built, capacity was gained, procedures were developed, and the Makuleke developed an image and reputation that now stretches across southern Africa and beyond. These achievements were not because of the contractual park process, as such. They were rooted in the particular social and political features of the community, and the way in which they reacted to an array of threats and opportunities. But the contractual park has been a key mechanism with which to build upon the initial success of the land claim, and a challenging tool with which to forge the strategies and capacities needed to respond to the conditions on which the land was awarded.

The most fundamental way in which communities need to 'win' with this kind of CBNRM is by material improvements in their livelihoods. So far, the people of the Richtersveld have won a few jobs in the park, mostly on low salaries. Occasional opportunities for eco-tourism work as guides, guest-house operators or handicraft makers make a marginal contribution to area livelihoods. The contribution to social welfare made through the community trust by SANParks rental payments is welcome, and SANParks also supported the community through social ecology projects and the employment of a social worker in the area. But these contributions were smaller than those made by the much wealthier local mining industry. Incomes from livestock grazing in the park have been maintained, but probably have not increased in real terms. Economically, Richtersvelders have won very little from this contractual park. The best they can say is that their assets have not been taken away from them.

The Makuleke's development programmes for their contractual park, and related eco-tourism initiatives, have succeeded in attracting large amounts of donor and government funding. Private-sector capital has been attracted to invest in joint eco-tourism ventures in the Makuleke region. Government grants have been provided for eco-tourism and infrastructural investments in the Makuleke's existing village area. Donor funding has supported the Makuleke's planning and capacity-building for their role in management and use of the contractual park. Significant revenues have already been earned from trophy-hunting concessions in the region, and are lodged in the CPA's bank account to pay for operating expenses and planned community projects. However, while a few leaders have been able to develop their capacities and careers and have received modest salaries for the dedicated work that they have done over the years, the ordinary citizens have yet to see material benefits flowing from the contractual park. They have not moved back onto the reclaimed land to farm it. Collection of wild plant resources there remains a problematic issue, and hunting is, of course, prohibited. The economy of Makuleke households has not yet been enhanced by the park, and there is increasing public impatience that so much struggle, so many plans and so many projects have, so far, yielded so few tangible benefits.

Do the Richtersveld and Makuleke contractual parks constitute a win–win kind of CBNRM? Not yet. The foundations for achieving the threefold target of sustainability at the economic, social and ecological levels have been laid; but much remains to be done. The Richtersveld and the Makuleke have made better progress than many other CBNRM initiatives in the region, and the contractual parks are preferable to alternative institutional and land-use arrangements for these areas. Furthermore, there have been some intangible benefits, and these should not be underestimated. But neither the communities nor the conservation agency have yet achieved significant tangible benefits, despite the communities' real or imminent ownership of the land on which these parks operate. The potential for a win–win situation is certainly there. It remains to be realized.

ACKNOWLEDGEMENTS

We thank Steve Collins for his comments on a draft of this case study, but retain sole responsibility for any errors or omissions.

REFERENCES

Isaacs, M and Mohamed, N (2000) 'Co-managing the commons in the "new" South Africa: Room for manoeuvre?' Paper presented to the Eighth Biennial Conference of the International Association for the Study of Common Property, Bloomington, Indiana

Reid, H (2001) 'Contractual national parks and the Makuleke community', *Human Ecology* 29: 135–155

Richtersveld Transitional Council (2000) 'Interim Integrated Development Plan for the Richtersveld'. Richtersveld TLC, Lekkersing

Shackleton, S, Campbell, B, Wollenberg, E and Edmunds, D (2002) 'Devolution and community-based natural resource management: Creating space for local people to participate and benefit?' *ODI Natural Resource Perspectives* 76, ODI, London

Chapter 17

The Luangwa Integrated Rural Development Project, Zambia

BRIAN CHILD

INTRODUCTION

This chapter describes the community-based natural resource programme (CBNRM) developed in Zambia's Luangwa Valley as one component of the Luangwa Integrated Resource Development Project (LIRDP). Referred to as the Lupande programme, this initiative is targeted at the 50,000 Kunda people living in the remote Lupande Game Management Area, which borders onto the South Luangwa National Park (SLNP), Zambia's premier wildlife attraction. The Lupande programme was initiated to control poaching through community involvement and poverty alleviation, but has, in recent years, taken on a much stronger rural development role.

The programme in Lupande is of particular interest for several reasons. Firstly, it has two distinct phases, allowing a direct comparison between what we might term first- and second-generation CBNRM, respectively. Prior to 1996, it resembled other southern African community wildlife management initiatives, such as Administrative Management Design for Game Management Areas (ADMADE) in Zambia and Communal Areas Management Programme for Indigenous Resources (CAMPFIRE) in Zimbabwe, in that authority and benefits were focused at the district level, and benefits usually emerged from approved projects. After 1996, the emphasis was changed to giving organized villages full control over 80 per cent of wildlife revenues. In this respect, it resembles CAMPFIRE's aspirations, and is designed to apply (and test) what have become known as the 'CAMPFIRE principles' (see Table 17.2).

These principles postulate that democratically organized local communities will conserve wildlife if they have the authority to manage and benefit from it and are constituted at the right scale. Ribot (2002) independently supports these principles when, in referring to rural development in general, he suggests that 'downward accountability' is of critical importance to programmes based on devolution or decentralization. In his review of 40 years of such programmes in Africa, Ribot laments that he was unable to find any cases of downward accountability. Similarly, the collection of papers on African experiences of community conservation, edited by Hulme and Murphree (2001), emphasizes the importance of devolutionary principles. Hulme and Murphree are, however, frustrated because the initial promise of these programmes has never been allowed to blossom. This, they claim, is because of 'aborted devolution', by which they mean the resistance by those in power to the emergence of a more equitable mechanism for the control of rural resources. The Lupande programme offers valuable insights because it has succeeded, at least during its second phase, in institutionalizing downward accountability. This important concept is used in this chapter to describe and analyse the evolution of the programme over time.

FIRST-GENERATION CBNRM

During the mid 1980s, giving communities any benefits from wildlife was a major innovation. The devolution of control of wildlife to private landholders had worked so well in parts of southern Africa that the next logical step was to apply the same principles to communal lands. The first attempt, during the late 1970s, was Zimbabwe's Wildlife Industries New Development For All (WINDFALL) programme, whereby the district council could apply to use the benefits from hunting and culling to construct government-approved projects.

At the time, there was wholesale poaching of rhinos and elephants in the Luangwa Valley. Specialists concluded that this could only be addressed by contending with the development needs of the rural people who survived through poaching. This notion led conceptually to the ADMADE programme, and also to the Norwegian Agency for International Development (NORAD) providing funds for the LIRDP programme to address wildlife management and the development needs of rural people in the southern Luangwa Valley (Larsen and Lungu, 1985).

As its name implies, LIRDP was an integrated resource development project. Spending some US$15 million in its first five years, its major achievement was the control of poaching in the project area. Rural development was also tackled through a wide range of measures. The project funded water development, agricultural research and extension, some road building, women's clubs, agricultural credit, food relief and even rural transportation. Unfortunately, too much money was spent on overheads and too little on results, the 'mini-government' character of the project was often criticized, and its effectiveness was often strangled by the complex committee structures imposed upon the project to ensure that all government departments were involved.

The community was allocated 40 per cent (later 60 per cent) of all revenues derived from hunting in the game management areas (GMAs) and from tourism in the park. At meetings of local leaders, the project was instructed on how to use these revenues. Examples included the purchase of a bus for transportation, which did not make a profit and was then used commercially outside the project area. A few schools and clinics were also supported. However, it was almost impossible to differentiate between projects supported by NORAD donor funds and those deriving directly from wildlife revenues. There was also little transparency and accountability in the use of these revenues. For example, there are no records of what happened to the income from selling the bus, though local people assumed that their leaders retained this money for their own use.

In 1996, community mapping, questionnaires and semi-structured interviews were used to assess the impact of the programme (Wainwright and Wehrmeyer, 1998). Ordinary people had little clear information about it, and the general feeling was that they had hardly benefited. Most of the few projects of which they were aware were associated with instances of misappropriation of money or materials. The chiefs effectively controlled the revenue flows, for which clear accounting was seldom required. Meetings between the chiefs and donor project managers were often antagonistic, with the chiefs demanding more and the project team having to say no. This confirmed that the top-down approach did not empower people; rather it tended to make them suspicious and resentful. The project had failed to achieve much in the way of development of social infrastructure, such as clinics, schools and roads. It certainly did not link wildlife to a perception of benefit, and thus failed to improve community attitudes to wildlife conservation.

SECOND-GENERATION CBNRM

A 1993 external review of the project (Scanteam, 1993) also identified these problems, and recommended that the larger project be scaled down from a financially unsustainable integrated resource development project to focus on managing the park and implementing an upgraded community programme. Its recommendations for the community programme reflected the powerful influence of the CAMPFIRE programme and its principles.

Following a trip to CAMPFIRE and a series of workshops within the project, a new policy was proposed for the community programme. This was a four-page document that incorporated a simple statement of devolutionary principles, and defined the roles of village action groups (VAGs), area development committees (ADCs), chiefs and the local leaders' committee, and the project. At its core lay the statement that all revenues generated in the GMA would belong to the community, and that 80 per cent of this revenue would be controlled democratically at the VAG level.

Given the political economic implications of this policy, it is surprising how quickly it sailed through the Zambian government's policy committee – which was largely comprised of the permanent secretaries of several ministries – and the review committee – which was effectively the project board, chaired

Table 17.1 *Principles embodied in LIRDP's 1996 CBNRM proposal,
stipulating conditions for the release of wildlife funds*

Conditions	Means of verification
1 Decisions regarding use of 80 per cent of the revenue must be democratic, transparent and participatory.	Decisions must be made at general meetings attended by at least 60 per cent of household heads and confirmed in written minutes.
2 People must have full choice of the use of their money, including household dividends (cash), projects and activities.	Confirmed by minutes and attendance of SLAMU at general meetings.
3 All finances must be used in the manner agreed at general meetings and must be fully accounted for by keeping proper financial records. This does not apply to the 6 per cent allocated to chiefs.	Full financial records will be compiled and submitted quarterly by VAGs and ADCs to SLAMU. They must also be presented to general meetings.
4 Each body should report regularly to its constituents (ie downwards) and to its supervising body (ie upwards).	Committees must report regularly on project implementation and finances at general meetings, and must also submit quarterly written summaries to their parent body and, ultimately, to SLAMU.
5 VAGs and ADCs must be properly constituted and democratically elected.	Each ADC and VAG must have a constitution and hold regular elections.
6 Money should be allocated according to the principle of producer communities.	Monies will continue to be shared equally among areas until such time as there is adequate consensus to change this situation.
7 Revenues should be disbursed by May in the year following that in which it is earned.	

Note: Principle 6 is a contentious issue. The chiefs have ruled that money will be shared equally. However, efforts are being initiated to develop wildlife everywhere in anticipation of the eventual implementation of the principle of producer communities.
Source: LIRDP (1996)

jointly by the Ministry of Tourism and NORAD representatives. It was, however, strongly resisted by the local chiefs who stood to lose the most. In the case of the Lupande community programme, its foundation was this project-level policy decision of decentralization, which was later built into the NORAD–Government of the Republic of Zambia (GRZ) co-operative project agreement to protect the principles set out in Table 17.1. A new body, the South Luangwa Area Management Unit (SLAMU), had emerged.

COMMUNITY ORGANIZATION

Within each of the six chiefs' areas at Lupande, the local population was subdivided into village action groups. Each of these groups developed its own constitution, the essence of which was that individual members were entitled to decide how revenues were used, and would elect a committee to carry out and regularly report on the instructions of the community. Although such a bottom-up approach was obviously foreign and clashed with the traditional hegemony, it was strongly supported by ordinary people. The constitution also incorporated procedural rules, such as frequency of elections and reporting, and defined the VAG as the primary action level using 80 per cent of wildlife revenues. Initially, there were 26 VAGs; but, over time, these have been split to make them more workable. There are now 43 VAGs, which still leaves them with an average of 476 adults each. General meetings, which are the heart of the programme and where all people can participate in decision-making and in holding their elected officers accountable, are, essentially, manageable. The ADC comprised several members of each VAG committee depending upon the size of the area. The chiefs, who had previously controlled the system, usually chaired the ADC, but were gradually persuaded over a period of five years that this was inappropriate since the chairperson was accountable and auditable and chiefs were neither.

REVENUE DISTRIBUTION

With two hunting concessions and occasional income from hippo culling, the Lupande GMA generated some US$220,000 annually. In the middle of the year, each VAG holds its two-day annual meeting. The first day is given over to training and awareness building, covering such topics as the constitution, wildlife off-take and income, how the new policy works, problem animals and so on. The second day is a formal annual general meeting, at which the committee presents its report and accounts, the project staff present an audit report, all posts are subject to re-election, project proposals are presented and discussed, and the income of the VAG is apportioned. On average, about 40 per cent is set aside for projects, such as school blocks, clinics, teachers' houses and wells; 10 per cent is allocated to run the VAG; 10 per cent is used to employ community-based scouts; and the remaining 40 per cent is allocated as cash to individual members.

Once the project agrees that the previous year's finances are correct, and that the community has followed procedures correctly, the most important aspect is the holding of four general meetings, at which finances and activities are properly reported, a certificate is signed and the cheque is released from a joint project–community bank account. Each VAG has a bank account and set of books. It usually pays the cheque into the account, and immediately withdraws cash to pay members their dividends. Thus, some 20,500 adults get a direct payment of US$5.37 from wildlife annually. Financial training of the committees usually follows immediately after revenue distribution (as new committees are often in place), and this is reinforced by quarterly rounds of auditing.

POLITICAL ECONOMICS

Initially, the revenue distribution programme met with strong resistance from the chiefs. The conflict raged for nearly five years. Some chiefs 'encouraged' their subjects to allocate a substantial part of the revenues to such activities as the chief's vehicle or projects managed by them.

Several interesting points emerged. Firstly, in the areas where the chiefs were especially predatory, the community allocated almost all of its income to cash and almost no projects were built. Where chiefs cooperated with people, they took far less cash and completed many more projects. Secondly, the new policy was extremely popular with the majority of the people. Indeed, one attempt to break the impasse between the chiefs and the new policy was an instruction from the policy committee to ask the people to vote on the policy. This was done in one VAG, where 130 people supported it and only seven, predominantly old women, opposed it. Thirdly, the community regularly tried to convince the project managers to resolve this conflict directly with the chiefs. The project staff refused to intervene, although they insisted on reporting all financial transactions transparently. Consequently, there was no ambiguity about how much money was missing and where it was.

Pressure built up in the communities and after five years, chiefs were less able to extract community revenues at will. The project also facilitated the involvement of senior regional politicians in brokering an agreement with the chiefs where they agreed not to take community revenue, in return for an additional payment of 1.5 million kwacha (US$1500 at the time). This informally negotiated shift in power relations was probably more healthy and more sustainable than if the project had used strong-arm tactics to get the chiefs to comply, which would have been impracticable.

POSITIVE RESULTS

At the time of writing, the results have been positive:

- There are now 43 working VAGs that meet regularly.
- In 1999, only 0.8 per cent of the money allocated to VAGs was misused, a remarkable achievement which confirms that village-level transparency works. In contrast, about 40 per cent of the money allocated to ADCs, which includes money that the VAG has forwarded for the management of community-based scouts, was unaccounted for.
- In four years these VAGs have constructed over 150 projects: 16 houses for teachers; 35 schools constructed or renovated; 14 clinics/health posts; 26 VAGs completed over 100 wells; and 60 other projects, including employment of teachers, food relief, shops and electric fences.
- After four years, the community has begun to appreciate its wildlife. Poaching has reduced and 76 community scouts have been employed. The proportion of revenue allocated to wildlife management has increased with

time: 1996 (0 per cent); 1997 (1.4 per cent); 1998 (4.4 per cent); 1999 (13.3 per cent). The next challenge for the project will be to train these scouts and teach communities to manage a law enforcement programme.

- The people of Lupande are now well organized. This makes it easier for them to work with other development agencies and government ministries. As a result, they are finding it easier to access money from other sources, such as the World Bank's Social Investment Fund. They have embarked on a land-use planning exercise to help them do so.

A comparison of attitudinal surveys shows that in 1996, 88.2 per cent of the community neither supported safari hunting, nor understood LIRDP policy. They believed that community development came from donor aid channelled through LIRDP and were unaware that funding for projects derived from 40 per cent of revenues from the park and GMA (Wainwright and Wehrmeyer, 1998). From unpublished LIRDP participatory rural appraisal (PRA) assessments, we also know that they were critical that projects were few, incomplete, inappropriate and tended to benefit the chiefs alone (unpublished LIRDP records). However, by 1999, more people appeared to support the programme (A Tembo, pers comm). Similar surveys also show that people were not really benefiting before 1996 despite the rhetoric of 'revenue-sharing', whereas after 1996, 20,500 people received cash each year and a large number of projects were undertaken.

ANALYSIS AND INSIGHTS

The early LIRDP CBNRM programme (see Figure 17.1) focused primarily upon the area level, and followed a false (but logistically simpler) assumption that traditional chiefs represented their people equitably. The primary mechanism for community interaction was a regular formal meeting with the six chiefs, which decided what to do with 'the 40 per cent' – that is, the proportion of all wildlife income owing to the community from tourism and hunting in the project area. With the refocusing of the project in 1996, all GMA revenues were returned directly to communities, while park revenues were retained for park management. This is illustrated in Figure 17.2.

Figure 17.3 pulls these concepts together. In a first-generation CBNRM programme, benefits flow downwards. This has many disadvantages. The linkages between wildlife and the community are weak, while people are subject to the decisions of their leaders and do not necessarily participate in them – they remain subjects rather than citizens. In the second-generation programme, villagers control and decide on the use of wildlife revenues. This creates a strong link between wildlife and benefits in the eyes of local people. It also empowers people and promotes democratization. Thus, in the second phase of the programme, 22,500 people decide how to use the money, instruct the 430 committee members what to do and require quarterly report-back meetings. A total of some 60,000 person days is committed to the project.

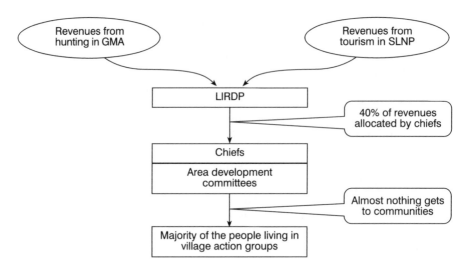

Figure 17.1 *The pre-1996 top-down structure of the community programme*

Compare this to the earlier phase when six people made all of the decisions – and even if the ADCs were fully involved and met monthly, only 60 people participated in decision-making (or some 800 person days). It is little wonder, then, that surveys showed that people had not understood the concept of the project prior to 1996.

Data clearly supports the superiority of the latter system. Although 40 per cent of the revenue was used as cash and 20 per cent for wildlife management and administration, over 150 projects were completed. This compares well with the less than ten projects in the earlier phase. This is a powerful indicator of improving community involvement and managerial capacity, as well as a turnaround in attitudes towards wildlife. Perhaps the most significant data is that only 0.8 per cent of VAG finances were not fully accounted for, and even then the communities had records of who owed them what, as well as repayment plans. This compares well with the figure of 40 per cent at the ADC level. Before 1996, all we know is that there was no financial accountability and much suspicion about the use of funds. The remainder of this chapter develops explanations for these differences in performance.

DOWNWARD VERSUS UPWARD ACCOUNTABILITY

In the first-generation model, a body at the area or district level is held accountable upward to a government agency or the non-governmental organization (NGO) that is implementing the programme. One explanation for aborted devolution is that when the implementing agency loses interest in the programme, few checks and balances remain, and the area- or district-level organization has ample scope to operate in a predatory manner. Contrast this to downward accountability. When each and every adult member of

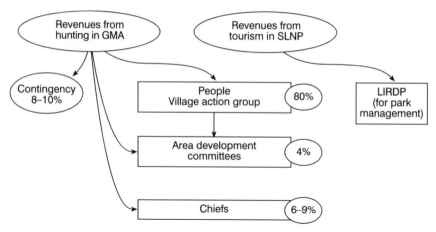

Figure 17.2 *Changes to the programme following the introduction of a policy emphasizing fiscal devolution at village level in 1996*

a community has the right to a proportionate share of wildlife revenues, they control the flow of resources to the various committees. As a result, they control the committees. When implementing agencies move on, the checks and balances remain in place.

THE ECONOMICS OF FIRST- AND SECOND-GENERATION CBNRM

In first-generation programmes, communities may have a say in the use of revenues; but use is generally restricted to social infrastructure and is often heavily influenced by more powerful individuals. For instance, in both the LIRDP and ADMADE programmes, projects tended to cluster around the interests of the chiefs, while in Zimbabwe's WINDFALL programme, projects reflected the interest of the district council. In short, wildlife revenues remain a public asset.

In second-generation programmes, communities debate and exercise choices over the use of wildlife revenues. As a group, they are entitled to keep all of the money as cash, should they collectively choose to do so. Thus, wildlife becomes a private or group asset and is valued more highly for this reason. This is illustrated in Figure 17.3a, where the histogram illustrating the value of tangible benefits in the form of cash, social infrastructure and activities, and management from wildlife revenues, is significantly higher for second-generation programmes. Possibly more important than these tangible benefits is the organizational capacity and empowerment created by the process of revenue distribution – that is, the 43 operational VAGs, all with regular elections, bank accounts, six-monthly audits and a high level of participation in both decision-making and community projects (for example, volunteer work making bricks, carrying sand and water, etc).

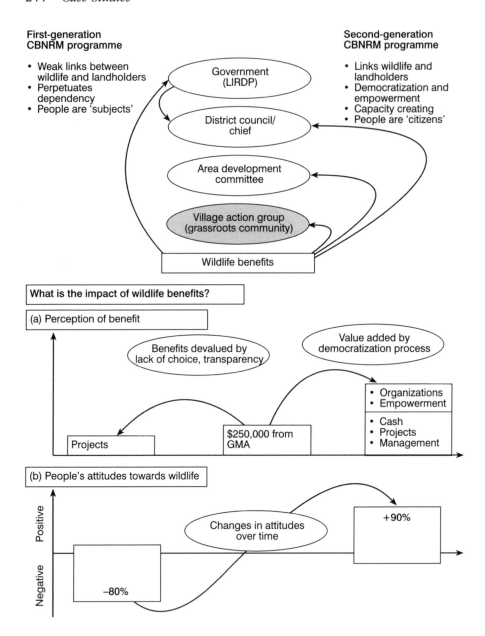

First-generation
CBNRM programme

- Weak links between
  wildlife and landholders
- Perpetuates
  dependency
- People are 'subjects'

Second-generation
CBNRM programme

- Links wildlife and
  landholders
- Democratization and
  empowerment
- Capacity creating
- People are 'citizens'

Government
(LIRDP)

District council/
chief

Area development
committee

Village action group
(grassroots community)

Wildlife benefits

What is the impact of wildlife benefits?

(a) Perception of benefit

Benefits devalued by
lack of choice, transparency

Value added by
democratization process

- Organizations
- Empowerment

- Cash
- Projects
- Management

Projects

$250,000 from
GMA

(b) People's attitudes towards wildlife

Positive

Negative

Changes in attitudes
over time

+90%

−80%

Figure 17.3 *Illustration of the difference between first- and second-generation CBNRM and its impacts on the public–private nature of resources and community attitudes*

Presuming that the change in attitudes (Figure 17.3b) reflect the communities' valuation of first- and second-generation programmes, the latter appears to be an order of magnitude more beneficial.

Table 17.2 *The application of the CAMPFIRE principles of CBNRM to the Lupande project*

Principles of CBNRM	Their application in Lupande
1 The unit of production should be the unit of management and benefit.	Regarding benefit, all revenues generated in the Lupande GMA are returned to these communities in a bottom-up manner. Regarding management, participation is increasing with time (eg quota-setting and allocation; law enforcement).
2 Producer communities should be small enough that all households can participate face to face.	This is achieved through a focus on VAGs where the whole community decides on the use of 80 per cent of revenues.
3 Community corporate bodies should be accountable to their constituency.	Revenue is contingent upon VAGs reporting quarterly to their constituency (downward accountability). They also report to the ADC/chief and the project.
4 Functions should be conducted at the lowest appropriate level.	Most activities are conducted by VAGs who implement projects and, increasingly, employ community-based scouts who are then seconded to the ADC.
5 The link between production and benefit should be transparent and immediate.	This is achieved by returning income to communities at general meetings, where records of wildlife off-take and income are also supplied. Regarding the principle of producer communities, monies are currently shared equally among all areas. This does not reflect production, but is workable and is constantly being debated.
6 Communities must have full choice in the use of wildlife revenues, including being paid out as cash.	This is ensured by allocating income at general meetings, including choice of cash.
7 All marketing should be open and competitive and should be conducted by the wildlife producers themselves.	This comprises the greatest weakness. Hunting is controlled centrally in Zambia and transparency is lacking. Communities do not negotiate with safari operators and are disempowered in this relationship.
8 The rates of taxation of wildlife should be similar to that of other resources.	Wildlife was heavily taxed, with LIRDP retaining approximately half of GMA income. Today, 100 per cent of income is returned to the communities.
9 Activities or investment should not be undertaken unless they can be managed and sustained locally.	The top-down phase generated acute dependency. Today, communities receive nothing from the project except knowledge, training and transparency. They must fund all other activities themselves.

Table 17.2 *continued*

Principles of CBNRM	Their application in Lupande
10 Government is the ultimate authority for wildlife.	Government monitors procedural compliance (financial, institutional and wildlife) and the impact of the devolved approach.
11 Devolving authority and developing community management capacity is a process.	Accept that there will be mistakes and misappropriations, but proceed if a genuine effort is made by communities to rectify such problems.
12 Co-management is necessary, especially in the shift from central to community management systems.	LIRDP cannot drop management such as law enforcement immediately, but is phasing out as community efforts are phased in. There will always be a role for government, which, as a regulatory agency, should monitor compliance with conditions attached to devolution and which, as a development agency, will need to provide supportive inputs such as training, combating commercial poaching, etc.

CONCLUSIONS

Table 17.2 compares the Lupande programme to a set of principles that are common to CAMPFIRE and are contained in the recommendations provided for the community programme by a review mission in 1993. The community programme improved dramatically as a result of implementing these recommendations, indicating that these principles have some value in the planning phases of CBNRM. However, this requires the development of management systems to translate principles into action. The development of these systems, including a good performance management system and the recruitment of a small team (10 to 14 people) of locally recruited community workers was a strength of the Lupande CBNRM programme. The total annual cost of supporting the community project was between US$50,000 and US$80,000 annually, or less than US$2 for each person in the community. This is far less than many other programmes in the region – for example, CAMPFIRE, Namibia's Living in a Finite Environment (LIFE) project, and Botswana's Natural Resources Management Project (NRMP) – and suggests that getting down to village level is not only more effective, but that, in the long run, it is a much cheaper approach.

REFERENCES

Hulme, D and Murphree, M W (eds) (2001) *African Wildlife and Livelihoods: The Promise and Performance of Community Conservation*. James Currey, Oxford

Larsen, T and Lungu, F (1985) *Preparation Report for the Luangwa Integrated Rural Development Project*. NORAD, Lusaka, September 1985

LIRDP (1996) 'Proposals and principles for the institutionalization of the Lupande Integrated Resources Authority'. LIRDP, Chipata

Ribot, J C (2002) *Democratic Decentralization of Natural Resources: Institutionalizing Popular Participation*. World Resources Institute, Washington, DC

Scanteam (1993) *Luangwa Integrated Rural Development Project: Project Appraisal*. NORAD, Lusaka, October 1993

Wainwright, C and Wehrmeyer, W (1998) 'Success in integrating conservation and development? A study from Zambia', *World Development* 26: 933–944

Chapter 18

Community wildlife management in Zimbabwe: The case of CAMPFIRE in the Zambezi Valley

BACKSON SIBANDA

INTRODUCTION

Zimbabwe's Communal Areas Management Programme for Indigenous Resources (CAMPFIRE) has received international publicity and acclaim as an innovative approach to natural resources management. This chapter reviews some of the key findings of an evaluation of ten years (1988 to 1998) of the CAMPFIRE programme that was carried out between 1996 and 1998. It focuses on three key issues, namely:

1   the impact of indigenous knowledge and intangible forces on conservation;
2   the limited impact of CAMPFIRE on local people's livelihoods; and
3   the uneven distribution of revenues from CAMPFIRE initiatives.

While my arguments here could be supported by evidence from most of the CAMPFIRE districts, I make particular use of Nyaminyami District as a case study for a more in-depth and detailed examination of the concept and the practice of CAMPFIRE. I look at the strengths, successes and weaknesses of the Nyaminyami case and suggest that the case study approach is most helpful for achieving a deeper understanding of some of the more site-specific issues that have arisen during the implementation of CAMPFIRE.

Zimbabwe's Department of National Parks and Wildlife Management (DNPWLM) developed CAMPFIRE in response to failed wildlife conservation approaches that relied primarily upon policing and law enforcement. The department had also realized that the law enforcers were thinly spread on the ground and that a lack of interest in wildlife conservation on the part of local people might be resolved by giving them ownership and control over wildlife resources. According to Murphree (1991) and others, CAMPFIRE is an approach to natural resources management that fosters development but also protects the environment. In search of the Holy Grail of 'sustainable development', CAMPFIRE represents an attempt to find new ways of enabling communities to develop and prosper without depleting our natural environment. It seeks to enable communities to utilize natural resources, to grow crops and to build roads and settlements without destroying forests, wildlife and degrading our soils (Sibanda, 2001).

THE LAND CRISIS IN ZIMBABWE

While the evaluation of CAMPFIRE documented here was completed before the land crisis and farm invasions that started in 2000 in Zimbabwe, it has long been clear that, given the obvious and visible pressures on land, the land crisis was a disaster waiting to happen. There can be no doubt that the land issue is central to the debate on natural resources ownership and management and, hence, also to CAMPFIRE. For this reason, I have argued (Sibanda, 2001) that any evaluation of CAMPFIRE must be based on a thorough understanding of land ownership, tenure systems and property rights in Zimbabwe, and particularly on how these affect communal land and the resources on it. The reluctance of the Zimbabwean government to give ownership of land to communities has failed to address a fundamental issue of equity and has encouraged dualism in the rural economy, making the sustainable management of natural resources such as wildlife extremely difficult. For the same reasons, the failure to address the issue of land ownership in Zimbabwe impacted negatively upon the implementation and success of CAMPFIRE. Communities have failed to fully support CAMPFIRE because the administration of land and other resources was decentralized, in terms of the concept of 'appropriate authority', to the district councils rather than to communities themselves. Ownership and decisions about resource use thus remain centralized in the hands of the state.

Appropriate authority was adapted from the 1975 Wildlife Act that gave private landowners the right to use wildlife on their lands. Given that the independence struggle was fought using land ownership as a platform, the black majority had expected that they would get back their land and own it once the country became independent in 1980. Unable to confer ownership of land to the communities, the authorities went on to coin the term 'producer units' when establishing CAMPFIRE. Producer units presented local people with the illusion that they were producers of benefits from indigenous resources on state land. The intention was to provide the officials with an easy formula for distributing benefits from wildlife in the absence of local ownership. The government was thus able to give a semblance of local control to rural people without giving up effective power. CAMPFIRE needs to be understood in this context. The communities soon understood that, as during the colonial era, land ownership and, therefore, power remained in the hands of the state. In 2000, when the government was desperate for votes, it used this land hunger to encourage the black majority to invade commercial farms, creating another illusion that it was giving land to the people.

In fact, the land resettlement programme was stillborn. The Zimbabwe government failed to introduce radical land reform measures that would have given land ownership to the people, either as individuals or as groups. Instead, it opted to give them licences of occupation, which are even less secure than the usufruct rights enjoyed by communal farmers. The granting of these licences of occupation also meant that the resettled farmers would have to manage state land and the resources on it as common property resources. Communal farmers became unwilling to invest in land that did not belong to them, which had a negative affect on CAMPFIRE.

Today, as populations continue to grow and the land issue remains unresolved, it is increasingly difficult to justify wildlife protection at the expense of agricultural development for local communities, especially when wildlife appears to have little direct tangible value. While district councils are seen as democratically elected institutions that represent the interests of communities, they are not able to deliver substantial benefits in the absence of meaningful resource ownership. The promised devolution of land and decision-making to local people never took place. As a watered-down substitute, CAMPFIRE could never hope to compensate for the lack of meaningful land reform. The case study shows how this inability by government to transfer land ownership to the communities has impacted negatively upon people's willingness to fully invest in CAMPFIRE.

THE STUDY AREA

The Zambezi Valley is an area of great biodiversity interest and is home to hundreds of wildlife species, such as elephant, buffalo, eland, zebra and wildebeest among the large mammals, and is also rich in other natural resources. The valley contains many tourist attractions, such as the Victoria Falls, Lake Kariba and Mana Pools, and national parks such as Matuzviadona and Chewore that have abundant wildlife. Wildlife is also abundant in the communal areas where about 2000 elephants and 5000 buffalo are known to inhabit the areas outside of the national parks. It is estimated that 70 per cent of the Zambezi Valley is untransformed wildlife habitat (Sibanda, 2001).

The wildlife in the Zambezi Valley owes its survival to the tsetse fly and mosquito infestations that have made human habitation difficult and have kept human and livestock populations low. The Tonga people who inhabit the valley have historically been neglected and marginalized. Infrastructure such as roads, schools and health facilities are poorly developed. CAMPFIRE was introduced here with the hope that the Tonga would benefit directly from the revenues generated by the programme, a situation that would begin to address some of the past neglect and injustices suffered by the Tonga people, particularly following the construction of the Kariba Dam, which displaced most of them from their homes in the valley to the escarpment.

Nyaminyami District in the Zambezi Valley is the poorest and most marginalized district in Mashonaland West Province and one of the poorest in the country. The district has 16 administrative wards but only 10 fall within the area covered by this study. Tourism is mainly confined to the national parks and Lake Kariba, where local people are not allowed to settle. Private proprietors who do not hail from or live in the district enjoy benefits from the lodges that they have built. As a result, there is considerable dissatisfaction from local people who want to manage and benefit from national parks, as these are seen as the jewels of the tourism industry. During my research, 43 per cent of the people interviewed felt that national parks should be owned and managed by a combination of the district council and local communities.

A brief history of the Tonga people

The Tonga are a once prosperous group of people who were marginalized and underdeveloped through a process of war and subjugation (Colson, 1971; Tremmel, 1996). The Tonga lost most of their wealth to the Ndebele, Kololo and, to a certain extent, the Rozwi. By the advent of European colonialism, the Tonga were already a weak people (Tremmel, 1996). The colonial administration paid little attention to the Tonga until the building of the Kariba Dam, a process that resettled the Tonga and further impoverished them. Until the Kariba was built, the Tonga had at least enjoyed the use of wildlife and had managed it using their indigenous knowledge and belief systems. Their resettlement denied them the use of wildlife resources, including fish and their gardens that were on the banks of the Zambezi River.

Tonga cosmology

In the Tonga worldview, the natural world, the spirit world and the human world are on the same continuum and life is not compartmentalized. The spirit is in nature and in human beings; hence, the natural world and the spirit are an extension of humanity. Life is celebrated through the use of natural resources; therefore, natural resources are conserved to guarantee the continued celebration of life. Life is not seen as existing outside the supernatural because it is the supernatural that controls all life processes. People do not die. They move from one form to another; they become shades, ancestors and spirits and watch over the living, as well as intercede with God on behalf of the people (Reynolds and Cousins, 1993).

The Tonga believe that all natural resources belong to God, and humans have a responsibility (not a right) to use them in a manner that does not displease God. People can never own natural resources but only have access to them. The Tonga thus believe that a bountiful harvest depends not only upon the biophysical elements of soil, water and light, but also upon using the resources in a manner that is in harmony with nature and pleases the ancestors and God. The hunting spirit guides the hunters not only to be successful, but also to avoid killing sacred animals or those that personify spirit beings. Under Tonga belief systems, eating the flesh of one's clan animals is sacrilegious. Thus, Tonga cultural values greatly influence the way in which they make consumptive use of wild animals.

Indigenous knowledge and traditional practices

One of the initial CAMPFIRE programme documents (Zimbabwe Trust, 1990) regards indigenous knowledge and traditional practices as being of paramount importance to its goal of natural resource management. The programme philosophy acknowledges that people will only participate in the management of natural resources effectively when their own values, knowledge and traditional practices are recognized and incorporated within the new strategy (Zimbabwe Trust, 1990). The Nyaminyami project document incorporates the Tonga values, indigenous knowledge and practices, and recognizes them as crucial to the success of CAMPFIRE.

According to the Tonga, May to September is the period when hunting produces the least harm to wildlife. Animals generally produce offspring between October and November, just before the rains start, so that hunting before that period avoids killing animals that might leave behind unattended offspring. Furthermore, the killing of female animals with young offspring is prohibited as this obviously affects breeding patterns. Mushayatumbu, one of the elderly people interviewed during the course of my research, illustrated the spiritual aspect of Tonga conservation by giving this explanation:

> We hear a lot about people who say the Tonga will exterminate wild animals; to us, this is foolish talk. How can the Tonga do that when we have protected these animals all along? For us, the Tonga, when I die and become the muzimu (ancestral spirit), I will continue to protect my family. How can I protect them if I do not leave behind resources for them to celebrate life with?

The legend of Nyaminyami was described by Mapfunde as an animal or fish that was believed to control the flow of the Zambezi. The same legend was also used to illustrate the Tonga resource use philosophy. Nyaminyami, it was said, would reveal itself from time to time and in different places in order to allow people to go and cut meat from it. But one was allowed only to cut as much as one could carry without assistance. It was believed that if one cut more than he could carry, the meat would rot even before the person got home. The practice was called *njeka wa cheka*, which means that if you only harvest as much as you need the resource will not be exhausted. According to this legend, Nyaminyami was able to regenerate the flesh that had been cut and the people had this perpetual supply of meat. The legend is supposed to illustrate sustainable resource use.

Mapfunde also gave another illustration using the eland, which is considered sacred by the Tonga. An eland could not be killed by just anyone and if, by mistake, it was caught in a snare and was killed, the chief and spirit medium would hold a cleansing ceremony and intercede to the ancestral spirits on behalf of the people for the wrongdoing. The spirit medium was consulted all the time over land and wildlife issues. This minimized destructive approaches, such as trapping and hunting during the rainy season. According to the Tonga, the spirit medium received these instructions from the ancestral spirits.

Traditional Tonga wisdom guided wildlife management: everyone observed the hunting seasons and respected protected species and protected areas. The hunters had to account for what they killed via a system of giving certain portions of meat to the chief as proof. The chief received and consumed such meat as a measure of public accountability, but also to invoke goodwill from the ancestral spirits. The taboo system was another control measure. It was taboo to go out and hunt and kill an animal before the meat from the previous hunt was finished, and it was believed that anyone who did not comply with this cultural norm would lose their children and livestock to wild animals. The case of the lion that killed a total of 12 people and many livestock during the early 1980s, which earned it the nickname *Masvera seyi*, was used as an example of punishment for such wrongdoing. A system of totem animals was used to ensure that clan animals did not become extinct, which would spell doom to that clan.

THE APPLICATION OF TRADITIONAL KNOWLEDGE IN CAMPFIRE

CAMPFIRE has incorporated Tonga beliefs about hunting seasons and prohibitions on the hunting of female animals within the hunting guidelines of the programme. Tonga knowledge about animal migrations has also been used in the management guidelines. Furthermore, consultations with communities and chiefs take place about local participation in the conservation of wildlife. However, a survey of 224 households and an in-depth study of the life histories of seven elderly people showed that, in practice, very little other indigenous knowledge, traditional practices or local values have been incorporated within the programme. For example, CAMPFIRE failed to incorporate the Tonga spiritual needs for hunting that have to do with the healing of the mentally sick, as well as their needs for worship. CAMPFIRE's failure to recognize this while granting permits for sport hunting has created serious misunderstanding and mistrust. Mr Dezwa, one of the seven elderly people interviewed, had this to say:

> *Our people now die from mental illness because they can no longer hunt, as this is prohibited. We are told that we cannot kill animals; but we see white men coming and killing even the most sacred animals, such as elephants and the eland. We wonder if the white men from overseas are coming to kill these animals in order to meet their own spiritual needs or maybe to heal their*

> *own mental illness. The law forbids the Tonga from killing animals. Why are white people allowed to kill animals and we cannot? If it is bad for Tonga to kill animals, it is bad for white people to kill animals.*

This illustrates the problems and conflicts that result from non-recognition and understanding of local people's values.

But traditional knowledge has its own shortcomings. The younger generations are influenced by Western concepts of democracy, private ownership and equity, and do not always see the value of indigenous knowledge. These young people want to own private property that they can individually control and from which they can derive direct benefit. They appear to be less interested in managing common property. Many of them view traditional institutions as undemocratic and, hence, not in tune with their own aspirations. Their exposure to traditional practices is limited as these practices are no longer widely used.

Thus, most Tonga people younger than the age of 50 have insufficient residual knowledge of these practices to be able to contribute to the programme. A survey revealed that 73 per cent of the community had gained some traditional ecological knowledge from older people, but had no practical experience in applying that knowledge. Even the older people had not fully utilized their indigenous knowledge since they were moved up the escarpment. Mapfunde, one of the Tsonga elders I interviewed, sums this up: 'Our dignity is long lost, our language is fast disappearing, even concepts of resource management which were part of Tonga culture are not even understood by the Tonga today.' This begs the question: should CAMPFIRE rely upon an incomplete and disappearing knowledge base? It should be borne in mind that CAMPFIRE had committed itself to not only promote indigenous knowledge, but also to contribute to its revival. CAMPFIRE should have encouraged local people to put their knowledge into practice and should have used it to augment modern conservation approaches. Mapfunde's statement shows that CAMPFIRE has not restored that respect for local knowledge. Evidence from the case study, however, suggests that there is still residual knowledge among the Tonga that can be used to complement current conservation efforts. Many of the traditional practices that are known to be environmentally friendly can still be revived to the benefit of sustainable resource management today.

As shown earlier, many of CAMPFIRE's initial objectives have not been met because of various constraints that have impacted upon their implementation. The current internal debates about land and resource ownership need to be fully examined as part of the way forward. Furthermore, evidence from this study suggests that local knowledge is still important and available and should be seriously considered in the further development of CAMPFIRE.

THE IMPACT OF CAMPFIRE ON LIVELIHOODS

Direct cash and material benefits from CAMPFIRE to local communities are viewed as major incentives for conservation. Murphree (1991), Rihoy (1992) and others see a direct link between benefits and people's participation in the conservation of wildlife. I examined the role played by cash and other material benefits as incentives for community participation in wildlife conservation. Cash benefits at the household level were found to be small and to have little impact upon people's participation in conservation. According to Bond (2001), more than 50 per cent of the total revenue generated by CAMPFIRE has been earned by three of the 27 CAMPFIRE districts. In my own research, only 30 per cent of the households in those CAMPFIRE wards had received cash benefits. In the wildlife-rich wards, such as Masoka and Mahenye, cash incomes have been distributed to 100 per cent of the households. However, these are exceptions. In Nyaminyami, some people earned cash as well as received other benefits; but almost 50 per cent of respondents did not receive any benefits. Farmers earn much more from their other activities than the average Nyaminyami annual household incomes from CAMPFIRE (Sibanda, 2001). For example, an average farmer in Nyaminyami earned 350 Zimbabwe dollars from small-stock sales in 1996, with a goat selling for 100 Zimbabwe dollars. In the same year, the mean household cash income from CAMPFIRE was 55 Zimbabwe dollars. It should, however, be noted that CAMPFIRE had contributed significant other benefits, such as grinding mills, education and health to people's livelihoods.

While cash and other benefits contribute to people's willingness to participate in CAMPFIRE, these may not be the major motivating factors for conservation. Almost 46 per cent of those interviewed had not received any benefits from CAMPFIRE; yet, they participated in conservation. Only 10 per cent of the people interviewed thought CAMPFIRE was about sharing benefits from natural resources, against 53 per cent who understood the programme to be about conservation of natural resources. There was also a significant 18 per cent who did not know what CAMPFIRE was about. The reasons for the participation of those who did not understand the programme or did not receive cash benefits were that CAMPFIRE's values coincided with their own traditional values; they did not want to be on the wrong side of the law; and they wanted to be part of the community. The view promoted by CAMPFIRE proponents – namely, that communities participated in wildlife conservation because of tangible benefits – is too simplistic.

The extent to which people benefited directly did, however, influence their perceptions. The people of Mola, for instance, who received 55 per cent of CAMPFIRE revenue distributed in Nyaminyami had a much better understanding, with 82 per cent knowing what the programme was about. On the other hand, only 31 per cent of the people of Nebire, who received just 9.5 per cent of the CAMPFIRE revenue distributed in Nyaminyami, had a reasonable understanding of the programme. Many of those who misunderstood the programme viewed CAMPFIRE as being about selling wildlife to white people. Another common misunderstanding was that wildlife management and conservation was the responsibility of central government. The minority correctly understood it to be about conservation of natural resources by the local people who share benefits from these resources.

Heads of households received and controlled most of the revenue (65 per cent), and women often argued that they did not know how this income was used. Only 9 per cent of the revenue is distributed directly to other members of the households. Adult females received as little as 3 per cent of the distributed income. Even the community projects did not benefit the poorest and elderly individuals, who had neither school-going children nor access to, or any use for, such facilities as grinding mills. This means that the wealthier members of the community, who earn incomes from other sources, are better able to utilize facilities such as schools and grinding mills that are provided by the income from wildlife. The poorer or elderly community members, who do not benefit from these facilities, are required to make an equal sacrifice in conserving wildlife.

The unequal distribution of revenues and benefits within and between the wards is a result of different interpretations of CAMPFIRE's constitutional principles. The DNPWLM and non-governmental organizations (NGOs) promote a system that rewards only those villages that are considered to be directly affected by wildlife. The strategy rewards those communities or villages where wildlife is killed during the hunting season because they are viewed as the ones who have protected the animals, and because they are considered to have been affected by problem animals. These benefits are supposed to motivate the communities to support conservation. This approach creates inequality in the distribution of benefits because wildlife is mobile and sometimes migrates to different areas during different seasons. There are other wards in the district who are equally affected by wildlife who do not receive any income or benefits as a result of this approach. The approach has serious shortcomings. In Nyaminyami, for example, the wildlife occupies areas further away from the lake and the river during the wet summer months (November to April) than during the winter because water and food are abundant. During this period wildlife destroys people's crops in these areas; but there is no demand for trophy hunting. During the months of May to October (the dry season), wildlife moves closer to Lake Kariba. This period coincides with the peak in sport- and trophy-hunting activity, and these wards end up receiving the bulk of the revenues from sport hunting because they are viewed as the protectors of wildlife. The villages that do not benefit obviously see the system as unfair.

CONCLUSIONS

Wildlife is a resource that generates considerable interest at the local, national and international levels. Governments are interested in it, as are NGOs, donors and international organizations. Local communities want to own it and control its use, as well as derive benefits from it. As a result, debates rage on about how wildlife can be managed and how as many people as possible can gain access to it. CAMPFIRE is one innovative approach to natural resource management that attempts to address some of the issues of accessibility. The underlying concept is sound; but the implementation has met with limited success, primarily because of the issues of resource ownership and the failure of the programme to incorporate more local knowledge. Some of the successes of CAMPFIRE in places such as Nyaminyami, Guruve and Mahenye are directly attributable to the abundance of wildlife in those districts; but these are very localized cases and their wider impact will always remain limited. Some success is also attributable to the many innovations brought in by CAMPFIRE, such as the introduction of some elements of local management, the use of indigenous knowledge and traditional practices and the policy of allowing local communities to benefit directly from wildlife. However, CAMPFIRE's major limitation is its inability to create a more equitable distribution of benefits from wildlife.

This chapter suggests that the Tonga conservation ethic, indigenous knowledge and cultural and traditional practices relating to resource use are, for the most part, guided by a particular Tonga spirituality and worldview. Conventional science excludes spirituality and spiritual growth and, hence, cannot help us in understanding or adopting these issues. Driven by conventional science, CAMPFIRE seems to have no capacity to deal with the spiritual dimension of natural resource management and conservation. Furthermore, CAMPFIRE has not been able to fully utilize this Tonga cosmology for the benefit of sustainable use of natural resources. Local knowledge has not contributed to wildlife management as had been envisaged when the programme was initiated. This also means that CAMPFIRE has not contributed to the rebuilding of indigenous knowledge.

REFERENCES

Bond, I (2001) 'CAMPFIRE and the incentives for institutional change', in Hulme, D and Murphree, M W (eds) *African Wildlife and Livelihoods: The Promise and Performance of Community Conservation*. James Currey, Oxford, pp227-243

Colson, E (1971) *The Social Consequences of Resettlement: The Impact of the Kariba Resettlement Upon the Gwembe Tonga*, Kariba Studies vol 4. Manchester University Press, Manchester

Murphree, M (1991) *Decentralizing the Proprietorship of Wildlife Resources in Zimbabwe's Communal Lands*, CASS Occasional Paper Series NRM. Centre for Applied Social Research, University of Zimbabwe, Harare

Reynolds, P and Cousins, C C (1993) *Lwano Lwanyika: Tonga Book of the Earth*. Panos Publications, London

Rihoy, E (1992) *Community Institutions, Population Movement and the CAMPFIRE Programme in Zimbabwe*. Zimbabwe Trust, Harare

Sibanda, B (2001) *Wildlife and Communities at the Crossroads: Is Zimbabwe's CAMPFIRE the Way Forward?* SAPES Books, Harare

Tremmel, M (1996) *People of the Great River*, Siberia House Series No 9. Mambo, in association with Silvera House, Gweru

Zimbabwe Trust (1990) *The CAMPFIRE Programme in Zimbabwe*. Zimbabwe Trust, Harare

Chapter 19

New configurations of power around Mafungautsi State Forest in Zimbabwe

BEVLYNE SITHOLE

INTRODUCTION

The literature on community-based natural resource management (CBNRM) and rural development, in general, abounds with examples of decentralized projects that have failed to involve local communities effectively (Bratton, 1994; Guijt and Shah, 1998). One of the key reasons cited for this failure relates to the continued monopoly of power by ruling elites or by particular families within development projects. Examples of such monopoly of power, even in situations where inclusive democracy appears to be working, suggests that Western notions of democracy and governance may be at odds with local notions of democracy in the rural villages in southern Africa.

This chapter examines a project in south-west Zimbabwe where the government has sought to involve the local community in the joint or collaborative management of a state forest. The term 'community' is used loosely here to refer to the villages around this forest. The chapter shows that formal democratic processes have been implemented only by accommodating pre-existing configurations of power that favour particular families and/or ruling elites. It thus addresses a critical question in CBNRM: the degree to which democratic institutions of a type that have evolved in Western societies can merge with traditional power structures in rural areas so that they become representative of all interests in a local community. The chapter suggests that there are a number of local forces, many of them deeply rooted in local culture and tradition, that shape the way in which this articulation of formal and informal institutions takes place in CBNRM.

MAFUNGAUTSI STATE FOREST

Mafungautsi State Forest Reserve is found in Gokwe District, in Mashonaland West Province. The forest is about 82,000 hectares in size and was reserved in 1954. The forest is surrounded by numerous villages, the people of which have ethnically diverse identities, comprising the Shangwe, Ndebele and the Shona people. The Ndebele and the Shona are immigrants while the Shangwe are native to the area. Most of the settlement is at the forest margin, although communities use a wide variety of products and services from inside the forests. In general, communities are allowed subsistence use of the forests but need permits to collect certain products.

There is much literature on communal use of forest products in Mafungautsi and detailed accounts and analyses of the relationships between the forestry authorities and the communities have been made over the years (Vermeulen, 1994; Matose, 1994). The relationship between the forestry authority and the local people over the years is best described as characterized by suspicion, conflict and, sometimes, violent confrontation (Matose, 1994). In an attempt to deal with these problems, the forestry authorities at Mafungautsi have been involved in a pilot co-management project since 1992.

The collaborative management project

In order to involve local communities, the forest authority set up resource management committees (RMCs) constituted by 'democratically elected' individuals. This chapter is based on research conducted in Batanai RMC, one of 14 RMCs around the forest. Batanai RMC comprises Mrembwe, Chanetsa and Vizho, all three being fictitious names for real villages in order to protect the identities of my informants. Batanai RMC is one of the three active RMCs that has frequent contact with forest authorities. There are a number of factors that have pushed the forestry authority towards more people-oriented programmes in the area. Chief among these is donor pressure, though long-standing contestations in the Mafungautsi region have also forced the forestry authority to investigate ways of involving local people in a co-management programme.

During the research, local people were cautious about describing the partnership as 'mutually beneficial', while forestry officials expressed the view that the collaborative management arrangements were genuine. Officials claimed that there was, at the time of writing, a new willingness by the authority to acknowledge people's use of forests as a legitimate livelihood need rather than as 'poaching'. There was also a realization among officials that without local cooperation, effective management of the forest would not succeed. Implicit in their desire to develop partnerships is the belief that local involvement (even when not clearly defined) implies some measure of joint proprietorship over the forests resulting in use behaviour that promotes sustainable use of the forest.

But the collaborative project faced a number of challenges, which can be summarized as follows:

- communication in remote areas;
- merging identities of the organization and individuals;
- questions over whether adversaries can become partners;
- conflicts with other local organizations;
- assumptions that RMCs represent local people; and
- difficulties in defining physical boundaries and beneficiary groups.

Communication in remote areas

Evidence based on village meetings and key interviews suggests that after ten years the forestry authority has not yet successfully integrated local people through their RMCs within effective co-management. There is infrequent contact between district forestry officials and RMCs. Thus, local people describe the forestry authority as being inaccessible, even though the authority has offices close to the forest at the district centre in Gokwe. The more remote the village, the less access people from that village have to forestry officials based at the district centre. Officials admitted, during interviews, that the degree of remoteness influences the extent to which they can interact with different RMCs and sub-committees. However, even in the areas near the district centres, local people suggested that officials prefer certain areas to others and tend to visit those more regularly. As one elder stated: 'Partnerships are like a fire in the kitchen. You must periodically add wood or poke at the embers to keep it burning, otherwise the fire will die.'

Merging identities of organizations and individuals

During the interviews it became clear that local residents' attitudes to the state forestry authority are critically shaped by their perceptions of the performance of the project coordinator. Respondents stated that 'Since she took over nothing has happened; she just does not seem to be interested. The forestry authority participation in the project is dead.' Furthermore, other researchers working around the state forest insist that the problem is 'that woman' and claimed that 'the project coordinator has always shown suspicion towards other researchers, fearing that they will pick on her alleged disinterest in doing work on the ground'. In another interview, a resident stated that 'Personalities in the project are problematic, especially working with that woman; the relationship is simply not working!'

Another interviewee said that 'If the project coordinator continues to run away from her roles, it is feared that she will be overtaken by events, possibly fail to cope with demands from the community.' These attitudes to the forestry authority, defined in relation to perceptions about the behaviour of a key official, demonstrate how easily the image of a new CBNRM institution can be shaped by perceptions of individual behaviour. Such overlapping perceptions about organizations and individuals suggest that institutional analysis in CBNRM should go beyond an outline of organizational charts, roles and activities and deal also with the critical influence that the behaviour and attitudes of key individuals can play.

Questions over whether adversaries can become partners

On paper, and in many official pronouncements, the forestry authority at Mafungautsi sounds committed to developing mutually beneficial partnerships with local people. But has the authority abandoned its top-down management practices?

The RMCs were created and facilitated by the authority and there is a requirement that women should be elected to the committees. Many people complained that they are often not aware that these committees are being constituted because elections meetings are called suddenly and, sometimes, remote villages hear about the meetings too late. Generally, there is a perception that this allows the friends of the district forest or party officials to get elected to all the key positions. There is also a widespread complaint that local people who get elected to these positions generally then come to consider themselves as quasi-employees of the forestry authority. Previous members for the dissolved Batanai RMC claim to have been paid 500 Zimbabwe dollars (US$33.33 in 2000) each, received overalls and got annual allocations of resources from the authority. Some local respondents described these elected people to be 'more forestry authority than the officials of the forestry authority itself'. They stated that *mwana we nyoka inyoka*, or 'an offspring of a snake is a snake'.

Consequently, the RMC has come to be regarded by many as an extension of the forestry authority at the local level, rather than as a people's committee. Furthermore, the forestry authority has maintained forest monitors who continue to prosecute 'poachers'. Most of these forest monitors come from other parts of Zimbabwe, fuelling allegations of malpractice, extortion and selective prosecution. Local people resent the continued presence of these monitors and describe their continued presence as an example of how little things have changed despite the operations of the RMCs.

Even on the issue of how to spend the revenue collected, local people, and even RMC committee members, suggested that the desires of the authority or its officials are imposed with little consultation or negotiation. Once the revenues are collected, the RMC and the forestry authority call meetings to decide which projects should be financed. Respondents claimed that forestry officials prefer certain types of projects and encourage local people to select these, even when such projects are a low priority for residents. Within the social forestry programme of the forestry authority, the main activities are tree planting (especially of gum trees by individuals or groups) and beekeeping projects. Thus, in most of the meetings, officials tend to push for these projects.

Local people complain that 'The forestry authority says the money is yours, but tells people do this and do that. We ask where is our ownership in that...the money generated by the RMC is controlled by the forestry authority. The money from the RMC is not our money; that is why people poach. They say the resources belong to the forestry authority and they are not being used.'

According to one informant, residents are often told by officials that 'You have lost focus; what you plan to do has nothing to do with the forestry authority.' But, added the respondent, 'This rejects people's desires; beekeeping is not popular. We told the authority that we wanted to build a school; but they also said we lost focus. Beekeeping is not sustainable; we want things that will last. No one survives on the gum trees, which they want us to plant.' Does it make sense to local people to plant trees when they see the forests as having abundant tree resources? Does it make sense to the community to become beekeepers when there is low consumption of honey in the diet and when there is no market for honey? Engaging local communities in collaboration must go further than asking them to rubber stamp ideas or activities that clearly do not further their livelihood goals.

Conflicts with other local organizations

The creation of RMCs is highly contested by other local organizations, such as village development committees, the rural district council and traditional leaders. Some of these organizations do not understand the need to have new structures when several of the existing organizations have roles that overlap with those of the RMC. Forestry officials argue that existing organizations are weak and ineffectual and others are dominated by elites. They indicate that they want a committee truly representative of the local people to be involved and democratically elected without external interference from local politicians and district council officials. In the case of Batanai, the RMC has no clear relationship with any local organization and the district council thus challenges the legitimacy of RMC. The district council argues that for policies in other sectors, such as wildlife, the council should constitute the committee. The forestry authority argues that the forest is outside the jurisdiction of the council and that the latter merely pretends interest in the RMC so that it can appropriate funds, as has been the case in a number of Communal Areas Management Programme for Indigenous Resources (CAMPFIRE) districts, where there is district council control over wildlife.

Assumptions that the RMC represents local people

As mentioned above, three villages constitute Batanai RMC. Attendance of RMC meetings is very low. Participation in public meetings by women in this area is even lower than in other parts of the country due to what researchers in the area have dubbed 'cultural controls'. In one of the villages, we found that people in the very rich and the very poor categories had little or no interest in participating in the co-management project. Recent migrants also feel excluded from decision-making and exist outside of the process. For example, one immigrant into the area states: 'I do not actively participate in the RMC. When you are an immigrant, you have little say in what goes on in the RMC. You will never be elected leader to the RMC; they elect each other.' Sometimes immigrants do get involved but their voices are discounted. For example, one school official states that 'There are many people among the locals who can spearhead development in this area. Unfortunately, they are not allowed to speak at meetings or even attend meetings. When they suggest something at meetings, no matter how good, people discount it on account of your origin. If

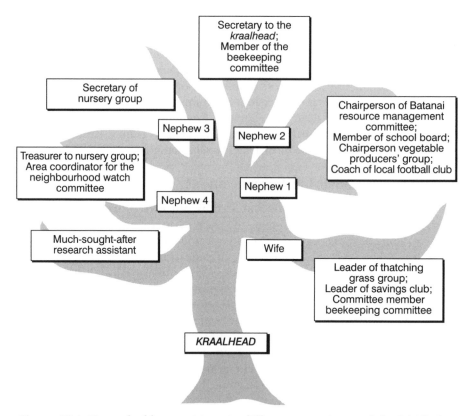

Figure 19.1 *Control of key positions in different committees of the RMCs by the* kraalhead's *family in Mrembwe village*

you persist and try to get involved, they threaten you with eviction or witchcraft.' Early immigrants are more accepted than recent immigrants whatever their ethnic group and they do sometimes get elected to higher positions. Analysis of the Batanai RMC and its two sub-committees (beekeeping and thatch grass collectors' group) shows that the relatives of *kraalhead* (village leader) Mrembwe hold most of the positions (see Figure 19.1).

However, other villages in the RMC are also represented in the committees. People from Mrembwe village hold the key positions of chairperson and treasurer in the RMC. Other committee members indicate that most decisions are made by these key people in consultation with the forestry authority, with little or no input from other members. Based on key interviews and group discussions, we identified the most influential person in the community as the wife of *kraalhead* Mrembwe (see Figure 19.2). This fact challenges notions and previous work by other researchers, suggesting that women do not take part because the dominant cultural norms do not allow them to get involved. This woman holds many more positions than other women in her area.

The *kraalhead*'s wife is the most vocal woman in public meetings and gatherings. She is rumoured to be the real influence and force behind her

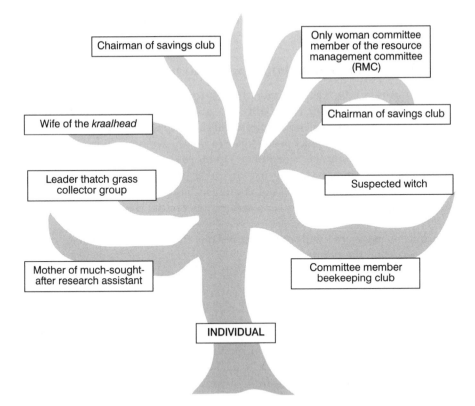

Figure 19.2 *Positions held by the most influential person in Mrembwe village*

family members. She is also widely feared as a suspected witch. Being a suspected witch means that most of her decisions go unchallenged. This is one reason why the former treasurer of the RMC was able to embezzle money with impunity. The belief in witchcraft is very strong in the area, especially among some of the Shangwe, who are regarded as having stronger animistic views than other ethnic groups such as the Shona and the Ndebele. However, local beliefs in witchcraft are evident among members of all of the ethnic groups, although these are often phrased in vague and metaphoric terms. In terms of their worldview, indifference towards, or disagreement with, a witch can evoke illness, death or any manner of bad luck. Thus, it is quite likely that, under the banner of open and democratic elections, people suspected of being witches may be voted in simply because of the fear that they invoke in others.

Respondents also suggested that the monopoly of power by families or elites is culturally accepted by many local people. They also noted that there was a tendency among the Shangwe to avoid holding elected positions. Some respondents from this ethnic group suggest that being elected 'cheapens' the traditional institutions that put people in power, and thus leads to disrespect and disapproval from other local residents. The fact that the democratic process is mostly flawed and controlled by outside influences also diminishes the respect given to the people in these positions.

Difficulties in untangling boundaries and beneficiaries

Previously, any use by local villagers of non-forest timber products (NTFPs) was regarded as poaching. Today, the state authority has recognized a list of uses as livelihood requirements. However, local people need to obtain permits issued by the RMCs to collect products or to use the forests. Evidence suggests that 'poaching' is as much a problem as before despite the RMCs and the respect for livelihoods based on use of forest products. Some respondents argue that poaching in some areas of the forests has actually increased. Various reasons are given for this increase; but three key factors were identified:

1   problems associated with obtaining permits (for example, extended delays in processing the permits);
2   the inaccessibility of some forest areas designated for each RMC relative to settlements where local people live; and
3   continued restrictions over access to valuable forest products, such as timber.

One villager who lived on the edge of the forest stated:

> *Sometimes I do not go to get the permit. I just go into the forest. As you can see, I live on the forest boundary. The RMC members live far away and when I do not have time to visit them, I just go into the forest and get what I want. Also, some of the RMC members are too full of themselves and they take their time processing the permits as if to make you feel their authority. Once I got caught and they took all the grass.*

While the change in attitudes towards local use is identified as positive, local people complain that the state charges them for resources that other villagers can get from commercial farms at no cost. One elder said: 'Often, you expect the state to look after you, not the commercial farmers. But, in reality, we wish the forest belonged to a white farmer.'

Different RMCs control different areas of forest alongside their villages. Although these areas are clearly defined administratively, boundaries are not observed. Thus, villagers can extract products or use areas of forests designated for other RMCs. In general, local people go to the nearest RMC rather than to their own. They also go to RMCs that are most likely to have the products that they are looking for in the quantities they need. Differential endowment and accessibility of forest areas has resulted in users criss-crossing boundaries. Consequently, some RMCs in resource-rich portions of forests tend to generate more revenue than others. RMCs that generate little revenue have begun to raise questions about who should benefit. For example, in Batanai RMC, people from villages far from the RMC argue that villages that fail to generate revenue for their RMC should not be included in projects financed by this revenue. Currently, the revenue is used for development projects that benefit all villages under the RMC. Those people generating revenue feel that it is unfair that people from distant villages benefit from the income generated in Batanai, when they harvest resources from another RMC and send their money to those RMCs. This demonstrates the problems that can arise from a bureaucratic tendency to use boundaries that bear no relation to actual resource-use patterns of the villages involved.

Despite its expressed intentions, the state still dictates conditions under which the forest is used. It retains all of the revenue from (restricted) valuable forest products, while local people have access only to the smaller revenues generated from their ability to harvest less-valuable forest products. Local people expressed dissatisfaction at being consulted over use of some forest products, while they had no say in the extraction of valuable products, such as timber. The forestry authority issues permits for these valuable products without consulting the RMCs.

Comparisons were drawn between RMCs and CAMPFIRE districts. It was pointed out that CAMPFIRE involves management of all game, not just small or big game, and that CAMPFIRE communities can sell valuable trophy species to safari hunters. A local respondent observed that 'Wet trees are the wives of the forestry authority. It is not possible for anyone to ask to harvest that tree; it is similar to asking a man to copulate with his wife.' Valuable timber is harvested only by outsiders (private companies and urban entrepreneurs), and some respondents alleged that the forestry authority 'wants to look after people who come from far and neglects people who live here. You would not buy a uniform for another's child when your own has nothing. You would first clothe your child, then clothe the other.'

CONSEQUENCES

This chapter has sought to address the question of where power lies in the co-management project and to establish the extent to which the RMC represents diverse interests in the villages. Recent amendments to policy in Zimbabwe, both in forestry and other sectors, present the 'right of participation' as creating opportunities through co-management arrangements for actors to participate in formulating and implementing management strategies.

However, in reality, there are vastly varying patterns of interaction between officials from the forestry authority with different villages and with different people in the RMCs. Most residents feel that active participation by residents, in general, is weak and that the authority is so distant to them 'it might as well be located in another country'. For collaboration to happen, partners need to know each other well (Petrzelka and Bell, 2000). Effective collaboration occurs when all partners listen, understand each other and compromise on their particular interests for the greater good. However, data presented suggests that, at least in the view of many local people, the elected

Batanai RMC finds itself more accountable to the forestry authority than to its constituency, and has now assumed the characteristics of the forestry authority.

In addition, the forestry authority determines the parameters under which individuals can be elected to a committee and the constitution of the committees, especially regarding the participation of women, what products can be harvested and the types of projects that the RMC can fund. This amounts to top-down management legitimized by local people through the existence of RMCs.

One of the problems affecting the partnership is the merging of identities of the organization and the individual. Local perceptions of the forestry authority reflect frustrations that local people have working with an individual. Murphree (1994) finds that personalities can sometimes overwhelm an organization, resulting in the individual becoming synonymous with that organization. Consequently, though partnerships are formed with organizations, one must always be aware of the enormous influence that individual rather than organizational traits have in shaping relationships and projects.

The development literature cautions against any creation of new structures where existing organizations have some capacity to carry out the roles of these new structures. The fact that power continues to be monopolized by the same families and ruling elites in the Batanai RMC would suggest that, rather than replace existing structures and processes, democratization has been accommodative and merely acted to accentuate the power differentials already in existence.

Although the forestry authority justifies the formation of the RMC on grounds of equity, transparency and greater participation, data presented in this chapter suggests a different reality. The RMC is not as representative as the authority would have us believe. In fact, of the three villages in Batanai RMC, one village is known to have more influence than the others since its members hold key positions in the RMC and its sub-committees. Further analysis reveals the monopoly of leadership positions by relatives of *kraalhead* Mrembwe and, within that family, the community identifies a woman as being the most influential person in the project.

While current orthodoxy suggests that women are excluded from decision-making structures, and, in particular, while literature from this area suggests that cultural constraints limit women's participation, we find that one woman is powerful in spite of these cultural constraints. This demonstrates that women can and do hold power perhaps in ways that are not always visible to researchers. The association of power with witchcraft, in this case, suggests that researchers and practitioners should be sensitive to less obvious determinants of power in rural societies. Moreover, the data indicates that local people generally accept the monopoly of power by particular households. Such cultural acceptance questions the relevance of Western notions of democracy and equity in some CBNRM situations.

The data also shows that the recent acceptance that use of the forest is important for livelihoods has not significantly changed the patterns of 'poaching' and resource use in the forest. While some revenue accrues to the RMC, the bulk of the revenue accruing to the forestry authority is neither disclosed nor shared with the other partners. Sharing the benefits and the costs of management is one of the important conditions for collaboration identified in common property literature (Ostrōm 1997). Costs and benefits from the forest are therefore not equitably distributed among the partners, thus limiting prospects for real collaboration.

Within the RMC itself, increased calls to restrict use by villages to designated areas of their RMC underlines the problems of defining boundaries that bear no relation to people's real patterns of resource use or adaptive behaviour. Consequently, there is a need to recognize that externally derived boundaries, while neat on paper, often overlay a complex tapestry of indigenous patterns of resource use.

CONCLUSION

Co-management presupposes that partnerships are contingent on shared interests. Data from Mafungautsi suggest that co-management is complicated, firstly, by relationships between the main actors and then by relationships within particular categories of actors. The RMC is meant to be the melting pot or intersection of interests between the forestry authority and local people; yet, it is clearly a source of dissent and dissatisfaction. While access to the forests for livelihood needs has been improved, access for commercial purposes has not. Development opportunities based on exploitation of the forest remain inaccessible to local people.

At the resource level, the forestry authority continues to wield power over the use of the forest, though it does so under the guise of a co-management project. At the level of the RMC, we see how familial control of the institution governs most development activity within the project. The analysis shows that in an RMC comprising three villages, one village has more power than other villages and, within that village, one family monopolizes key positions in the RMC and its sub-committees. Within that family, there is a single powerful woman who is said to be the real driver of all aspects of the project. Thus, we can conclude that what is purported to be a community-based intervention is, in reality, a family-level intervention. Yet, these family members were elected through democratic process by three villages. The acceptance of this monopoly of power by kin challenges Western ideals about equity and participation.

REFERENCES

Bratton, M (1994) 'Peasant and state relations in post-colonial Africa: Patterns of engagement and disengagement', in Midgal, J S, Kohli, A and Shue, V (eds) *State Power and Social Force: Domination and Transformation in the Third World.* Cambridge University Press, New York, Melbourne, pp231–255

Guijt, I and Shah, M K (1998) *The Myth of Community: Gender Issues in Participatory Development*. Intermediate Technology Publications, London

Matose, F (1994) *People's Use and Perceptions of Forest Resources: An Analysis of State Property Regime in Zimbabwe*. MSc thesis, University of Alberta, Edmonton

Murphree, M W (1994) 'The role of institutions in community based conservation', in Western, D and Wright, M (eds) *Natural Connections: Perspectives in Community Based Conservation*. Sland Press, Washington, DC, pp403–427

Oström, E (1997) *What Makes for Successful Institutions To Govern Common Pool Resources?* Center for the Study of Institutions, Population and Environmental Change, Indiana University, Bloomington

Petrzelka, P and Bell, M (2000) 'Rationality and solidarities: The social organization of common property resources in the Imdrhas valley of Morocco', *Human Organization* 50(3): 343–352

Vermeulen, S (1994) *Consumption, Harvesting and Abundance of Wood Along the Boundary Between Mafungautsi State Forest and Gokwe Communal Area, Zimbabwe*. MSc thesis, University of Zimbabwe, Harare

Conclusions and recommendations: What we have learned from a decade of experimentation

CHRISTO FABRICIUS, EDDIE KOCH, STEPHEN TURNER, HECTOR MAGOME AND LAWRENCE SISITKA

This book has presented a critical overview of the way in which community-based natural resource management (CBNRM) programmes in the past decade have evolved and been implemented in southern Africa. A basic question threads through the synthesis and case studies: 'Has the movement described in the book reached the point of failure or is it merely in need of a number of adaptations?' Or, to use a phrase that was repeated by the editors during the planning sessions for the book: 'Has the CBNRM brew been burnt on the fires of experience or does the recipe need some tinkering with?' Our answer has been consistent. The question is methodologically and chronologically inappropriate. We argue there is not linear movement from inception to success or failure. Both the movement and the individual projects that comprise it go through cycles, long and short, that involve experimentation and adaptation. In the process, lessons are learned that can help cement the 'epochal' articulation between traditional and formal, communal and private, that is being forged as CBNRM proliferates and unfolds on the subcontinent.

In this Conclusion, we provide a conceptual model of 'how CBNRM works', followed by a number of operational lessons that we have learned from the preceding chapters and our own experience. Here, the grammar differs from that in the previous parts. Out 'to-the-point' writing style is deliberate, and aimed at those at the CBNRM coalface.

HOW DOES CBNRM WORK?

The functioning of CBNRM, and its different components, is presented diagrammatically in Figure 20.1. The *basic building blocks* of CBNRM are ecosystems and people (box I). The other basic building blocks are local institutions (codes of conduct, rules); skills and the general capacity of all role players to engage in CBNRM; and essential tools and equipment with which 'to do the job'. These are the inputs into CBNRM that feed into CBNRM *processes.* These processes are *external events,* such as floods, droughts and political surprise (box II); *external interventions,* such as policies, donations, negotiations and law enforcement (box IV); and *local management activities and strategies* – the things local people do with natural resources, and with each other (and outsiders) when they access and use natural resources (box III). These processes create a series of *outputs* from CBNRM – for example, wealth, greater resource security, improved livelihoods and improved or impaired ecosystem integrity (box V).

Facilitators, local people and policy-makers are, to a large extent, able to influence the outputs of CBNRM through their interventions and management actions and strategies. Bearing in mind that much of what happens in CBNRM is beyond the control of local players (the external events in box II), role players (communities, facilitators and policy-makers, in particular) are faced with a single challenge. How can they play their roles in such a way that the outputs of CBNRM are optimized? Which principles can they follow and implement, to increase the likelihood of the CBNRM movement and its programmes achieving their specific and general objectives? And which guidelines can be provided to make the most of CBNRM?

RECOMMENDED GENERAL PRINCIPLES

After more than a decade of experimenting with CBNRM principles and approaches, a number of broad principles have emerged among many CBNRM practitioners, including the authors of various sections of this book. Here it should be stressed that principles are merely the fundamental rules that should be followed in implementing CBNRM. They are what guide one's thinking and actions in a very generic way; they are not blueprints for success and they cannot replace interventions based on concrete, specific and sensitive analysis. Having said that, we have identified seven principles that, if ignored, dramatically increase the likelihood of CBNRM to produce more failures than successes. They are:

1   *A diverse and flexible range of livelihood options is maintained:* People continue to use a range of different opportunities to make their livings. They grow food, keep livestock, sell eggs, make craft products, hire their labour, collect medicinal plants, harvest thatching grass, collect food from the water, and provide services for tourists, as well as many other things.
2   *The production potential of the resource base is maintained or improved:* The amount of natural resources available not only stays the same, but increases through good management. There are more mussels growing on the rocks, larger areas of grass of better quality, seedlings and saplings of preferred plants are growing in the forest and woodland, and animal numbers are increasing.

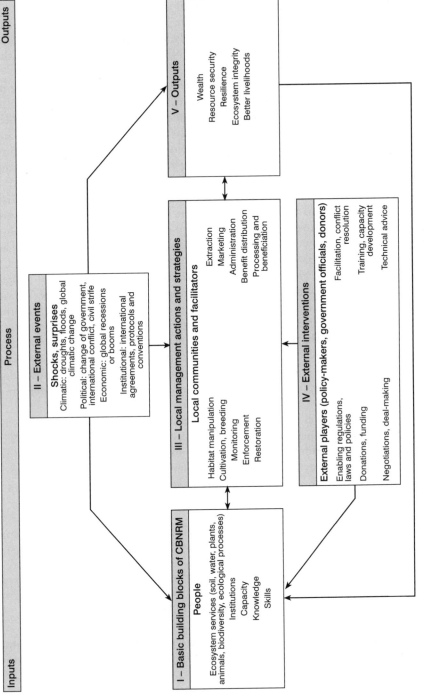

Figure 20.1 *A CBNRM systems model*

3 *Institutions for local governance and land and resource management are in place and are effective:* There are local rules and they are implemented. The local management organization works well and takes its responsibilities seriously. It works closely with community members and outside partners to ensure that the CBNRM initiative is benefiting the people and the natural resources.

4 *Economic and other benefits to provide an incentive for the wise use of resources exist:* People are properly rewarded for the efforts they make to look after their natural resources. They stick to the quota agreed for their harvesting, receive a good market price for their products, and make some extra money through expanding their work to other areas. Community guards patrol the forest, grassland or lake to prevent outsiders from taking plants or animals.

5 *There are effective policies and laws, they are implemented and authority is handed down to the lowest level where there is capacity:* The laws are observed and enforced, and people are given the right and responsibility to make their own decisions about the use of their resources. The harvesting quotas are set by the community with advice from specialists.

6 *There is sensitive and responsible facilitation from outside:* Local people have the right to work closely with advisers and experts who understand the social and cultural context well, and have real experience in the management of the resources in the area. These outside agents have a commitment to sharing the skills and knowledge with local citizens and are able to respect local knowledge and integrate it where appropriate with their technical expertise. The approach is one of sharing knowledge and encouraging the community to contribute its experience and understanding.

7 *Local-level power relations are favourable for CBNRM and are understood:* The people in the community who have the most influence, the traditional leadership and the older men, are genuinely committed to making sure that everyone benefits as equally as possible. They work hard to ensure that the stronger members do not dominate the process. Everyone is aware of who the influential people are.

In addition to the above, we have identified a few additional practical and overarching principles that apply to all outside interventions that aim to alleviate poverty.

ADVICE FOR PRACTITIONERS

Implementing CBNRM always involves meeting a number of challenges. Some of them are fairly common to all CBNRM initiatives. Before starting on any initiative it is worth remembering these:

• Expect a huge amount of variation and difference in each case.

- Don't apply any guidelines as a blueprint. Be willing to experiment and contribute through adaptation. But avoid being fickle and confusing everyone.
- Expect local conflicts. CBNRM is sometimes a bit like a revolution, so don't be surprised by conflict. Try to predict it through good monitoring and then try to prevent it. Don't be worried if it happens anyway. This is normal. Shocks and surprises are part of the game.
- Tread lightly with local power relations. CBNRM is an explicitly egalitarian programme. It will inevitably threaten some. Sometimes there needs to be a pragmatic accord with the rich and powerful who may be threatened by the democratic agenda of CBNRM. It may be possible to persuade those whose interests are opposed to the principles of CBNRM to cooperate. At other times it may be necessary to confront those who obstruct the implementation of programmes that promote the rights of the poor and marginalized. In all cases, unneccessary conflict should be avoided and intervention should be sensitive and based on careful analysis.
- CBNRM is about people. All people have strengths and weaknesses, hopes and ambitions, needs and wants. Bringing together many different people to work together towards a shared goal is extremely challenging and it is never easy. All initiatives, particularly those involving funding and the prospect of income generation, tempt people to promote their own interests. CBNRM should never become a vehicle for promoting the personal or political ambitions of individuals or groups in any sector.
- Let go of control. Real participatory decision-making, and the devolution of authority (cornerstones of CBNRM), mean 'letting go' and handing over authority. This often leads to outcomes that were not predicted or intended. These are not necessarily worse than the original intentions, but can present quite a challenge to those used to being in control of situations.
- Be more patient than normal. Expect participatory natural resource management to be a slow, incremental process. Donors and government agencies need to recognize that the process of defining and registering community-based organizations, and developing competent institutions, is slow and arduous with lengthy time horizons of up to ten years, requiring long-term commitment and ongoing support.
- Keep in mind that people value natural resources in different ways. Some are concerned with economic values, others about cultural values, and yet others about conservation values. Don't assume that local people are always strategic and rational in the corporate sense. Furthermore, don't expect them to always share the non-monetary values that conservation planners place on species or ecosystems.
- Monitoring of all aspects at all times is essential. Evaluation should be seen as integral to the whole process. Clear evaluation processes must be included in the design of any CBNRM initiative. Everyone should be responsible for evaluating their area of activity, including their own performance. The approach should be both 'participatory' (involving everyone) and 'formative' (to inform changes to the programme).

- Communication between all stakeholders must be maintained throughout the process. Formal communication channels must be established at the outset, and there must be room for additional informal contacts.
- All stakeholders should be prepared to be flexible in their approach and adaptable to the changing circumstances.
- All stakeholders should apply themselves to the initiative with complete professionalism. This should extend to all aspects of their involvement, including full attendance at meetings, submission of reports, provision of necessary and agreed support, and evaluation of their roles.

MORE ACTION-ORIENTED GUIDELINES

The sectoral role players in CBNRM (especially local people, practitioners such as field workers, consultants and researchers, and policy-makers) need action-oriented guidelines that are directly applicable to their specific line of work.

Twelve working principles for local people and their leaders

1   *Work with as many people as possible – remember that this is for the whole community.* It is very important that all voices are heard and respected at all stages. In particular the less forceful groups and individuals should be encouraged to contribute their ideas. Be careful about particularly strong groups and individuals trying to use the initiative for their own purposes. It is especially important to find out who is most involved in the use of natural resources. Their input will be crucial and their interests must be properly represented.

2   *Use a strong and truly representative organization (such as a committee) to represent local people.* If a strong institution which has shown that it does a good job, already exists, then use this rather than creating a new structure. If not, then choose honest, reliable and active people from the different sectors in the community to lead the process on behalf of the community. One representative who can write well should be appointed to record all of the activities and events that take place in the initiative. Other representatives can be responsible for other aspects of the initiative. These aspects may include working with the other partners, monitoring the resources and supporting the development of different enterprises.

3   *Be very clear about what is expected and required from the initiative.* Establish a clear vision of what people expect; but be realistic about the benefits that are likely to come. Make sure that all other partners from outside understand and share this vision. Take care that your own ideas are not ignored or overridden by the other partners.

4   *Be aware that there are different kinds of benefits, and that some are short term and others longer term.* Most people will, naturally, be interested in direct financial benefits early on. Other benefits that are often more

difficult to see can include a better living environment; skills development (practical and educational); cooperation within the community and with others; and improved livelihood opportunities. Benefits that can come with government, donor or non-governmental organization (NGO) support include long-term security and rights to resources and land; protection against outside threats; access to loans; and assistance with negotiations with the private sector. Negotiate these benefits.

5 *Recognize that the benefits from CBNRM will not solve all of the problems in the local area.* CBNRM can only provide a few opportunities to help people meet their needs. It should be seen as adding to the other ways in which the community members make their living. People should be encouraged to continue with their different activities and not rely completely upon the benefits from CBNRM.

6 *Those who make the biggest sacrifice should benefit more than others.* The people who will lose most because of the way in which CBNRM changes how they use the resources should be supported in developing other income-generating activities. They could also receive some compensation (perhaps by being employed in the project). Some people will always benefit more than others, often through being employed in some way. This must be discussed and agreed by everyone right from the beginning as it may cause conflict if left until later in the process.

7 *Work with the other partners to develop a realistic management plan for the resources.* Bring together people's understanding and knowledge of the resources and the information from the partners when drawing up a clear and workable plan. Include in this plan agreed rules about the use of the resources. Also include a strategy to monitor the use and condition of the resources. People should be involved in all aspects of developing and implementing the plan, as well as monitoring its success.

8 *Expect some tensions and conflicts to develop.* In any group of people, especially when there is money involved or controls are put in place on how people use resources, conflicts will occur. Be prepared for these and try to deal with them before they become serious. It helps to keep good and open communication, and to allow people to voice their concerns and complaints. These must always be discussed openly and responded to in appropriate ways.

9 *Make sure that everyone is aware of what part they should play in the initiative and of their responsibilities.* Hold regular meetings to ensure that everyone knows how they should contribute to the initiative and is doing what has been agreed. Draw up a constitution early on in the process, or adopt or amend an existing constitution.

10 *Keep close contact with others in the community and with the outside partners.* There must be good communication between everyone involved at all times. In addition to more formal meetings, the main community representatives should be available to other community members and partners. This will help in dealing with problems or new developments as they occur.

11 *Recognize that it will take time for major benefits to appear.* In CBNRM projects, a great deal of work is usually needed before real benefits can be reaped. An important role of the community representatives is keeping the community motivated and involved while no obvious financial benefits are being produced. In the meantime, negotiate with government and other partners for more immediate benefits.

12 *Make sure that people are aware of the 'bigger picture'.* Seek the help of partners and supporting organizations to achieve this. People should also be aware of the government's policies concerning natural resources and their use and management. People should understand how their contribution fits into the broader CBNRM movement in the country, in Africa and throughout the world.

Twelve working principles for practitioners

1 *Keep your options open.* The range of resources that can be utilized, the different types of labour contributing to CBNRM and the many different sources of income to the household help communities to cope. It is therefore important to ensure that a range of livelihood options continues to be available to local people. Big, homogeneous interventions are risky because markets fluctuate and global events are unpredictable. Maintaining a diversity of options helps people to recover after unexpected political, economic and ecological change because their 'eggs' are not all in one basket.

2 *Manage and monitor natural resources carefully.* The natural resource base is the fundamental building block of CBNRM. If this base is destroyed, the option to engage in CBNRM no longer exists. Get reliable information about the resource-use patterns (what is used and for what; who uses it; how much and how often is it used) and production potential of the ecosystem before making formal agreements. Invest a reasonable and appropriate part of any profits back into natural resource management, and assist local people in developing and implementing their own monitoring systems.

3 *Build local organizations.* In order to ensure a strong sense of local ownership, a local management body must do the administration and make decisions. This body will need proper support and, often, appropriate training to carry out these duties. It will need to be constantly nurtured. In some cases, if there are serious problems, it may need to be reconstituted. As far as possible, use existing organizations rather than creating new ones. However, make informed decisions about this and don't compromise on the objectives of CBNRM if new bodies are essential.

   Be aware that capacity-building is always a long-term process. Training of local organizations must have clear and agreed objectives and should be monitored. Once the objectives of the training are achieved, the local body should take full control and responsibility.

4 *Make sure that CBNRM produces real benefits, now and later, for local people.* Make sure that the direct benefits to local people compare

favourably to the local costs of conserving and managing natural resources. Local people lead busy lives, and land is in short supply. They will not invest time, land and other resources in CBNRM unless there are clear and direct benefits. Ensure that there is a market for the goods produced or services offered from CBNRM. Outside assistance will probably be required to develop a clear business plan for the project. This will need to examine what the real demand is for the product, how much can be produced on a sustainable basis and what returns can be realistically expected from the sale of the product. The plan will also address questions of quality control and the consistency, or seasonality, of supply.

5 *Expect a huge amount of variation in each case and manage each situation uniquely.* Establish local rules, codes of conduct and 'ways of doing' by constantly learning and adapting. But be aware of national, provincial and local policies and strategies and use them to your advantage. There is no blueprint for CBNRM. Apply the lessons learned from past experience and monitor regularly.

6 *Compile a management plan.* Start with a basic, locally developed, plan, set of rules or constitution and build on it. Get specialist advice; but make sure the plan meets local needs.

7 *Use skilled facilitators and other supporters and advisers that you can trust every step of the way.* The ultimate aim is for CBNRM initiatives to be sustainable without outside facilitation; but this can take a very long time. In some cases, specialist services (such as marketing) may always be provided by an outside partner. This happens in many business situations.

8 *Make sure the right people are involved in CBNRM.* Involve individuals with skills, enthusiasm and empathy who easily connect with others. Each actor (for example, communities, government participants, supporters) must appoint a dedicated 'champion' for each main task or step. Increase the leadership pool by giving inexperienced people responsibilities.

9 *Expect conflict and power struggles and plan for this upfront.* Local power struggles raise their head once there are tangible benefits, and communities are never completely unified. Deal with conflict early.

10 *Build alliances and work hard at maintaining them.* Work with other organizations in government and the private sector and make space for them. They have their own special skills and areas of work, and are valuable partners. Make sure they also benefit from working with you. Be aware that this can create new hitches. If outside partners (third parties) are involved in fundamental aspects of the programme, such as harvesting the resources, work closely with them to manage and monitor their activities.

11 *Budget realistically.* Extra time and money are needed to make participation and collaboration work. Joint management costs more, and takes longer, than conventional management; but it is more effective in the long run. The main benefit is that joint management provides different perspectives and helps with integrating the many different aspects of CBNRM.

12 *Be open and honest.* Spend a lot of time on negotiations and try to find honest compromises. But don't be held to ransom by groups with a vested interest. Communicate your intentions, plans and strategies often, and clearly, to everybody right from the start.

Encourage openness, questioning and debate at all times. Make sure that feedback from all parties is integrated within future planning.

Eleven working principles for policy-makers

1 *Ensure that the policy process is adaptive and flexible.* It should be possible for policies to be refined in a step-wise way. Build in annual revisions and evaluations from the start. Draw strongly on local experience in making and refining policies.

2 *Policy papers must be easy to understand and easier to get to.* Keep the key elements simple. Avoid jargon and complicated orders.

3 *Create broad, overarching national or sub-national policies that provide the foundation upon which to build local rules.* A commonly stated principle of CBNRM is the need to devolve management and decision-making to the smallest and most local unit of people who use natural resources. There is much debate and controversy, though, about the way in which this principle should be implemented in the different contexts that apply in each country of the region. In many countries local authorities intercept benefits that should flow to residents of a local area. In others, the institutions of local government have the necessary policies and capacity to help implement CBNRM programmes. Thus sometimes it is necessary to push for devolution away from local government agencies to local democratic institutions. In other cases it is possible to create viable partnerships between local governments and local democratic institutions. The principle of devolution needs to be tempered with the advantages, where these exist, of working with local governments. Leave room for local people to make their own regulations, using local knowledge and customs.

4 *Aim to hand down authority to the resource users themselves, once they have the necessary training and skills.* But ensure that no local role player is left out. Recognize the role of traditional leadership in areas where they have influence. Give people long-term security and rights to resources and land. People need to know where they stand and what is at stake before they will invest time and money in managing their resources.

5 *Policies must have teeth.* Fines and other sanctions must get progressively stricter when rules are broken. Allow officials on the ground to use their discretion when applying the law. Each situation is different.

6 *Formulate clear conditions for local people before the authority over natural resources can be delegated to them.* These include having an elected management authority in place; establishing a legal entity; demonstrating a minimum level of management capacity; and having a monitoring system in place. Make provision for outside technical support to help communities establish this.

7　*Establish a CBNRM training programme.* This programme should be aimed at developing the skills of local users to manage their own resources, and at encouraging other local role players, including municipal authorities, to remain part of the process.

8　*Break down barriers between agencies, or create bridges to cross those barriers.* Each agency should define its role in integrated land use and be clear on how it will play its role. Agencies should establish special CBNRM posts at different levels, and provide appropriate training and funding for these. But be careful of establishing new, complex and cumbersome bureaucracies that hamper rather than stimulate progress in CBNRM.

9　*Get hold of the right information before signing formal agreements.* The economic and ecological feasibility of benefit-sharing agreements, joint management and the transfer of land and other assets must be beyond doubt. Feasibility studies should be conducted before initiatives are launched or announced.

10　*Make it easy for communities to reap financial benefit from CBNRM.* Examples include allowing the transfer of saleable assets to communities; allowing permits or licences to be sold to third parties (such as a private-sector partner) under certain conditions; and easing fiscal regulations for certain groups (especially educationally disadvantaged people who don't speak English).

11　*Guarantee people certain non-financial benefits.* These benefits include support and legal protection of territories against outside threats; technical, financial and political support for local people's own management activities; sustained capacity-building for local communities to help them manage their areas and resources effectively; facilitation services; access to loans and other capital; and assistance in negotiating deals with the private sector.

It is hoped that the guidelines in this chapter, and the examples and more in-depth synthesis that came before it, will help officials, facilitators, local people and policy-makers in improving local people's lives, while at the same time improving the natural resource base. CBNRM, compared to 'conventional' natural resource management, is still in its infancy. Much more experimentation and ongoing assessment is therefore needed to better understand the factors that 'drive' CBNRM, and the conditions for success or failure, in different contexts.

In reality, the future of many species and ecosystems in southern Africa is in the hands of rural people. Governments and donors have embarked on a process of devolution and democratization of natural resources from which there is no turning back. CBNRM is as integral to the subcontinent as its famous wildlife and diverse and rich cultures are. The achievements of these programmes, like the region's dynamic ecosystems and unpredictable politics, change constantly. Success and failure varies from one season, year or decade to another. In southern Africa, nothing is known for certain except that there will be change and CBNRM.

Index

Page numbers in *italic* refer to figures, tables and boxes

access rights 216, 220–1
accountability 235–6, 237, 239, 242, 242–3, *243*, *244*
adaptive renewal cycle 160–2, *161*, 171
ADMADE (Administrative Management Design for Game Management Areas, Zambia) 235, 236, 243
agriculture 5, 50, 51, *55*, 57, 105, 143
armed conflicts 66–9

Basarwa (San) people 9, 104, 153–4, 160, 162, *163*, 171–2
  impact of CBNRM 167–71
  land rights 164, 165–6
  traditional lifestyle 4, 32, 34, 164–5, 172
  vulnerability 165–6
Basotho people 177–9
Bawa *see* Tchumo Tchato
beach village committees *see* BVCs
beekeeping 24, 127–34, 262–3
belief systems 3, 21, 32, 116–18, 120–2, 265, 268
  Tonga people 32, 34–5, 251–2, 257
  see also spirit mediums
benefits, state 52, 170
benefits (from CBNRM) *19*, 25, 27, 33, 213, 274, 278–9
  cause of conflicts 80, 81
  distribution 81, 172, 215, 277
  financial 22, 55–7, *56*, 99, 155–6, 276, 281
  intangible xiv, 22, 33, *34*, 99, 276–7, 281
  need for tangibility xiv, 211, 215–17, 221
  sharing 83, 269
  'win-win' benefits 55, 231–4
  see also revenues
biodiversity 10, 21, 93–100

Botswana 35, 52, 56, *56*, 58, 68, 72
  CBNRM in 36, 147–50, 154–8, 166–71, 171–2
  rangelands 13, 51
  role of government 36, 71
  tourism revenues xiv, 99
  see also Basarwa (San) people; Okavango Delta
boundaries 32, 266–7, 269
bushmeat 98, 100, 138, 214
BVCs (beach village committees) 33, 184–5, 186–8, 189, 191–2

CAMPFIRE (Communal Areas Management Programme for Indigenous Resources) 14, 70, 70–1, 89, 90, 248–51, 267
  benefits from 33, 53, 56, *56*, 99, 100, 105, 139
  division of benefits 58, 60, 71–2, 84, 215, 255–6, 257
  impact on livelihoods 255–6, 257
  as model for other projects 10, 195, 212–13, 235, 237
  principles 15–16, *16*, 235, 245–6, *246*
  and traditional knowledge 253–4
capacity-building 23, 145, 158, 229–30, 278
Caprivi (Namibia) 33, 70–1, 104–5, 196
CBD (Convention on Biological Diversity, 1992) 10, *11*, 75, 96
CBNRM (community-based natural resource management) xiii–xiv, 39, 102–3, *102*, 271–2, *273*, 281
  assumptions 157, 158
  Basarwa dissatisfaction with 169–71
  and beekeeping 129–30, 134
  CAMPFIRE principles 15–16, *16*, 235, 245–6, *246*
  conflicts and 79–80, 88–91

and conservation 100–3, *102*, 106–7, 142
costs 57, 246
as democratic movement 73
and everyday resources 143–5
first-generation 16, 236–7, 241–4, *242*, *244*, *245*
formal 24–7, 46, 52–3, 53–7, 62–3, 99, 106
and globalization 23, 157
historical background 3–14
informal 46, 52, 53, 129, 174
and livelihoods 45–54, 57–61, 142, 213
motives in 54–5, 62–3
objectives xv
and peace dividend 66–7, 69–70
political aspects xiv–xv, 14, 70–2
and poverty xv, 58–9, 198, 211
principles 15, *16*, *18–19*, 72, *238*, *245–6*, *272–5*, *276–81*
recommendations 272–81
second-generation 15, 237–8, *238*, 241–2, 243–6, *243*, *244*, *245–6*
and traditional leaders 123–4
value 48–53, 55–6, *56*
weaknesses 19–23, 214–21
see also benefits (from CBNRM); CAMPFIRE; conflicts; revenues (from CBNRM)
CBOs (community-based organizations) 25, 167
CDOs (community development organizations) 83
chiefs 4, 82–3, 117, 118–20, 197, 239, 253
conflicts with 84, 240
in Lesotho 174–5, *176*, 178
see also headmen; leaders
CITES (Convention on International Trade in Endangered Species of Wild Fauna and Flora, 1973) 71, 93
CMAs (community management areas) 150–1
co-management 183–92, 228–30, 260–9, 279
common property theory *see* CPT
Communal Areas Management Programme for Indigenous Resources *see* CAMPFIRE
communal conservancies 9, 14, 35, 62, 72, 73, 194–8

community definition 31–2
intangible benefits 33, *34*
opposition to xiv, 70–1, 82, 197
principles 15, *17*
revenues from 99, 196–7, 205, 206, 207, *207*
role of facilitation 30, 197
role of government 36
tensions within 36, 47, 82, 83–4, 197
see also Torra Conservancy
Communal Property Associations *see* CPAs
communities 79–80, 83, 85, 89, 90–1, 145, 157
conflicts within 21–2, 78–82, 87–91, 157, 211, 217–18, 240
identifying 22, 30–2, 150
identity 82, 217, 232–3, 253–4
community development organizations *see* CDOs
community management areas *see* CMAs
community-based natural resource management *see* CBNRM
community-based organizations *see* CBOs
conflicts 8–9, 16, 47, 106, 212–13
among institutions 170–1, 188, 191–2
armed conflicts 66–9
local 78–91, 151–2, 153–4, 170–1, 185–8, 261–6, 275
management of 27, 37–8, 74, 157, 229, 277, 279
with wildlife 203
within communities 21–2, 78–82, 87–91, 157, 211, 217–18, 240
conservancies *see* communal conservancies; Torra Conservancy
conservation 5–8, 54–5, 63, 95–6, 177, 180
and CBNRM 93–4, 100–3, *102*, 106–7, 143
costs 102, 103–6, 107, 215, 279
and development xv, 156
incentives 216, 255–6, 274
contractual parks 223–34
Convention on Biological Diversity *see* CBD
Convention on International Trade in Endangered Species of Wild Fauna and Flora *see* CITES

CPAs (Communal Property
   Associations) 227–8, 231, 233
CPT (common property theory) 14–17,
   16, 17, 58–9, 155
culture 24, 32, 63
   see also belief systems; spirit mediums

democracy 90, 194, 217, 259, 263–6
democratization 10–14, 73–4, *74,* 211,
   241–2
Deutsche Gesellschaft für Technische
   Zusammenarbeit *see* GTZ
development xv, 59–61, 121–2, 156
   agencies 177
devolution 16, 72, 221, 228, 274, 275,
   280
   failures 236, 249, 259
diversification, of livelihoods 74–5, 130,
   167–8, *169,* 272
diviners 118, 119, 121–2, 123
donors 10, 24–5, 93, 142, 186, 189–90,
   213, 275–6
   role xiii, 179–80, 186, 211, 218, 219,
   233

economic instrumentalism 55, 62, 215,
   216
elites 58, 80, 81, 157, 259, 265–6, 268,
   276
   interception of benefits 21, 22, 47, 80,
   194, 211, 220
empowerment 63, 155, 156, 158, 186,
   198
   achieved by CBNRM *19,* 53, 232–3,
   241
enforcement 8, 25, 101–2, 189, 274, 280
   lack of resources for 13, 69
entrepreneurs 83–4
environmental entitlements 25–7, *26*
everyday resources 23, 135–8, *137,*
   141–5, *144*
   economic value *137,* 138–41

facilitation 24, 36, 37–8, 90, 145, 157,
   279
   key ingredient in CBNRM *19,* 27, 30,
   74, 272, 274
fisheries, Malawi 62–3, 182–92
food security 97–8
forced removals 8, 9, 79–80, 227
Ford Foundation 213, 218–19

GAs (grazing associations) 176–7, *177*
gender issues 47, 80, 87–8, 143
   see also women
globalization 23, 36, 157, 171
governance 46, 46–7, 118–20, 178–9,
   208, 212, 274
governments 24–5, 49, 275–6
   local 84, 280
   role 70, 71, 157, 179–80, 212,
   218–19, 280
   see also state
grazing associations *see* GAs
GTZ (Deutsche Gesellschaft für
   Technische Zusammenarbeit) 133,
   184

harvesting 49–50, 196
headmen 4, 184, 185, 187–8, 189,
   191–2, 197
   see also chiefs; leaders
healers, traditional 98, 100, 123
human capital 44, 46, 172
human rights 74
hunting 4–5, 6, 34–5, 93, 99, 252–3
   by Basarwa people 153, 166, 169–70,
   172
   illegal 100–1, 201, *201–2,* 212
   licences 101, 166, 215
   quotas 24, 105, 153–4, 196, 202–3,
   205–6
   trophy hunting 100, 101, 105, 154,
   196, 201, 205–6
   see also bushmeat; poaching

identity 82, 217, 232–3, 253–4
illegal hunting 201, *201–2,* 212
   see also poaching
incentives 32–3, 187, 216, 255–6, 274
incomes 55–6, *56,* 255–6
indigenous knowledge *see* traditional
   knowledge
infrastructure 45, 61, 237
institutions 46–7, 274
   building 22, 63, 73–4, 197–8, 208–9,
   213, 217, 278
   conflict among 170–1, 188, 191–2
   local 4, *18,* 22, 27, 38–9, 228–9, 271–2
   new 168–9, 170–1, 268
   traditional 22, 24, 38–9, 170–1, 254
Integrated Rural Development and
   Nature Conservation *see* IRDNC

international agreements *11–12*, 36, 75, 93
  see also CBD; CITES
IRDNC (Integrated Rural Development and Nature Conservation) 13, 201, 204, 208

joint management 228–30, 279
  see also co-management
JVAs (joint venture agreements) 150–5, 158, 204–5

Khwai (NG18, Botswana) 153–4, 157, 165, 167–71
Kruger National Park (South Africa) 69, 103, 105, 227–8
  see also Makuleke people
KwaZulu-Natal 115–16, 124

land 5, 7, 7–8
  claims 13–14, 22, 70, 227, 232, 233
  ownership 48, 145, 174, 232, 249–50
  rights to 27, 164, 165–6, 172, 216, 232, 249–50
land reform xiv, 70, 74, 78–9, 90, 141, 249–50
  South Africa 59
landscape 124
leaders 38–9, 46, 83–4, 276–7, 279
  spiritual 80, 85–7
  traditional 4, 39, 82–3, 84, 117–18, 123–4, 138
  see also chiefs; headmen
leases 150–2, 155, 158
legislation 7–8, 37, 71, 166, 189, 209, 274
Lesotho 38, 46, 53, 59, 68, 180
  range management 4, 7, 174–80
LIRDP (Luangwa Integrated Rural Development Project, Zambia) 13, 14, 60, 70, 100, 235–6, 236–46
  principles *24–6*, 238–9, *238*, *245–6*, 246
  revenues 33, 99, 236–7, 239–40
  traditional authorities and 73, 82, 84, 240
livelihoods 44–5, 52–3, 54, 62–3, 81–2, 177–9, 180
  Basarwa people 164–5, 166
  beekeeping and 127–34
  CAMPFIRE's impact on 255–6, 257

CBNRM and 48–52, 54–61, 62, 233
  diversification 167–8, *169*, 272
  everyday resources and 136–8, *137*, 140–1, 145
  NTFPs and *137*, 260, 262, 266, 266–7, 268–9
  role of biodiversity in 97–100
  see also benefits (from CBNRM)
livestock production 50, 51
  see also range management
local government 84–5, 280
Luangwa Integrated Rural Development Project *see* LIRDP
Lupande programme *see* LIRDP

Madikwe Game Reserve (South Africa) 83, 85, 87–8
Mafungautsi State Forest (Zimbabwe) 13, 53, 60, 84, 85, 86, 260–9
Makuleke people 9, 46, 71, 73
  co-management by 228–9, 231–4
  conflicts among 79–80, 81, 84, 89
  land agreement 14, 70, 103, 105, 227–8
  revenues achieved 57, 99
Malawi 14, 68, 72
  beekeeping 129, 130, 133
  fisheries 33, 38–9, 62–3, 83, 182–92
Malombe, Lake (Malawi), fishery 182–4, *183*
mediation *see* facilitation
Mid-Zambezi Rural Development Project 121–2
migrant labour 140, 178, 226
monitoring 156, 158, 219, 221, 274
Mozambique 7, 68, 72, 90, 215
  beekeeping 128, 129
  Tchumo Tchato project 72, 84, 86, 89, 210–22

Namibia 9, 47, 52, 57, 58, 68, 70–1
  IRDNC 13, 201, 204, 208
  role of government 36, 201–3
  tourism 201, 202, 203, 204–5
  wildlife 195, 196, 200–1, 201–2, *202*
  see also Caprivi; communal conservancies; Torra Conservancy
national parks 14, 177
  see also Kruger National Park; Richtersveld National Park
natural capital 44, 45–6

natural resources *see* resources
nature 63, 124
NG18 (Ngamiland Area 18, Botswana)
    153–4, 157, 165, 167–71
NG32 (Ngamiland Area 32, Botswana)
    104, 163, 164–5, 167–71
NG34 (Ngamiland Area 34, Botswana)
    56, 61, 81, 83, 99, 151–3, *153*, 157
NGOs (non-governmental organizations)
    xiii, 10, 93, 142, 171, 197, 198,
    256
  in Botswana 152
  in Namibia 201, 208
  role 13, 24
  in South Africa 230
NTFPs (non-timber forest products) 2,
    97, 135–6, 260, 268–9
  see also everyday resources

Okavango Delta (Botswana) xiv, 35,
    148–9, 160, 163
  CBNRM in 52–3, 55, 56
  Khwai village 153–4, 157, 165,
    167–71
  Sankuyo village 56, 61, 81, 83, 99,
    151–3, *153*, 157
  see also Basarwa (San) people
ownership 30–2, 69–70, 216, 257
  land 48, 78–9, 93–4, 145, 174, 232,
    249–50

participation 13, 17, 20–1, 27, 28–30,
    29, *31*
  and democracy 73, 82, 217
  guidelines 275–6, *276*
  incentives for 32–3, 186–7
  in LIRDP 239, 241–2
  in RMCs 263–4, 267–9
  of women 263, 264–5, *265*, 268
partnerships 22, 74, 211, 220, 221
  see also JVAs
'people and parks' programmes 50,
    56–7, 135
personalities 261, 268, 279
poaching 8, 9, 100, 218, 235, 236
  of NTFPs 260, 262, 266, 268–9
politics xiv–xv, 14, 70–2
population (human) 89, 101, 190
poverty xv, 58–9, 61, 198, 211
power 229–30, 262–9, 274, 275, 279
preservation 5–8

protected areas 6–7, 8–9, 14, 67–8, 143,
    177
  see also national parks

range management 24, 50, 51
  Lesotho 4, 7, 174–80
range management areas *see* RMAs
regulations 25, 36, 185–6, 274
  infringement of 183, 184, 186
resource management xiv–xv, 14, 16,
    70–2, 116–18, 140, 142–5
  see also CBNRM; traditional systems
    of resource management
resource management committees *see*
    RMCs
resources 45–6, 93, 97–100, 206
  access to 169–70, 217, 251
  and people xiii, 23–4, 27, 234
  production potential 272, 278
  rights of use 69–72, 78–9, 165–6,
    202, 211, 249
  state control of 8, 48, 212
  value 48–52, *51*
  see also belief systems; land;
    ownership; traditional systems of
    resource management
revenues (from CBNRM) 151–3, *153*,
    168, 196–7, 205, *207*, 211
  distribution 59–60, 207, 239–40,
    243–4, *255*–6, 257, 266–7
  interception 84, 215
  use 59–61, 152–3, 168, 207, 236–7
Richtersveld National Park (South Africa)
    73, 223, 226–7, 228, 229, 230
  benefits from 56, 57, 99, 231–4
rights 74, 75–6, 202
  of access 216, 220–1
  to fisheries 189
  to land 27, 164, 165–6, 172, 216,
    232, 249–50
  of resource use 69–72, 78–9, 165–6,
    202, 211, 249
  see also ownership
rituals 117, 136
RMAs (range management areas) 176–7,
    177
RMCs (resource management
    committees) 260–1, 262–9, *264*,
    265
rural development 141–2, 143, 235, 236

San people 22
see also Basarwa (San) people
Sankuyo (NG34, Botswana) 56, 61, 81,
83, 99, 151–3, *153*, 157
SANParks (South African National
Parks, *formerly* SANP) 223, 225,
226, 227–30, 231–3
SL (sustainable livelihoods) framework
44–5, 46
social capital 44, 165
South Africa 4, 9, 13, 52, 58, 68–9, 143
everyday resources 136, 139–41
land reform 59, 141
Madikwe Game Reserve 83, 85, 87–8
resource valuation 48, 50, 51, *51*
role of state xiv, 48, 68, 71
see also contractual parks; Kruger
National Park; Makuleke people;
Richtersveld National Park
South African National Parks *see*
SANParks
spirit mediums 4, 21, 86, 118, 119,
121–2
and natural resources 122, 214, 216,
218, 253
spiritual ecology 116–18, 120–2
spiritual leaders 80, 85–7, 119, 121
state 8, 20–1, 27, 36–7, 48, 51–2, 267
see also governments
state benefits 52, 170
sustainable development 120, 121, 123
sustainable livelihoods *see* SL
sustainable use 93, 123, 216

taboos 4, 100, 122, 164–5, 172, 252,
253
Tanzania 90, 128, 129, 132
Tchumo Tchato (Mozambique) 72, 84,
86, 89, 210–22
tenure rights *see* rights
territorial cults 86, 120–1
Tonga people 32, 34–5, 53, 250–4, 257
top-down approach 16, 237, 241–4
Torra Conservancy (Namibia) 52, 55,
56, *56*, 197, 200–1, 202–9, *202*
tourism 13, 49, 69, 105–6, 197, 211,
250
Basarwa people and 168, 170
community-based 180, 197–8
eco-tourism 228, 233
joint ventures 150–5, 204–5, 233

in Namibia 201, 202, 203, 204–5
revenues from 57, 99, 196, 226
wildlife tourism xiv, 151, 153, 154,
166
traditional authorities 82–3, 197
traditional healers 98, 100, 118, 123
traditional knowledge 24, 25, 27, 33–6,
38, 169, 252–5, 257
traditional leaders *see* chiefs; headmen;
leaders
traditional systems of resource
management 3–4, 5, 7, 58–9, 62,
95, 145
range management 174–5
see also Basarwa (San) people; belief
systems; leaders; traditional
knowledge
transhumance 175, 176, 178, 179

Umnga (South Africa) 86–7, 123
USAID (United States Agency for
International Development) 149,
153, 156, 157, 180

VAGs (village action groups) 237,
238–9, 240–1, 242, 243, *243*, 244,
245
values 21, 49, 63, 252, 276
VDCs (village development councils)
174–5
village action groups *see* VAGs
VTCs (village trust committees) 167,
169, 170–1

wars, environmental impacts 67–9
wild resources 97–100
wildlife 67–9, 103–5, 203, 256–7
Botswana 148–9, 156, 163, 166
management of 55, 56–7
Namibia 195, 196, 200–1, 201–2, *202*
Tonga people and 252–4
Zambezi Valley 250–1, 256
wildlife tourism xiv, 151, 153, 154, 166
'win-win' benefits 55, 231–4
women 86, 87–8, 139–40, 256, 262
Basarwa people 168, 169
beekeeping by 130, 131, 133–4
as chiefs 174–5
and everyday resources 47, 136–8,
143
participation 263, 264–5, *265*, 268

worldviews 3, 21, 121, 218–19, 251–2,
    257

Xaxaba (NG32, Botswana) 104, 163,
    164–5, 167–71

Zambia 7, 53, 56, 68, 72, 215

beekeeping 128, 131, 133
    see also LIRDP
Zimbabwe 7, 9, 50, 57, 68, 72
    beekeeping 128, 131, 132, 133
    land crisis xiv, 249–50
    spiritual beliefs 121–2
    see also CAMPFIRE; Mafungautsi
        State Forest; Tonga people